Bill Evans: How My Heart Sings

PETER PETTINGER

Bill Evans: How My Heart Sings

YALE UNIVERSITY PRESS NEW HAVEN & LONDON

Published with assistance from the foundation established in memory of Philip Hamilton McMillan of the Class of 1894, Yale College.

Designed by James J. Johnson and set in Gill Sans and Electra types by Ink, Inc., New York, New York. Printed in the United States of America by Thomson-Shore, Inc., Dexter, Michigan.

Library of Congress Cataloging-in-Publication Data

Pettinger, Peter, 1945–
    Bill Evans : how my heart sings / Peter Pettinger
        p.   cm.
    Discography: p. ****
    Includes bibliographical references (p. ****) and index.
    ISBN 0-300-07193-0 (alk. paper)

    1. Evans, Bill, 1929–80. 2. Pianists—United States—Biography. 3. Jazz musicians—United States—Biography. I. Title.
ML417.E9P53   1998   781.65'092—dc21
                              [B]   97-49991 MN

A catalogue record for this book is available from the British Library.

The paper in this book meets the guidelines for permanence and durability of the Committee on Production Guidelines for Book Longevity of the Council on Library Resources.

10 9 8 7 6 5 4 3

For Ros

Contents

Part IV. The Last Trio, 1977–80

Preface

…a rather simple person with a limited talent and perhaps a limited perspective.
—*Bill Evans on himself*

In 1958 I was thirteen years old, pursuing classical studies in piano and violin. And, like many a British teenager of the time, I was listening to the latest rock 'n' roll hits dispensed from the heart of Europe by Radio Luxembourg. A schoolfriend had enterprising taste in jazz, though, and we started to swap 45-rpm singles and EPs, which were all we could afford. Our appreciation progressed through the traditional bands to the truly "with it" Dave Brubeck. For that artist at least, a tiny audience in the east of England was running parallel with student appreciation on the wide American campus. Our ears matured quickly to the "cool" sophistication of the Gerry Mulligan Quartet—in particular, that magenta-sleeved Vogue EP with "Bernie's Tune" and "Walkin' Shoes"—and when Miles Davis came our way (excerpts from *Miles Ahead* and *Milestones*), our course was confirmed.

Then my friend brought along the trumpeter's latest—something called *Jazz Track*. The piano on this stunning record was being played by an unknown musician with an ordinary name: Bill Evans. But the way he was shading his tone was anything but ordinary; he sounded like a classical pianist, and yet he was playing jazz. I was captured there and then—the archetypal pivotal moment. The concept of the "Bill Evans sound" instantly enshrined and distilled what I had always hoped to hear. It was the plaintive harmony, the lyrical tone, and the fresh textures that captivated so; it was the very idea that one style of music could be played with the skills and finesse normally only brought to another; it was a timeless quality, a feeling that the music had always been there; and above all, it was a yearning behind the notes, a quiet passion that you could almost reach out and touch.

I began to collect the records. So, I later learned, had hundreds of other people. But at the time I felt, strangely, that I was the only one who knew and responded to this music. Many Evans connoisseurs have had this experience, and jealously guard what they regard as their exclusive found treasure. It surely stems from this artist's ability to communicate at a very personal level, a quality emanating from his character, which was quiet, introverted, and modest. He was not a glamorous person, and he appeared to play not for the masses but for himself. A listener felt like an eavesdropper, communing on a privileged, one-to-one level. Through this quality—this "presence"—Bill Evans today gets through to listeners from all walks of life in a way that many other musicians do not.

My desire to acquire more of this playing on disc soon became an obsession. I pursued every secondhand outlet that I could think of, on the outside chance of unearthing some undiscovered sideman recording—for I soon realized that Evans could be every bit as rewarding in small print as he was in large. It was all very hit and miss, the luxury of Peter H. Larsen's monumental discography, *Turn on the Stars*, being still almost twenty years away. As a fledgling classical pianist, I had the good fortune to begin traveling, and I discovered that issues appeared on the Continent before they did in England. Whenever I went to Paris, for example, I went straight to the Lido Musique on the Champs Elysées, and my Riverside copy of *Portrait in Jazz* still carries the stickers of "36 Francs" and "Déclaré à la S.D.R.M." on the back. Later the quest extended to New York basement emporiums.

Evans's artistic development was long, slow, and, as he put it, "through the middle." It is fitting that his recognition today progresses in a similar way. Over the years since his death in 1980, his niche on the retail shelves has grown slowly but steadily, so that now the big stores offer a generous selection of his CDs. Gradually, the message of this giant is being valued for its true worth; one senses a slowly developing appreciation. He is especially "big" in France—but then, he always was—and it was there rather than in England or America that a portrait for television was made in 1996.

He was a supremely natural pianist. Indeed, he even looked like part of his instrument—an extension of it, rather than someone sitting at it. Or rather, *it* was an extension of *him*; he did not so much play upon it as coax it into life. His diffident and slightly awkward appearance when walking onto the bandstand was transformed when he began to play; then, somehow, he was complete.

His influence is pervasive, extending generally throughout jazz and specifically to countless instrumentalists. The interactive, chamber-music concept of the Bill Evans Trios has even permeated an entire recording label (one for which he never recorded); the whole aesthetic of Manfred Eicher's ECM company has been defined by the Evans approach to economy and

Maxine Evans, Bill's stepdaughter, receiving the pianist's Lifetime Achievement
Award for 1994 from Michael Greene, President of N.A.R.A.S.
Zavatsky, courtesy estate of Bill Evans, copyright © Nenette Evans 1996

silence. Many of Evans's trio members, as well as other musicians he influenced, went on to record for the label.

The story of his life is the story of a working musician on one long round
of clubs, concert halls, and studios. When not on the road, his musical home,
the backbone of his working life, was the Village Vanguard club in New York,
and his playing there over the years was captured by one particular fan, in
anguish over vanishing sounds: Mike Harris's clandestine recordings, released
by Fantasy in 1996 as *The Secret Sessions*, preserve the man on the job.

I never knew Evans the man, but I did hear him countless times at
Ronnie Scott's in London, the Village Vanguard, and elsewhere. I regularly
flouted Manhattan's reputation as the mugging capital of the world, tramping
home on foot between 3:00 and 4:00 A.M. from Greenwich Village to some
midtown hotel. In London, too, I would stay out for every note, night after
night. Reticent, and holding Evans in awe, I could never pluck up the confidence to speak to him (apart from a wild musical request one night, graciously

fulfilled). Courage apart, though, part of me did not really want, or need, to meet him. It may sound sentimental to say so, but the music was enough, and I do not regret the anonymity.

⋐ ⋐ ⋐

In writing this book I have enjoyed the immense privilege of meeting in person, and learning from, some of the musical icons of my youth. I refer in particular to Art Farmer, Bob Brookmeyer, and (a later hero) George Russell. Other musicians who played or worked with Evans and who have helped me with my inquiries are Jack DeJohnette, Chuck Israels, Mundell Lowe, Ron Mathewson, Helen Merrill, Palle Mikkelborg, Michael Moore, Claus Ogerman, Tony Oxley, and Eliot Zigmund. I thank all these artists for lending authenticity to the pages that follow. To this list I would add the composer Earl Zindars, whose works held a particular place in Evans's heart, and I offer a special appreciation to Zindars's wife, Anne, for unwittingly supplying the title of this book. When I asked Phil Woods about working with Evans, though, he answered politely, with an artful glint in his eye, "I'm not divulging anything. It's all going in *my* book." Fair enough.

Pianists who knew Evans and have shared their memories include Gordon Beck, Michael Garrick, John Horler, Art Murphy, and Jack Reilly, and I am especially grateful to one who knew him well: his good friend Warren Bernhardt.

My thanks go to Judy Bell at the Richmond Organization, for supplying detailed information of Evans's publications; Win Hinkle, for allowing me to use numerous excerpts from the articles in his journal *Letter from Evans,* most of them resulting from his indefatigable interviewing; Ron Nethercutt, for supplying me with unique material from Evans's college days at Southeastern, and Dr. Peter Titelman of Northampton, Massachusetts, for providing a personal memory of the First Trio at the Village Vanguard. Blank spaces in the nooks and crannies of my research were variously filled out by Robert Hogan, Jean-Michel Reisser, Alain Mehrenberger, Jan van Schellen, and Gladyse Saul—to all these I give my thanks. Barry Kernfeld was an early reader of the manuscript, and I appreciate his valuable suggestions.

At Fantasy Records I am grateful to Orrin Keepnews, for allowing me to raid his chronicles of the years at Riverside, and to Terri Hinte for numerous kindnesses. Thanks also to two English West Country enthusiasts, Colin Kellam and Brian Hennessey, to whose private tape collections I have been granted access. Hennessey, who holds the Bill Evans Memorial Library, and sometimes looked after Bill when he was in England, has illuminated my pages with his recollections. I have learned much also from the Oreos Collection Jazz book, *Bill Evans: Sein Leben, Seine Musik, Seine Schallplatten,* by Hanns E. Petrik.

The distinguished author and lyricist Gene Lees, another close friend of Evans's, injected an early boost of confidence by reprinting an article of mine in his *Jazzletter.* His advice and encouragement set me on the right road. Later, when the text became at least presentable, Evans's longtime manager and producer, the late Helen Keane, gave generously of her dwindling energy to answer my questions and to comment on the manuscript chapter by chapter. Gene and Helen were indispensable pillars to my quest.

Last but not least, I wish to thank Dr. Earle Epps for generously sharing the history of the Soroka family line, and Nenette Evans, administrator for the estate of Bill Evans, for her interest, support, and generosity in providing unique family photographs.

Bill Evans: How My Heart Sings

Prologue

I have always hoped to visit Russia, to feel at first hand the roots of this part of myself.

— *Bill Evans*

William John Evans, the younger of two brothers, was born on August 16, 1929, in Plainfield, New Jersey. Although little is known of the forebears of his father, Harry Leon Evans, born in Philadelphia in 1891, Harry instilled in his sons a strong sense of Welsh Protestant ancestry. In the renowned vocal tradition of Wales, he gave rein to his own musical talents by singing regularly in a barbershop choir. The family of Bill's mother, Mary, came from Russia, a country nurturing a rich choral heritage of its own, and one with a mighty pianistic pedigree as well. Mary Soroka (the name means "magpie") savored the music of her Orthodox church and amused herself as an amateur pianist. Harry and Mary's sons—Harry Jr. and Bill—both went on to make music their profession. For Bill the outcome was priceless; the jazz pianist Chick Corea, for one, paid homage to his accomplishment: "Bill's value can't be measured in any kind of terms. He's one of the great, great artists of this century."[1]

⧉ ⧉ ⧉

In the early 1960s Brian Hennessey, a British fan of Bill Evans, visited New York on business and went to meet the pianist at the Village Vanguard jazz club, where he was playing. Hennessey was in a position to organize some playing dates in England, an offer that Evans immediately accepted. Besides the professional opportunity, he saw a chance to visit his Celtic fatherland. The first of many trips to England ensued, but he was never quite able to include a westward pilgrimage to Wales.

Late in the sixties, as well as once again at the end of his life, he was equally intent upon visiting his other ancestral homeland, Russia. On the first occasion there was a last-minute hitch at Kennedy airport. A second opportunity arose in 1980, and although he was hesitant about an extended

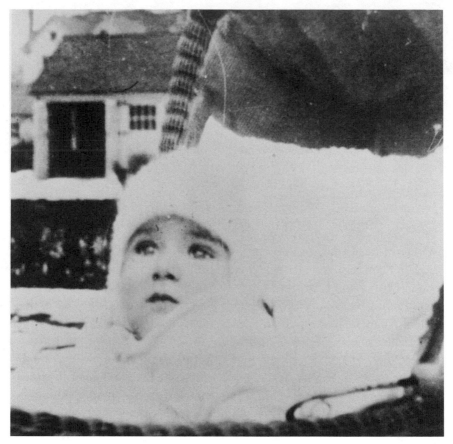

Baby "Billy," as they called him, 1929.

tour under spartan conditions on the Russian provincial road, he was eager to include a handful of major concerts to satisfy his large Russian following. But in the wake of Soviet military intervention on behalf of a puppet regime in Afghanistan, he found himself faced with an agonizing decision. In autumn 1980, not long before he died, he called off the trip. In a letter to the editors of the American jazz magazine *Down Beat* and other prominent publications, he made clear his stance on the politico-artistic regime in the Soviet Union, a decade before glasnost:

> I am a jazz pianist of international reputation. My name, Evans, is obviously Welsh, but my mother's name (Soroka) and heritage is Russian. Memories of my childhood are warmly crowded with the singing and spirit of this heritage of frequent family gatherings—a priceless gift of enrichment to a growing child.

Consequently, I have always hoped to visit Russia, to feel at first hand the roots of this part of myself. Reports for many years that I had many dedicated fans there were confirmed recently, when my trio was invited for five concerts in Moscow, late in September of this year.

Perhaps even without the catalyst of Afghanistan, I might have arrived at the following conclusion, for I had often lamented the tragedy of people living in a society where one's opinion could bring about long suffering, imprisonment, and where an artist's purest inspiration was expected to conform to outside criteria. The very denial of the essence of art today! But the event of Afghanistan propelled my thinking.

I wrestled with the problem for a few days, and came to the firm decision that I must cancel the concerts. I hoped that by the grapevine, perhaps those fans that learned of my reasons for not appearing would be aroused philosophically, and therefore energy might be created, opposed to the perpetuation of this oppressive government.

The obvious counter argument to my conclusion would be that we should bring them our cultural message. I think this is a bit too convenient. If all performing artists examined this issue and refused to perform wherever an environment of oppression exists, perhaps great revolutionary energy could be created. To perform there voluntarily, after all, is to walk passively in the atmosphere of the degradation of the human spirit.

My gesture will have little or no significance, but I follow my code and am at peace with myself.[2]

Those final words read like an epitaph, and indeed Evans knew that he was dying. He had suffered throughout his life from hepatitis. The condition had been exacerbated by drug use over more than two decades, which led to bleeding ulcers and malnutrition. As one close friend, the writer Gene Lees, told me: "His was the longest suicide in history." In the final years the self-destructive pianist was weak and was shooting cocaine; surely he suspected, when he renounced the tour of Russia, that he might not survive the trip — whether because of ill health or drug trouble — even had his humanitarian convictions allowed it.

⊂⊦ ⊂⊦ ⊂⊦

Mary Soroka, Bill's mother, stopped her own mother from teaching him Russian, afraid that he would not learn enough English. Evans later regretted his mother's protectiveness on that count. Once, during the 1950s, he received some letters from a Russian jazz pianist. Mary, who read and wrote Russian with difficulty, managed to translate them and, at Bill's urging, wrote replies. He once received a memorable letter from a group of fans in Leningrad, written in perfect English. Later, the same group sent him a large, exquisitely bound book by a historic Russian poet-philosopher, which he treasured, giving it pride of place in his home. In Russia, Evans's records are issued on the Melodia label, and his fans there do not hesitate to claim him as their own.

The Soroka line of descent can be traced to an area of Ukraine that was once part of the Austro-Hungarian Empire. Mary, in a letter to a cousin, described the lifestyle of her forebears around the 1870s: "They lived under horrible conditions. Only the parents had beds. They had an oven for cooking, but no chimney for the smoke to get out, and the children slept on top of the oven. In winter, they had to bring the cattle indoors, so that they wouldn't freeze."[3]

Many lived in turf huts with earthen floors. Bill's first cousin, Dr. Earle Epps, has said: "They were dirt poor. And that was in an area where the boundary lines just kept changing with every war. One time it was Russia, another time Hungary and then it would be Germany. These poor people didn't know whom they belonged to. They were Russians living in Austro-Hungary, being ruled by Poles."[4]

On today's political map, Ukraine is cradled geographically by the borders of Romania, Moldova, Hungary, Slovakia, Poland, Belarus, and Russia, and culturally by a deep artistic heritage, rich and various, with a particular emphasis on music. From these lands in the nineteenth century came two of the greatest pianist-composers of all time—the Hungarian Franz Liszt and the Pole Frédéric Chopin. It is fitting that Bill Evans, a poet of the piano—once dubbed the Chopin of jazz—traces one side of his ancestry to this part of the world.

⋵ ⋵ ⋵

Bill's grandfather Ivan Soroka came from the town of Brunarya, in the province of Galicia, near Lvov in present-day Ukraine. Ivan's wife-to-be, Anna Matichak, was born in Charna, a village lying in the shadow of the Carpathian Mountains. In their teens, Ivan and Anna emigrated separately to the United States. Only then did they meet and marry, settling in Old Forge near Scranton, Pennsylvania.

The Sorokas were a part of one of the pockets of society that characterized the American immigrant's experience—a small, tightly knit community, in this case a little piece of Russia. The community still thrives in the Scranton area, and to this day there are people living there who hardly speak English and for whom the Russian church is the focus of their lives. The history of the area is dominated by its abundance of anthracite coal; mine owners welcomed all immigrants and the cheap labor they provided. The Russian influx began as a trickle in 1865, but by the time that the Sorokas went over in the early 1890s, more than thirty thousand of their compatriots were coming to the United States each year. Ivan and Anna had six children who reached adulthood: Antoinette, Mary, Julia, Justine, Michael, and Nicholas (a seventh died in infancy). The second child, Mary, mother of Bill Evans, was born in Old Forge on February 12, 1896.

A frequent cause of mortality among the miners was black lung disease, but Evans's grandfather Ivan was accidentally killed when dynamiting coal in 1904. No system of compensation had yet been adopted, and the Soroka family was left destitute. For three or four years, two of the children, Mary and Justine, were raised in a nearby orphanage run by Orthodox priests. There they spoke only Russian, and only when they left as adolescents did they begin to learn English at the American school.

Epps, one of Justine's sons, recounts: "The Epps family, the Soroka family, and others ended up in Manville, New Jersey, the home of the Johns-Manville Asbestos Corporation, which manufactured shingles and pipes. Apparently, all the workers that were coming over were Russian and Polish, and nobody could speak English. But there were lots of laboring jobs in Manville. My uncle Michael became a personnel director there, and I suppose he got jobs for everybody. Mary worked in the accounting department."[5]

Many inhabitants of the small country town of Manville journeyed to their places of work in lower Manhattan on the New Jersey Central and Pennsylvania Railroads. A few stations nearer New York City, across open fields, lay Dunellen, where Harry, Bill's father, worked. The next stop was the workaday town of Plainfield, where he and Mary lived and where Bill and Harry Jr. were born and raised.

Harry Sr. entered the printing trade, producing magazines at Art Color Printing in Dunellen. He was remembered by friends as gentle and easygoing in character—when sober, that is, for by all accounts he was a heavy drinker. Mary, in contrast, was strong and determined. Earle Epps remembers a tumultuous marriage: "Harry was always a playboy, and pleasure was more important to him than his family, which he frequently neglected. After his alcoholic abuses he would cry and say how sorry he was, but two days later it would be the same old story all over again. He loved singing and barbershop harmony, and he and his buddies would get together with a bottle and start singing and drinking. Mary said that her life was hell for most of their married years, until they retired."[6]

Mary's great love was the music of the Russian Orthodox Church, music that she had heard every day while growing up at the orphanage with

The brothers Harry and Bill with parents, Harry and Mary.
Courtesy estate of Bill Evans, copyright © Nenette Evans 1996

Justine. Another sister, Julia, had a sufficiently good singing voice to tour professionally in musicals and light opera. Indeed, the whole Soroka family displayed musical feeling, and they would sing monastic chants a cappella, intuitively switching parts at will. Their traditional singing on festive occasions (following the Old Style calendar), or after dinner at home, was some of the first music that Bill Evans heard, and they passed along to the youngster their reverence for fine music.

Part I
Birth of the Sound, 1929–58

CHAPTER 1

The Kid from Plainfield

I've always preferred to play something simple than go all over the keyboard on something I wasn't clear about.

—*Bill Evans*

Harry and Mary's firstborn, Harry Jr., inherited the solid, chunky features of his father, but Bill, born two years later, took on the narrow bone structure and sharper countenance of his mother. He became her favorite. When Harry Sr.'s drinking bouts brought abuse and financial strain, Mary often took the boys to stay in nearby Somerville with her sister Justine and the Epps family.

Here, too, there was music. In the evenings, Earle Epps's father, who held a bachelor of music degree in piano and organ, would sit down at the piano and play through the great classics, an indulgence that had a crucial effect on the visiting Evans brothers. Earle Epps recalls the boys' earliest attempts at music: "Somewhere between five and seven Harry started playing the piano, but there was no thought of giving Bill piano lessons; he was too young. In those days the piano teachers came to the home. Bill used to crouch over in the corner and listen. When they had finished and left the room, he'd go over, sit down, and play what he had heard."[1] The precocious Bill was already challenging Harry when, at age six and a half, the younger brother started his own lessons.

Evans always acknowledged the influence of his brother, not only in music but also in sports: both were natural athletes, and with a dash of hero worship Bill always tried to minimize the two-year gap. Soon they succumbed to the family passion, golf, spending much of their early years on the greens; indeed, either might have pursued a professional career on the circuit. Other sports and recreation ran in the family, as well: for several years in the late 1920s, Harry Sr. and his brother-in-law Michael were

Age eight, soon after starting violin lessons.
Courtesy estate of Bill Evans copyright © Nenette Evans 1996

business partners in a combined pool and billiard hall and bowling alley in Dunellen. Then, with a sure eye for business, they set up a summer-season golf driving range across the highway from the busy Hadley Airport near New Brunswick. In the winter they ran a similar one on Route 1 at Vero Beach, the Florida coastal resort to which Harry and Mary eventually retired.

The Evans brothers began to cycle from their white-boarded home on Hunter Avenue in Plainfield to piano lessons in neighboring Dunellen. Their teacher, Helen Leland, rated Harry the better pianist. Evans remembered her with affection and gratitude for not insisting on a heavy technical approach—which, with his temperament, might have turned him against music. Instead, she encouraged him to explore the printed note at sight. He soon found it easy to play what was put in front of him, an aptitude which later gained legendary status. There was a fair selection of sheet music at home, and he would plow willy-nilly through marches, polkas, songs, and classics, selecting favorites as he went.

The ability to sight-read is hard to explain, being in varying degrees innate, acquired by osmosis, and begotten by healthy curiosity. The true reader settles for imperfection en route, being impelled to attain the end of the phrase at all costs. Thus the reader views the concept of "practice"—the perfection of one's party piece—with deep suspicion. Evans exasperated his college teachers with imperfect renditions of the set scales and arpeggios. Practicing such items could never engage the youth's musical instincts. To be sure, he *played* a lot—three hours or so a day in childhood—but he focused the energy unconventionally. "Everything I've learned," he said, "I've learned with feeling being the generating force. I've never approached the piano as a thing in itself, but as a gateway to music."[2]

At the age of seven Evans embarked on violin studies, and although ultimately the instrument gave him little satisfaction, the experience of holding, even increasing, the sound on the string may well have contributed to his lifelong obsession with "singing" on the piano, the sensitive pianist's ultimate challenge, and one that he met supremely. Over the years he tackled several instruments, studying the flute and piccolo, for example, under the guidance of Joseph C. Schaedel, his high school music teacher. But the piano, on which he could attack and sustain with crystal clarity, remained his one true love. Much later he reflected on the cardinal position that the instrument had occupied in his early life: "The first time I realized that I really loved playing was when I was about ten and I broke my wrist climbing a tree. And I realized I missed playing the piano. It was a strange enlightenment. I'd taken it for granted."[3]

⋐⋐ ⋐⋐ ⋐⋐

The family moved to 490 Greenbrook Road, the brothers now attending North Plainfield High School. At home Evans enjoyed some formative listening experiences, reflecting his enthusiasm for contemporary European repertoire: "I can remember, for instance, the 78 album of Petruschka which I got early on in high school as a Christmas present—a requested Christmas present. And just about wearing it out, learning it. That was the kind of music that at that time I hadn't been exposed to, and it just was a tremendous experience to get into that piece. I remember first hearing some of Milhaud's polytonality and actually a piece that he may not think too much of—it was an early piece called Suite Provençale—which opened me up to certain things."[4]

Like most music lovers of his generation, Evans grew up through the

1940s with network radio. His musical mind was open, and his absorption of the radio's diverse fare was one reason for his later insistence that he had learned from everybody. His own training and repertoire, though, were strictly classical, and for six or seven years he played nothing but the notes on the page. Moreover, although he was an accomplished player, he had no understanding of how the music was constructed. In an educational video made in the sixties he reminisced with his brother about their school days: "From the age of six to thirteen, I acquired the ability to sight-read and to play classical music, so that actually both of us (as you know) were performing Mozart, Beethoven, or Schubert intelligently, musically. Yet I couldn't play 'My Country 'Tis of Thee' without the notes."[5]

This kind of musical blockage, a common result of habit and conditioning, was soon released. Evans recalled first hearing jazz at the age of twelve or so: the big band recordings of Tommy Dorsey and Harry James, followed by the great jazz instrumentalists. His brother, who was already absorbing the idiom, was learning the trumpet and playing in the school rehearsal band. When the piano player got the measles one day, Bill sat in, relishing his new-found role: "When I joined that rehearsal band I read the stock arrangements exactly as written, and once in a while I'd have a bell-tone in the third chorus—ding!—and I'd wait for that, because I had a little something."[6]

Then came a singular occasion, marking precisely the beginning of his jazz career: "One night we were playing 'Tuxedo Junction,' and for some reason I got inspired and put in a little blues thing. 'Tuxedo Junction' is in B♭, and I put in a little D♭, D, F thing in the right hand. It was such a thrill. It sounded right and good, and it wasn't written, and I had done it. The idea of doing something in music that somebody hadn't thought of opened a whole new world to me."[7]

He rapidly grasped the jazz idiom, and soon he made a cardboard disc, playing the "fastest boogie-woogie in Central Jersey." This natural facility awed his friends, whose letters began with salutations like "Dear Bill (drop dead) 88 keys, Evans."

His sight-reading skills led to opportunities at the local theater. He began playing his first professional jobs, at dances, weddings, and other events from Elizabeth to New Brunswick, working several nights a week as well as weekends. His schoolwork deteriorated somewhat as a result.

One mainstay local gig was at the Manville Polish Home, where there was a good polka band. The drummer and bandleader sat high above the bandstand on a riser of his own, playing with one hand and holding the microphone in the other. Evans recalled that this impresario knew "thousands of polkas" in Polish. As if the Sorokas had not suffered enough in the past at the hands of the Poles, Bill would take the train to Manville and churn out these dances for a dollar an hour.

He formed a trio with his friends Connie Atkinson on bass and Frank Robell on drums. During the summer, there was resort work around New Jersey. On gigs with a local group of older musicians, he would return home in the small hours, his first taste of the jazz life. The multi-instrumentalist Don Elliott, who was two or three years Bill's senior, dropped by from neighboring Somerville to sit in. Evans recorded with Elliott some fifteen years later at the Newport Jazz Festival, as well as on a studio album called *The Mello Sound*.

Evans wanted to find out how music was constructed, and he worked away in private at things he had not been taught. He took his cue from George Platt, the bass player in that local band. Evans recounted:

> He knew chord changes very well, and understood harmony and wrote arrangements, and had the patience of Job, I guess, because he called chord changes to me for a year and a half without ever saying, "Haven't you learned them yet?" Finally, instead of thinking of them as isolated changes, I worked out the system on which traditional theory is based: I just used numbers—I, V, VI, and so on—and began to understand how the music was put together.
>
> Also the band was more of a jazz band than the high school band. I had to play solos. On some of the jobs, the people expected to hear jazz, so I just dived in and tried it. I have recordings from the very beginning that show I was very clear in what I was doing. I've always preferred to play something simple than go all over the keyboard on something I wasn't clear about. Back then, I would stay within the triad.
>
> I was buying all the records... anybody from Coleman Hawkins to Bud Powell and Dexter Gordon. That was when I first heard Bud, on those Dexter Gordon sides on Savoy. I heard Earl Hines very early and, of course, the King Cole Trio. Nat, I thought, was one of the greatest, and I still do. I think he is probably the most underrated jazz pianist in the history of jazz.
>
> I'd play hookey from school and hear all the bands at the Paramount in New York or the Adams in Newark. Or we'd try to sneak in the clubs on 52nd St. with phony draft cards, just to hear some jazz. I got a lot of experience with insight that way.[8]

Evans was still in high school when the new music of bebop began to erupt in New York in the early 1940s. He was perhaps just too young, and not yet enamored enough of jazz, to adopt the new language. Then, precisely when he might have been ripe for conversion, he left the area to continue his studies in Louisiana. The end of the decade was spent a thousand miles away from the flourishing art of bebop, a simple geographical fact that led him to pursue other forms on his own.

⋐ ⋐ ⋐

So it was, in September 1946, that Evans, along with several other students from New Jersey, continued his musical studies on a scholarship to Southeastern Louisiana College at Hammond, some fifty miles from New Orleans. Just seventeen, he savored being on his own for the first time, and in such a place. "It's an age when everything makes a big impression," he said. "And Louisiana impressed me big. Maybe it's the way people live. The tempo and pace is slow. I always felt very relaxed and peaceful. Nobody ever pushed you to do this or say that. Perhaps it's due to a little looser feeling about life down there. Things just lope along, and there's a certain inexplicable indifference about the way people face their existence."9

The double life that he had established in high school—student and night owl—continued to flourish in Hammond. From a base on Magnolia Street, New Orleans, he went jamming almost nightly around the Crescent City and the surrounding countryside with his regular group, the Casuals. Later he described the sort of pocket-moneymaking gig the band undertook. One, for example, was an outdoor affair for seventy-odd folk: "It was a church in the middle of a field—a boxlike structure about forty by twenty with nondescript paint on the outside and none on the inside. It was more like a rough clubhouse than a church. I think they built it themselves. You wondered where the hell they came from because you couldn't see any houses around. It was a dance job. We played three or four tunes for them, and then blew one for ourselves. They didn't seem to mind. Everyone had a ball. The women cooked the food—it was jambalaya—and served it from big boards. Everything was free and relaxed. Experiences like these have got to affect your music."10

Back home, during summer vacation after his first year, he played in a group that included Russ Le Gandido on clarinet and saxophone, Connie Atkinson on bass, and the singer Eleanor Aimes. A private recording made at Point Pleasant on the New Jersey coast in August 1947 is a fascinating document of the teenage pianist. Already he was able to sustain a string of block chords underneath a newly created top line. Rhythmically, he began to insert broad triplets into a solo, a very personal touch. Harmonically, he kept things simple, departing from the triad to embrace sixths and thirteenths, occasionally adding the slightly more adventurous sharp fourth. In introductions, vocal backings, and solos alike, each component was earnest. For Evans, even at that age, there was no such thing as the glib, ready-made gesture. In the clarity of the thinking, and the simplicity of the material and its presentation, lay a shining promise for the future.

He assimilated "a thousand influences," from musicians at the clubs where he played to nationally prominent figures—not just pianists like Dave

The marching band (Connie Atkinson far left, Bill Evans far right).
Courtesy estate of Bill Evans copyright © Nenette Evans 1996

Brubeck, George Shearing, Oscar Peterson, Al Haig, and Lou Levy, but
hornmen as well, like Miles Davis, Dizzy Gillespie, Charlie Parker, and Stan
Getz. He took something from each. "Bud Powell has it all," he said, "but
even from him I wouldn't take everything. I wouldn't listen to a recording by
Bud and try to play along with it, to imitate. Rather, I'd listen to the record
and try to absorb the essence of it and apply it to something else. Besides, it
wasn't only the pianists but also the saxophones, the trumpets, everybody. It's
more the mind 'that thinks jazz' than the instrument 'that plays jazz' which
interests me."[11]

     The biggest influence on Evans at this time, though, was the pianism of
Nat "King" Cole—in Bill's estimation "one of the tastiest and just swingin'est
and beautifully melodic improvisers and jazz pianists that jazz has ever
known, and he was one of the very first that really grabbed me hard."[12] Evans
was particularly struck by the way Cole would expand just one idea through
a large span of chorus, citing his 1944 trio record of "Body and Soul" as an
example. It is easy to see the appeal: clarity and freshness of ideas, sparkling
fingers, flawless execution, pearly tone.

Evans frequently acknowledged his debt to Cole, but in one important respect they differed: attractive as the Cole sound was, the imagination of the young Evans sought something extra. Cole played delicately, "on the surface" of the keys, an approach perhaps cultivated from playing behind his own singing. That would not do for Evans, who, influenced in part by his ongoing classical training but mostly by his own expressive soul, demanded a deeper, more engaging tone, firmly extracted from the bed of the key.

⫤ ⫤ ⫤

Back at college, he was playing first flute in the concert band. If playing the violin had fostered a depth to his midregister piano tone, the flute promoted a pearly treble. His piano technique evolved, meanwhile, and he soon became known as the "king of the fast-lock tens," a reference to his left-hand "walking" tenths. In later life he reflected nostalgically on that formidable keyboard prowess. Such facility came naturally, for his attention was engaged by things higher than études, scales, and "practice." His end-of-term reports indicated as much, swinging between such comments as "fine talent," "unlimited possibilities," and "wonderful potential" to "needs brushing up on arpeggios," "technique, as such, deficient but certainly no hindrance in performance."

Evans's studies in the classical repertoire, two weekly lessons of an hour and a half each, took in sonatas by Mozart and Beethoven and works by Schumann, Rachmaninoff, Debussy, Ravel, Gershwin (the Piano Concerto in F), Villa-Lobos, Khachaturian, Milhaud, and others. Performances of some of these pieces were broadcast, and prizes came his way under the guidance of his piano teachers, Louis M. Kohnop, John Venettozzi, and Ronald Stetzel.

For his senior recital on April 24, 1950, Evans began with Bach's Prelude and Fugue in B♭ minor (from Book I of the "48"), Brahms's Capriccio, Opus 116, No. 7, and Chopin's B♭ minor Scherzo. Not surprisingly, a Russian composer was represented, Evans choosing a group of Kabalevsky's recently published Preludes. The program finished with the opening movement of Beethoven's Third Piano Concerto; Evans's teacher, Ronald Stetzel, played the orchestral part. Later, as honor graduate on Senior Class Day, he played the whole concerto with the college orchestra.

The constructional knowledge of music that Evans later brought to jazz was firmly rooted in this European tradition, as was his thoroughly trained and exquisitely refined touch at the keyboard. In later years, when interviewers observed that certain aspects of technique—his pedaling, for instance—were unusually polished for a jazz musician, Evans was invariably baffled, for the whole process had been quite unconscious for as long as he could remember.

But even as he mastered the classics, jazz was conquering his heart. He worked for hours on end at the grammar of jazz, refining his knowledge of what he was doing when playing it. As colleagues from his student days who had seemed more gifted—the ones with the "easier" talent—dropped out of the profession, Evans kept working, and playing.

He studied theory and composition with Gretchen Magee and became deeply appreciative of her guidance. With a piece called "Very Little Suite" he appeared on the college platform as composer-performer.

In about his third year he produced a small masterpiece in waltz time that he called "Very Early." It is a highly disciplined piece of writing, its melody comprising a two-bar falling, and then rising, germ; it can withstand the most rigorous structural analysis. It exemplifies a fundamental lifelong characteristic: the application of logic to a creative musical process. That approach was the backbone of the form and content of Evans's art. And yet when we listen to his music, we are conscious not of the compositional process but only of the resultant poetry. Played "straight" from the page "Very Early" is a lyrical gem; but it also provided its composer with a fruitful sequence for improvisation, the earliest of many compositions that sustained him around the globe for three decades.

He developed a love for the works of Thomas Hardy, becoming something of an expert on them. He also identified strongly with the visionary eighteenth-century poet and painter William Blake. Later, in discussing Blake's art, he propounded an artistic ideal:

> He's almost like a folk poet, but he reaches heights of art because of his simplicity. The simple things, the essences, are the great things, but our way of expressing them can be incredibly complex. It's the same thing with technique in music. You try to express a simple emotion—love, excitement, sadness—and often your technique gets in the way. It becomes an end in itself when it should really be only the funnel through which your feelings and ideas are communicated. The great artist always gets right to the heart of the matter. His technique is so natural it's invisible or unhearable. I've always had good facility, and that worries me. I hope it doesn't get in the way.[13]

Evans's talents were diverse—he was accomplished with pen and brush, for example, and his understanding of musical theory expanded into the sciences. His enthusiasm and skill in sports, notably football, came to the fore. He played quarterback in the winning side at the school's intramural tournament, his team representing the local chapter of the Phi Mu Alpha fraternity. On January 14, 1950, he was triply honored, receiving certificates for becoming president of that chapter, for his election to the Thirteen Club, and for earning an entry in "Who's Who Among Students in American Colleges and Universities."

With his music fraternity brothers on the steps of Southeastern Louisiana College, 1950.

Used with permission of Ron Nethercutt, Southeastern Louisiana University

Evans graduated from Southeastern in May 1950 with two degrees: bachelor of music with a piano major and bachelor of music education. In letters to his teachers years later, he expressed his deep appreciation of their patience, perseverance, and personal attention. Thirty years after he graduated, when he returned to play with his last trio, he told the audience that his last two years at the college had been the happiest of his life.

Ralph R. Pottle, head of the Department of Music, wrote several letters of recommendation for Evans upon his graduation, including one to a bandleader he knew in California named Freddy Martin:

I should like to recommend that you audition a young man who graduated here last week on piano. We brought him here four years ago on scholarship on piano primarily for dance work in our scholarship dance band. He became such a superb pianist that he finally played the Third Piano Concerto by Beethoven....

He was an excellent improvisor with a clean technique when he came here and had a flair for the smoothest modulations from key to key I had heard from one no older than he was then, about seventeen. Being an honor student throughout his four years of college, majoring in music, and an intent student of the modern idioms in piano playing, he developed to perhaps the finest all around dance pianist I have heard in the profession. This has been confirmed by other professionals who have visited our campus, among the name dance bands. When we made professional phonograph records recently (Vonna Records of Hollywood made them), the recording engineer told me the boy played the smoothest piano he had ever heard. Incidentally, his playing is so completely effortless that you can hardly believe what you hear. He covers the keyboard with a sense of rhythm and harmony and speed and orchestral balance which is remarkable. He told me just before leaving, after graduation, that he would endeavor to follow the profession of playing with dance orchestras. Surely a spot can be found for one so superior. He is a nice looking boy, always cooperative, good morale, clean morally—no drinking problem and so unassuming that he might be mistaken if one weren't on the lookout for him.[14]

One brief encounter early in his career at Southeastern augured well for Evans's future. A young guitarist who was making a name for himself, Mundell Lowe, had gone to school in Hammond and returned there straight from military service in the South Pacific. He was due to go on tour with Ray McKinley's enterprising swing band. With only a day or two to spare in Hammond before leaving, he managed to hear Evans at the college. Deeply impressed, he said, "When you come to New York, you find me and call me, because after I spend a while with Ray, I want to form a group and I'd sure like for you to play piano in it."[15]

Evans was elated, and he resolved to follow up on Lowe's offer should he head in that direction. Meanwhile, he had his teaching degree and was equipped to follow in his brother's footsteps if he wished. Harry had married and settled in nearby Baton Rouge, and eventually he became supervisor of musical education in the public schools there. But Mundell Lowe had recognized something special in Bill's playing, and he could not imagine the pianist as a teacher. Lowe's invitation to try his luck in the big city prompted the boy to give rein to more creative aspirations.

CHAPTER **2**   Swing Pianist

...when the moment came, bang! I went out into jazz.

—*Bill Evans*

Evans took up Mundell Lowe's trio invitation and called him in New York. The guitarist recalled: "So we met at the old Café Society downtown, Bill Evans and a young kid from New Jersey he had known, a bass player by the name of Red Mitchell. We put this trio together, and it was really a good group. The only problem was it was so good we couldn't get booked. Val Irving tried to book us for a while. He booked us in Dean Martin's hometown, Calumet City, Illinois. We played there for two weeks in one of those places where they literally had chicken wire around the bandstand so they couldn't hit you with the beer bottles. We continued together for a while but we had a rough time getting enough work."[1]

Thus for a brief period Evans joined in the line of piano, bass, and guitar trios pioneered by Nat "King" Cole in 1939 and notably upheld by Art Tatum, Ahmad Jamal, and Oscar Peterson. Lowe was an exploratory guitarist, and Red Mitchell was revealing fresh ways of articulating lines with a hornlike individuality. When I asked Mundell Lowe what it was about Evans's playing that struck him most in those early years, he answered in just two words: "So fresh." He remembered that Evans was already using block chords, George Shearing–style; it must have been an intriguing group.

⮢ ⮢ ⮢

At the end of July 1950, Evans landed the piano chair with the clarinetist and bandleader Herbie Fields, another colleague from New Jersey. This band's music went commercial during the fifties, but not before Fields had been voted New Star on alto by *Esquire* magazine. Evans maintained that he

learned how to accompany from Herbie Fields. The keyboard played a crucial role in the band's arrangements, and piano solos were prominent.
Occasionally everybody would join the leader in a unison vocal, and this was
when it sounded most like a jump band, rhythm-and-blues and boogie-woogie being integral to its makeup. Later Bill recalled, "In some ways he had
been a forerunner of rock 'n' roll. He was wiggling, jerking."[2] But the band
could embrace a gentler sophistication, too. When Evans joined he was a
master of all these styles.

That year the band undertook a typical itinerary, ranging from San
Francisco to Washington, taking in St. Paul and Detroit on the way. In New
York City they played the Paramount and Apollo Theaters and the 49th &
Broadway Club. A regular venue was the Silhouette Club in Chicago, and
from there, on October 10, the twenty-one-year-old Evans wrote to Dr. Pottle
at Southeastern to say how happy he was in the band. He added, though, that
he needed to brush up on piccolo: his selective service physical examination
notice had just arrived, and he fervently hoped that he could discharge his
patriotic duty musically.

After many months with Herbie Fields, Evans knew one thing: it was
hard work. "You know, I have often been condemned for not playing
strongly," he said. "But when I was with this band I would come off the stand
with split fingernails and sore arms. We worked hard trying to sound like the
full Lionel Hampton Orchestra."[3]

One other engagement stuck in his memory forever: he played in
Buddy Valentino's big band opposite Nat Cole in the Renaissance Ballroom
in Harlem. An awed Evans wrote to his brother, who was in the navy: "I sat at
the same piano and played the same keys as Nat King Cole," he said. "It was
reverential."[4]

⋵ ⋵ ⋵

In 1951, as the United States waged war in Korea, Evans was inducted
into the Special Services section. His recruitment in the army began, confus-
ingly, at the Navy School of Music in Washington, D.C., where musicians
from all the armed forces were trained in military music before dispersal to
their various posts. Jack Reilly, a pianist in the navy at the time, has never forgotten hearing Evans practicing at the music school one day. "It sounded like
a mixture of Bud Powell, George Shearing, and Teddy Wilson," Reilly told
me. "But more than that I was completely taken aback by the sheer joy and
above all the 'swing' element in his right-hand lines and his ability to coordi-
nate both hands as he improvised; that is, the left hand was never a mere

Bill Evans as a G.I.
Courtesy estate of Bill Evans copyright © Nenette Evans 1996

accompaniment, but always rhythmically integrated in and around the right-hand 'figures.' This was a *new* synthesis of what we mean by 'swing,' and the uniqueness of Evans in embryo."

Also enlisted in the navy was a young percussionist and composer from Chicago named Earl Zindars, with whose compositions Evans was to become uniquely associated. Zindars recalls their first meeting: "I had this arrangement of 'September in the Rain,' and I gave it to Bill, who gave it to the guys in the Army band. The Army and Navy bands were in heavy competition with each other—a band fight. He wrote to me when I got back to Chicago and said, 'We won the fight, and your arrangement was fantastic!'"[5]

Evans was posted to Fort Sheridan just north of Chicago, making sergeant and playing flute and piccolo in the Fifth Army Band. He had been relishing his newfound freedom on the road with Herbie Fields, and the army was a frustrating career interruption. He hated it, and it took him years to get over the experience. Later he had nightmares about having to do three extra years because his papers were lost.

He did make a friend for life in the army, though. Evans and the singer and bass player Bill Scott grew so close that each eventually was best man at the other's wedding. With a group of the other soldiers they ran a jazz show on the camp radio. Days off were spent playing through "fake" books of jazz sequences or going to the movies, where Evans first fell in love with some of the Disney tunes that he treated so distinctively later. He somehow continued to mature musically, listening and playing as a civilian around the clubs in Chicago. At one of these, the Streamliner, he got together for the first time with yet another New Jerseyite, the clarinetist Tony Scott.

ᘓᘒ ᘓᘒ ᘓᘒ

Evans was discharged from the army in January 1954. His confidence had been undermined, and he felt the need for a period of review and musical consolidation. "I was very happy and secure until I went into the army," he said. "Then I started to feel there was something I should know that I didn't. . . . I was attacked by some guys for what I believed, and by musicians who claimed I should play like this pianist or that. Pretty soon I lost the confidence I had as a kid. I began to think that everything I did was wrong."[6]

But it was not only insecurity that delayed his plunge into the outside world; it was also a clarity of vision about what it would take to succeed. "After the army, I went home to my parents and took a year off. I set up a little studio, acquired a grand piano and devoted a year to work on my playing. It did not come easy. I did not have that natural fluidity, and was not the type of person who just looks at the scene and through some intuitive process, immediately produces a finished product. I had to build my music very consciously, from the bottom up. My message to musicians who feel the same way is that they should keep at it, building block by block. The ultimate reward might be greater in the end, even if they have to work longer and harder in the process."[7]

This deeply probing homework gave Evans the foundation needed to sustain him through the toughest of professions, and it resulted in his always knowing what he was doing musically. He had been advised at Southeastern Louisiana that he had the makings of a concert pianist, and he was still suffering an inner conflict about which direction to take. He felt slightly guilty about favoring what he viewed as the easier option: jazz. It was scarcely easy: he still spent all day "woodshedding" in the soundproofed studio, having to be coaxed out simply to eat. His sister-in-law Pat, who frequently came up from Louisiana, recalls, "He often said to me that if he had anything to give, he could only give it through his music. It was his way of expressing himself as a person, his very being, through his music."[8] During this self-induced sabbatical, Bill also went down to Baton Rouge to see Pat and Harry. The brothers remained very close, and they maintained a mutual respect, Harry for Bill's playing and Bill for Harry's skill as a teacher.

Bill also envied the family side of his brother's life, and one of his joys on these family visits was spending time with his three-year-old niece, Debby. He often took her to the beach, and his fondness for her inspired him to write what became his most famous tune, "Waltz for Debby." His affinity for triple meter, then still unusual in jazz, fostered the natural flow of this lovely, lilting melody, which carries the listener effortlessly over its long lyrical span. Its construction is impeccable, the modulatory scheme exemplary, and those factors provided a strong basis for improvisation. But as with "Very Early," these techniques do not claim our attention. On the contrary, we are simply captivated by the song's charm and beauty.

ᘓ ᘓ ᘓ

Evans's parents retired to Ormond Beach in Florida, to the sun, the ocean, and golf; Harry Sr. had mellowed with maturity. For Bill it was time to make or break in New York City, and in July 1955 he rented a tiny apartment on West 83d Street. He had the proverbial few dollars in his pocket and a Knabe grand piano occupying most of the living room; its music stand held pieces by Chopin, Ravel, and Scriabin, as well as "The Well-Tempered Clavier" by Bach.

His appetite for musical knowledge led him to enroll downtown at the Mannes College of Music for three postgraduate semesters in composition. He filled notebooks with twelve-tone rows in all their permutations, at one point distilling from them an intense and frantic four-voice canon. He was well pleased, too, with some songs he wrote to poems by William Blake. These were to be his final studies in classical music, but he continued to play it for pleasure. A few years later his girlfriend Peri Cousins witnessed his daily fare: "He would usually play classical music. Of course, you know, he was a romantic. He played Rachmaninoff, but he also played Beethoven and Bach. He would play that and then just drift into jazz in a very fluid kind of way. It was wonderful to hear this—that was my privilege."[9]

Whether he made it in jazz or not, Evans knew that he could get work as a musician. He had decided to take stock after five years and make a choice: risk all for a career in jazz, or settle into studio work. During this first chancy, out-on-a-limb year he played some crazy jobs. There was the Friendship Club in Brooklyn three nights a week, and the Roseland Ballroom on Wednesday afternoons. He chased a bewildering variety of "Tuxedo gigs": society balls, Jewish weddings, intermission spots, and, most depressing of all, the over-forty dances. He rode down to Rockaway on the subway and played in some bar or other till five in the morning for a pittance. These jobs paid his rent, but he found the occasional real jazz gig, too: a week here, an odd concert date there, nights filling in — "depping" — a bonus in his diary.

Having learned his trade with the swing bands, he was ripe for the piano role in a small group. The bebop jazz combo, heralded by Oscar Pettiford and Dizzy Gillespie at the Onyx, had arrived in New York just more than a decade earlier, and the new music was in vogue. In the brownstone basements of 52d Street, jazz clubs and strip joints vied for supremacy. It was a heady time for jazz, with Art Tatum appearing at Basin Street, George Shearing at the Embers, and Bud Powell in residence at Birdland. Thelonious Monk played at the Café Bohemia. At places like the Hickory House and the Composer, Evans sat in, like everyone else, absorbing the scene and the songbook.

One engagement gave him a prophetic taste of the venue that was destined to mean most to him: the Village Vanguard. He remembered the gig as his first real break in New York City, working solo opposite the Modern Jazz Quartet:

> Nobody knew me, of course, and you could hear a pin drop during their sets, and despite the fact that Milt Jackson gave me a really fine introduction every time, this intimidated the audience into about five and a half seconds of silence, and from then on it was thunderous din. But I just kept playing. . . . Now one gratifying thing: one night I looked up, opened my eyes while I was playing, and Miles [Davis]'s head was at the end of the piano listening.
>
> But a more humorous part of it: the way the Vanguard is built, it's a triangular club and the bandstand is in the apex of the triangle and there are a few seats that are sort of behind the bandstand, just a bench against the wall and a thin table. And while I was playing one night, the maître d' brought a party of four up while I was playing — I stopped, he said excuse me — and he led them *between me and the keyboard* to that table. So that's about the way that first job was.[10]

Evans's abilities were instantly recognized by his colleagues, who were already predicting big things for him. There was a definition and a reliability about his playing that made him a ready choice for a gig. He found himself playing again with Don Elliott, as well as with Tony Scott, who was to become a guiding force over the next four years. As a result, he renewed contact with Mundell Lowe, who was featured in Scott's group, and they played clubs in Greenwich Village like the Dome and the Café Society. Harry Evans sometimes dropped in. Scott, who was arranging and conducting for Harry Belafonte, tried to persuade Evans to become the singer's accompanist. He declined, lacking confidence and feeling that it would interfere with his attendance at Mannes College.

⋐ ⋐ ⋐

One of Evans's regular jobs was with Jerry Wald, a popular clarinetist and bandleader who fronted a succession of good ensembles through the 1940s and 1950s. The previous year his band had recorded a program of Al Cohn arrangements for MGM's new Designed for Dancing series of ten-inch LPs. In some discographies Evans has been listed as the probable pianist, but he was surely incapable of such vapid tinkling.

He was instantly recognizable, though, on the twelve-inch Kapp LP *Listen to the Music of Jerry Wald*, which offered well-behaved arrangements for an instrumental sextet plus strings. On the surface Evans's numerous solos used conventional dotted rhythm and conformed to the swing-band manner, but within that framework he planted a variety of rhythmic devices, their timing always precise and, on a more jazz-driven "Love for Sale," decidedly snappy. He created fresh and clean-cut melodic lines, and on "Lucky to Be Me," from Leonard Bernstein's musical *On the Town*, he sounded an individual note. The key was F, and he ushered in the melody with a swiftly rising scale before the beat. This was no ordinary flourish, however, for after the introductory bell note, C, he used a minor scale on D♭, a more colorful solution than the conventional scale of F used later by the strings.

In the typical swing-band folio of the day it was a rare chart that did not modulate at least once. Here, too, for its final phrase, the Bernstein score moved up a minor third to finish out in the key of A♭. Evans was very much at home in these highways and byways, but that particular move was one lesson in structure that he always remembered.

In view of the remarkable collaboration that was to come, it is odd to register this as the pianist's first recorded session with the drummer Paul Motian, playing here in singularly polite style.

⋐ ⋐ ⋐

In the course of his night-time forays from Chicago's Fifth Army barracks, Evans had become friendly with a sensitive singer named Lucy Reed, to him one of the warmest nightclub attractions in the Windy City. She sang a regular spot at Chicago's Lei Aloha Club, in a threesome with the pianist Dick Marx and the bassist John Frigo. Early in 1955 this group came to New York to play the Café Society and the Club Chi Chi. Billed as Lucille Reed, the singer started a run of several weeks at Max Gordon's Village Vanguard club. She was being advised at the time by a young agent, Helen Keane, who had recently moved from Music Corporation of America to CBS. She put Reed into Gordon's other club, too: the Blue Angel. Evans met Keane, who seven years later became his agent, while hearing Reed at one of her gigs during this visit to New York.

When Reed returned to New York later in the year to record *The Singing Reed* for Fantasy, she used a group that included her friend Bill Evans at the keyboard. Evans served as singer-accompanist and pianist-arranger for a repertoire that was typical of Reed's Chicago shows. All those nights on the dance-band podium had equipped Evans with a bagful of piano licks, including a few personable, darting stabs of his own. The Johnny Mercer–Harold Arlen classic "Out of This World" elicited from Evans a striking Latin arrangement, his keyboard asides confirming the hint of menace in the guitar ostinato. The lucidity that he brought to this treatment carried over into his brief solo on Jimmy Van Heusen's "You May Not Love Me," which was delivered with a distinctive lyrical touch, revealing a blossoming ability to create atmosphere with beautiful sound. The double-tracking of the voice on Frank Loesser's "Inchworm" may be noted in passing, the singer using the recording technique to convey the illusion of two vocal characters. Evans became fascinated by this procedure, which would lead to supreme musical results in his own work.

For a time, Tony Scott's quartet had included the New York–born electric guitarist Dick Garcia, who came from a pedigree line of Spanish guitarists. He toured and recorded with the George Shearing quintet, playing on the hit track "Lullaby of Birdland." His first recording under his own name, as Richie Garcia, was *A Message from Garcia* on the Dawn label. Evans made a brief appearance, his first on record as a small-group sideman. On "Like Someone in Love" he again intimated a special sympathy with the songs of Jimmy Van Heusen, complementing the reflective mood with simple ideas delivered in the gentlest of manners.

ᚗ ᚗ ᚗ

Evans's career began to take off in 1956, largely through the efforts of the indefatigable clarinetist Tony Scott. Born Anthony Sciacca of Sicilian stock in Morristown, New Jersey, in 1921, Scott attended the Juilliard School of Music before studying with the grandiose eclectic Stefan Wolpe, a composer and teacher held in high esteem by the New York modernists in the 1950s. A mutual classical background helped to draw the budding jazzmen Scott and Evans together.

With a voracious appetite for jamming, Scott blew his way from joint to joint through the 1940s, elbowing his way into sessions with engaging audacity. All-night sessions on 52d Street and uptown at Minton's Playhouse were his way of life. As a pianist himself, and arranger to Billie Holiday and Sarah Vaughan, as well as Harry Belafonte, Scott was well attuned to the fundamental qualities in Evans's playing. He always claimed to have discovered Evans—he made the same claim with regard to the pianist Dick Hyman—maintaining that he had been trying to "snap him up" since 1949.

Scott was enjoying considerable fame as a leader in his own right and was able to offer Evans regular club work for several years. In the summer his quartet (with Evans, Les Grinage on bass, and Lennie McBrowne on drums) went on tour, taking in Chicago, Detroit, Trenton, Toronto, and Washington, winding up at a new club in Greenwich Village called The Pad. Evans was getting a feeling for the road, for a lifestyle that eventually ruled his career.

Meanwhile, Scott was being backed by RCA, and in July this quartet contributed four tracks to his showcase album, *The Touch of Tony Scott*. The location was one of New York's great recording venues, the neobaroque Webster Hall on the Lower East Side. Evans also joined two starry big band lineups for the rest of the album, which kicked off in great style with "Rock Me But Don't Roll Me," Scott screaming high over the top of his own tune and arrangement. Evans was no stranger to rock 'n' roll, having been exposed to all forms of pop during a decade on the dance circuit, and he could just be heard slotting in behind Mundell Lowe's raunchy guitar. Elsewhere, his comping touch was readily identifiable and precisely weighted. Some chords were held down longer than others, the timing of the cutoff as important as the attack.

It was on the quartet tracks, though, that Evans delivered his most fully formed work to date, displaying several facets of his rapidly developing talent. "'Round About Midnight" was notable for its reticence, Scott and Evans taking a refined view far removed from the rough-hewn original. Bill's classical training helped him layer the tone, the opening melody warmly projected, the accompanying chords touched in ever so lightly underneath.

On two other tracks he employed that artful, double-handed technique known as "locked hands," which he had been pursuing since his college

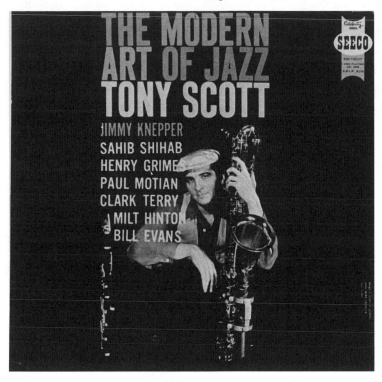

Clarinetist Tony Scott provided Evans with much late-fifties club work in New York.

days, each note of the melody played and harmonized by the right hand whilst simultaneously doubled at the octave below in the left. In this manner all the harmony notes became sandwiched between two parallel lines an octave apart. Derived from close saxophone-section voicings, the technique was pioneered at the keyboard by Milt Buckner in the Lionel Hampton band and popularized by George Shearing in his quintet recordings.

On "Aeolian Drinking Song," though, the aim was entirely different: to create single lines, either solo or in counterpoint, in the Aeolian mode—a scale from A to A on the white notes of the piano—based in this case on the note F. There was hardly a chord to be heard in the piece. In the first of several similar excursions in his early career, Evans met the challenge head-on. He was stark, deadly, and intellectually daunting. This track belonged to a separate strand in the pianist's makeup and will be better understood in the light of a radical session that had taken place in the same venue some three months earlier. On that occasion, the seminal figure in charge was the composer and arranger George Russell.

RCA rapidly set up sessions for a follow-up, to be called *The Complete Tony Scott*. The leader was to produce an entire big-band disc for the first time in his career. He not only dedicated his new swinging, danceable album to William Basie of Red Bank, New Jersey, but he secured the services of more than half of the Basie Band itself, including Freddie Green on guitar, as well as a couple of Duke Ellington's players.

Evans acquitted himself as the complete swing pianist with an unerring instinct for context, but the enterprise also gave him an opportunity to display his big-band arranging talent. His arresting score of "Walkin'" incorporated the traditionally played intro and tag perpetuated in the classic 1954 version by Miles Davis, which Evans would have known. Traits to emerge in Evans's playing were present in the writing—such things as rhythmic displacement and the temptation, ingrained from the swing charts, to change key. Reed voicings were sensuous, wah-wah syncopations tripped one over another, and imitations shadow-sparred.

In the middle of all this, Evans and the Scott group played the Preview's Modern Jazz Room in Chicago from Christmas until mid-January 1957. Then, after the final session for *The Complete Tony Scott*, there came a temporary break in their association. The intrepid clarinetist was off on a lengthy overseas tour, playing his way Pied Piperlike across Scandinavia, central Europe, and South Africa. As a talisman for all that was new in music, he dispensed a jazzed-up English language to the people: "Oop-bop-sh-bam, a-kloog-a-mop, Charlie Parker, Bird."

3

New Jazz Conceptions

All I must do is take care of the music.

—Bill Evans

The whole idea behind "Aeolian Drinking Song" was revolutionary and lay entirely outside the scope of the average swing musician. The one pianist on the scene in the summer of 1956 who was most likely to assimilate the idea and come through with flying colors in the execution was Bill Evans. His first recorded leap into that particular void had already occurred at the end of March, in a sextet led by the composer George Russell. *Down Beat* magazine had announced that Russell, who had not been active in jazz since 1951—when he had done "Ezz-thetic" and "Odjenar" for a cool Lee Konitz sextet nominally led by Miles Davis—was now writing for several forthcoming Victor jazz albums. Kenny Dorham was projected (prematurely, as it turned out) as the trumpeter, and Bill Evans was advertised as the pianist.

One hot day the previous summer, while recording *The Singing Reed*, Lucy Reed, who was an old friend of George Russell and his wife Juanita, called to say that she would love to visit with a friend called Bill. George suggested they all take a ride on the Staten Island ferry. His first impression of Lucy's friend was not encouraging—"plain looking fella, very quiet, very withdrawn"—and Russell felt that he was in for a tough time socially. *This is going to be like pulling teeth all day*, he thought.

Eventually they returned to the Russells' place at the Beechwood Hotel, where the stove, bed, ironing board, and piano were crammed together into one room. George was paying his dues working behind a lunch counter while working on his theoretical magnum opus, the *Lydian Concept*. As it happened, some of his arrangements had already come Bill's way in a concert with Lucy. The ironing board was moved onto the bed so that Evans could play, while Russell, expecting the worst, hovered at the door ready to make an excuse. Instead, "It was one of those magic moments in your life when you expect a horror story," he now recalls, "and the doors of heaven open up—I knew then and there he wasn't going to get away."[1]

⊑⊧ ⊑⊧ ⊑⊧

George Allan Russell was born in Cincinnati in 1923. He remembers singing in the choir of his African Methodist Episcopal Church, and he grew up to the sounds of Fate Marable's Kentucky riverboat music. Art Tatum spent some time in the city, and Russell sometimes heard him practicing. As a teenager he was impressed by Tatum's sounds, but he was equally struck by his first experience of modern symphonic music, a record of Debussy's "Fêtes" from the orchestral *Nocturnes*. He never let go of that sound, and the amalgamation of jazz with European forms was crucial to his musical philosophy. Like Tony Scott, he came under the influence of Stefan Wolpe for a while.

In 1941, after failing the draft because of spots on the lung, Russell entered the hospital for the first time with tuberculosis. It was during subsequent extended spells in the hospital, and between drumming with Benny Carter's band, that he formulated his theoretical work, fully entitled *The Lydian Chromatic Concept of Tonal Organization for Improvisation (for all instruments)*. The concept exposes an existing principle rather than inventing something new; Russell's revelation is based on the conviction that the Lydian scale on, for instance, C (C D E F♯ G A B) is more compatible with the tonality of C major than is the familiar C major scale. The logic of this, as explained in the book, is irrefutable, and Russell's thesis convinces not only theoretically but in the compelling brilliance of his own creations. "George composes things which sound improvised," Evans said. "You have to be deeply involved in jazz and understand all the elements to be able to do that."[2]

Evans became exposed to this world soon after he settled in New York in 1955, and he quickly absorbed its language. (Like the French genius, Olivier Messiaen, George Russell stakes out his own vernacular.) Evans's active participation began the following year, soon after RCA began a new series of recordings called Jazz Workshop. One of the recordings, led by the alto saxophonist Hal McKusick, included a piece by Russell. Encouraged by McKusick, Jack Lewis, the artists and repertory man for RCA Victor, offered the composer his own record date in the series. Russell already wanted Evans, and Hal McKusick recruited the other musicians, including trumpeter Art Farmer, guitarist Barry Galbraith, and bass player Milt Hinton.

Three recording dates were set up and a series of intensive Sunday rehearsals, usually at Hinton's house in Queens, took place before each session. The bassist played his part as written, but Art Farmer told me that the other musicians "took the parts home from the rehearsals and tried to come to terms with them. All George Russell's music was taken very seriously by the musicians. That Victor album took a year to do."

There was a calm and quiet confidence about George Russell that inspired trust in his players. RCA Victor sessions did not come easily, but Farmer remembers that the composer never panicked or raised his voice—and everyone knew there would be no overtime pay. Afterward Miles Davis told Farmer, "Man, that was very nice work. It can't have been easy." Called *The Jazz Workshop*, it was George Russell's first big-break album as leader, and for the first time he could swap a penurious lifestyle for the relative comfort of a small apartment on Bank Street in the Village. Russell and Evans became good friends, George and his wife nicknaming Bill "the minister," he looked so unlike a jazz musician.

The melodic and harmonic world created (or discovered) by Russell was hauntingly original. Hal McKusick, who sounded thoroughly at home in the sessions, nevertheless declared that it was like learning another language. The album should be assessed in terms of music history, for though undoubtedly a jazz record, it is also a twentieth-century classic, to be considered alongside the wind chamber works of Stravinsky or Varèse.

At the first session at Webster Hall in March, Evans turned in some solid work, firm of tone and with a spring in the fingers. Russell's most-played piece at the time was "Ezz-thetic," a tortuous bop line on the restructured chords of "Love for Sale." Bill's solo on it here gleaned from Bud Powell and Horace Silver but had a direction and purpose all its own.

Evans was not blessed with natural self-assurance, but by the time of the second session in October he had just completed his first trio album, *New Jazz Conceptions*, and his confidence was boosted as well by the presence of Paul Motian on "Round Johnny Rondo," "Witch Hunt," and, most of all, "Concerto for Billy the Kid." The "Concerto" was his real opportunity, designed especially by Russell "to supply a frame to match the vigor and vitality in the playing of pianist Bill Evans."[3] At the start, in the two-handed octave passage over bucking-bronco rhythm, Evans played from the written score, but soon stretched out, fully exposed, on the chords of "I'll Remember April." The precision of the fingerwork controlled the backing band, abetted by the alert Russell on the podium. This was one of the pianist's early tours de force, on a par with the more notorious "All About Rosie," composed by Russell about a year later.

The musicians knew that they had a sensational performance of "Concerto" in the can, but Art Farmer recalls that either Evans or Russell was dissatisfied with some element, and it was decided to have another crack at it during the final December session. On that take Evans incorporated a quote from Thelonious Monk's "Well, You Needn't." He had come under the wing of Monk, staying at his place once, just when he needed friends and contacts in New York City. He had no doubts about the quality of that eccentric genius's playing, and his favorite recording was the Prestige album from the early 1950s, mostly Monk originals in definitive versions. Evans particularly liked the humor in the playing. Later, in the sleeve note to the 1964 Columbia album *Monk*, he wrote: "Monk approaches the piano and...music as well, from an 'angle' that, although unprecedented, is just the right 'angle' for him."[4]

The Jazz Workshop was the first of a handful of stunning collaborations between Russell and Evans. The pieces were superbly structured, at once compositions and settings. Evans himself always stressed the importance of form and structure in his own work, whether it be the overall framework of a number or the shape of a solo. He was in his element participating, and one wonders what other pianist working in this context could have accomplished what Evans did: creating such assertive right-hand lines unaided by left-hand comping, integrating the invention stylistically, and reading the written parts with such skill. Art Farmer said, "The more difficult the music was, the more he made of it. He could deal with the weirdest chord changes and really respond to a challenge."

⊏⌷ ⊏⌷ ⊏⌷

The work of the pianist Lennie Tristano, with his cool approach to a line, permeated Evans's contribution to this music. Tristano came from Chicago, but when he arrived in New York in 1946 his radical thinking attracted a cult following, and in 1951 he set up his own studio from which to teach. His main disciples—Lee Konitz, Warne Marsh, Billy Bauer, and Sal Mosca—assisted in circulating his ideas, which were highly individual, not to say controversial. Students came from all over the world, and it is worth reflecting that Evans could have chosen to study with Tristano instead of enrolling for postgraduate study at Mannes College. Evans's faith, though, lay in the work of the established masters rather than the vision of one individual.

Tristano appeared infrequently in public, but in the latter half of 1955 he had been playing at his own Sing Song Room over the Confucius Restaurant in New York, and it is likely that Evans heard him there. In any case, Tristano's early quintet recordings had spoken to Bill directly as a student, their clear architectural thinking and emotional intensity inspiring him to write out charts of his own for alto and tenor saxophones. Evans cited tunes like "Tautology," "Marshmallow," and "Fishin' Around," saying, "I heard the fellows in his group building their lines with a design and general structure that was different from anything I'd ever heard in jazz. I think I was impressed by Lee and Warne more than by Lennie, although he was probably the germinal influence."[5]

Tristano was dismissive of others, outspoken and irascible. He once got up and left during a Bill Evans Trio performance, much to the embarrassment of Lee Konitz, who was obliged to leave with him.

The influence of the older pianist on the younger is clearly audible: Tristano, the sonic architect and ascetic, argued for soundness of construction but shied away from romantic inflection. Evans, the passionate romantic, nevertheless identified immediately with Tristano's logical approach. Thus a satisfying amalgam was achieved as Evans pursued Tristano's long, snaking, but rhythmically bland lines, injecting them with cross-rhythms and oblique accents of his own, the execution controlled with tightness and panache.

Evans's studio dates in 1956 lined up in such a way that he was switching back and forth, chameleonlike, from the language of George Russell's combo to that of Tony Scott's big band. Regardless of style, a finished aspect shone out consistently from his playing. Even at his most spontaneous, his choice of notes was never casual, always precise. The effect was of a top copy, produced after lengthy consideration, which impressed with its inner confidence.

In fact, though, the twenty-six-year-old Evans was far from confident, as evidenced by his reluctant approach to the setting up of *New Jazz Conceptions*, his first recording as a leader—and his first in the trio format of piano, bass, and drums, the lineup he was to make most significantly his own. The bashful pianist had to be pressed into action by a kind of subterfuge.

With some variations, the story goes that Evans was playing a gig with his old guitarist friend Mundell Lowe and the bassist Herman "Trigger" Alpert, who taped some of the session with an Ampex portable recorder. Lowe had been making some records for a newly emerging independent label called Riverside, whose production partners were Bill Grauer, in charge of business affairs, and producer Orrin Keepnews. Lowe knew that Evans would resist making a traditional demo of his own, so he played Alpert's tape to Grauer and Keepnews over the telephone.

Keepnews and Grauer were sufficiently struck by the low-fi sound coming down the line that they resolved to catch Evans live. After hearing him in

Evans got his first recording contract (with Riverside) after guitarist Mundell Lowe played a tape of him over the telephone to producer Orrin Keepnews.

the Village a few times, mostly with Tony Scott, they tendered him a contract: although it was a no-fringe contract at scale wages, the offer displayed an astuteness from a small company that the larger ones often lacked. Keepnews had some trouble convincing Evans that he was ready to record under his own name, and with a trio; usually, of course, it is the artist trying to persuade the producer.

It was standard practice in those days for a small jazz company to economize by recording an album in a single day, but Keepnews made an exception for Evans, giving him two well-separated sessions for his first trio recording. The pianist picked two of his erstwhile colleagues from the Tony Scott quartet with whom he felt at home: Teddy Kotick on bass and Paul Motian on drums. Evans chose the repertoire and had the idea for the three short piano solos. It was a groundbreaking record not only for Evans himself but for the prevailing jazz scene, bursting with variety and energy and containing four of Bill's own compositions.

The first of these was "Five," based on the chords of "I Got Rhythm."

Under cold analysis, the clever tune takes on the nature of an arithmetical puzzle. It is in four time, but quintuplets occupy each of the first sixteen bars. Evans himself was undecided how to notate the more complex middle eight, consisting of descending four-note scales (with an occasional rest in between); it was, in short, as Evans's pupil and friend Warren Bernhardt says, "a bitch to play." These four-note scale groups move down in thirds (a typical feature of the pianist's right-hand style) and they go *five* times into each half of the middle eight. On paper the intellect is satisfied, and in sound, as befits the Evans sense of humor, the piece emerges as a musical conundrum. In later years, he drove it hard, frequently playing it as a signature tune at the end of sets. He could be off the bandstand in half-a-minute flat with this frantic Speedy Gonzales play-out; it was his way of saying *That's it for tonight, folks!*

He was constantly preoccupied with the displacement of notes and phrases against the meter, and on his tune "Displacement," few notes indeed are on the beat. Its clipped, disjointed nature kindles a matching kind of improvisation in which brief, catchy ideas succeed one another, the left hand staccato-prompting the right. A couple of years earlier, Horace Silver was playing like this with Miles Davis—Evans and Silver were ardent mutual fans.

"No Cover, No Minimum" was a blues, "written" by Evans for the date. It has often been said that Evans was not at his best playing the blues, and he admitted as much himself. The rawness and simplicity of the idiom was generally incompatible with his musical character, but there was some strong playing here nonetheless.

The fourth original on the album, "Waltz for Debby," was one of three solo tracks, beautifully executed miniatures recorded after the sidemen had been dismissed. Written two years earlier for his niece, it was headed for jazz-classic status from the start, though Bill later expressed surprise at such an early piece achieving such a rank. This prototypical rendering was classical in another sense, being comparable to a piano vignette of, say, Robert Schumann's. Some six years later, at the composer's request, his friend Gene Lees added a touchingly perfect lyric.

Elsewhere, Paul Motian nudged and prodded, his extroverted character a fine match for the pianist's vigor. Motian's contribution was important, for in it were sown the seeds of the essential Bill Evans trio of the future, fostering chamber music among equals. Teddy Kotick, on the other hand, laid a firm walking foundation, fulfilling the traditional bass-playing role of the time. Evans's tone was chunky and positive and as sensitive on ballads as the instrument and acoustic would allow. There was accuracy and exuberance in those wiry fingers, and the brain behind them "composed live" with both imagination and intellect, adding "bop pianist" to his résumé in the process.

Evans always stressed that he learned from everyone, especially horn players, but there were specific influences at work, too. Nat Cole and Lennie Tristano have already been cited in his pianistic lineage, and Tristano frequently played opposite the great Bud Powell, freely acknowledging his influence. Powell's own long and energetic lines needled their way deeply into the playing of the young Evans, too, and their far-reaching effect is explosively evident on this album. If pushed into naming the influence of one pianist over all others, Evans nominated Bud Powell. Structurally, a typical Powell performance was framed by what might be called bookends, or precise settings for top and tail. Evans, formally disciplined from his dance-band days, seized on this strategy to set up a number of his tracks.

His work was acknowledged now by discerning jazz ears, but it had yet to reach the jazz-listening public. *New Jazz Conceptions* was released in January 1957, but despite good reviews from *Down Beat* and *Metronome*, it sold only about eight hundred copies during its first year. Evans had no qualms about this. His only goal was to improve his own private standards.

He said later, "I can remember coming to New York to make or break in jazz and saying to myself, *Now how should I attack this practical problem of becoming a jazz musician, as making a living and so on?* And ultimately, I came to the conclusion that all I must do is take care of the music, even if I do it in a closet. And if I really do that, somebody's going to come and open the door of the closet and say, *Hey, we're looking for you.*"[6]

CHAPTER **4**   Sideman

...just a bunch of friends playing together, having a good time, who respected one another as players.

—Milt Hinton

For a year and a half, Evans's life in New York had been hectic, including much club work and appearances on some half-dozen stylistically varied albums. Tony Scott, whose quartet had provided a regular booking in the pianist's diary, was now overseas, and Evans retired somewhat from the live scene. After *New Jazz Conceptions* he spent endless hours sight-reading Bach as an aid to developing tone control and technique.

Near the end of his life Evans told Jim Aikin: "Bach changed my hand approach to playing the piano. I used to use a lot of finger technique when I was younger, and I changed over to a weight technique. Actually, if you play Bach and the voices sing at all, and sustain the way they should, you can't really play it with the wrong approach. It's going to straighten you out in a hurry if you have a concept of what it should sound like."[1]

Evans needed good tone and independent fingers, among other qualities, to meet the challenge of his next group of engagements. In 1957 Brandeis University appointed the composer Gunther Schuller as artistic director to its Festival of the Arts. While lecturing there, Schuller coined the term "third-stream" for the fusion of the European musical tradition with jazz. In this context the university commissioned one composition from each of six composers, three from jazz (George Russell, Charles Mingus, and Jimmy Giuffre) and three from the classical world (Schuller, Harold Shapero, and Milton Babbitt). Bill Evans, as a well-rounded musician, was engaged as pianist for the event.

George Russell's contribution, a suite in three movements called "All

About Rosie," was previewed on NBC-TV's *Tonight Show* a week before the festival. For the core of his fourteen-piece lineup Russell drew on the talents of four musicians who had been at the heart of *The Jazz Workshop* LP: Evans, Art Farmer, Hal McKusick, and Barry Galbraith. The piece went well, Evans in particular rising to its considerable challenge; the power of television led to hallowed references in jazz circles to a "legendary" performance by an unknown pianist called Bill Evans.

All six works were played outdoors on the campus on June 6; Schuller conducted, and Nat Hentoff introduced the composers and their pieces. It was cold and damp, the audience was restless, and the performance of this demanding music reflected the inhospitable conditions. Listening closely was a twenty-year-old Brandeis student, Chuck Israels. Afterward he played bass in a trio at a reception; his colleagues were an even younger pianist, Steve Kuhn, and the drummer Arnold Wise. Evans liked what he heard from the trio and chatted with the players, little suspecting that both bassist and drummer would feature in his own group within the next few years.

The concert program was repeated more successfully indoors the following morning, and it was soon recorded as *Brandeis Jazz Festival* for Columbia. In the third movement of "All About Rosie," Russell spotlighted the pianist as he had in "Concerto for Billy the Kid": in both pieces tempo and feel were the same, "Rosie" taken perhaps a notch up from "Billy." Again the band dropped out on cue to leave Evans's coruscating right hand exposed in solo, his choice of notes uncanny, the rhythmic verve bracing, his fingerwork relentlessly muscular. Aside from the brilliance of the playing, the most notable element was the assured integration of improvised and written material, credit due in equal parts to composer and performer.

This stimulating attribute also characterized Evans's role in Schuller's piece, "Transformation," in which the composer made a gradual and brilliant transition from a nonjazz passacaglia form into jazz proper; complementing the composer's strategy, Evans moved smoothly from the written part to his improvised solo. In preparing the first movement of "Revelations" by Charles Mingus, Evans tasted the composer's working method, which was to rely more on oral explanation than on the written score. As befitted music arising out of a ritual event, Mingus's vocal exhortation, "O Yes, My Lord!" was followed by a rousing, "old church-style" piano solo. Later, Evans's down-home piano set up the ensemble "preaching" session at the heart of the movement. Undoubtedly Evans's classical training qualified him for invitation onto these grueling sessions; few musicians could offer the ability to read the atonal score of Milton Babbitt's "All Set" on the one hand and to provide free jazz improvisation on the other.

⊂⊫ ⊂⊫ ⊂⊫

While working on the Brandeis project, Evans was invited onto a small-group session for Jubilee Records. The electric guitarist Joe Puma— *Metronome* magazine's New Star poll-winner—was making *Joe Puma/Jazz*. He, too, had played in the Jerry Wald band, where he had met Paul Motian, also booked for this recording.

Bill rode to the studio with his army friend Earl Zindars, who told me this story:

> One very late evening, three musicians—Bill Evans, Bill Perry, and I—were sitting around and talking for a long time, when I suddenly said, "Let's have a contest right now for the best melody." We all agreed and after it had been very quiet for a while we took our tunes to the piano and played them back. Perry's melody was disqualified immediately because it didn't make any musical sense. Then Bill, who had written a twelve-tone melody (different from his later recorded "T.T.T."), played his, but he didn't care for it. Bill took my tune, which turned out rather well, and kept playing it over and over again until he said, "I'm gonna take Earl's tune to the Joe Puma session tomorrow." Of course I was delighted. It was at that session that Joe Puma christened it "Mother of Earl."

On the record this tune inspired Evans to an oblique less-is-more approach—much of the harmony was implied rather than explicit. This added an intriguing dimension, as though a more telling comment might be made by avoiding the obvious. Then, emerging imperceptibly on "I Got It Bad (and That Ain't Good)," Evans nudged a progression of graded, liquid-dropped chords, sixteen bars of perfectly conjured piano.

His potency of timing, which remains generally underrecognized, was as vital as his choice of notes, an acknowledged strength. The two went hand in hand, enhanced by a third element—tonal emphasis, so that the shape of a line, the rhythmic surprise within it, and the varying intensity of sound were intuitively created as one. These intimate tracks displayed Evans's most relaxed and subtle playing to date.

⊂⊫ ⊂⊫ ⊂⊫

Earlier in the year, Evans had been playing in a group led by Don Elliott, his old friend from Somerville. Elliott had become the most versatile of players, winning *Down Beat*'s Miscellaneous Instrumentalist award five years running (1953–57). Besides singing, he was adept on at least vibes, trumpet, bongos, and mellophone. The mellophone was his specialty, an easier-to-play, jazz substitute for the French horn. With a nucleus of Elliott, Evans, Bill Crow on bass, and Al Beldini at the drums, the combo toured the colleges in the Northeast on weekends.

This group, but now with Ernie Furtado on bass, was booked for an appearance at the Fourth Annual Newport Jazz Festival on Rhode Island in July. George Wein, the entrepreneur who directed the festival, was later responsible for including Evans on many "package" tours. The quartet shared the Saturday afternoon billing with Cecil Taylor's quartet, Jimmy Smith's trio, and the Horace Silver quintet. Don Elliott did a humorous set, with vocal impersonations and a vibraphone parody; like everyone else he was introduced by Willis Conover, the jazz voice of Voice of America.

Verve Records issued a series of LPs from the festival, and on one of these, *Eddie Costa, Mat Mathews, and Don Elliott at Newport,* are three numbers from the more sober beginning of the Elliott set. They furnish the first examples of Bill Evans's "live" playing on disc. He comped, as ever, with care and thought, and turned in two sparkling solos buoyantly propelled by his colleagues on bass and drums. The depth of piano tone was subtly varied within the line, even at these relatively up tempos. On his trio spot for "I Love You" he retained the chunky delivery and idiosyncratic coda of his performance on *New Jazz Conceptions*. He had fixed a format as a blueprint for the presentation of the number, a procedure he would apply to the whole of his regular repertoire. Three energetic solo choruses served as a reminder of the punishing work that he had done with Herbie Fields.

⊂⋢ ⊂⋢ ⊂⋢

A few weeks later, Evans was called upon to substitute for Dave McKenna in the popular Al Cohn–Zoot Sims Quintet at the Café Bohemia. One night in August he came home at about 4 A.M. to find a wire: "Can you make a record date this morning at 10 A.M. with Charlie Mingus?" For some reason Wade Legge, current pianist in the Mingus group, was not going to be there for the session. Perhaps Evans's contributions to "Revelations" at Brandeis had stuck in Mingus's mind. As a result of that experience, the pianist had at least an idea of what to expect. He made it to the session (for Bethlehem Records) and sight-read the parts — as Gil Evans used to say, Bill was a quick study.

The disc was issued as *East Coasting,* and there was no question who was at the helm: except on the two ballads, the powerhouse combination of Charles Mingus and Dannie Richmond got into its prodigious stride and swept all along before it. This wonderfully integrated group was perfectly attuned to the wavelength of its guiding spirit. Mingus generated sparks that ignited everyone into highly individual solos that were at the same time in a unified groove. Evans found an appropriate emotional footing every time, boldly stamping his own low-key imprint on proceedings.

Mingus expressed his approval when referring to the track "Conversation": "Notice he didn't come in and just play. He could have come in and run all over the piano; he has the technique for it. But he started his solo by developing from what the horns had said, and he kept building on that."[2]

On "West Coast Ghost," Evans's aural imagination again dictated to him that sound quality was as important as material, in this case resulting in an exemplary synthesis: as played here, and sustained in the pedal, the music tugged at the listener with a plaintive cry. Mingus was well pleased with the stand-in pianist's work and remained a staunch supporter of Evans over the years.

⋶ ⋶ ⋶

Earlier in the year the Charles Mingus Jazz Workshop had welcomed trombonist Jimmy Knepper to its ranks, a challenge that both fortified Knepper's individual voice and consolidated his reputation. Originally from Los Angeles, he had become disillusioned working in big bands on the East Coast and hungered for the smaller unit's potential for individuality. He made his first recording as leader on Mingus's Debut label in July, and for his second, *A Swinging Introduction*, on Bethlehem, he called upon the pianist whom Nat Hentoff had recently termed "urgently imaginative" and "increasingly arresting." This Evans certainly was on "Idol of the Flies," one of three originals from Knepper and the title of a later issue of the album. On this Stan Kenton–inspired piece Evans achieved a quirky mix of the linear and the chordal, the latter in a string of darting, rhythmic surprises.

⋶ ⋶ ⋶

Evans was being heard more and more around metropolitan New York, and in October 1957 he was able to boast a billing as the Bill Evans Quartet, splitting a long weekend with the hugely popular Anita O'Day at the Cork 'n' Bib on Long Island. Soon after, during two weeks at the Five Spot with Oscar Pettiford's group, Evans was taken ill, no doubt with one of his recurring liver complaints; it must have been a bad bout, because he always got up and played if he possibly could. Sharing the front line with Red Rodney in that combo was the baritone saxophonist Sahib Shihab, who had played in the pianist's arrangement of "Walkin'" on *The Complete Tony Scott*.

Evans joined Shihab for some tracks on *Jazz Sahib*, the saxophonist's recording debut as leader for Savoy. The session took place at Rudy Van Gelder's studio across the Hudson in Hackensack, New Jersey. In his converted living room, where he had a small Steinway grand, the engineer recorded for Savoy on Wednesdays and Thursdays, Prestige on Fridays, and Blue Note on Sundays. It was Evans's first visit to the Hackensack venue, and, perhaps because of the studio dryness, perhaps due to a lack of depth to the piano, he felt slightly uncomfortable. The recorded piano sound was distinctively "boxy." He sounded conspicuously himself, though, when simply taking four bars of the tune in Melba Liston's "Ballad to the East." Here, although Evans did nothing to alter melody or tempo, there was no mistaking that poised timing and weighting of tone.

⊏⊧ ⊏⊧ ⊏⊧

The following week, Evans had recovered sufficiently to join Shihab in a different group. Tony Scott was back from his overseas trip, and with typical enthusiasm he set up a marathon "blowing" and recording session with some of his favorite colleagues. He had parted amicably with RCA, feeling unable to conform to their terms; the musical gypsy in him needed to freelance. Commandeering a studio, he and his group laid down no fewer than twenty-five tracks, amounting to about two and a quarter hours of music. Tony Scott, Bill Evans, and Paul Motian were there for the duration, the other players drifting in and out of the studio. In 1991 the material was compiled on a double CD entitled *Tony Scott and Bill Evans: A Day in New York*.

The session probably came at the end of a running gig, as the simple head arrangements were confidently tight in execution. Paul Motian, playing more and more in the New York clubs, confirmed his status as one of the best of the small-group drummers, and Evans sounded happy to be back with his ebullient beat, reacting with smoothly flowing ideas. In this mix of standards and blowing themes by Scott—sometimes little more than token pegs hung on routine sequences—Evans found room for a variety of approaches, often adopting a characteristic stance for a number and sticking to it. He played, in turn, an affectionate George Shearing takeoff, a blues solo in octaves in slow motion against the fast beat, and superior cocktail commentary on ballads. Up-tempo he was deft and resilient, the fluency laced with invention.

The collection typifies his gigging at the time, such meetings flowing under the bridge nightly. Milt Hinton, talking in the early 1990s to Alyn Shipton on the BBC, put the whole feeling of those days nicely into perspective: "To you now those sessions seem like an extraordinary thing, but to us it was just a bunch of friends playing together, having a good time, who respected one another as players."[3]

⋐⋐ ⋐⋐ ⋐⋐

During the 1950s, something of a rash of baritone saxophonists blossomed onto the scene, and Evans had his fair share of playing with them. The run continued now with Pepper Adams, Evans joining the Prestige All-Stars in the Van Gelder studio for a long workout on the title track of *Roots*.

⋐⋐ ⋐⋐ ⋐⋐

Nineteen fifty-seven had been steadily rewarding. Evans had consolidated his reputation as one of the brightest and most reliable newcomers on the New York scene. The next year got off to a sunny start, in the studio with Eddie Costa. Costa, who had just been voted *Down Beat*'s New Star in both piano and vibes, hailed from Atlas, Pennsylvania, on the same coal-mining belt as Old Forge, the Soroka family's American roost. Growing up some fifty miles farther down the Susquehanna River, Costa had breathed the same contaminated air as Bill Evans's grandfather. Costa may well have been the vibraphonist on *Listen to the Music of Jerry Wald*, on which Evans had played, and they appeared as sidemen together a few more times after their 1958 studio session.

In 1956 Shelly Manne, André Previn, and Leroy Vinnegar had made a smash-hit LP of songs from the Broadway musical *My Fair Lady*. Now, in the same vein, Eddie Costa and his quartet tackled Frank Loesser's 1950 hit show *Guys and Dolls* for Coral Records. Eddie Costa was the nominal leader on *Guys and Dolls Like Vibes*, but the solo spotlighting was shared equally with Evans. The arrangements, too, were a joint effort.

"If I Were a Bell" proved itself the best jazz vehicle of the set, the whole quartet sparkling happily, Evans's solo adroit and delightfully cheeky. The other songs illustrate his earliest grapplings with show business material. On the ballads he went straight out for quality of sound, candidly hugging the melody with beautiful tone, his ear intuitively working the tonal differentiation between the hands. The exemplary and natural use of the sustaining pedal that Evans exhibited here was by no means a prerequisite of the jazz pianist, but he had long been able to shade Debussy and Ravel to a fine degree. He also started to develop in rudimentary fashion his signature touched-in block chording supporting the rhythm of the top line. This was the beginning of one of Evans's great stylistic innovations and once or twice, just for a radiant bar or two in the "Adelaide" solo, it could be heard in embryo.

⊑ ⊑ ⊑

The all-embracing Don Elliott was always on the search for new outlets and, inspired by the work of the great vocal arranger Jud Conlon, he now planned a mood album with voices. For his instrumental department he went right to the top, choosing, coincidentally, four of those musicians—Bill Evans, Hal McKusick, Barry Galbraith, and Paul Motian—who had been fundamental to George Russell's radically different work.

Elliott's album for Decca, *The Mello Sound: Don Elliott and His Choir*, is hardly a jazz record, but it is a delightful curiosity, an amiable period piece. Evans immersed himself in the "hi-fi mood" with understanding and respect. On this aptly titled disc everyone was exceedingly polite to everyone else, Don Elliott surpassing all with his mellow vibrato. Only on "Play Fiddle Play" did proceedings stir briefly into jazz life with a string of improvised choruses.

⊑ ⊑ ⊑

It is a small, almost incestuous world, the musical community. At times, especially on the jazz scene, it seems that everybody has played with everybody else somewhere or other, or has at least kept mutual company. The attractively husky ballad singer Helen Merrill, for instance, whom Evans now found himself backing in a recording session, had worked occasional club dates with his old swing band, the Jerry Wald orchestra. That band was quite a training school over the years.

Merrill was born in New York in the same year as Evans. She had always surrounded herself with the finest jazz musicians, jamming in the late 1940s with Charlie Parker, Bud Powell, and J. J. Johnson, and "sitting in with people like Diz and Miles," before signing a recording contract with EmArcy (Mercury's new jazz-only label) in 1954.

She counts herself fortunate to have grown up within a close-knit jazz fraternity. "There was an enormous amount of talent in New York City, and we naturally gravitated toward one another," she told me.

> We were both sure of ourselves, and at the same time painfully insecure. Bill was no exception. We created a cloistered world where we exchanged beautiful tunes, chord changes, and encouraging words. It was a comfortable place and one by one we made our way into our own fortune and fate. Bill would call me for tunes and I would happily suggest songs I thought were worthy of attention. I suggested "Beautiful Love" to him, and he listened to my record and faithfully played the melody I sang, which was not the original melody. We both had a good laugh about

that. He would call me on other occasions. Once, just before going with Miles, he wondered if he would be "good enough," and I assured him he was. He also called me the night before our recording together and asked the same question. Of course, the answer was the same.

Evans was engaged for a handful of tracks on the last of Merrill's EmArcy albums, *The Nearness of You*. The sleeve, in the fashion of the time, spelled out the sort of thing to expect from your latest purchase: "Type of Music: Warm, jazz-based vocalizing with backing from flute and rhythm. Intimate fare."[4] Helen Merrill had asked George Russell to do the arrangements, which remained uncredited. Sleeve and discographies list Russell on guitar, but he assures me that the guitarist was Barry Galbraith, whom he always used in his writing. With the exception of "Just Imagine," which he did not touch, Russell's distinctive voice was evident in the spare language of the settings. Merrill, enticingly warm, molded the intensity of her tone like a horn, coloring her line with a tastefully controlled vibrato. Evans commented dreamily on the title track. "Bill was a wonderful accompanist," she added. "But is that any wonder since he was so very sensitive and endlessly musical?" The Belgian tenor saxophonist Bobby Jaspar, here a full-bodied soloist on flute, went on to guest with the Bill Evans Trio at the Showplace during the following year.

⋐ ⋐ ⋐

The indispensable Evans next took part in an important Hal McKusick album, *Cross Section–Saxes*, on Decca. Three sessions were clearly differentiated in character according to the arranger involved. Jimmy Giuffre, for instance, created three highly original vignettes, by turn cellular, linear, and sparse. Then Ernie Wilkins and George Handy provided more traditional fare, employing a saxophone quartet with a suppleness to match McKusick's own playing. On the Charlie Parker blues "Now's the Time," Evans followed on after Wilkins's sumptuous section scoring of Parker's original 1945 solo—the nearest we shall get to hearing Evans jamming with Parker. The three remaining tracks were from George Russell, who was continuing along the path of *The Jazz Workshop*. On Russell's original, "Stratusphunk," Evans's fine, darting solo extended as a filigree behind the returning theme statement.

He was becoming well known for his ability to play "contemporary" music—third-stream and avant-garde—and, encouraged by critical praise, he was tempted for a while to concentrate his career in that area. The Brandeis album was about to be released, and now came a further television exposure. It was June 1958, and George Russell was the guest star on the

NBC-TV series *The Subject Is Jazz,* introduced by Gilbert Seldes. The musical director for the series was the jazz pianist and scholar Billy Taylor. He had been so impressed with the Russell-Evans escapade on RCA's "Concerto for Billy the Kid" that he built the final installment of the program, called "The Future of Jazz," around another performance of it.

Within a year the range of Evans's playing had expanded to embrace the far-flung worlds of the cocktail lounge and Milton Babbitt. At points in between, a flash of insight would fleetingly evoke a new voicing, one that worked perfectly and revealed itself as fresh not only to Evans but to the language of jazz. A new harmonic world glimmered on the horizon toward which he would ever strive. At other times the novelty might lie as much in the emphases within the chord as in the chord itself. A sense of structure was steadily developing in his solos; an accumulating series of related gestures might be crowned with a resolution that was both unexpected yet satisfyingly pressed home. The unpredictability of the rhythmic mold into which his notes were cast was increasingly attractive. He seemed incapable of anything indiscriminate or inconsequential, even when comping. Indeed, remarkably, he could often be identified from his comping alone, a sample eight-bar section emerging like a carefully thought out miniature arrangement.

Evans was, it seemed, ready for anything. Good thing he was, for one night he suddenly found himself down in Brooklyn playing hell for leather in the Miles Davis band.

Part II
The First Trio, 1958–61

CHAPTER **5**   A Call from Miles

Boy, I've sure learned a lot from Bill Evans. He plays the piano the way it should be played.

—*Miles Davis*

The trumpeter Miles Davis, after working through a succession of short-lived ensembles, had finally, toward the end of 1955, formed what turned out to be a settled group, called the New Miles Davis Quintet. The other players were John Coltrane on tenor sax, Red Garland on piano, Paul Chambers on bass, and Philly Joe Jones on drums. It is hard to imagine a more impressive quintet than this one, with Davis and Coltrane riding high on its supremely integrated rhythm section. Garland, although he played flamboyantly, always used his prodigious technique to imaginative ends. He became the perfect complement to Davis, ever alert when backing, and contributing energy and content in his own right. This group had been together on the road for two and a half years and had made a series of classic albums—including *Workin'*, *Steamin'*, *Relaxin'*, and *Cookin'*—when its leader, for various reasons, began looking for a new pianist.

For all its brilliance, the group had its problems, largely drug-related; Garland was becoming increasingly unreliable, and the replacement of Philly Joe Jones with Jimmy Cobb was imminent. A musical question also hovered: on one of the *Milestones* sessions in April 1958, Red Garland's indisposition had left Davis to double on piano in his own composition "Sid's Ahead." The cryptic chords that the trumpeter used on that occasion reinforced a "modal" pull—a move away from diatonic harmonies and their relationships—that he had been feeling intermittently for some years.

Needing a pianist both reliable and in tune with this imagined world, Davis approached his friend George Russell for advice. After *The Jazz*

Workshop, the Brandeis concert, and *Cross Section–Saxes,* Russell readily suggested Bill Evans. That recommendation confirmed Davis's own inclination.
The trumpeter had been keeping an ear open for Evans's work over the past year
or two, and the pianist knew it, for his friend Julian "Cannonball" Adderley,
who had joined the Davis band late in 1957, kept him posted. Evans, for his part,
had known Davis's work well since the earliest Savoy records of 1945. But apart
from a brief hello at the Composer's club, the two had never met.

Davis, the master of understatement, was also looking for a pianist who
would complement his feeling for space. Garland tended to drop his chords
in at regular intervals and sometimes insistently, admitting space in a general
way. Evans, in contrast, did so specifically, his carefully judged silences integral to a structure which acted like a scaffolding of immense but rarified
strength. Such cool clarity, without sacrificing flexibility, appealed to Davis,
as did the fresh harmonic slants that Evans brought to his voicings. Davis also
may have been ready for a quieter voice from the keyboard. Garland was a
hard act to follow, but what Evans had to offer was something completely different. It has been said that when Evans and Cobb joined, the energy went
out of the Davis band, but what Evans contributed in its place was of deeper
value and farther-reaching consequence. It was recognized as such by Davis,
and indeed by the history of jazz.

George Russell told me exactly how the two players came together:

> Miles was having a problem with substance abuse in his band and asked me if I
> knew of any pianist who could play the job. I recommended Bill.
> "Is he white?" asked Miles.
> "Yeah," I replied.
> "Does he wear glasses?"
> "Yeah."
> "I know that motherfucker. I heard him at Birdland—he can play his ass off.
> Bring him over to the Colony in Brooklyn on Thursday night."
> The Colony Club was a small neighborhood joint in Bedford Stuyvesant, a
> black area of Brooklyn, gang-dominated then—in those days not the sort of place
> you wanted to break down in your car if you were white. I called Bill and piled him
> into the Volkswagen along with Barry Galbraith and drove him down to the club.
> The full sextet was playing—Philly Joe Jones, Paul Chambers, Red Garland,
> Cannonball Adderley, John Coltrane, and Miles Davis. Bill sat in after the first set.
> At the end, Miles said, "You're hired."

Evans gave a different account, Miles's growl and all: "Although I'd
never really met the man, the phone rang one day and I picked it up and said
hello and I hear, 'Hello. Bill, this is Miles—Miles Davis. You wanna make a
weekend in Philadelphia?' I almost—you know—fainted; I made that weekend and he asked me to stay with the band."[1]

That weekend in Philadelphia—earned by Bill's "hot seat audition" in Brooklyn—kicked off several months of a relationship amounting to a mini-epoch in the evolution of jazz. The pianist's self-assurance was given a huge boost by the posting. "I had always had a great respect for Miles Davis," he said later. "And when he asked me to join him I realised that I had to revise my views about my own playing. If I continued to feel inadequate as a pianist, it would be to deny my respect for Davis. So I began to accept the position in which I had been placed."[2] As it turned out, he was able not only to distinguish himself in one of the greatest small bands in history but also to exert his own influence upon its leader.

⋵ ⋵ ⋵

Evans joined Davis in April 1958, and for the first few weeks he relished having Philly Joe Jones at the helm. Their mutual respect developed into a momentous and lifelong association, both personal and professional. Saturday night radio broadcasts were the fashion, and on May 3 the Mutual Network's *Bandstand USA* carried the new lineup playing "Woody'n You," "In Your Own Sweet Way," and "A Night in Tunisia" from the Café Bohemia in New York. This was Oscar Pettiford's club on Barrow Street, where Adderley had played his New York debut shortly after it opened in 1955. It was a long, narrow space with a bar at one end and the bandstand at the other, and Evans knew it well as a member of the Tony Scott group. The following week the sextet played the Storyville Club in Boston, again making the Saturday night broadcast.

The pattern continued a week later still, with the group back at the Bohemia on May 17. *Bandstand USA* again featured the "controversial" Miles Davis. The session appeared on the Chakra label as part of an album called *Makin' Wax*, the first-issued document of Evans with the Miles Davis band. On this particular night Adderley could not make it, so the lineup was the basic Miles Davis Quintet, with Garland replaced by Evans.

The tunes were standard fare for the group, material that Evans had by then gotten into a familiar bandstand groove. Only slightly awed by his surroundings, the pianist sustained his spot on the up-tempo "Walkin'" by lacing his personal turns of phrase with blues inflections. Davis kicked off "Bye Bye Blackbird" in the "wrong key" of G (rather than F), a deliberate tease in which Evans conspired. A radio broadcast in those days was not geared to posterity and suffered at the sound engineer's whim; microphones were turned up and down like yo-yos to accommodate the current soloist. As a result, some tantalizing chordal backing from Evans was all but lost.

The Village Vanguard club in New York, Evans's "home" territory.
Toby Appel

Over the closing radio-tag playout of "Two Bass Hit," the master of cere-monies plugged the Sunday afternoon concert sessions at the club: "You just go in, pay your admission price and that's all—you don't have to buy any-thing else." As Evans's blues title from *New Jazz Conceptions* put it, no cover, no minimum. Dom Cerulli, the New York editor of the Chicago-based *Down Beat*, was on hand to identify the musicians for the listeners.

⊏⊨ ⊏⊨ ⊏⊨

The following week the sextet moved into the Village Vanguard, Jimmy Cobb taking over at the drums. The club was closed on Monday, so May 26 was a good day to go into the studio for Columbia. The resulting album is usually known as *Jazz Track*. No one could have anticipated the outcome of this session, which produced playing of such intensity, spirituality, and Olympian beauty that it ranked as one of those crucial moments in the his-tory of art after which things were never quite the same again.

For all kinds of reasons the musicians coalesced in an extraordinary way. Evans's burning message—lyrical, textural, sensual—had to be released; it had long been smoldering within him, the very core of his musicality. His first studio setup with Davis gave him the freedom to express himself with some refinement away from the rough and tumble of the bandstand, and this, along with a fresh repertoire of intriguing chord sequences, lent the atmosphere an air of untapped promise. Until this moment, the world did not know the magic that Evans was holding. Perhaps only Davis suspected.

Davis liked both Garland and Evans because they played a "sound" rather than a chord. In his solo introduction to "On Green Dolphin Street" Evans lovingly molded that sound, crystallized from all his efforts to date. With the very first chord he hit his true vein, refuting those piano technicians who maintain that the instrument is incapable of individual expression. There *is* a way of weighting the touch, distributing the timbre, and breathing the approach that says, *listen*. The imagination *can* manipulate ivory, felt, steel, and spruce to sublime ends. Evans called it putting emotion into the piano, and he proved that it can be done; it is the artist's mind over matter. The sounds he created on this date were so incredible that he might have invented a new instrument. This was no ordinary piano but a new breed of animal, the familiar instrument transcended. As a matter of fact, the studio piano was sadly out of tune, but we hardly notice; on the contrary, the enduring impression is of beautiful piano sound, such is the depth of the player's message. For the first time it may be said: one sustained chord from Evans says more than a thousand words.

This artist had a vision, and the technique to realize it. Always articulate in musical matters (whether playing or speaking) Evans outlined his definition of technique: "Technique is the ability to translate your ideas into sound through your instrument. This is a comprehensive technique which goes beyond scales and so on. It's *expressive* technique...a feeling for the keyboard that will allow you to transfer any emotional utterance into it. What has to happen is that you develop a comprehensive technique and then say, 'Forget that. I'm just going to be expressive through the piano.'"[3]

His apprenticeship at Southeastern had stimulated his ear for tone color, the potency of harmony, as well as for mood and emotion, in a way that only the European classical repertoire could. Now, with the technique he describes, his fingers were free to strive for the music behind the notes: "You have to spend a lot of years at the keyboard before what's inside can get through your hands and into the piano. For years and years that was a constant frustration for me. I wanted to get that expressive thing in, but somehow it didn't happen. When I was about twenty-six—about a year before I went with Miles—that was the first time I had attained a certain degree of expressiveness in my playing. Believe me, I had played a lot of jazz before then. I started when I was thirteen. I was putting some of the feelings I had into the piano. Of course, having the feelings is another thing, another matter."4

Evans had those feelings in abundance, and on this day he became the catalyst for Davis. Attentive, Miles responded with his muted song, in a new-found lyricism of his own. Bill, beautifully poised, returned the compliment with limpid tone, his touch immaculate, the voicing superb.

The mood of the session was pervadingly lyrical, the first three numbers new to Davis and almost new to jazz. "On Green Dolphin Street," by the Polish composer Bronislau Kaper, and Victor Young's "Stella by Starlight" were both from forties films—*Green Dolphin Street* and *The Uninvited*, respectively—and have provided satisfying improvising vehicles for jazzmen, including Evans himself, ever since that seminal day.

"On Green Dolphin Street" (apparently suggested by Adderley) was a gift for Evans, with its chromatically falling chords over a pedal bass. Just before the take, Miles leaned over Bill's shoulder to make a rare specific demand. "I want this here," he said: rather than the pedal point in Kaper's songsheet (and for the introduction only) he wanted the piano's bass line to rise a minor third, and then to fall by three semitones. Evans's visionary interpretation of this overture and subsequent solo helped make this float-ing, medium-tempo version the one by which all others have since been judged, for it became a jazz standard after this. In that solo, his top line developed into a fine melodic invention—no single voice though, but a shifting block of organic sound, melody and harmony fused. That "pull" exerted by the pedal note on the changing chords above was a very old device and was particularly exploited by a contemporary of Kaper's, the Armenian-Russian composer Aram Khachaturian. It appealed both to Evans's harmonic sense and the Russian quota in his genes, and he went on to introduce Davis to the music of Khachaturian and Rachmaninoff (as well as Ravel).

On "Fran-Dance" Evans matched the nasal trumpet tone with piquant chords, again specified by Davis, and in his brief and simple solo he demon-strated the voicing of harmony as the piano's most expressive tool. These chordal requests hallmarked each number's character, and Evans later cited them as two of maybe four or five that Davis ever made; Adderley said that in his two years with the band they probably had about five (very succinct) rehearsals, two of them when he first joined.

On the very slow "Stella by Starlight" Jimmy Cobb was inspired, the conveyance of levels faultless; his move to sticks behind Coltrane instilled a moment of high drama. The drummer elevated and propelled majestically,

Coltrane responding with lyrical power. Evans loped along behind, effort-lessly manipulating the space of the inexorable progression.

These three tracks marked the first great milestone in the pianist's lyri-cal development and in turn set the tone for the more famous album, *Kind of Blue,* to be made by the same musicians ten months later. There followed in the studio "Love for Sale," with a spring in everyone's step. When this track was first issued in 1975, Evans recalled: "Paul Chambers and Jimmy Cobb were getting edgy having to hold back, and wanted to cook on something. Miles just turned and said, 'Love for Sale,' and kicked it off."[5]

ⅽ⊱ ⅽ⊱ ⅽ⊱

The previous year the young French composer Michel Legrand had gone to New York to arrange and conduct a series of "mood" albums for Columbia. To appease his passion for jazz in general, and Miles Davis in par-ticular, a record of jazz classics called *Legrand Jazz* was planned. For this, Legrand's first attempt at writing for jazz musicians, three orchestras were booked, one led by Miles Davis, who had the prerogative of bringing in a nucleus of players. He took four from his current sextet, including Evans, who had no idea what to expect; Davis just said, "Come on in and do a date."

It was appropriate that the composer of "Waltz for Debby" should find himself booked to play the ballroom-orchestra piano part on Legrand's set-ting of "The Jitterbug Waltz." He invested it with a tasteful rubato, wafting down in romantic fashion backed by the harp. His subsequent single-line solo, though, reverted to his true Davis-band mode of the moment, confident and crisp. Legrand's opening to "'Round Midnight" was a complete red her-ring, Evans's tinsel-bedecked arpeggios (rendered as if in white tie and tails) defying any notion that Miles was about to enter playing Monk. John Lewis's "Django" boosted the Gallic content of this transatlantic potpourri, Bill accompanying Miles with semistaccato droplets in deference to its com-poser's piano style.

ⅽ⊱ ⅽ⊱ ⅽ⊱

In June the Davis sextet played one-week residencies at the Spotlite Lounge in Washington, D.C., and at Small's Paradise in New York City. By this time, the leader's prestige was such that he was able to offer his band the best-paid job in jazz. But he worked only when he felt like it, and the side-men were paid per gig (a trial offer of retainers having not worked out), so they were either tempted or forced to take other work.

One such job, a Riverside recording, was slotted in by Adderley and

Evans on July 1, just before the sextet's Newport Festival appearance. For *Portrait of Cannonball,* as the album was called, Adderley called on two of his friends from Florida: trumpeter Blue Mitchell and bass player Sam Jones. Philly Joe Jones (now running bands of his own) and Bill Evans were natural choices to complete the quintet.

From Evans's point of view, the session was important for the first performance of "Nardis," specially written for Adderley and this session by Miles Davis. The trumpeter never recorded it, but Bill Evans took it over for life. Davis "came along to the studio with it," Evans recalled. "It was certainly different; it moved differently, and you could see that the guys were struggling with it. Miles wasn't happy either, but after the date he said that I was the only one to play it in the way he wanted. I must have helped his royalties over the years, because I have never stopped playing it. It has gone on evolving with every trio I have had."[6] On the originally issued take, he formed his solo with care and typical logic, floating gently prodded chords from another time dimension over the bridge, and finally working a two-note cell for the close.

Nearly two years had passed since he had inaugurated his solo career in this very studio—on what sounds like the same piano—with *New Jazz Conceptions.* The development in his playing can be heard on "Straight Life," a new ballad from Adderley (not to be confused with Art Pepper's bebop tune of 1951). There was now an added lyrical dimension in the voicings, tone quality, and depth of feeling. The mood created was spellbinding, the minimum selection of notes speaking for itself; why play ten when two can say more? The listener is mesmerized by the living presence of the understatement. A year or two before, even Evans could not have done this. Additionally, throughout this Tuesday session he experimented with brief right-hand snatches in octaves, perhaps thinking of the Thursday to come in Newport, when the extra force engendered might come in handy in the wide-open spaces of Freebody Park.

⊏⊱ ⊏⊱ ⊏⊱

The Miles Davis band made the trip to the coastal resort of Newport, Rhode Island, for its Fifth Annual Jazz Festival. Evans and Davis often traveled together on such trips. The festival began with Salute to Duke Ellington Night; the session was notable for a plethora of press attention, general chaos backstage and onstage, and delayed starting times. Miles and his sextet concluded the first half. At the previous year's festival Evans had played his own trio spot in Don Elliott's set. This time, though there was no such focus, his star status was assured by the distinguished company he was keeping, his position the envy of just about every jazz pianist in America.

The set was recorded by Columbia and released, complete (for the first time) with Willis Conover's introduction and the full theme at the end, on a 1994 double CD called *Miles Davis & Thelonious Monk: Live at Newport 1958 & 1963*. Davis seemed determined to show that, even without Red Garland and Philly Joe Jones, the band's energy level was still high. And indeed, they produced a magnificent, highly charged set.

On the opener, "Ah-Leu-Cha," the tempo was well up, the three horns in wild form. Evans, excused a solo turn in the midst of this onslaught, largely restricted his comping to the middle eights. Scarcely drawing breath, the leader instructed the band into a lively "Straight, No Chaser," Paul Chambers half-timing his beat under the beginning of each solo. Evans and Chambers cooled things down with two fine solos, preparing the way for "Fran-Dance" at the heart of the set, the only concession from the group's regular club fare to the new lyrical repertoire. Coltrane went off on a trip of his own as usual, and then Evans turned in a real gem, blossoming into full flowering maturity with an exquisite sample of his newfound gospel. His inner conviction strengthening, he took risks with ideas, playing beyond himself and his material.

⋲ ⋲ ⋲

Later in July the sextet played two weeks back at the Village Vanguard, followed by a week at the Spotlite Lounge in Washington. For many years a poor-quality, private tape of "Walkin'," "All of You," and "'Round Midnight" has been in circulation. It may have been taken from this Spotlite engagement on August 9. In 1995 this material was included on an Italian CD called *Four-Play*. The document preserves something of the audience prejudice that Evans had to contend with on the road: for his solo on "Walkin'" he received noticeably less applause than the other soloists, and for that on "All of You" none at all—and they were both good excursions. Bill referred to this as the "silent treatment," meted out by black listeners who resented him replacing Red Garland. The group went on to the Comedy Club in Baltimore.

⋲ ⋲ ⋲

Cannonball Adderley, now on a five-year contract to Mercury Records, again took time off from the Davis band to enter the studio in his own right. The subject was Duke Ellington's ill-fated show *Jump for Joy*. Mercury had drafted the composer Bill Russo to arrange ten numbers from the score for a small jazz combo plus string quartet. From the Davis sextet Adderley took with him Bill Evans and Jimmy Cobb, but the spirit on *Jump for Joy* remained largely stifled. Evans was neither encouraged nor inclined to be himself, and his talents were wasted.

ci ci ci

Two days later, on August 23, the Davis sextet appeared at the New York Jazz Festival on Randalls Island. Then on September 9, Columbia Records held a party to celebrate its current stake in the jazz record industry. The invitations specified a five o'clock start, and the Miles Davis Sextet was invited to perform between sets by the Ellington band, Billie Holiday, and Jimmy Rushing. Risers had been constructed, and amidst scattered baggage the Davis group took up positions to conclude the first half of the party. Opinions vary as to whether Philly Joe Jones or Jimmy Cobb was at the drums; Evans remembered it as being Jones, but his memory was frequently at fault on such facts. It was only a party, said Columbia, and it was being recorded merely as a memento. Nevertheless it was issued fifteen years later as *Jazz at the Plaza (Volume 1)* — a marketing decision cited by Evans as typical of the record companies' exploitation of artists. In an interview with the Canadian jazz broadcaster Ted O'Reilly in 1980, Evans recalled that when the album was released in 1973, those musicians that were still alive were offered payment at the 1958 scale. Chronologically, it is the last issue of Evans playing in the Davis band.

The players staggered raggedly into a fast "Straight, No Chaser." For long stretches behind Davis and Coltrane, Evans dropped out altogether, Coltrane's onslaught in particular leaving little room for diatonic comments. At the end of his solo Adderley transferred a handy phrase to Evans, rather like an Olympic relay baton. Evans, carried on the relentless tide of the drummer's wash, matched him in note-by-note proliferation. A quote from "Blue Monk" finally got him back to the theme. The privileged party goers seemed well pleased, and Coltrane and Adderley retired to sit the next one out.

Evans transports us to a world a million miles away, ruminating moodily into "My Funny Valentine," a tune that he rarely played, which here provides a vehicle for one of his most remarkable utterances. Somehow conjuring magical colors out of the resident "honky-tonk," he molds timeless waves of harmony. Without breaking the spell, Chambers solos perfectly and Miles, as always, makes us feel that this is *the* moment, the unique time we will hear these notes and only these notes.

After this blissful oasis, the party atmosphere resumed with a joyous "If I Were a Bell," from the group's Bohemia Club repertoire. The band played out on "Oleo," Evans working his own "Five" motif hard in his brief, purposeful, all-structure solo.

⊂⊱ ⊂⊱ ⊂⊱

In his autobiography Davis summed up his feelings about Evans: "Bill had this quiet fire that I loved on piano. The way he approached it, the sound he got was like crystal notes or sparkling water cascading down from some clear waterfall. I had to change the way the band sounded again for Bill's style by playing different tunes, softer ones at first. Bill played underneath the rhythm and I liked that, the way he played scales with the band. Red's playing had carried the rhythm but Bill underplayed it and for what I was doing now with the modal thing, I liked what Bill was doing better."[7]

It is said that music is an international language, and certainly many a fine performance has resulted from multinational or mixed-race ensembles. But what was happening in the Miles Davis sextet, due to the presence of Bill Evans, was an amalgamation on a creative level of disparate cultures. The white pianist's offering, dripping with the history of the European classics, brought the band members up short with astonishment. They had never heard anything like it; jazz had never heard anything like it, and the whole world was unprepared for its marriage to contemporary black American music. Better than third-stream, the miracle was worked not from the head, but from the heart.

⊂⊱ ⊂⊱ ⊂⊱

During the forties in the jazz world, hard drugs, notably heroin, became rife through association with a cadre of prominent users. If Charlie Parker could be an addict and a genius, it had to be worth a try. On the scene, there grew a kind of romantic association with the masters, the guru setting the trend for the disciples.

In his army days Evans had tried marijuana and had continued to smoke it even though it interfered with his memory. Contrary to most current medical evidence, he believed that marijuana led to heroin—and, as if to prove his point, he tried that, too. Not until he played with Miles, though, was his heroin use more than experimental; he was determined not to isolate himself from the drug-grounded fellowship of that band. In fact, not content with being a mere addict, he was determined to be the worst junkie in the band. The drummer, Eliot Zigmund, who played with Evans much later, considered one possible cause: "I almost think that his involvement with drugs (early on, anyway) was to get away from the fact that he really was a very American kind of guy. I think the drugs for him made him more mysterious, or got him to a more mysterious place, got him out of his background."[8]

Evans, with his Montgomery Clift looks, had no trouble attracting women, but he prided himself on his discerning taste. Since the late fifties he had been living with Peri Cousins, a young black woman who had fallen for the intelligent, gifted ex-college kid. Bill was madly in love with her. Peri knew Bill when he was "learning" heroin, before he started using a needle, and she provides a penetrating analysis of his rationale: "It was self-destructive. Of course, that was the bane of our existence, because he was a person who was so aware that there was no argument that I could give him. Because he knew. He knew what he was doing and part of him felt that was something he had to do and that when he was finished he'd stop. I suppose lots of people felt that way. But I don't mean that he said, 'Oh, I can just stop anytime I want to.' He knew it was destructive but it was almost as if he didn't want to stop." If it was a deliberate ploy it was also a defense mechanism: "I have a theory about his addiction," she continues. "When Billy (I was the only person who called him Billy, which he didn't particularly like but accepted), when he came down, when he kicked it, which he did on numerous occasions, the world was—I don't know how to say it—too beautiful. It was too sharp for him. It's almost as if he had to blur the world for himself by being strung out. I had that impression all the time."[9]

As soon as he joined Miles, accumulating circumstances induced Evans to blur that world. He encountered racial discrimination, he suffered from feelings of inferiority and the physical effort of touring, and he received enticement from colleagues already hooked. Among those colleagues, Philly Joe Jones was probably most to blame; it certainly was not Davis, who was upset by Bill's craving and tried to discourage him. Leonard Feather's words are painfully apropos: "A leader who hires one junky may soon find himself with a whole band of them. For the addict, the presence of a fellow user not only brings a mental communion but ensures the presence at all times of a ready supply of dope."[10] Bill and Philly Joe became great junkie-buddies over the years.

⸙ ⸙ ⸙

Evans was uncomfortable in the band for a number of reasons, not the least being his status as a racial minority of one. It was hard to endure the racial teasing from this established gang. Davis, who loved Evans, could nonetheless be cruel, and Coltrane never quite approved his presence. Audience reaction in club after club carried an undertow of prejudice. In this black band Evans cut an incongruous figure, but Davis's criterion for selecting his colleagues was always precisely musical, and the list of his white band members is long—Lee Konitz, Victor Feldman, Joe Zawinul, Dave Holland, John McLaughlin, Mike Stern, the saxophonist Bill Evans, and many more—to say nothing of his deep friendship and close association with the arranger Gil Evans.

Davis said: "Some of the things that caused Bill to leave the band hurt me, like that shit some black people put on him about being a white boy in our band. Many blacks felt that since I had the top small group in jazz and was paying the most money that I should have a black piano player. Now, I don't go for that kind of shit; I have always just wanted the best players in my group and I don't care about whether they're black, white, blue, red or yellow. As long as they can play what I want that's it. But I know this stuff got up under Bill's skin and made him feel bad. Bill was a very sensitive person and it didn't take much to set him off."[11] In a caustic twist, Davis later accused Evans of not hiring black musicians—which would come as something of a surprise to Philly Joe Jones, Alan Dawson, and Jack DeJohnette, to name only drummers in Evans's trios.

From the black patrons in the clubs Evans received a lot of flak for not swinging as hard as Garland. When this happened, for all their internal baiting, the band would rally round to defend him. Wherever fans demanded to know why he was there, they were told, "Miles wants him there—he's *supposed* to be there."[12] Although he kept his end up pretty well, the hard-blowing, marathon-type numbers favored by the band (and easily accommodated by Garland) were not his preferred repertoire, and the endless gigs of that nature took their toll.

Sensitive to the last, he took the criticism to heart. But there was a reverse side to the coin: he saw the band members as superhuman, and the reality of survival among them and the bestowal of respect from the current titan of jazz had fed his ego. In one sense he had reached the zenith of his profession, occupying the piano chair in the top group of the day. Moreover, he had put his own stamp on the band and had steered its repertoire into new lyrical paths, becoming in the process one of the few white jazzmen ever to influence black colleagues. Great music had been made, and he had catalyzed new depths in Davis's own playing. Most important for Evans, dealing with the honest personalities of Davis's band had endorsed his own singularity and made him realize that being himself, both musically and personally, was the only route to take. Davis maintained that he "made" Evans by having him in his band. This was not the case, for although that exposure brought his name more readily before the public, he was already on course and would have come through clearly on talent alone.

In touring the country to fully booked venues, and in being thrust into such prominence, Evans endured enormous pressure. He must have done much of it in a kind of running shock. In October 1958, after about seven months on the road playing with the best, and earning good money, he left the band. The parting was amicable and entirely his own decision. In addition to everything else his father was ill; exhausted physically, mentally, and spiritually, Evans flew to Florida to stay with his parents for a few weeks at Ormond Beach. He needed to recuperate, relax, play golf, and clear his mind, all of which were best undertaken in the comforting refuge of the southern climate that he knew, far away from the recent, uncongenial spotlight.

CHAPTER 6

Everybody Digs
Bill Evans

Why didn't you get a quote from my mother?

—*Bill Evans, to Riverside Records*

Thanks to his albums with George Russell, Charles Mingus, his own *New Jazz Conceptions*, and his exposure in the Miles Davis band, Evans won the *Down Beat* International Critics' Poll for the year 1958, in the New Star category. By contrast, the Readers' Poll placed him only twentieth in the piano section, tidily illustrating the gulf between critical and public reaction to the new pianist. As it happened Miles Davis had won both the Critics' and the Readers' Polls for the year, and when he received his plaques from Dom Cerulli during an engagement at the Village Vanguard, he also accepted on behalf of Evans, who by then had left the band.

⧡ ⧡ ⧡

Back in September 1958, while continuing to play on the road with the Miles Davis Sextet, Evans had fulfilled a handful of other recording dates. Among these was a quintet album—the brainchild of the new head of jazz at United Artists, Monte Kay—which was undertaken the day after Columbia's party at the Plaza. The trumpeter Art Farmer and the tenor saxophonist Benny Golson were also New Star winners that year, and Kay's idea was to make a sort of poll winners' showcase. Art's twin brother Addison joined on bass, and Dave Bailey (then with Art Farmer in the Gerry Mulligan Quartet) completed the group on drums.

The recording took place in the intimate atmosphere of the Nola Studios in New York, a vintage venue situated on top of Steinway Hall, in use since the thirties. At the end of the sessions, it was decided to issue the album under the trumpeter's name as *Modern Art*. With this quintessentially happy combo, the feeling of a mutual admiration society at work came through strongly. Evans's playing throughout was alert, exploratory, and clearly enunciated. On the leader's blues, "Mox Nix," the players' fine credentials were displayed both singly and collectively, with Evans sparkling in rock 'n' roll mode on the head arrangement. On Jimmy Van Heusen's "Like Someone in Love" the pianist's half-chorus of subdued autumnal color was perfectly scaled to the intimate feel. Of all the albums on which he played, this was one of his favorites.

In 1995 I chatted with Art Farmer during a gig in my hometown, and he mentioned that however relaxed *Modern Art* may sound, it was not an easy record to make. He remembered Tommy Nola, the recording engineer, with particular affection. "He was like a sixth member of the band," Farmer said. The trumpeter also confided an incident that sheds fascinating light on Evans's state of confidence. In spite of his newfound expressivity at the piano and the reassurance of self-identity acquired with the Miles Davis band, Evans visited a psychiatrist to find out whether he really wanted to continue as a pianist; under the influence of a "truth drug," he invariably answered yes.

⊂⊱ ⊂⊱ ⊂⊱

For most of November, burned out after leaving Miles Davis, Evans relaxed on his father's driving range in Florida. He reportedly took great satisfaction in shooting 41 for nine holes of golf. He also visited his brother Harry in Louisiana. "One of the reasons I left Miles was because my father was ill," he said. "I spent some time visiting my folks, and went through a rather reflective period. While I was staying with my brother in Baton Rouge...I remember finding that somehow I had reached a new inner level of expression in my playing. It had come almost automatically, and I was very anxious about it, afraid I might lose it—I thought maybe I'd wake up tomorrow and it wouldn't be there."[1]

He need not have worried. When he got back onto his own piano in New York, he found the new expressive feeling to be consistently on tap. He now occupied a three-room apartment at 310 West 106th Street, mostly taken up with his Knabe grand and enhanced with a painting by Paul Motian's wife, Gwyneth. Evans, too, aspired to the visual arts, adopting the self-encouraging tongue-in-cheek credo that he could be at least as good as Paul Klee. In restaurants and clubs he would doodle on anything that came to hand: here a cartoon, there a finished and colored abstract.

Sport was a keen interest, and Evans spent most afternoons checking the current scene on television, in particular, baseball, football, golf, and bowling.

In later years he gambled on the horses, avidly following form and winning often. Sometimes he would put hundreds of dollars on a race. Michael Moore, his bassist for a while in the late seventies, commented with a twinkle that Bill made more a year at the racetrack than Moore did as a bass player.

Evans loved to read, in particular humorous books, his beloved Thomas Hardy, and philosophy. His bookcases held works by Plato, Voltaire, Whitehead, and Santayana, as well as the worldly speculations of Freud, Margaret Mead, Sartre, and Thomas Merton. He had introduced John Coltrane to the works of the Southern Indian spiritual leader and philosopher Krishnamurti. Middle and Far Eastern religions held a fascination for him, including Islam and Zen. His interest in Zen — before it became fashionable, and along with many other religious philosophies — amounted only to curiosity, but it had slipped into a magazine article once and haunted him, a typical affliction of the interviewee.

In December 1958 Evans appeared on NBC-TV, recording a very fast "I'll Remember April" in a quintet that included Tony Scott and the trombonist Eddie Bert. That was a golden year for jazz on television. With the springtime performance of "Concerto for Billy the Kid" and this appearance, Evans had played his small part. Eddie Bert had been with the Herbie Fields band for about four years before Bill joined it, and with the Charles Mingus Workshop shortly before Evans contributed to *East Coasting*. If the two reminisced on the NBC date about old times, their thoughts would have been tinged with sadness: Fields, their erstwhile bandleader with whom the pianist had served an invaluable apprenticeship, had died recently of an overdose of sleeping pills while playing commercial jobs in the Miami area.

⋐ ⋐ ⋐

Try as he might, Orrin Keepnews at Riverside had not been able to coax Evans back into the studio for a trio date. It had been more than two years since *New Jazz Conceptions*, and before joining Miles the pianist felt that he hadn't anything fresh to say; by the time he knew that he had, he was too busy traveling with the band. As was obvious from his sideman recordings, his adaptability was infinite, but deep down there was a stronger compulsion. He had found his voice: now he must speak again through the choicest medium — the trio — and after further thoughtful practice he reentered the studio to make *Everybody Digs Bill Evans*. For this, he chose to work again with the drummer and bassist from *Portrait of Cannonball*, Philly Joe Jones and Sam Jones.

It was his first trio disc with Philly Joe; subsequently, whenever he was without his regular drummer, Evans called on Jones, and over the years they would do several tours and residencies together. Sam Jones, like Teddy Kotick before him, implemented for Evans the traditional, solid, bass-of-the-trio role.

Evans's performance represented a significant advance on *New Jazz Conceptions*. At once, the feeling was more relaxed, due in part to Philly Joe's laid-back yet "dug-in" beat. On "Night and Day" (the drummer's showcase) the pianist enjoyed playing around and against the laid down pulse. For sheer invention he was out on his own. On one of the eights his snaking flight covered the keyboard like a deflating balloon; one can almost see the incredulity on the faces of his colleagues as they gamely try to come in again on the apparently vanished beat.

For once, Evans took Sonny Rollins's "Oleo"—a frenetic mainstay of the Davis band—at moderate pace. Philly Joe Jones held back for three choruses, half-releasing with brushes, but when he finally exploded, Evans launched into a sustained salvo of pivotal turns with a driving force unmatched to date. The pianist Billy Taylor reacted enthusiastically to this track in his *Down Beat* Blindfold test: "Sounds very much like Bill Evans— very adventurous. I like his playing. He's one of the few guys around now— even though he plays quite a lot in hornlike lines when he's playing with drive like this—who has two very good hands.... Actually, he has two styles at the moment—a ballad style and an up-tempo style. His work is very personal. Five stars for this."[2]

The unaccompanied solo idea from *New Jazz Conceptions* was continued here with four numbers, again done at the end of the session. One was "Some Other Time" from Leonard Bernstein's *On the Town*, not included on the original album. At Evans's first attempt an extraordinary thing happened. Having initiated the two-chord background ostinato, he found himself hypnotized into a "one-off" pursuit of a line, increasingly decorative, based on those two chords alone. That this happened quite spontaneously is confirmed by Orrin Keepnews, who of course was there at the time. Evans himself said: "What happened was that I started to play the introduction, and it started to get so much of its own feeling and identity that I just figured, well, I'll keep going."[3]

Others have conflicting memories: Gretchen Magee, Bill's theory teacher at Southeastern, attests that this exploration (or a variant of it) was written out as a composition exercise, a homework assignment when Evans was a student. His longtime girlfriend Peri recalls that he would drift, when playing at home, into "Peace Piece" (as the new creation came to be called) out of "Some Other Time," a tune that she often asked him to play. The true source of this stream, like countless others in art, will probably never be pinpointed. The bass player Chuck Israels, for instance, suspects that it might have been a "practiced improvisation."

There is surely some truth in all these suggestions, and Chopin's Berceuse in Db, Opus 57, a piano piece that Evans knew well, was a clear precursor as well. That gentle reverie is precisely parallel, being based throughout on a two-harmony left-hand ostinato, which, like "Peace Piece," never varies until it makes a cadence at the end. The right-hand line starts simply, each succeeding two- or four-bar section introducing a fresh decorative idea; in performance it should sound like a written-out improvisation. As Evans progressed through "Peace Piece," he may well have been spiritually and formally conscious of Chopin's work.

Furthermore, we know he was a Scriabin enthusiast, but did he know Olivier Messiaen, whose "Catalogue d'Oiseaux" for piano was just appearing? No matter; there is, in any case, much birdsong incorporated around the apex of the Evans arch, where the bitonal texture scintillates in the manner of the French master (ex. 1).

Evans felt unable to oblige subsequent club requests for "Peace Piece." It was a unique performance—or almost so, for after a first take Orrin Keepnews wrote on his recording sheet that Bill was not quite happy, and the next take was used. "It's completely free-form," Evans said. "I just had one figure that gave the piece a tonal reference and a rhythmic reference. Thereafter, everything could happen over that one solid thing. Except for the bass figure, it was a complete improvisation."[4]

It was Evans's idea to finish each side of the LP with the brief tag called "Epilogue," which thoughtfully melded stark intervals onto a folklike line. One discography has seen fit to regard the repeated track as an error, but its duplication on the CD reissue, overseen by Orrin Keepnews, the original producer, confirms that it was intentional.

With the two remaining ballads, Evans creates an illusion that overcomes the simple fact that tone dies on his instrument. Working this magic requires a certain mental attitude; it is necessary to "think through" a phrase to connect dying notes. On "What Is There to Say?" and "Young and Foolish" he is the master at this, sustaining the lines with intensely yearning tone and melting harmony. On both these tracks a new technical trick is introduced consisting of a sort of inverted spread (filling in the lower notes of the chord after the melody note is struck). But it is his ravishing use of tone that makes "Young and Foolish" his first truly lyrical trio track and one of those that goes deepest; played with muscular strength in the singing it touches the heart.

Ex. 1. The closing bars of Evans's improvisation "Peace Piece," from *Everybody Digs Bill Evans*. Olivier Messiaen's *Catalogue d'Oiseaux* was just coming out. The left-hand chords are those of Leonard Bernstein's "Some Other Time."

Transcribed by Jim Aikin

⫥ ⫥ ⫥

When the album was released in May 1959, the twenty-nine-year-old Evans found himself showered with accolades on the unique "all quotes" cover. From Miles Davis: "I've sure learned a lot from Bill Evans. He plays the piano the way it should be played." From George Shearing: "Bill Evans is one of the most refreshing pianists I have heard in years." From Ahmad Jamal: "I think Bill Evans is one of the finest." And from Julian "Cannonball" Adderley: "Bill Evans has rare originality and taste and the even rarer ability to make his conception of a number seem the definitive way to play it."[5] The phlegmatic pianist took all this with a hefty pinch of salt. His reaction was typical of his modesty, diffidence, and sense of humor. He quipped to his producer, "Why didn't you get a quote from my mother?"[6]

Gene Lees had just joined *Down Beat* in Chicago as managing editor. In due course he accepted an article on the pianist by Don Nelsen that *Esquire* had rejected, and subsequently he put Evans's picture on the front cover of his magazine. The exposure no doubt elevated Evans's career at the time, but—as Gene Lees would be the first to agree—like the public acclaim with the Miles Davis band, it was merely a boost for an already accomplished artistry. Nonetheless, Evans was grateful for the "high" provided by this airing, along with the starry plaudits on his new album cover. As Orrin Keepnews wrote later, rave reviews also appeared in *The Jazz Review* and *McCall's*, not to mention *Scholastic Magazine* and the men's magazine *Rogue*.

Here is Evans's own assessment, looking back in 1975: "I've always felt pretty good about that record, because I know there was a strong feeling to it, and that's the hardest thing about recording to begin with. You know, you go in at a certain time on a certain day, and you hope you're going to have that kind of peak. No matter what happens, you play, you do a job, and to most listeners it probably doesn't make that much difference. However, when you do have that special day, it penetrates—I mean this album has gotten a certain kind of reaction from people through the years; it seems to have a lot to do with that very special feeling I had then."[7]

⫥ ⫥ ⫥

Lennie Tristano talked about how his finger sank into the note, all the way to the bottom of the keyboard until it went *pow!* This was the Bill Evans way, as well, and it was integral also to the touch of his friend Sonny Clark, who had come to New York the previous year and whom Evans acknowledged as an important influence.

Evans's close friend Gene Lees
wrote lyrics to "Waltz for Debby,"
"My Bells," and "Turn Out the
Stars."
Courtesy of Gene Lees

Clark was a straight-down-the-middle bopper of real quality, absolutely
in the Bud Powell tradition. There was a deal of refinement in Clark's playing, too, not least in his actual sound. He was one of those pianists who feel,
and show, respect for the instrument; one who collaborates with it rather
than acts the aggressor upon it. Such a player is immediately in a position to
judge and vary sound quantity (while maintaining quality), and thereby to
control tonal nuance within a line. For this reason alone, it is easy to understand the attraction Clark held for Evans. There was the clearly articulated
fingerwork in up-tempo lines, some of them very long indeed; and an inclination to needle away at a solo with concentrated mental energy. Then there
was the economy of notes, the use of sequential motives in cross-rhythms and
the hardly touched-in left hand.

All these things either influenced Evans or confirmed artistically what
he was trying to do. Like Evans, Clark was a thinking pianist, with ideas clear
and to the point. Both players had a way of being lyrical and at the same time
muscular, and both integrated elements of Lennie Tristano and Horace

Silver. For all these common virtues, however, neither could ever be mistaken for the other.

The two pianists became good friends, and musical matters were not the only indulgences they shared: Clark's dependency on drugs went deeper than Evans's and was exacerbated by alcohol consumption. In 1963 he died, at age thirty-one, of a heart attack while playing a gig at Junior's night club in New York.

CHAPTER 7

Miles Calls Back

I took a tune of mine called "Blue in Green."

—*Bill Evans*

Any day can be a working day for a musician, and the day before New Year's Eve 1958 was one for trumpeter Chet Baker and his assembled group. The occasion was the completion of a Riverside album with the singer Johnny Pace, *Chet Baker Introduces Johnny Pace*, and the location was Reeves Studios, the company's regular recording venue.

Afterward Baker—along with Herbie Mann, who had been playing flute—stayed on into the evening for a further session. A fresh group, now including Evans (who indeed is mistakenly listed in some sources as having played on the earlier record), convened around them to begin an album of ballads called *Chet*. Pepper Adams played baritone saxophone, and the rhythm section was completed by Paul Chambers and Connie Kay. It was a sleepy occasion, but the pianist excelled with a chunky, two-fisted solo on the slow blues "Early Morning Mood." One fascinating detail emerged: at the beginning of "Alone Together," Evans's harmonies hinted strongly at the first chords of "Blue in Green," soon to be aired on *Kind of Blue*. The resemblance is too close to admit coincidence; apparently Evans was already doodling with the new tune.

On January 19, 1959, at another session for the same album, Kay was replaced by Philly Joe Jones, resulting in the reassembly of a one-time (if brief-tenured) rhythm section of the Miles Davis Sextet. "Time on My Hands" yielded a half-chorus of integrated playing from this trio, with floating "scrunch" chording in the classic Evans mold, a momentary plateau almost worthy of *Jazz Track*.

⋐⋐ ⋐⋐ ⋐⋐

The recording for *Chet* was completed, but the evening was far from over. When Evans, Chambers, and Jones started playing a little trio number at the end just for kicks, Orrin Keepnews suggested that they should at once make a trio record. The three musicians looked at one another and thought *another check*.

The fruits of the rest of the evening were eventually issued on the "twofer" (as double-LPs were called), *Peace Piece and Other Pieces*. The three players immediately got down to business, and "You and the Night and the Music"—done rather mournfully with Chet Baker—was injected with new life. A favorite recording of Bill's was "How Am I to Know?" made by the "New" Miles Davis Quintet in 1955, and the trio tried this number next. Earl Zindars has a homemade tape of himself and Evans playing a long "work-out" excursion on this tune. Win Hinkle, who interviewed Zindars for his magazine *Letter from Evans*, describes how he discovered it:

> When we went into Earl's house, he immediately played a tape of Bill playing the piano with Earl accompanying on brushes, playing on a phone book since no drum-set was around. Bill plays for about twenty-five minutes, just on this one tune. At one point, he gets up from the piano at the end of a chorus to go get a Coke or some-thing and says, "Take it Earl," meaning for Earl to solo till he gets back. We all crack up with laughter when this happens, as if Earl could manage a great solo with only brushes and a phone book. Bill comes back and walks around the room. "Where's the top?" he asks Earl. On a phone book, how much form can you make?[1]

After two shots at Dizzy Gillespie's "Woody 'n You" the trio did "My Heart Stood Still" on which, warming to the task and cheering up by the minute, Evans cheekily inserted a phrase or two of "Santa Claus Is Coming to Town," in keeping with the season. In the absence of Davis, he made "On Green Dolphin Street" singularly his own, sustaining a tour de force of midregister block chording over four choruses. By this time everyone had had enough, and they packed it in for the night with less than an LP's worth of material.

Having those three musicians together in the studio was potentially a wonderful thing, but Evans was bothered by the difference between that potential and the performance. He regretted that the session had been thrown together so quickly. Admitting that the work needed better-organized topping and tailing, he nevertheless agreed to its final release in 1975. "It's very interesting to hear simply because of the great musicians involved with me," he said. "I think Philly Joe and Paul were pretty much at their peak at that time, and as far as I'm concerned these are two of the most underrated musicians in the history of jazz, much greater influences than they're given credit for. You really don't hear Paul Chambers mentioned that much in the history of bass playing, but I know personally that he was an influence on Scott LaFaro and Eddie Gomez—and I'll bet just about any bassist who plays well will mention Paul."[2]

Orrin Keepnews suggested to Evans that for the first time he was getting his remarkable personal form of expression fully under control. Evans responded: "I think there's always an identity in your playing, but to make it more broad requires a different kind of maturity. I could play you a tape I made when I was in the army in about 1953 that has the seeds of the way I build lines and all that, but what you're talking about is that deeper level I suddenly just found around the time I left Miles. It's something that's very elusive and doesn't happen very often, but all you can do is to strive for it every time you play. At that period it seemed to be there all the time."[3]

⫴ ⫴ ⫴

A week before, Evans had been booked for three days of big-band Gershwin. Samuel Goldwyn's film production of *Porgy and Bess* was due out in June, and the entire music business was holding open season on the score. Jack Lewis, now with United Artists and the recent producer of *Modern Art*, planned his own version, choosing to focus the distinctive talents of arranger Bill Potts onto the latest "jazz *Porgy*." Clean and incisive, Potts's charts for *The Jazz Soul of Porgy and Bess* blew all the cobwebs away from the familiar tunes.

Evans contributed his quota to the milelong roster of brief but star-studded soloing. His contributions were to some extent obliterated by the backing, but that was an attractive part of the unremitting arrangement produced by the no-nonsense Potts. In the course of his part-reading duties, Bill took the melodies of "I Loves You, Porgy" in single notes, and "Strawberry Woman" in octaves. Art Farmer recalls that these were very happy sessions: "They had to be," he told me, grinning. "With Harry Edison and Charlie Shavers laughing and joking throughout, not to mention Zoot Sims and Al Cohn, I could hardly play sometimes!"

⫴ ⫴ ⫴

Down in the Village on Hudson Street, near the mouth of the Holland tunnel, the Canterino family managed the Half Note Café, presenting some of the best jazz in town, a new group every two or three weeks. The previous fall Lennie Tristano had opened there after a prolonged absence from the scene. He disapproved of the resident stiff-actioned Steinway, though, and picked out a two thousand–dollar Bechstein for the club.

In February, Tristano went in for a whole month with his disciples Lee

Konitz and Warne Marsh on saxophones, plus Jimmy Garrison on bass and Paul Motian on drums. The Italian brothers who owned the club appealed to Tristano's roots, Mike Canterino serving the tables, Sonny tending the bar, and their sister Rose extending a welcome at the door. The pianist did not often appear in public, but some gentle persuasion from his compatriots made all the difference, and he returned several times to the Half Note.

On the last two Tuesdays of this engagement, Tristano had teaching obligations so Konitz invited Bill Evans to sit in. Konitz was under contract to Verve, and the company engaged Peter Ind, an English bass player who had already played regularly in the Lee Konitz Quartet, to record the group on state-of-the-art equipment (Presto). In 1994 the material surfaced on a double CD from Verve called *Lee Konitz: Live at the Half Note*.

Evans's debt to Tristano was already recognized, but now, for the first time, he met up with the "cool school" itself, as personified by Konitz and Marsh. Konitz recalls Evans's role: "I think he was extremely affected by knowing that he was sitting on Tristano's chair. And he was very quiet and did very little. The people at Verve never released those recordings because they didn't think they were good for Bill. Actually, what he played when he did play was very good, but it was obvious that he had many considerations about playing with us."[4]

Evans approached the musical environment in which he found himself with respect and his habitual astuteness. He acknowledged Lennie Tristano, whose gig it was and whose place he was taking, as the living figurehead for a whole school of musical thought, at once contemporary and valid. Evans's sparse contribution resulted from an acute assessment of how he could most effectively contribute to the situation. Without directly assuming the mantle of Tristano, he nevertheless found a way, in such company, of complementing the older master's driving spirit.

The frontline pairing of Konitz and Marsh, inaugurated some years earlier, enjoyed a rare revival. On their theme statements the richness of their two-part interweaving (now becoming three-part with Garrison's firm line) stood up well without the incursion of harmony, and on these, as well as under the bulk of the frontline solos, Evans mostly laid out; when in, his comping was some of the most judicious and pertinent in the business. Likewise, when soloing, he either omitted harmony under his own right-hand line, or touched it in lightly, as if on another instrument, another timbre.

The musicians ranged through the "Tristano book," the school's own repertoire based on standard changes. Of the two horns, tenorman Marsh was the more committed to a uniform tone on the line, thus faithfully upholding the Tristano philosophy, but Evans felt more akin to the tonally inflected and harder-edged Konitz on alto.

Self-absorbed, the pianist produced some of the most original and at the same time physically relaxed soloing of his career, one sign that he was enjoying Tristano's choice of Bechstein. His lines were spare and sinewy. Never had he conjured more minimalist material, or put it to more telling use; never had he incorporated space more meaningfully, as being essential to structure; and never had he sculpted more barbed, darting fragments or effected more lightning pounces out of silence. One may liken him in these tracks to a panther lying in wait at the keyboard, infinitely patient, the master of his domain.

For the aficionado of the quintessential Evans, it is the wondrously timed chording on "How About You?" that craves particular attention. The voicing of the chords is dense, their relevance to the chord sequence absolute; yet, paradoxically, it is the subtle underplaying, the unpredictable and pregnant spacing, and the supremely sensitive touch that speak such volumes. If ever genius would go unnoticed, this is how, for the whole performance is covert, uttered in shadow, as if it were not really there at all.

⋐⋐ ⋐⋐ ⋐⋐

Evans continued to make a living by playing the thriving New York scene, where jazz clubs were on the increase for a time. He went into the Half Note again, this time in a quintet led by Tony Scott with Jimmy Knepper. Evans was almost taking over the piano seat at this club, for he was next featured there in Bob Brookmeyer's quintet. The valve trombonist had been one of Bill's first friends in New York, and around this time they shared several studio dates. In March 1959 they were scheduled by United Artists for a quartet recording, and *Down Beat* announced a forthcoming LP with the bassist Wilbur Ware. Brookmeyer nurtured a capricious line in piano playing, however, a talent that was now to blossom unexpectedly.

When I caught up with him on tour recently, he clarified events for me: "The two-piano idea was a complete surprise for both Bill and me—the session was scheduled as trombone and rhythm section. Bill, Wilbur Ware, Elvin Jones, and I had gone into the studio very late the night before, to no final end—I played a piano trio tune and, at the end of the session, Bill and I did a one-piano, four-hands version of "Whispering–Groovin' High," as I recall—I'm not even sure it was taped."

The producer, Jack Lewis, prepared his surprise, and Evans and Brookmeyer arrived the next morning to find two grand pianos rolled into position. Not only that, Percy Heath and Connie Kay (on bass and drums, respectively) were now ready to play. A uniquely fascinating disc, *The Ivory Hunters: Double Barrelled Piano*, was in the offing.

Jack Lewis obviously had faith in Brookmeyer's musicianship, and he knew enough about Evans to trust his adaptability, having produced several albums on which he played. That it would be a meeting of two thinking musicians, each with a sense of humor, was assured, but would the piano styles jell? As it turned out, Bob's diffuse palette juxtaposed well with Bill's nutty bite, their respective fantasies interlocking neatly. Neither had done anything like it before, and with no routine to fall back on, the call and response varied, the spontaneity heightened by the unexpected situation.

It was decided to try some exploratory maneuvers on "I Got Rhythm" and then to lay it down. Fun turned out to be the key: Evans's solo was all in octaves, making a clean frame—the admission of air and light into a double-keyboard texture is of paramount importance—while Brookmeyer accompanied in quarter-note triplets, a leaf out of Evans's rhythmic book. Augmentation, diminution, double-timing, cumulative pedaling, close imitation—all were thrown into the last crazy chorus. On "As Time Goes By," Bill's tremolo backing at the opening and close may have been prophetic in terms of another unique venture to come: *Conversations with Myself*. Indeed, the entire day's work may have sunk in subconsciously to that end, sowing the seeds for some three years' gestation.

Evans likened his colleague's style to a prism, revealing, instead of the actuality, something that has been turned through a slight angle. Reviewing Evans's work as a whole, Brookmeyer saw a unique synthesis of bebop and the American melodic songwriting style. "Bill and I were friends then," Bob said, "and—to this day—I'm glad he put up with an amateur piano player. We were both surprised and pleased." Bob Brookmeyer, the weaver of clean lines—witty, energetic, and warm—never did unpack his trombone that day.

⊂⊱ ⊂⊱ ⊂⊱

In the same month, besides making *The Ivory Hunters*, Evans completed work on George Russell's first full album for Decca, *New York, N.Y.*, which had been in progress for some time. The composer had asked Jon Hendricks to write four poems, to be recited by the author at strategic points on the album.

The first track, "Manhattan," had been recorded the previous September while Evans was in the middle of recording *Modern Art*. One of Russell's intentions was to display some of the solo talent on the current New York

scene, and Bob Brookmeyer, soft-muted and playful, led off. After Evans's
satisfying solo came John Coltrane's, a performance that had come only after
the saxophonist had brought the rehearsal to a puzzling halt.

As George Russell recalls:

> There are all these expensive musicians sitting around, and we got to his solo and he
> just stopped everything and went over in a corner with the chords. Now this is on a
> tune called "Manhattan," a really traditional tune. After about a half-hour, the A&R
> people are looking very concerned because this is costing them a lot of money. And
> 'Trane is working out *something*. It took me years to figure it out, but what Coltrane
> was doing was making a lot of chord substitutions—which I'd already done—to
> "Manhattan." So he had to go in and try to make substitutions on my substitu-
> tions—and figure that out, because he hadn't seen the music. I think I told him,
> "John, you'd better look at the music." So right in the middle of the date, that's what
> he did...so I just made his job a lot more difficult, and he never liked that solo, you
> know, but he played the hell out of it.[5]

In November 1958 Evans returned to New York from his post-Miles
recuperation to play on two more tracks: "A Helluva Town" and "Manhatta-
Rico." On "Manhatta-Rico" the piano solo turned out just a tad elegant—
taking a spin, as it were, in an unaccustomed neighborhood of New York.

Finally, in March 1959, Russell's own "Big City Blues" was recorded.
Out of a brass fanfare Evans's solo piano cascaded downward into this vivid
evocation of the city that never sleeps. Without a score it is hard to know
what is Russell and what is Evans—which is just as the artists would want it.
The pianist's controlled yet scintillating upward glissando ushered in
Hendricks's next poem and the brooding blues proper, on which the
predawn atmosphere of the coda recalled the Mingus book of "Revelations."

Throughout this tapestry of the metropolis, Evans played his part to perfection, as in his finely accumulating cadenza into "East Side Medley," his
own vehicle on the album. On its lyrical "Autumn in New York" section this
track induces the heady sensation of an imaginary album: *Everybody Digs
Bill Evans* plus big band. Then the mold was snapped and Evans delivered
"How About You?" with chunky chords and tautly flashing rhythm, the
theme statement ending with a whiplike cascade of fingers into the band.
With a combination of intelligence and spiritual rapport, Evans had once
again tailored his playing to the George Russell sound-world.

ᴄᴈ ᴄᴈ ᴄᴈ

After Evans left the Miles Davis band in November 1958, Red Garland
was called back for a short period. In February 1959 the Jamaican-born
Wynton Kelly officially became the group's new pianist. Davis wrote in his

autobiography: "Wynton joined us just before I was going into the studio to make *Kind of Blue*, but I had already planned that album around the piano playing of Bill Evans, who had agreed to play on it with us."[6]

Kind of Blue was made in March and April 1959. As it turned out, Wyn Kelly played on one track only, "Freddie Freeloader," named after a well-known Philadelphia character. Evans thought it a beautiful track, and Davis's blues solo on it was one of his favorites. Kelly's bright, sparkling style on this basic four-chord blues was in vivid contrast to Evans's more studious manner. The number was recorded at the first of the two Columbia sessions. According to Jimmy Cobb, this was not the first time that Davis had booked two musicians for a single date if the material was diverse enough to demand it. Evans had held Kelly in high regard since hearing him in Dizzy Gillespie's big band, responding to his particular blend of clarity and exuberance. This reaction was typical of Evans's appreciation of the work of his fellow pianists; from Oscar Peterson to Cecil Taylor, he was full of admiration for their diverse talents and generous in his praise.

Miles Davis's general goal on the new album was to explore a "modal" language. More specifically he sought to tap the possibilities latent in any one mode: he would improvise on its scale and the chords derived from that scale rather than relying for interest and stimulation on a progression of related chords (or chord sequence). Evans, through the George Russell connection, was able to embrace this concept in his own playing, as Davis well knew, and his presence became crucial to the character of the album. Nevertheless, Evans did not go on to pursue the model in his own career.

With one honorable exception, the first complete performance of each number went onto the record—though as Jan Lohmann's comprehensive discography, *The Sound of Miles Davis*, indicates, a handful of substantial attempts at most numbers, quite apart from niggling false starts, were begun and abandoned before a complete take was achieved.[7] The exception was "Flamenco Sketches," whose second take was accepted, the first appearing later on a retrospective package called *The Columbia Years, 1955–1985*.

This high rate of extempore success prompted Evans's imagination as he wrote the much-quoted original sleeve note:

> There is a Japanese visual art in which the artist is forced to be spontaneous. He must paint on a thin stretched parchment with a special brush and black water paint in such a way that an unnatural or interrupted stroke will destroy the line or break through the parchment. Erasures or changes are impossible. These artists must practice a particular discipline, that of allowing the idea to express itself in communication with their hands in such a direct way that deliberation cannot interfere....
> This conviction that direct deed is the most meaningful reflection, I believe,

has prompted the evolution of the extremely severe and unique disciplines of the jazz or improvising musician.[8]

⊏⊟ ⊏⊟ ⊏⊟

The mode chosen for "So What" was the Dorian—the white notes on the piano from D to D. After a brief introduction, composed by Evans and suspended in time, the bass went into rhythm, carrying the melodic content with a repeated two-bar motif. The piano's (and then the band's) answering "amen" (or "so what") riffs were built up largely in fourths, as opposed to the thirds that are basic to the tonal system, as exemplified by Bobby Timmons's comparable composition "Moanin'," recorded by him some four months earlier. The improvising frame of "So What" was simplicity itself: an AABA form, the B of which merely slid the Dorian scale up a semitone like a geological fault. When this point came in his solo, by way of answering the "preaching" band riffs, Evans took on the role of a one-man big band with dramatic relish.

The authorship of the brooding masterpiece "Blue in Green" became a matter of some dispute. In the late sixties Evans recalled: "I had been out of the group for a few months, but Miles called me to make this date. He said he had some things sketched out, and I should call round to his apartment on the morning of the date. I took a tune of mine called 'Blue in Green.' Now I know that on the album it is credited to Miles, but he did the same thing with two of Eddie Vinson's tunes, 'Tune Up' and 'Four.' It's a small matter to me, but when someone asks me about it I tell the truth."[9]

More specifically, he explained: "One day at Miles's apartment, he wrote on some manuscript paper the symbols for G-minor and A-augmented. And he said, 'What would you do with that?' I didn't really know, but I went home and wrote 'Blue in Green.'"[10] This meeting probably occurred about two months earlier, shortly before the first session for *Chet*, when Evans had gotten into "Alone Together" with exactly those chords.

When Win Hinkle asked Earl Zindars whether the tune was exclusively Bill's, he replied: "Definitely. I know it is, because he wrote it over at my pad where I was staying in East Harlem, fifth floor walk-up, and he stayed up until three o'clock in the morning playing those six bars over and over. It was lovely, but it turned out to be only six bars! But still it was all perfect, it's all there. Those are Bill's changes in there."[11] Earl has sketches to prove it.

But Davis, not Evans, copyrighted the tune. Although Evans referred to the attribution as "a small matter," it nevertheless stuck in the back of his mind for life. It resurfaced at the end when, as if to set the record straight, he

The second *Kind of Blue* session in 1959; Evans cut an incongruous figure in the all-black Miles Davis band.

Don Hunstein

told his friend Herb Wong that Davis had given him a check for twenty-five dollars when Evans had suggested that he might be in for a share of the royalties. "Now, that's what Bill told me," Wong said. "He was very serious about it and I believe that's probably what happened. Maybe Miles did it as a joke, as if to say, 'Come on, are you kidding? Here, take this.'"[12]

One special feature of "Blue in Green" was defined by Evans as its "ten-measure circular form," so devised as to leave the uninformed listener unable to discern the beginning and end of the sequence.[13] The form was further disguised in this performance, first by the short piano introduction and then by succeeding choruses doubling up the changes, going through the sequence of chords twice as quickly, Jimmy Cobb's brushes nevertheless maintaining the initial rate of pulse. Adderley sat this one out, but Coltrane evoked a starkly searing tone. Miles squeezed out his spare, muted line exquisitely, Evans's richly floating sonorities all the more poignant by contrast. The music remains haunting and ageless.

In 1992 Columbia/Legacy issued a special MasterSound Edition of *Kind of Blue*. In the sleeve note, Amy Herot sheds light on a matter of some curiosity. Referring to the 1959 recording sessions, she writes:

Columbia's recording policy at that time was to run two tape machines simultaneously, a master and a safety. At the March 2 sessions, the master machine was running slow, so that when the tapes were played back at the correct speed, the music was slightly faster—sharper—than the April 6 session. Over the years, many musicians have noticed that the first side of Kind of Blue—"So What," "Freddie Freeloader" and "Blue in Green"—is about a quarter-tone sharp, and wondered what Miles could have had in mind. According to Teo Macero, the speed change was not intentional, and it is corrected here for the first time, using the safety tapes.[14]

This is an important reissue, as the corrected tempo subtly affects the loping feel of the first two numbers and intensifies the languorous atmosphere of "Blue in Green."

⇌ ⇌ ⇌

The Columbia production department caused more raised eyebrows with a label-editing slip in its first LP issue. On the original label the titles of "All Blues" and "Flamenco Sketches" were reversed, Evans's track descriptions on the sleeve fitting this reversal. Although the label order was quickly corrected, the sleeve-note was not, and it made garbled reading for many years.

"All Blues" then, in its true persona, is a twelve-bar sequence (with additional four-bar interludes) of beguiling simplicity and hypnotic flow. The rising, semitonal slide of harmony employed for the middle-eight of "So What" recurred here, but fleetingly, as a piercingly "blue," half-bar coloration. Only in the studio did Davis hit upon the six-beat subdivision of the bars, Evans immediately upholding the idea with his measured, background "trill" put in on the spot; in his key position above Chambers's one-bar riff, he maintained careful control of the sustaining texture with this fluttering figure. His own musical comments were pungent and meaningful, the stabs behind Davis as hard as can be. Afterward his solo blossomed gently out of the mold while remaining integral to it; here the listener is asked to consider the value of sound as such, to savor gradation of tone expressed with economy of material.

The pianist's pivotal role on the album was nowhere better demonstrated than in "Flamenco Sketches," where he was responsible for the alternating two-chord pattern operating on four of the five "levels" of its sequence (there was no theme). This pattern was identical in harmony, tempo, and initially in key to his openings to "Some Other Time" and "Peace Piece." In fact, Davis had wanted to use "Peace Piece" for the session. (Evans must have given him the gist of it or played him a tape, for it was not yet issued.) Only that morning at Davis's apartment did Evans suggest the five-tiered development of "Flamenco Sketches"; they worked the levels out together at the piano. The fourth level was characterized by a different two-chord pattern, this time a semitonally adjacent pair imparting the Spanish tinge implicit in the title. Rarified and introspective, the solos were born out of the concept and mood of "Peace Piece"; without that precedent "Flamenco Sketches" would not be. The alternate take (reissued on Columbia/Legacy in 1997) revealed an even sparer Evans, the focus of his sound melting in and out of silence.

Evans wrote out the chords for "Flamenco Sketches" for the band, as well as the melody and changes for "Blue in Green." Nothing was written for the other three numbers except a single-line sketch of the introduction to "So What" for Paul Chambers to play, to which Evans added harmonies. Essence and detail merge imperceptibly on the album to contribute to the whole. When the ruffled waters of who composed what have flowed away, the album will remain as a truly collaborative achievement by two mutually respectful artists. Many years later, when trying to account for the album's continuously phenomenal success, Evans would point to the simplicity of the charts and the "first-take" freshness of the playing, as well as hinting modestly that the chemistry might have been a little better than usual that day.

"I suppose that *Kind of Blue* has been a far-reaching influence," he said. "But when we did the album we had no idea it would become that important. I have wondered for years just what was that special quality, but it is difficult for me as a contributor to be objective about it. Of course, just to record with a band like that was a special experience for me. You can wait a lifetime for such opportunities. It was one of the most comfortable times I had with that rhythm section. There was always some kind of magic and conviction with Miles. Whatever he did became a point of departure for so many people."[15]

Over the years, the album has reached more listeners than possibly any other jazz recording, due in no small measure to the lyrical essence of Bill Evans.

CHAPTER **8**

Portrait in Jazz

Especially, I want my work—and the trio's if possible—to sing.

—*Bill Evans*

In the summer of 1959 Evans found himself in an artistic limbo. He was thrilled by the discovery that he could express himself emotionally through his instrument, but he had no ongoing outlet for that promise. What he needed now was his own trio, the ideal forum for any pianist with something to say—and Evans had more to say than most. For the time being, though, like all musicians, he had to earn a living from his talent. Biding his time before the next creative ignition point, he undertook a number of sideman jobs.

On the delightful *Lee Konitz Meets Jimmy Giuffre* for Verve, Evans kept his playing cool, airy, and laced with humor; his outing on "Cork 'n' Bib," for instance, was dedicated to the pursuit of the crushed note. Two days later he was in the studio for Columbia, contributing to the compilation *Something New, Something Blue*—part of the ongoing search for working integrations of jazz and straight composition—but he found little substance for inspiration. He then went into the Composer on West 58th Street for an indefinite run opposite the George Wallington group.

John Lewis, meanwhile, had been writing the score to Robert Wise's new movie, *Odds Against Tomorrow*. For the original United Artists sound track recording Lewis was free to choose the players in the full orchestra he had at his disposal. As a rhythm-section nucleus he called on his colleagues of the Modern Jazz Quartet. Occupied on the podium, he handed over his piano chair to the most versatile candidate of the time, Bill Evans, for be it big band or small group, jazz or straight, third-stream or film, Evans could cover them all.

Bill was disappointed by one outcome, however: "In the movie, there's a seduction scene between Robert Ryan and Gloria Grahame. I improvised on it," he explained. "I was looking at the picture while improvising and I'd coordinated my improvisation with what was going on on the screen. When I saw the movie, I realized the music had been edited with a four-second time lag. It didn't mean anything any more."[1] Nevertheless, sitting in as pianist of the Modern Jazz Quartet delighted him no end, as did playing the steam whistles of the calliope in a section called "The Carousel Incident."

Finally, in this summer spate of work, he was called upon—as one of Riverside's resident pianists—to contribute to *Chet Baker Plays the Best of Lerner and Loewe*, a kind of follow-up to *Chet*.

⊆⊱ ⊆⊱ ⊆⊱

The long-standing relationship of Evans and Tony Scott continued with an early August run at the Showplace, a club in the Village. Twice during the gig Scott organized some recording on modest equipment, but the results seemed rough and the tapes were set aside. By the 1970s Scott had moved permanently to his native Italy, but in 1978, on a rare visit to New York, he gave the tapes to producer Ray Passman. The material was released by Muse Records in the early eighties on two LPs called *Golden Moments* and *I'll Remember*.

The records open with a relaxed, trio-only version of "Like Someone in Love," Evans's eight-bar introductory descent simple and classical. After this lovely track, Scott moved into a hard-swinging "Walkin'." A good time beckoned, Evans displaying an unexpected but effective crudity in the blues. On "I Can't Get Started," leading back to Scott's reentry, he scurried all over the keyboard, the choice of every note meaningful, logical, and delivered with unfailing accuracy. Such purpose equally characterized his excursion on "Free and Easy Blues" as the torque on his coruscating line was gradually increased.

"My Melancholy Baby," the final track on *Golden Moments*, exhibits one of the pianist's tours de force, planned, technically speaking, as an exercise in parallel octave playing—the same single line in each hand, an octave apart. He can be heard warming up the technique in the background under Scott's solo, trying out motives, scales, figurations, and cross-rhythms for later use. The ensuing solo is interspersed with self-encouraging moans of the kind we have come to expect from some artists but seldom hear from Evans. Among classical performers, the Spanish cellist Pablo Casals and the Canadian pianist Glenn Gould are rare examples of artists who do this, but in jazz the phenomenon is more widespread, as might be expected from the less formal art. Pianist Keith Jarrett has taken this behavior to the farthest extreme, his almost continuous verbal exhortations seemingly indispensable to the creative process. Evans's self-coaxing on "My Melancholy Baby" was intermittent, a way of connecting

the thought processes, of injecting the invention. At the end of the improvisation, he went out on a final twinkle in tenths as if to say (in all modesty), *how
about that?*

Whereas the classical interpreter serves the composer and his work, the
jazz musician projects his own creative personality. On *I'll Remember*, Scott
made "Stella by Starlight" as hot as Miles Davis—on *Jazz Track*—had made
it cool. These two renditions (with Evans on each) have only tune and chord
sequence in common, but their equal validity is part of the meaning of jazz,
as dictated by the player's disposition.

The prevailing mood on these dates was one of joyous jamming, all the
more so as Evans and Scott knew that this might be one of their last collaborations. They had been friends for more than eight years and had played scores
of tunes together, but Evans was on the brink of becoming his own man,
while Scott was off on a two-year concert tour of India and the Far East. This
was a unique odyssey for an American jazz musician: as a kind of United
States ambassador to music, he would visit exotic locations throughout the
Orient, his appetite for playing anything, with anybody, continuing unabated.
But Evans's own journey, though for the time being geographically limited,
was destined to shape more profoundly the course of Western musical history.

⋹ ⋹ ⋹

During the 1950s academic attention to jazz in America increased enormously. The most important development in that trend was the short-lived
Music Inn School of Jazz at Lenox, in the Berkshires of western Massachusetts, established in 1957 by Stephanie and Philip Barber, with John Lewis as
its artistic director. For the last three weeks in August 1959, Evans was invited
onto the faculty of the school. In this rambling summer resort, just down the
road from the long-established classical courses at Tanglewood, and in sea-
sonably hot weather, Evans tried his hand (for the only time in his life) at
teaching jazz.

The 1959 sessions were run by Gunther Schuller and John Lewis, and
the faculty also included George Russell, Herb Pomeroy, Kenny Dorham,
Max Roach, J. J. Johnson, Bob Brookmeyer, Jimmy Giuffre, Bill Russo, Jim
Hall, and the rest of the Modern Jazz Quartet. It was quite a year for students,
too: attending were Al Kiger, Dave Baker, Freddie Hubbard, and Gary
McFarland, as well as Ornette Coleman and Don Cherry, who were to hit
New York for their famous run at the Five Spot in November. For these play-
ers, the designation *student* was, as George Russell once put it, referring to
Coleman in particular, "a kind of a gross error."

Evans was engaged to help John Lewis with the piano students, who included Ran Blake and Steve Kuhn, the youngster whom Evans had heard in the foyer at Brandeis. Dave Mackay was there, too. "We talked about music a lot," he recalls of Evans. "He was reticent to 'teach' because I think that was his nature. I don't think he probably ever taught other than there. Except though to share talking about music. It was such a pleasure. He was fun. A lot of people don't know how funny Bill was."[2] For the final students' concert, tutors Evans, Jim Hall, and Connie Kay offered a septet that included trumpeter Al Kiger, vibraphonist Gary McFarland (both later recorded with Evans), and a young pianist from Bombay, already well known in India, called Dizzy Sal. Elsewhere in the concert, the piano playing of Steve Kuhn was exceptional.

One other student attending that year was Bill's brother, Harry. Several years later, they made an educational video together called *The Universal Mind of Bill Evans*, and one of a range of topics covered was the teaching of jazz. Bill reflected on his experience at Lenox:

> When you begin to teach jazz, the most dangerous thing is that you tend to teach style.... I had eleven piano students, and I would say eight of them didn't even want to know about chords or anything—they didn't even want to do anything that anybody had ever done, because they didn't want to be imitators. Well, of course, this is pretty naive...but nevertheless it does bring to light the fact that if you're going to try to teach jazz...you must abstract the principles of music which have nothing to do with style, and this is exceedingly difficult. So there, the teaching of jazz is a very touchy point. It ends up where the jazz player, ultimately, if he's going to be a serious jazz player, teaches himself.[3]

Evans celebrated his thirtieth birthday at Lenox. In just four years as a professional musician he had accumulated a wealth of experience. In his new role as adviser he concentrated on a common error among young players: many students, he observed, get a generalization in their minds of how top-flight pianists handle their material. Rather than being satisfied with working simply and honestly within a framework, they try to approximate what they hear in a way that is so loose they cannot build on it. You cannot progress on top of vagueness and confusion, he declared. He was living proof of his own classic maxim: "It is true of any subject that the person that succeeds...has the realistic viewpoint at the beginning, knowing that the problem is large, and that he has to take it a step at a time, and he has to enjoy this step-by-step learning procedure."[4]

ᑕᗱ ᑕᗱ ᑕᗱ

Tony Scott was leaving America. All the people he cared about were dying. "Bird was the big shock," he said. "Pres [Lester Young] in 1958 and Lady Day [Billie Holiday] in 1959. I wanted to get out. New York was like a big cemetery."[5] Before leaving for the Far East, he went into the studio to record a whole series of tributes, including material finally issued in 1986 on the Sunnyside LP *Sung Heroes*.

For a self-confessed gypsy, Scott was a disciplined composer. He and Evans played his two pieces for clarinet and piano, "Israel" (not to be confused with Johnny Carisi's classic number) and "For Stefan Wolpe," with consummate professionalism on this record. The pianist's classical pedigree came through on the opening of Scott's "Requiem for 'Hot Lips' Page," the first melody note in the right hand being placed a fraction of a second later than its accompanying chord in the left. This was no accident but was done to draw attention to the higher note, the gambit a legacy of the "old school" of classical piano playing. One artist much admired by Evans, Arturo Benedetti Michelangeli, was a particular exponent of this style; used subtly, as here, it works perfectly.

More important, the session marked the first studio collaboration of what was to become a historic threesome: Bill Evans, Paul Motian, and a twenty-three-year-old bassist named Scott LaFaro. "Misery," written by Tony Scott for Billie Holiday, is a four-minute gem, a deeply poignant composition given a fabulously beautiful opening by Evans, who focuses again on his lyricism, his spiritual domain. LaFaro plays a simple line while indulging a subtle variety of attack and timing, but the melding of that line with the piano, in its placement and tone, gives the number distinction. Not much happens, but a wavelength is established. For Evans, having drifted for some months, "Misery" offered a glimpse of a relationship to come.

The next day Evans was back in the studio for Verve (though with very little to do) for a follow-up to *Lee Konitz Meets Jimmy Giuffre* called *You and Lee*.

⋐⋐ ⋐⋐ ⋐⋐

Miles Davis, knowing that Evans wanted to form his own trio, spoke of him to some agents, at the same time recommending as collaborators bassist Jimmy Garrison (with whom Evans had played quite a bit lately) and drummer Kenny Dennis (who had played on *Legrand Jazz*). Indeed, for three weeks in November, after a little rehearsing, that trio was booked into the recently renamed Basin Street East club on East 49th Street, formerly the Casa Cugat. Talking to Lee Jeske, Evans described the extraordinary circumstances of that engagement:

We were working opposite Benny Goodman, who was making sort of a triumphal return, and we were treated so shabbily—they would turn the mikes off on us, etc., giving Benny's band state dinners with champagne (while) we couldn't get a Coke without paying two bucks and getting it ourselves. Anyhow, the guys' egos couldn't take it. Kenny Dennis and Jimmy Garrison left very shortly. I think the gig was two or three weeks. I think I went through four drummers and seven bass players, or something like that, during that gig.

Philly Joe was on that gig for a little while and we really started cooking. We started getting some applause and then they told me not to let Joe take any more solos. I said, "Well, I'm not going to tell him. If you want to tell Philly Joe Jones he can't solo, you tell him." That's the way it was.

Anyhow, in going through all these players, Scott LaFaro (who was) working around the corner on a duo job…came over to sit in a couple of times. Paul Motian, who I had been friendly with and knew, had been busy, but by the end of the gig both of these guys were available and interested and that's who I ended up with. They became the original trio and it was the *right* original trio. So sometimes those situations maybe are karmic or in some way fated, so that you eliminate the people that aren't committed and perhaps aren't right, and end up with the right thing.[6]

So the first Bill Evans Trio, with Garrison and Dennis, lasted about a week, sinking without trace beneath the Benny Goodman hype, the sheiks, and the chauffeured limousines. Even had it survived this jinxed engagement, though, a trio with Jimmy Garrison could not have succeeded for Evans. They had played well together at the Half Note and the Showplace earlier in the year, but the bass player's style was to lay down a rock-solid foundation—fine in itself, and an approach that had served Bill well up to now—but no longer sufficient to feed the pianist's flourishing imagination. Garrison was not interested in liberating the role of the bass, and soon he went on, via a brief spell with Ornette Coleman, to lend powerhouse support to John Coltrane's quartet. Kenny Dennis, although the gig had not worked out for him either, urged Evans to pursue the formation of his own trio, support that the pianist took to heart.

⋐ ⋐ ⋐

Evans had one or two ideas for the group he envisaged: "I'm hoping the trio will grow in the direction of simultaneous improvisation rather than just one guy blowing followed by another guy blowing. If the bass player, for example, hears an idea that he wants to answer, why should he just keep playing a 4/4 background? The men I'll work with have learned how to do the regular kind of playing, and so I think we now have the license to change it. After all, in a classical composition, you don't hear a part remain stagnant until it becomes a solo. There are transitional development passages—a voice begins to be heard more and more and finally breaks into prominence."[7]

In such a musical context, the standard jazz "blowing" format seemed somewhat simplistic. Evans wanted to escape this conventional approach to jazz form, and for good reason. He knew that if the stereotyped mold could be broken, beautiful music could be created. He was also conscious that he wanted to develop this ideal, not as a solo pianist, but with colleagues of like mind. Paul Motian had been on his wavelength for years, and now—Eureka!—Scott LaFaro was in the running as an equal voice.

The newfound trio landed an extended engagement at the Showplace, and by a process of trial and error began to develop the group concept on the job. "All I had to offer," said Evans, "was some kind of reputation and prestige that enabled me to have a record contract, which didn't pay much, but we could make records—not enough to live on, but enough to get a trio experienced and moving. I found these two musicians were not only compatible, but would be willing to dedicate themselves to a musical goal, a trio goal. We made an agreement to put down other work for anything that might come up for the trio."[8] The members formed, briefly as it tragically turned out, one of the most important, one of the best-knit, and one of the most subtly inventive groups ever to exist in music.

☙ ☙ ☙

Drummer Paul Motian, of Armenian descent, had already figured prominently in Evans's musical life. He was born in Providence, Rhode Island, in 1931 and, like Evans, had flung himself on the mercy of New York City after being discharged from military service. He studied at the Manhattan School of Music for a semester and a half, soon falling behind in his studies due to nightly engagements. A versatile musician, he played with many groups, including those of George Wallington, Lennie Tristano, Oscar Pettiford, Stan Getz, and the Al Cohn–Zoot Sims Quintet.

Bassist Scott LaFaro was born in Newark, New Jersey, in 1936. After starting out on clarinet and tenor sax, he took up the bass at the age of seventeen, traveling to Los Angeles with Buddy Morrow's band in 1955 and joining Chet Baker the following year. (Evans and Motian played for his audition, and Motian was distinctly unimpressed.) When he came to New York in April 1959, he toured briefly with Benny Goodman (ironically, in view of the Basin Street episode) before meeting up with Evans on *Sung Heroes*.

LaFaro was voted New Star on bass by the *Down Beat* critics, and Evans himself received that accolade on piano for the second year running. The Readers' Poll, meanwhile, rocketed him from twentieth in 1958 to sixth, behind only André Previn, Erroll Garner, Dave Brubeck, Thelonious Monk, and the people's favorite, Oscar Peterson. Here, then, was a musician's musician who also was rapidly becoming popular with jazz listeners.

Orrin Keepnews, ever watchful and supportive, set up a recording session for Bill's new group (subsequently known as the Original Trio or First Trio) in December 1959, the pianist's third date for Riverside under his own name. Called *Portrait in Jazz*, the LP became the first of only a handful of recordings of the group's work to survive. It is sometimes described as a transitional record, but it was also a remarkably valid, sincere, and affecting piece of work in its own right. From *New Jazz Conceptions* to *Everybody Digs* had been a giant step, but the plateau attained on *Portrait* was high indeed, its fresh vistas possessed of a new subtlety in the execution.

Aware that he was gaining some recognition from the general paying public, Evans entered the studio with fresh optimism. To a program of mainly standards he added one new composition of his own, "Peri's Scope." His girlfriend Peri, for whom it was named, remembers that he had written the tune early in 1958.

> "The first working title was 'Kid's Tune,'" she said. "And I had been complaining that no tune was ever written with my name. You know, there was 'Mary' and 'Ruby, My Dear' and so forth.... So, we toyed with naming it 'Perisphere.' He decided that wouldn't be right because Sphere was Monk's middle name. Then he came up with 'Peri's Scope.' That was in the summer of 1959 as I remember. And then later that year, toward the end of the year, he was recording an album and he called and said, 'Guess what we recorded?'
> "Of course, I couldn't.
> "'Peri's Scope.'
> "It was a great feeling, I felt immortal."[9]

Although it is written throughout in 4/4, a three-in-a-bar cross-feel is interpolated into the tune, a foretaste of alternating meters that will persistently recur in Evans's work. It was the first number to be recorded, and LaFaro immediately homed in on the pianist in a special way. When Evans breathed between phrases for a bar or so, LaFaro filled in with a plunging line, the sound ample and resilient. Significantly, at such moments, the bassist had taken the initiative for propelling the performance as a whole; he was already an equal partner. His choice of notes on a walking bass was intriguingly unconventional, and an infectious swing was generated by all three players in rapport.

Maintaining the medium-tempo feel, "Witchcraft" was next up. LaFaro created all manner of patterns from note one; during the first four bars alone he had climbed a ladder to dizzy heights, in sequences that sound roughly like triplets but are actually resolved in a quite independent meter. This sort of strategy bore out some remarks Evans made later: "My first impression of him, when we met during an audition for Chet Baker in '56 or '57, was that he was a marvelous bass player and talent, but it was bubbling out of him almost like a gusher. Ideas were rolling out on top of each other; he could barely handle it. It was like a bucking horse."[10]

It still was, but now he *could* handle it. Elsewhere on the record, never satisfied, he can be heard trying out chording, a procedure made easier by the way his bass was strung: by lowering the height of the bridge, he brought the strings closer to the fingerboard than was the norm, making possible a more guitarlike technique. This unfailing enthusiasm for experiment was just what Evans wanted—it was vital to his concept of interaction between the players. After the theme of "Witchcraft" both players soloed in tandem, Evans initially dropping in and out of short phrases to allow LaFaro into the dialogue. The concept was beginning to work. The pianist's invention on these two tracks, with its instant execution, was staggering, the ideas direct and clear.

The notion of "simultaneous improvisation," incorporating call and response, emerged as planned procedure on two versions of "Autumn Leaves." One take (on which the stereo equipment was malfunctioning) was put on the mono release, the other on the stereo. On the mono "preferred version," Paul Motian was a brilliantly equal third partner, and when the launch came he provided exhilarating drive. Equally, an up-tempo "What Is This Thing Called Love?" demonstrated some formally planned interplay, as well as tight piano-and-drums riffing behind the bass solo, evolved during their Showplace club engagement. Evans's main solo was a joy and it is no exaggeration to say that the presence of Scott LaFaro had given him a new lease on exploratory life. Perhaps for the same reason, the pianist was inspired on ballads to erupt from his lyrical base into ecstatic flights of energy as though, childlike, he was unable to contain his wonderment.

"Some Day My Prince Will Come" had worked beautifully in the context for which it was written in 1937, Walt Disney's animated feature cartoon, *Snow White and the Seven Dwarfs*. It became the first in a line of so-called "trite" film and show tunes that Evans played, though credit must go to Dave Brubeck for first using it (and other Disney tunes) in a jazz context. Evans became very attached to it over the years, seeing in it a freshness and a strength fit for probing.

ᚳ ᚳ ᚳ

Evans's "creed" carried an extension: "Especially, I want my work—and the trio's if possible—to sing. I want to play what I like to hear. I'm not going to be strange or new. If what I do grows that way naturally, that'll be O.K. But it must have that wonderful feeling of singing."[11] All pianists must strive for this on an instrument of percussion whose notes die immediately after being struck. Evans met the challenge on "Spring Is Here," a magnificent example of his lyrical touch. It is worth considering for a moment his first right-hand note, the melody note G (in the key of Ab). *How did he make it sing?*

Most vitally, the note had to come from the heart. His motivation to sing, his reason to care about sound at all, arose from his need to express emotion through his skill at the keyboard. Practically, it was delivered with weight—arm-weight—that is to say, natural gravity, and with no suggestion of forcing the sound. As any good piano teacher will advise the student, a relaxed arm will produce quality of sound, whereas tension in the musculature will cause a hard sound. Evans understood and practiced this principle absolutely, and his sound always had quality and depth as a result.

The note was delivered with a certain, judged *amount* of weight, in the light of advance knowledge of how long it was going to have to last (ring or sing) before the next one. Furthermore, it was delivered with understanding of the nature of the harmony that goes with it: in the tonal system, some harmonies are more discordant than others; these are the more expressive ones and, in terms of tone, they must be leaned into further. This particular note received that tone, being colored by one such harmony.

A still further singing quality was determined by the fact that Evans was inspired to ruminate underneath with gently moving left-hand chords; the main note had to ring through this extra part. This lightly touched-in accompaniment would help to shade the tone of the main note and also carry it through the very slow tempo of the bar. Simultaneous with the note in question, a barely audible middle chord was played. Because of the extreme delicacy of its touch, this harmony was more hinted at than stated; nevertheless, the relative tone assignation to main note and harmony notes was a fine consideration.

Finally, the note was delivered with total confidence in Scott LaFaro's richly supporting bass note, which was used as a cushion upon which to rest and blend the tone. *The note sang.*

Evans is able to move us today because of the way he played that note, making it live like no other. The sound is alive and breathing, and is heard, not as decibels at a certain pitch, but as a manifestation of an artistic spirit. He possessed that priceless attribute, the ability to communicate feeling through sound—in his case, a gift that was both innate and informed.

Some pianists feel into the bed of the key, using the arm as a shock-absorber to the sound, while others play more "at the surface." Evans was of the former persuasion, accounting for his intensity of tone and thereby his ability to sing. This expressive technique emanated directly from his studies of the classical repertoire. Because of his physically relaxed attitude at the keyboard he had every nuance of touch at his disposal, and was able to mix a rich palette of musical colors. He brought to a ballad as much light and shade as the finest classical artist and became one of the first to exploit this range in piano jazz.

From the start of their relationship, LaFaro hardly needed Evans's encouragement to be an equal voice. Just as the pianist had stimulated Miles Davis into new realms of lyricism, so now the bassist freed Evans's imagination into territories unknown, restoring him, after a dull patch, to his own dimension. *Portrait in Jazz* was a revolutionary recording for Evans, who was able for the first time to realize some of his ideals.

CHAPTER 9

Explorations

Those two guys brought tears to my eyes.
— Paul Motian, on Bill Evans and Scott LaFaro

As the sixties dawned a new form of music began to dominate the airwaves and jukeboxes of clean-living America. Born in the previous decade, it was a mutated amalgam of rhythm and blues, gospel, and country. As the nation's youngest elected president, John F. Kennedy, invoked the passing of a generational torch, the new youth craze swept all before it. But after he was assassinated, in November 1963, the floodgates were opened onto the vulgarity and excess of a musically permissive era.

Looking back in 1994, Art Farmer spoke for many in confessing that he regarded the late 1950s and early 1960s as the heyday of jazz. With the advent of pop and rock he felt that "the bottom was falling out of jazz in New York"; later in the decade he became just one of many Americans who settled in Europe for good. But for a few years in the early sixties, "pure" jazz remained unadulterated by jazz-rock incursions, and its diehard exponents continued to enjoy a healthy following.

Bill Evans began the decade with a brief reunion of that redoubtable Miles Davis rhythm section: himself, Paul Chambers, and Jimmy Cobb. They performed at Birdland with the singer Frank Minion and contributed with him to a hip LP for Bethlehem called *The Soft Land of Make Believe*. The number on it called "Flamenco Sketches" was really "All Blues" from *Kind of Blue*, despite the former title being clear on label and sleeve and Minion's own added lyric containing several references to "flamenco." Conjecture about these mixed-up tracks may continue, but in any case, with the aid of triple-tracking the singer emulated the original arrangement on *Kind of Blue*, essaying to become Adderley, Coltrane, and Davis all rolled into one; then, in true Jon Hendricks tradition, he added lyrics to the first two choruses of Davis's original solo. Evans, Chambers, and Cobb straightforwardly reproduced the original background. "So What" was similarly resurrected, Evans creating a two-chorus solo as a valid alternative to the original. His free introduction with Chambers from *Kind of Blue* was retained (he had kept the manuscript sketch).

On the full vocal version of "'Round Midnight," the introduction, link, and coda were borrowed directly from the arrangement that Gil Evans had made for the Miles Davis Quintet in September 1956. That setting had been absorbed by Bill when playing the piece on the road with Davis in 1958, and an example is preserved on *Four-Play*. He always incorporated those elements afterward when playing the number. On *The Soft Land of Make Believe* he took a strongly delineated solo, and it is a treat to review the classic sound of these Miles Davis anchor men, reunited for this bizarre but enjoyable enterprise.

⫷ ⫷ ⫷

The trio with LaFaro and Motian went on a cross-country tour early in 1960, the first time a Bill Evans Trio had gone on the road. Touring the world with his own trio was to become the central activity of the pianist's life. This first itinerary ranged from Boston to San Francisco, where Evans made his first appearance at the city's Jazz Workshop. Paul Motian recalls: "We played the Sutherland Lounge in Chicago and things really came together. One night during that engagement, Bill played Monk's ''Round Midnight' so beautifully that Scott responded in a way that I can still hear. Those two guys brought tears to my eyes."[1]

They returned to New York in February, appearing in a Town Hall concert package before settling into Birdland, the club on Broadway at 52d Street started by the publisher Monte Kay. He had recently set up the sessions for *Modern Art* and would soon manage Evans's career briefly. Birdland was Count Basie's New York headquarters, and his band was topping the bill for most of March, packing the club as usual, the Bill Evans Trio in support. Most of the patrons were in for Basie, and their reaction during the trio spots ranged from a fairly noisy lack of interest to quiet appreciation, the latter coming from those devotees occupying several lines of chairs facing the bandstand, a nondrinking area known variously as "the bleachers," "the bullpen," or "the peanut gallery."

Evans had already broadcast with Miles Davis on Mutual's *Bandstand USA* programs, but now his own group was on the airwaves for the first time.

From March to May they were featured on several early-hours transmissions from Birdland. In the early 1970s excerpts from these broadcasts came out on two bootleg LPs. The labels were Alto Records (*A Rare Original*) and Session Records (*Hooray for Bill Evans Trio*), just two in a huge series released by New York record collector–turned–executive Boris Rose. Like countless jazz musicians, Evans was dogged over the years by illicitly recorded and marketed material. Joe LaBarbera, his last drummer, remembered Evans's outrage upon finding one of those caricatured white LP jackets in a record store somewhere in Europe. He disapproved of his performances being issued without permission and always wished to maintain control of his releases. In 1992 Cool n' Blue Records of Switzerland reissued this material on CD as *The Legendary Bill Evans Trio: The 1960 Birdland Sessions*. In addition to the material on the LPs, this release included closing-theme ("Five") tags and the restored MC Sid Torin's voice introducing "the most talked-about young man of piano jazz" and plugging the just-issued *Portrait in Jazz*. These were the Friday night editions of the Symphony Sid Show, running until five in the morning, with phone-in record requests invited. The trio sets went out live between midnight and one o'clock—hence the Saturday dates listed.

On the transmission of April 30, LaFaro introduced a new feature into "Autumn Leaves," namely a pedal note on the first sixteen bars, and he structured his first solo chorus correspondingly. Such pedal points were ripe for development in Evans's playing, too, and increasingly of late the last two bars of a theme statement (the "turnaround") had received special treatment. In the vast majority of songs, the last note of the melody falls on the first beat of these two link bars. Evans understood the true function of this breathing space (literally so, if the melody is being sung), and foresaw how anticipation of the first solo could be heightened by exploiting the insistent pull of the dominant. By encouraging his bass player to set up a reiterated dominant pedal note against the harmonies that revolved back to the tonic, he propelled the listener from the end of the tune into the improvising.

Increasingly, the first solo was coming from LaFaro. That night he was in an extroverted mood, strumming his instrument like a guitar and violently rattling gut on fingerboard. On "Come Rain or Come Shine" his forging line pounded into the very earth. Evans always got straight down to business on this song, worrying away at the chords, wrenching them this way and that. Somehow, on a sustained "Blue in Green," Evans coaxed a tone out of the scraggy house piano.

Whatever one may think about the ethics of issuing these Birdland eavesdroppings, they do contain superb playing and provide the only other opportunity, besides the famous 1961 Village Vanguard sessions, of hearing this First Trio at work in a club.

ᗱ ᗱ ᗱ

On the recent cross-nation tour the musicians had felt their way into a "working book" of songs in viable tempos and formats. Along with their three-way activity, they were functioning as a smoothly integrated unit. Nicely established now, the group had work under its belt (a run at the Hickory House, for example) and an album released. The commitment in their playing was absolute, with no concessions either to entertainment or coasting, and if a trio booking came up they honored it in the face of more lucrative work. By its very nature, the group depended on the continuing development and rapport of its particular members and would not readily adapt to a stand-in musician.

Still, there was time and opportunity for all three to work in other directions, and both Paul Motian and Scott LaFaro were constantly in demand. Evans himself teamed up again with Paul Chambers and Philly Joe Jones for part of a hi-fi sampler from Warwick Records called *The Soul of Jazz Percussion*. One track, "Ping Pong Beer," justified the reunion, the uniquely bustling Jones propelling Chambers, Donald Byrd, Pepper Adams, and Evans through some good solos before swapping fours with Earl Zindars on timpani.

One evening in mid-May, the final concert in Charles Schwartz's series *Jazz Profiles* took place at the Circle in the Square in New York City. The Bill Evans Trio participated in the event, a concert profile of the composer Gunther Schuller, including a revival of his "Transformation" from the 1957 Brandeis program, featuring Evans as improviser. The pianist was involved in several other works, too, including two sets of variations that he recorded on an album called *Jazz Abstractions*. He took part in a similar concert later in the summer.

Another booking for the trio that summer was at the 1960 Newport Jazz Festival, the one that became notorious for its riots caused by thousands of beer-swilling college kids who knew little (and cared less) about jazz. The city council was panicked into closing down the concerts on the fourth day, which meant that the Monday afternoon's program organized by Marshall Stearns on the theme of "the doorstep of the future" never took place. Bill's trio was to have participated, along with Gunther Schuller, John Coltrane, and Ornette Coleman.

ᗱ ᗱ ᗱ

Bill's all-time favorite drummer, Philly Joe Jones.
Lee Tanner / The Jazz Image

Mankind had not quite taken its first step into space, but the Soviet sput-
niks had been going up, preparing the way, since 1957. To these cosmic
developments George Russell dedicated his new work for Decca, *Jazz in the
Space Age*. Thinking of Evans's ability to rise to a challenge, he had the idea
of pairing him with the avant-garde Canadian pianist Paul Bley. He foresaw a
two-way stimulus, both musicians steeped in history yet open-minded and
technically versatile.

From the start of the record, Russell had the magic touch, having only to
run beads on drum to transport the listener to his imaginative world. The two
pianists entered, playing out of time and therefore independently of Don
Lamond's shuffling background in 5/2 time. The composer outlined the roles
of the freely improvising pianists: "Bill and Paul were free to come close to the

tonality—sum total of the bass notes—relate to the 5/2 gravitational pull, or not. Tonally and rhythmically out in space, they were not victim to the tyranny of the chord or a particular meter. In essence, this is musical relativism. Everything can be right. The idea takes over. They worked in the realm of ideas, projecting one upon the other. This is pan-chromatic improvisation."[2]

Evans gave his freest playing yet on record, but outright freedom was not for him. While he could have fun and stretch his mind with such playing, it could never completely satisfy him. Given the mainstay support provided by Russell, though, he was prepared to take the plunge away from tonality. Rhythmically, in the two-piano exchanges on "The Lydiot," the freedom of Bley contrasted with the tightness of Evans, establishing a relationship similar to the previous year's keyboard excursions with Bob Brookmeyer (who, incidentally, played in the trombone section at one of the sessions for this album). On "Dimensions," Evans was at his most virile, building with inexorable logic over a long span, but his most potent statement came on "Waltz from Outer Space," a hypnotically floating George Russell creation incorporating many a sidestep. From his imaginative fund the pianist extracted a new brand of block chording, out of *Kind of Blue*, yet in the Lydian language.

⊟ ⊟ ⊟

Evans's *Down Beat* poll positions continued to be high. No longer eligible for the New Star category in 1960, he came third in the Critics' list and fifth in the Readers' (one up from the previous year). In the year's polls at *Metronome* and *Playboy* he rated second among pianists, and he was making an impact abroad, too: in the first Japanese *Down Beat* poll, the readers placed him tenth.

That summer, Evans signed a personal management pact with Monte Kay, who had already taken on the Modern Jazz Quartet and was soon to sign Ornette Coleman. Then, while working at a New York club called the Jazz Gallery, he was taken seriously ill with hepatitis. The condition caused his hands to swell, but that in itself interfered little with his playing; more debilitating nausea and fatigue, though, forced him to cancel a Birdland booking. Once again he went down to Florida to recuperate at his parents' home.

Meanwhile, his new agent arranged some recording dates with J. J. Johnson and Kai Winding, to be produced by Creed Taylor, who had progressed through Bethlehem Records on his way to ABC-Paramount. At ABC he founded the Impulse jazz label and invited Evans onto the first issue in the Impulse catalogue, *The Great Kai and J. J.*, as well as *The Incredible Kai Winding Trombones* and *The Blues and the Abstract Truth*.

Johnson and Winding had co-led their popular two-trombone quintet from its Birdland debut in 1954 to its final showing at Newport in 1956. After that, the group reunited for various projects, including *The Great Kai and J. J.* Sensing the flavor of the session, Evans responded to the novel lineup in sprightly form, keeping everything straightforward and easy on the ear. In vivid contrast to his ongoing trio work, he produced his most lighthearted playing to date; perhaps it was just the job he needed to snap out of his recent illness. "I Concentrate on You" furnished an early example of one of his later mannerisms during the 1960s and early 1970s: a rising chromatic trickle, very fast, repeated across the beat, the whole sequence falling. Every jazz musician has a fund of such clichés to fall back on from time to time, but with Evans they had so far been rare.

Evans completed one more job with Kai Winding, this time in the latter's four-trombone-plus-rhythm-section band, formed after his quintet with Johnson officially disbanded. On *The Incredible Kai Winding Trombones* the leader's arrangements produced a rich, dark-chocolate sonority. Winding was soon to become musical director to New York's Playboy Clubs, and his version of "Black Coffee" gave a taste, aided by Evans's sleazy piano, of what he might offer in that capacity.

⇇ ⇇ ⇇

In November 1960 the trio began two weeks at the Village Vanguard, playing opposite the Miles Davis band (which now had Wynton Kelly on piano). As a direct result of hearing Evans play "Someday My Prince Will Come" during that engagement, Davis added it to his own repertoire the following year; indeed, it became the title track of one of his albums.

There were to be other direct spin-offs from the music of Bill Evans: for a Carnegie Hall concert given by Miles Davis in May 1961, Gil Evans orchestrated some of the key elements in Bill's interpretation of "Spring Is Here" on *Portrait in Jazz*, preserving both the tempo and the spirit of the trio's original. He made particular use of the pianist's reharmonization of the theme with its "noodling" inner parts, as well as the descending jagged line of the first turn-around and the chordal idea at the start of the piano solo. For the same concert Gil transcribed Bill's introduction to "So What" from *Kind of Blue*.

Back in May, the "Jazz Profiles" concert had premièred two sets of variations by Gunther Schuller (on themes by John Lewis and Thelonious Monk, respectively), and these were now recorded by mostly the same musicians for an Atlantic album called *Jazz Abstractions*. Evans's contribution was small though telling, and unfailingly idiomatic. He was not called upon to solo, but rather to act as occasional anchor to the proceedings. On the impressive "Criss Cross" variants his stabbed chords behind Ornette Coleman's alto and Eric Dolphy's bass clarinet were in true Monkish spirit.

⇻ ⇻ ⇻

The trio reunited for a New Year's tour of the Midwest. At the end of the tour, in February 1961, they made a second album for Riverside called *Explorations*. According to Orrin Keepnews, there was tension in the air on the recording date. Evans and LaFaro were at loggerheads over some nonmusical matter, and Keepnews was fed up with their bickering. Evans was also complaining of a headache. Furthermore, LaFaro was grappling with a replacement bass while his usual Vermont-made instrument was being repaired. As a result, he was shy of the high register and indulged less than usual in his personal brand of chordal experiment.

For whatever reasons, there is a feeling of restraint in the trio's playing— an exploration of an elegant sound-world dedicated to the understatement. The sensitivity of the ear is heightened as Evans's delicate though probing touch draws the listener in. There is a cleanness to the sound, a pearl-like precision in the playing. In addition, subtly and ever so slowly, in accordance with his lifetime's pace of development, Evans introduces further twists into the chordal language, enhanced voicings, additions to the palette of harmonic shades.

The first number to be played was a newcomer to the Evans repertoire, a gem from the pen of Earl Zindars, called "Elsa." Evans began it with an air of mystery, like the unveiling of a secret, the gentle introduction melting imperceptibly into the tune, the listener hardly aware it has begun. This prototype "Elsa" had a precious quality—overt expression withheld—that set the tone for the session. Of Zindars's tunes, Evans had previously recorded only "Mother of Earl," but from now on the composer's work would occupy a special place in Evans's music making. "Bill always said he was a 3/4 person," Earl told me, "and I likewise agreed, that I was, too. Probably a good reason why he had 'Elsa' always ready wherever he performed."

Earl Zindars was born in Chicago in 1927 of mixed Irish, German, and Scottish descent. He grew up to master the full range of percussion and played for a time in the Chicago Symphony. But his true vocation was composing, and when he sent an orchestral piece to Evans the response was typically generous. "He discussed the music with me at great length and encouraged me to continue writing," said Earl. "That was, to me, the best of Bill, parallel to his genius; the way he would take time to totally immerse himself in somebody else's music in such a clear and non-affected way, and share his friendship, musically and spiritually. That is something I'll never lose or forget."[3]

After penning the exquisite "Elsa," Zindars wrote all his melodies, if not specifically for Evans, at least with him in mind. One of his tunes that Bill played in those days but never recorded was "Vasa." Miles Davis caught Evans doing it once and liked its adventurous harmonic flavor. "Puppet Party" was another, a tricky little polytonal number that Bill enjoyed playing around with. The pianist always lent a sympathetic and enthusiastic ear to anything Zindars offered.

On *Explorations* something of the rarified treatment of "Elsa" was afforded to "Nardis," the tone conjured with care on this, its first recorded trio version. There was a fragility to the concept that echoed Evans's written invocation of Japanese visual art on his *Kind of Blue* sleeve note. The theme statement led directly to a featured bass solo, setting a formal precedent for all future Evans performances.

Standards made up the rest of the program, "I Wish I Knew" amply demonstrating one of Evans's characteristic approaches: the large-scale substitution (in an organic way) of new harmonies for the songbook changes. The Gordon-Warren songsheet made do with half a dozen or so basic chords. Evans's reconstruction, on the other hand, employed nearly three times as many, changing mostly by the half-bar. In this way a simple song could be enriched, strengthened, and transformed. In collusion with the infinite shades of his tone production, the pianist was able to make, instrumentally, an affecting vocal statement. Typical of his ballad performances, it was played with feeling but was never mawkish.

At the end of the session came "How Deep Is the Ocean?" which was remarkable at the time for leaving the melody till the end, and Johnny Carisi's "Israel," which rose light and airy as a soufflé, epitomizing Evans's artistic position, vintage 1961. On this the trio meshed beautifully, tendering immaculate balances of intellect and swing, sophistication and poetry. Paul Motian, at his crisp best, pinched the cymbal brushwork on the theme, characterizing the coolly contained expressive range.

⋐⋐ ⋐⋐ ⋐⋐

At the core of Evans's thought was the abandonment of the root to the bass. He commented: "If I am going to be sitting there playing roots, fifths, and full voicings, the bass is relegated to a time machine."[4] He was not the first to adopt this strategy. As far back as the mid-forties Ahmad Jamal had experimented in this way, and through the fifties Erroll Garner, Red Garland, and others took individual plunges into this uncharted rootless territory.

Evans's achievement lay in consolidation, in the creation of a self-sufficient left-hand language—a "voicing vernacular" peculiarly his own—based on the logical progression of one chord to the next while involving the minimum movement of the hand. This resulted in a continuity of sound in the middle register (still implied even when momentarily broken) that opened up areas for invention not only above but below it. The pianist's left hand spent much of its time around middle C, a good clean area of the piano where harmonic clusters are acoustically clearest. Thus was paved the way for the bass player's contrapuntal independence, an opportunity seized by Scott LaFaro.

As exhibited freely on *Explorations,* Evans's very personal "locked-hands" technique had now attained a fully formed order. Exploratory right-hand lines were shadowed by left-hand harmonies suspended from and carried by the singing, leading voice, the choice and tone of each note consummately judged. The whole moved as a loping unit, a unified concept in which the harmonic cushion was harnessed to the rhythmic contour of the top line. "Sweet and Lovely" offers a superb example, the chordal solo adding a harmonic zest, twice removed, to the background sequence.

Evans could sustain entire choruses in this way with apparent ease, and the phenomenon was his most striking contribution to the language of piano jazz. But it was an element of style—the personal aspect of playing that he was at pains to avoid teaching at Lenox, for fear of encouraging the mimicry of an idiom rather than the emergence of that idiom from the student's own creative spirit. Individuality of style, Evans believed, must be arrived at through the application of fundamental principles, as he himself had done ever since trying to become a jazz musician. Precisely by working at the essence of his material had he arrived at a stylistic dialect through which to express it.

10 Sunday at the
Village Vanguard

*It bugs me when people try to analyze jazz as an intellectual theorem. It's not.
It's feeling.*

—*Bill Evans*

Before making *Explorations* in 1961, Evans had teamed up with Cannonball
Adderley, who wanted to make an album that would break away from his
own popular soul style, as typified by his work with the pianist Bobby Timmons. Although the Riverside record that resulted was nominally Adderley's,
the concept was built around his friend Bill Evans, and in a far more positive
way than on *Portrait of Cannonball*, their previous collaboration for that
company. Orrin Keepnews recalls that it was Adderley's idea to use Percy
Heath and Connie Kay from the Modern Jazz Quartet, as well as Evans, to
bring about a cooler style. This one-off lineup of musicians was drawn from
three busy working groups—Adderley and his Quintet, Evans with his Trio,
and the MJQ. Considering the life of a traveling musician, it was an accomplishment to assemble these four players for three sessions, in one place,
within the space of seven weeks, to make *Know What I Mean?*

Riverside's most recently acquired recording venue was Plaza Sound
Studio, but Evans preferred the piano at Bell Sound Studios, where he had
chosen to make *Explorations*, and Adderley readily agreed to record where
Bill was happiest. Proceedings began with the Gershwins' "Who Cares?" the
laid-back, motorized groove of their first attempt acquiring, on the next, an
extra couple of notches in tempo and buoyancy from drummer Connie Kay.
Evans settled into an irresistible solo that, with the aid of the MJQ airborne
propeller, must rank as one of his catchiest creations. Then, as composer, the
pianist came up with his own special concoction for the album, created in
the studio at Adderley's request. Like his "Flamenco Sketches" on *Kind of*

With Julian "Cannonball"
Adderley while making
Know What I Mean? in 1961.
Steve Schapiro, courtesy of Fantasy, Inc.

Blue, it was a succession of five chords or "levels"—in this case, minor sevenths on F♯, E♭, E, A, and C (four bars on each). Orrin Keepnews christened
it "Know What I Mean?" after one of Adderley's conversational signatures.

The second of the three dates produced a slinky-slow "Elsa"; Evans,
who had made his trio version a couple of weeks earlier for *Explorations,*
chose the piece for the session. Adderley gracefully stood aside to leave the
tune statements to the pianist before squeezing his own extra juice from the
fertile sequence. From the way Evans sank into the harmonies it was evident
that he found Earl Zindars's composition a perfect fit.

Completing the album in March, the quartet recorded Evans's own
"Waltz for Debby" as a jazz-blowing vehicle. Evans propelled his solo introduction inexorably toward the saxophone entry, changing into four time for
the melody chorus and the ensuing improvising. The tune was taken up in due
course by Ahmad Jamal and Oscar Peterson, who both adopted this format.
After Evans's death in 1980, Peterson included the number in many of his sets.

After a weekend at the Cork 'n' Bib club in suburban Westbury, Evans
teamed up for another session with Paul Chambers and Roy Haynes, both of

whom had been on *The Great Kai and J. J.* The mostly blues-based program of *The Blues and the Abstract Truth,* again for Creed Taylor's Impulse label, was impressively composed and arranged by Oliver Nelson. Nelson, offering his own brand of composer's tenor, also made a front line with Freddie Hubbard (trumpet) and Eric Dolphy (alto sax and flute). Evans was arguably miscast in this magnificent album; after all, blues influences were notably absent from the evolving, organic concept of his own trio, and he was at his best here when adopting the scrunchy, chordal approach, as on "Yearnin'."

Evans's bookings were now being managed by Rudy Viola of International Talent Associates, and the trio continued to get work—weeks at the Town Tavern in Toronto and the Sutherland Lounge in Chicago, for instance. It was uncanny how the Evans trio concept was falling into place, and a springtime engagement at the Showboat in Washington paved the way for the final evolution of this remarkable chamber group.

ⅇ⅀ ⅇ⅀ ⅇ⅀

During 1961 the Bill Evans Trio spent a good deal of time at 178 Seventh Avenue South in New York's Greenwich Village. The venue? Max Gordon's basement dive and live jazz mecca, the Village Vanguard. It had opened nearby as a focus for poets in 1932 as the Village Fair, then expanded to offer folk and popular music, cabaret, and comedy, only in the mid-fifties becoming best known for fine jazz. Since then most of the greats have performed there, but for Bill Evans the place was to hold a special significance.

In 1980 Max Gordon, the club's modest but uncompromising owner, wrote: "The first time Bill Evans played the Vanguard, twenty-five years ago, he was the intermission piano player opposite the Modern Jazz Quartet. When the MJQ was on, the crowd, who'd come to hear them, was quiet. When Bill took over, a buzz started 'round the room. Who in hell is Bill Evans? They'd never heard of him. He was filling space between sets for the star attraction. Today, Bill is the star attraction. He plays at the Vanguard four, five times a year. Now when he's on, the Vanguard is Town Hall."[1] Back in 1961 he was not yet the "star attraction," but his engagement at the Vanguard for two weeks in mid-June was an honorable, equal billing with the singing group Lambert, Hendricks, and Ross.

At this time, a teenage jazz fan named Peter Titelman was attending high school and living with his parents just around the corner from the Village Gate, another neighborhood club. He spent much of his weekend time at the Vanguard, the Gate, and the Half Note. He evokes a typical weekend:

The Vanguard was my favorite club: it was small and intimate, they didn't bother about me coming in as a minor, and the audience was most appreciative. One Sunday I had been uptown with my parents. I told them that I very much wanted to see Bill Evans at the Vanguard that afternoon. The show started at 4:30, and I urged my father to come down with me. We headed down to the Village and stood in [a long] line with a ... quiet and respectful group of fans. Once inside the Vanguard, we managed to get a small table for two in the second or third row—there were only a couple of tables across—directly facing the bandstand.

LaFaro, Motian, and Evans all had their own personal style; but they played in such a synchronous fashion. Each musician was focused and always seemed to be deep within himself, yet totally listening and interacting with the other two as if they were a hyperorganism—which of course they were—in the sense of being, or functioning, like any emotionally driven relationship. Bill was hunched over the keyboard, and his fingers always seemed very flat and unbent.

As to the music of that afternoon, it was sublime. There were a few numbers that I had not previously heard, and on these the trio really seemed to stretch out and play a little longer than on some of the pieces I was used to hearing. It was one seamless set, and of course it was too short. The audience was very diverse: young and old, black and white. They definitely had ears for the music that Bill Evans and his group produced.

Night after night at the Vanguard, Bill Evans, Scott LaFaro, and Paul Motian honed their craft and refined their art. They were obviously in superior shape, and Orrin Keepnews pressed Evans to make his first on-the-job recording. He had taped the pianist Junior Mance at the club earlier in the year, had liked working in the room, and knew it could provide a good keyboard sound. Evans liked its forty-year-old Steinway, and, as Keepnews said, "this type of session was a relatively painless way to extract an album from the usually foot-dragging pianist."[2] Riverside's resident engineer, Ray Fowler, was out of town, but when it was decided to aim for a recording on the last day of the engagement, Dave Jones, a specialist in two-track location work, was available.

The Vanguard's policy at that time was to schedule a Sunday matinée as well as an evening performance, and those afternoon sessions—like the one that Peter Titelman and his father attended—were a focus for the most discerning jazz audience in New York City. On June 25, 1961, the trio played five sets—two in the afternoon and three in the evening—each one comprising four or five numbers and lasting about half an hour. The long day afforded the Riverside team generous leeway for whatever recording hazards might arise on site. And so, with the pianist himself finally in favor of the project, the equipment was lugged downstairs and the scene set for a memorable day's recording. Two albums resulted at the time: *Sunday at the Village Vanguard* and *Waltz for Debby*, a further selection of takes appearing posthumously as *More from the Vanguard*.

During the afternoon, at home in his favorite locale, Evans relaxed and expanded, effortlessly engaging with his colleagues. One new number, "Alice in Wonderland," evinced his fondness for the Disney waltz, his delivery at once floating, lithe, and tensile. Another recorded first for him was "My Foolish Heart," from the 1949 film of that name. In the movie, Victor Young's full-bloodied score conveyed the love-theme as a leitmotiv, the melody welling up under every kiss. Here at the Vanguard, Evans's glowing ballad statement sustained a cooler romanticism, quintessentially his own. This sublime reading, the corporate sound unerringly molded, stands as one of the all-time classic Bill Evans Trio tracks.

In the second set "My Romance" was alive in detail, yet serene in progression, a feeling helped by LaFaro's emphasis on a half-note, rather than a quarter-note, pulse. The seeds of a new improvisational "lick" were sown in Evans's solo, a sort of squashed octave idea that was fleetingly attractive here, but which later became overused. The afternoon ended with "Solar" by Miles Davis, Evans's solo starting as a long, octave-doubled single line, parallel fingers flashing in all manner of rhythmic guise. Scott LaFaro resolutely refused to "walk" but improvised alongside, the duet tied together by Paul Motian's intertwining pulsations. Thus provoking astonishment and awe, the trio closed down until the evening.

The evening sessions opened with LaFaro's intriguing new composition, "Gloria's Step." Its irregular phrase lengths feel completely natural, testimony to LaFaro's creative flair. Evans was quite at home in it with his unassumingly melodic commentary and exemplary pedaling. On "My Man's Gone Now" the piano solo was typically understated, LaFaro's strummed underpinning responsible for the broodingly intense mood.

Evans usually left the tune of Cole Porter's "All of You" till the out chorus (if he played it at all), preferring at the beginning to work his way obliquely around it. Here, the opening "statement" was an adventure in itself, and the second chorus a lesson in motivic development (Ex. 2). As with his George Russell and Miles Davis collaborations, so with the trio he dropped out behind two choruses of LaFaro's solo. Aside from his keenness to feature those colleagues, there was a formal point to the decision. "I think in terms of a number having a total shape," he said. "For example, I try to avoid getting to full intensity too early. Any one thing done for too long gets tiring. Contrast is important to me. I even thought that drums would be a problem and we might be better without them. It was remarkable that Paul Motian came along and identified with the concept so completely."[3] The trio played out on "All of You" with a circular four-bar sequence, a tag for the tune that can be traced back through Miles Davis to Ahmad Jamal.

Ex. 2. The start of the second chorus of "All of You" from *Sunday at the Village Vanguard*. Several aspects of the Evans approach may be observed. The right-hand line develops motivically and integrates his idiosyncratic quarter-note triplet. The rootless left-hand voicings drop in irregularly around the middle-C area and incorporate (at the beginning) that "scrunch" minor second interval, so much a part of the "Bill Evans sound." Note in the last two bars how the left hand rhythmically shadows and supports the right.

Transcribed by Steve Widenhofer

By the middle of the evening a good crowd was in the club, and the place was buzzing. Evans said later, "They needed time to talk.... I just blocked out the noise and got a little deeper into the music."[4] Thus insulated, he gauged his tonal level to that of his colleagues. Miles Davis's famous comment that Evans played a sound more than a chord may be expanded to embrace the whole trio; by now, in vindication of the group credo, its magically unified sound was about to be engraved on the history of jazz.

Gershwin's "I Loves You, Porgy," at first loaded with feeling on its orchestrally swelling statement, subsequently relaxed into a caressingly swinging trialogue. The set ended with Evans's only recorded shot at Miles Davis's 1958 modal classic "Milestones," which in due course panned out as a bass feature. By now LaFaro had his Vermont-made instrument back in service after the *Explorations* date. When on tour, Evans had noted, "It had a marvelous sustaining and resonating quality. He'd be playing in the hotel room and hit a quadruple stop that was a harmonious sound, and then set the bass down on its side, and it seemed the sound just rang and rang for so long."[5]

The final set reworked earlier tunes, more deeply in the cases of "Detour Ahead" and "Gloria's Step," less so with "Waltz for Debby" and "All of You." It was late, it had been a long day, and the stragglers were drifting home. Few were left to hear the final selection, "Jade Visions." It was the second LaFaro composition that day and was played twice in succession, first as a light cocktail, the 9/8 pulse floating, the touch delicate; then slower, digging deeper, a more velvet claret.

The fruits of the group's imagination that day continue to reward repeated hearings—and to renew the listener's mental and emotional stamina. Each piece occupies its own crystalline world of magic. As Bill Goodwin, who drummed with the trio briefly in the seventies, put it: "When Bill and Scott and Paul Motian got together, it was as if they already knew what to do. They had instant sound; they had instant rapport."[6] This legacy has been called Bill Evans's finest hour, and few would disagree. Delving into the riches recorded (amounting to about two and a half hours of music) we witness a certain apogee in the development of the jazz piano trio, the medium pursued by Evans for his lifetime's achievement. For depth of feeling, in-group affinity, and beauty of conception with a pliant touch, these records will be forever peerless.

ᙍ ᙍ ᙍ

Ten days later, Scott LaFaro was driving back late to his parents' Geneva home in upstate New York. Heading east on Route 20, an unlit rural road, he veered off into a tree and was killed outright. Evans and Motian were both devastated at the news. Not only was LaFaro's death a terrible personal loss, but it was the end of Evans's ideal triumvirate, in which he embraced his bass player as a kind of alter ego. At a stroke, the brightening flame of the group's creativity was savagely extinguished, and the bass player's death killed something in the pianist himself.

In numerous interviews Evans has paid tribute to what he always considered to be his finest trio. He said:

> What is most important is not the style itself but how the style is developed and how you can play within it. Sometimes Scott, Paul and I would play the same tune over and over again. Rarely did everything fall into place, but when it did we thought it was sensational. Of course, it may not mean much to the listener, as most people in clubs do not listen on that level anyway. What gave that trio its character was a common aim and a feeling of potential. The music developed as we performed, and what you heard came through actual performance. The objective was to achieve the result in a responsible way. Naturally, as the lead voice, I might have shaped the performance, but I had no wish to be a dictator. If the music itself did not coax a response, I did not want one. Meeting both Scott and Paul was probably the most influential factor in my career. I am thankful that we recorded that day, because it was the last time I saw Scott and the last time we would play together. When you have evolved a concept of playing which depends on the specific personalities of outstanding players, how do you start again when they are gone?[7]

Evans did not play for many months, not even at home. The depth to which he was shattered reflected his esteem for LaFaro. Bill knew the scene; he knew the bass players. As the most versatile jazz pianist of his generation he had brushed with the full range of talent in New York. There were many magnificent players, but it was a question of wavelength — tuning in to a personal concept of playing. "Scott was just an incredible guy about knowing where your next thought was going to be," Evans said. "I wondered, 'How did he know I was going there?' And he was probably feeling the same way. The most marvelous thing is that he and Paul and I somehow agreed without speaking about the type of freedom and responsibility we wanted to bring to bear upon the music, to get the development we wanted without putting repressive restrictions upon ourselves."[8]

Riverside had been looking for only one album, but LaFaro's death changed the economics. *Sunday at the Village Vanguard* was subtitled *Featuring Scott LaFaro* and was rushed out by September 1961. Evans himself was eager to emphasize the bass player's contributions, including his compositions "Gloria's Step" and "Jade Visions." Orrin Keepnews asked Evans to write a few words for the sleeve, but he could not bring himself to

The First Trio, with bassist Scott LaFaro and drummer Paul Motian, right, at the
Village Vanguard, New York, 1961. Riverside producer Orrin Keepnews, left, looks on.
Steve Schapiro, courtesy of Fantasy, Inc.

do it. Had he done so, he might well have mentioned that "Scotty" had
finally made a record with which he was happy. The album earned Evans his
first Grammy nomination. A second album, *Waltz for Debby,* followed in
spring 1962.

The photographic portrait of Evans on the sleeve of *Sunday at the
Village Vanguard* shows starkly the effects of his heroin addiction. Indeed,
his decline in health may be traced through photographs, starting with the
robust, full-in-the-face pianist of 1957. The following year, photographs with
Miles Davis showed features as yet unravaged by the drug, but by the beginning of 1960, shortly before the release of *Portrait in Jazz,* loss of weight had
induced a gaunt and craggy look, an austere aspect of suffering that would
persist for the following decade. His appearance on the cover of *Down Beat*
in December of that year presented an image of inaccessibility and torment.

Seemingly uncommunicative and serious in appearance, at least until his later years, Evans was often thought of as an intellectual. So he was—staggeringly so—and yet he used rational command only as a vehicle for emotional expression, and therein precisely lay his strength. No one had toiled harder at understanding the mechanics of his medium, but his poetic motivation in performance was clear both in these tracks and in his complaint that "it bugs me when people try to analyze jazz as an intellectual theorem. It's not. It's feeling."[9]

He often likened his art to that of the painter who might in discussion refer only to perspective, composition, and color. "But the moment that he begins painting he will let his feelings explode, and now it is his human side that will show up in his works. It is exactly the same for me. I think in technical terms, but what I play is human."[10]

Because of his self-imposed grounding in jazz grammar and his deliberate application of that knowledge, he was incapable of sentimentality, the cozy way out or the "easy-listening" option. In his own words: "Discipline and freedom have to be mixed in a very sensitive way, creatively, to get a really great result. I believe all music is romantic, but if it gets schmaltzy, romanticism is disturbing. On the other hand, romanticism handled with discipline is the most beautiful kind of beauty. And I think that kind of combination was beginning to happen with this particular trio."[11]

Ever since his early lyricism Evans had tended toward his natural introspection, and even when projecting strongly he seemed self-absorbed. His first thought was to play music that would satisfy himself, hoping meanwhile that his audience would meet him halfway. Whitney Balliett saw this as Evans's personal dilemma, "a contest between his intense wish to practice a wholly private, inner-ear music and an equally intense wish to express his jubilation at having found such a music within himself."[12]

If, on these 1961 recordings, he made no effort to embrace his audience, yet he craved their communion. His inward-looking character, his disinclination to reach out to his listeners, and his seemingly detached stage attitude may have eliminated a potential audience during his lifetime. For these reasons he never became a household name like Oscar Peterson or Dave Brubeck. Such artists, in addition to their musical merits, entertained and openly communicated in ways that did not come naturally to Bill Evans.

Part III
On the Road, 1961–77

CHAPTER **11** Moonbeams

The muscular force that made his up-tempo work as a sideman so notable has now become an integral part of his ballad playing, giving him the delicate strength of silk thread.

—Joe Goldberg

After the death of Scott LaFaro, the summer of 1961 became one of the extreme low periods in the life and career of Bill Evans. "I didn't realize how it affected me right away," he said. "Musically everything seemed to stop. I didn't even play at home."[1] He became increasingly withdrawn, a condition reinforced by his drug use. The tragedy threw the significance of what the trio had been doing together—the infinite possibility that both Evans and Paul Motian had felt—into stark relief. They had achieved such a plateau of artistic communion that Evans was shocked and numbed, both personally and musically, by the loss. His brother Harry was in New York earning a Ph.D. at Columbia University, and Pat, Harry's wife, even recalls Bill wandering around the city wearing some of LaFaro's clothes.

In their August poll the *Down Beat* critics raised Evans into second place behind Thelonious Monk and were backed up in December by the magazine's readers, who placed him third. But it was scant consolation for the broken artist. Eventually, after several months' silence, he undertook one or two club appearances playing solo, and in October he was briefly enticed back to Riverside for an album in progress called *Rah* by the up-and-coming singer Mark Murphy. It was a token session for Evans. Wynton Kelly had already been the pianist on three dates with a handpicked brass ensemble arranged and conducted by Ernie Wilkins. For this fourth session, with a minimum musical brief, Evans was called in by Orrin Keepnews, as much to lift him out of his depression as anything else. Murphy was being managed by Helen Keane—who in due course would also manage Evans—and later, when Evans began playing at the Vanguard again, the singer would sit in with the trio at Sunday matinées.

At this point, Charles H. Israels, the young bass-playing student whom Bill had heard at Brandeis University, reenters the story. Israels had first heard Evans in 1955 at the Composer, the same small club on 58th Street in New York where the pianist had first heard Scott LaFaro. After graduating from Brandeis, this "middle-class Jewish kid from Yonkers and Cleveland Heights" had gone to Europe, working with Bud Powell, Kenny Clarke, and Lucky Thompson before returning to research acoustics in Boston.[2] Since 1959 he had been playing in the George Russell sextet.

During the period of the First Trio, Evans had felt Israels's affinity to his wavelength—enough to make him the natural choice as LaFaro's successor. Israels was in Europe at the time, playing jazz in the pit with the Jerome Robbins Ballet USA. When the news came, he experienced a bizarre mixture of sadness and exhilaration, for he knew intuitively that he was likely to be Bill Evans's next bass player. He was not surprised to find, on his return, a message calling him to play with Evans. Israels has variously been described as positive, aggressive, or arrogant—strangers wanting a friendly word could get short shrift—but he had a productive effect on the ailing pianist, giving him a needed jolt into action.

They had but one "rehearsal," which typically amounted to a play-through of a couple of tunes. Like Miles Davis, Evans disliked rehearsing. Israels, as a result of his chamber music training, asked the pianist to move his head or body to indicate changes of tempo in or out of rubato sections. He was told not to worry: "Just listen. You'll know how long to wait—you'll know when to play."[3]

"We tried it and he was right," recalled Israels. "We went to work in Syracuse. He played on a white upright piano in a black club in the black ghetto and stayed in a hotel right next to the Greyhound bus station and kind of hid out while we developed enough rapport for us to go into the Hickory House for a long run."[4] This was to become the pianist's routine in each location on the road, a reclusive existence of room service and television.

He was struggling on several levels at this time, still reeling from the summer, his career off the rails, and this new trio still at a formative stage. *Down Beat* reported that he had signed with Verve Records, though under the terms of his contract he would continue to record for Riverside for eighteen months. Meanwhile, a recording date had come up from Atlantic Records for an album called *Nirvana* with flutist Herbie Mann.

With its new bass player, the Bill Evans Trio became a very different group right from the start, but it would be unfair to judge it on the showing of this record. The three musicians, feeling their way, did not blend completely, either among themselves or with Herbie Mann. Although they made conscious attempts at joint improvisation, they remained *self*-conscious, and the integrated sound and concept of the Bill Evans Trio was missing for the time being.

The title track, a kind of 1960s-vintage New Age rumination of scant substance on two alternating chords, epitomized the pervading atmosphere, but with his thoughtful solo on "Lover Man" Evans salvaged from the session the good name of introspection. The inclusion of Erik Satie's "Gymnopédie No. 2" was a salutary reminder that modal aspirations away from tonality were already under way in the late 1880s (*pace* the ghost of Miles), when the composer's early piano works accorded the minor seventh chord a status in its own right, freeing it from its previously defined en route function in a sequence. Evans and Mann, while following the bass and harmony exactly, gently reformed the piece's melodic line, always mindful of Satie's peculiar brand of melancholy and stark innocence.

During 1961 Herbie Mann's group had taken on board the self-taught vibraphonist Dave Pike. He had recently moved from the West Coast to New York and now teamed up in his own right with Evans for a quartet session on the Epic label called *Pike's Peak*. Alert and involved, Evans can be heard picking up some of the threads of his calamitous summer. After the pinnacles reached with his defunct trio, he sounds to be in neutral mode, biding his time, waiting for something to happen. There was a certain aridity in the style, contrasting markedly with the integrated warmth of his first trio's rapport, but to his credit Evans was beavering away at ideas, supplying judiciously varied backings to his extroverted leader. "Why Not" was Dave Pike's answer to "So What," and Evans furnished his third recorded version (after *The Soft Land of Make Believe*) of this Miles Davis chord sequence, this time authoritatively chunky in the spirit of the original on *Kind of Blue*. Bill liked this record a lot.

Meanwhile, the new trio continued to coalesce on a string of New York club engagements, playing two weeks at the Village Vanguard opposite the MJQ before going into Birdland in February 1962. As before at that club, a black-market issue resulted, this time on the Chazzer label (three tracks released in the eighties alongside much later material). On *Bill Evans Trio: Rare Broadcast Material* it was another weekend at Birdland, and another radio broadcast from "the jazz corner of the world," as Sid Torin never failed to remind his listeners. With "Haunted Heart" digging deeper than before and "Nardis" taking on board a new degree of earnestness, the trio—suddenly a unit—showed signs of fulfilling a challenging succession.

Riverside was planning a major collaboration with the already legendary Tadd Dameron, who, since the 1940s, had been a vital arranger and pianistic messenger of the "new music." In the role of composer, for which he always wished to be remembered, he had never been represented to his own satisfaction on records. This project, called *The Magic Touch*, gave him a full-scale opportunity to mount his comeback. Evans, a natural choice for the role of big-band soloist, had included Dameron's "Our Delight" on *New Jazz Conceptions* and would soon take on "If You Could See Me Now" as one of his preferred ballads for the trio. On this marvelous disc—Dameron's last—one of the many joys is hearing Evans cooking again with Philly Joe Jones, this time with Ron Carter on bass.

While recording *The Magic Touch* at Plaza Sound, Evans overcame an earlier dislike of that studio's piano, and he returned to attempt a solo album. It did not work out well, though, in spite of the experience of some earlier solo club dates. The material surfaced posthumously in 1981 on the Milestone twofer *Conception*. It is the first time we hear Evans swinging unaccompanied on disc, and occasionally it can be unsettling. His rhythmic displacement seems like a deliberate attempt to throw the listener; it is not, but in the absence of the laid-down beat we must learn to trust the implied one. There seem to be gaps and we can find ourselves a beat out if we go with the off-centering instead of holding out against it.

The mood was strange—the pianist's mind half on something else—yet a mysterious depth was being probed. "Like Someone in Love," for all its apparently formless progress, somehow revealed Evans's private thoughts. He then recorded his first respectful nod toward Dave Brubeck, swingingly encapsulating one of his fellow pianist's best tunes, "In Your Own Sweet Way." Alas, he aborted.

A hectic period of recording was looming for Evans, and in the ensuing flurry both producer and pianist forgot about the session. Peter Keepnews sees the playing as "a kind of unofficial eulogy" to Scott LaFaro.[5] Testament or not, and imperfect though it is, it is a moving document.

⊂⊱ ⊂⊱ ⊂⊱

The world's first stereophonic high fidelity record had been produced and released by Audio Fidelity Records in November 1957. The same company had since developed Triple Play Stereo. This concept's flagship album, *Pop + Jazz = Swing*, was inspired by the fact that many bebop standards used the chords of popular songs. Selecting from this repertoire, Benny Golson contrived two separate combo arrangements for each—one popular, the other jazz—which worked either singly or together. The recording was offered for sale in two different versions: on *Pop + Jazz = Swing* various combinations could be created by adjusting the speaker balance control, whereas *Just Jazz* contained the jazz versions only.

A valiant rhythm section, with Evans on piano, supplied both servings simultaneously. In spite of the title and the employment of the finest musicians (an expanded version of Art Farmer and Benny Golson's original Jazztet), the music emphatically did *not* swing, the relentlessly mechanical beat suggesting the use of a click track; indeed, several multitrack recording sessions were needed. Evans seems to have been instructed, presumably by Golson, to keep his comping as snappy as possible so as to avoid harmonic conflict with the pop version. He carried this notion over into his solos, which were notably more disjointed than usual; but at least, on "Moten Swing," the "staccato burst" approach imbued each phrase with impulsive energy. The long-suffering Ron Carter and Charlie Persip were replaced by Paul Chambers and Jimmy Cobb for one track only—"Walkin'"—the last time the Evans-Chambers-Cobb triumvirate is heard on disc.

⊂⊱ ⊂⊱ ⊂⊱

At the end of April, two dates were set up at United Artists with the guitarist Jim Hall. Quite a coterie of musicians used to get together in New York at that time, as Hall recalled: "The circle that George Russell would have over to his place included Jimmy Giuffre, Bob Brookmeyer, Gil Evans, Zoot Sims, Bill and others. It didn't seem strange to me to do records together. Somebody always had a record date. I mean, this is what we did. It was very exciting in those sessions. We weren't thinking about making 'jazz history.'"[6]

One of the mysteries of music that defies analysis is the ability of two musicians to play especially well together, to feel and instinctively adapt to what the other is doing. The duet recording made by Evans and Hall, *Undercurrent*, exemplified this secret. In this sublime meeting, the artists shared a common ground of musical values, Hall confessing to having long been influenced by Evans. Both, too, had a strong feeling for chamber music: the interactive trio was the pianist's aspiration, and Jim Hall's small-group pedigree was high, especially within the intimate settings of the Jimmy Giuffre 3. Quality of sound encompasses a blending of timbres, in this case lovingly conjured; singing tone shines out from every note.

There is a hazard attached to combining piano and guitar, both essentially chordal instruments. Although jazz musicians use alternative chords with ease, the simultaneous choice of two valid but different chords may well not work. Evans and Hall had the intelligence and mutual awareness to escape this snare. And to avoid textural overcrowding, both were conscious of the value of space, every note being made to count in their joint tapestry.

On this, his first duo record, the pianist evinced a new background technique, uniquely suited to the medium. At ballad tempo he moved along gently behind the soloist with evenly spaced chords, functionally equivalent to guitar strumming, and simultaneously providing harmony, rhythm, and a cushion for his colleague. In so doing he glided smoothly without accents, demonstrating—along with the ability to sing—another nonpercussive use of his instrument.

The two takes of "My Funny Valentine" (one fairly romping) are remarkable; the tapes reportedly were left running while the musicians enjoyed an excursion beyond the United Artists all-ballad brief. On the livelier take, originally issued, the two-man band swung like mad, the guitarist providing batterie effects in abundance. Leaving the harmony to his colleague, Evans created long lines with his right hand only, at one point slipping a guitarlike (cross-string) up-and-down arpeggio idea into the line— Billy the Kid was back in town.

ᒣ ᒣ ᒣ

In spring 1962, Brian Hennessey, who later set up Evans's first London engagement, visited New York—and, like any jazz enthusiast arriving in the Big Apple, thought, *who's on?* "I purchased a copy of *Down Beat*," he said.

> Sure enough, the Village Vanguard was offering the Bill Evans Trio that week and not long after checking into the hotel, I took a cab to Greenwich Village. On arrival outside the Vanguard, I observed a long queue waiting to get in and soon discovered that it mostly consisted of Irish Americans who were there to hear the main act of the evening, the Clancy Brothers. To them, the Bill Evans Trio was merely an interval filler. After the Clancy's first set, the audience evaporated (the beer was cheaper around the corner), but huddled round the piano in what appeared to be a state of worship were a dozen studious devotees.
>
> Bill arrived, looking extremely ill. He was attempting to recover from a serious hepatitis infection. The dark glasses didn't hide the jaundice or the obvious malnutrition which was to put him into hospital again later. The music, however, was very healthy, and I soon realized that *Sunday at the Village Vanguard*, the album I had been playing so much at home, was no fluke. Chuck Israels had replaced Scott LaFaro, but Paul Motian was still on drums.
>
> At the interval I made a tentative visit to the back kitchen, where Bill was sit-

ting. I introduced myself as a young jazz fan from England making my first trip to New York and expressed my admiration for his music. Bill was most kind and hospitable—asked me to sit down, ordered me a drink, and we were soon chatting, as much about Thomas Hardy as about music, because when I told him I lived in the West Country he enquired about Dorchester, and I discovered that he was an authority on the works of Hardy. It was perhaps that we were able to talk about things other than music that made my company more acceptable—a change from the never-ending stream of people that merely wanted to find out about his music, which chords he played and when. He asked me if I was staying for the second set, and I said yes. He then said he would drive me back to my hotel, as a young stranger to New York should not be walking about at 3 A.M.

Naturally, I spent a few more nights at the Vanguard that week and joined Bill for a couple of restaurant visits—not that he ate more than a bread roll. His liver was so badly damaged from hepatitis that the doctors questioned whether he might last another year.

From the trio's point of view, that booking with the Clancy Brothers was a mistake. Max Gordon warned them that Tommy Makem and the popular Irish folksinging group would attract a nonjazz, hard-drinking, boisterous crowd. He said, "If you want the work, you can have it, but it's going to be a little rough." They did need it, and took it, but Evans referred ever after to the "roar" that set in during his own sets.

Around this time, the trio was recorded at Studio 8H in Rockefeller Center by WCBS-TV for the Sunday morning series *Camera Three*. The program revealed a quietly singing and increasingly healthy Evans and provided the first surviving tapings of two new originals: "Time Remembered" and "Re: Person I Knew." On television the trio projected a formal and civilized image for the art of jazz.

The writer Gene Lees received a credit for his contribution as consultant, but Helen Keane of CBS, who actually got Evans and the trio the booking, did not. She was already one of the most highly respected artists' managers in New York. Gene and Helen had just met, and she recalled, "He had just left his editorship at *Down Beat* magazine. After he came to New York we fell in love and were together for years. I knew Bill Evans's work, because I never stopped loving jazz and listening to jazz. I just was not professionally involved with it."[7] As it turned out, both of them were soon to be very close to Evans, both personally and professionally—in the case of Helen Keane, until the end of the pianist's life.

ⅽⅇ ⅽⅇ ⅽⅇ

After several months working with Chuck Israels in his group, Evans felt ready to record a new trio album. Three days after finishing *Undercurrent* for

Evans with his longtime manager, producer, and friend, Helen Keane, Tokyo, 1976.
Courtesy of Fantasy, Inc.

United Artists, he was back in the studio with Riverside. Orrin Keepnews tells how he planned the three sessions: "I had a special challenge for them: for some time I had wanted Bill to do a totally laid-back, all-ballads album, but feared that a steady dose of slower tempos might perhaps over-relax the group to the point of lethargy. My solution was to make a second, somewhat livelier record at the same time, literally alternating the two repertoires to provide enough variation to keep everyone alert."[8] The ballads eventually formed the album *Moonbeams*, and the more up-tempo numbers went to make *How My Heart Sings*.

Now that Israels was thoroughly integrated into the trio, some aspects of his playing may be examined in order to pinpoint the essential character of the new group. A classical lyricism was immediately recognizable, within which each note was carefully chosen and valued. His lines tended to move stepwise, or in close position, rather than in leaps. A sense of rhythmic adventure complemented that of Evans, and he was prepared to play freely around the implied beat, resulting—as the pianist said—in sympathetic interplay. He was more than willing to indulge in tenor-register duologues, and his solos were melodious, often branching out from an initial arresting motif.

Many of these qualities were displayed on the first recording of "How My Heart Sings," an Earl Zindars waltz with a 4/4 interlude. The idea of alternating time signatures within the span of a song and improvising on that set structure, chorus by chorus, was new to jazz; as a consistent procedure it was initiated here by Zindars. This was a prototypical performance for the group, which could now be regarded as the Second Trio. It was Israels's presence that resulted in a rendering so poised, sensitive, and well-mannered—though the same terms might also describe the writing of Earl Zindars. The interpretation was contained, not allowed to freewheel, as though presented to the listener in a carefully wrapped parcel. The composer wrote the tune for his fiancée, Anne, just before they got married, and she supplied the title that so happily encapsulated the musical being of Bill Evans.

Also captured on this first date was a refreshingly upbeat and swinging "Summertime" (the tune advocated by Israels), for which the bass player had devised a double-stopped riff, neatly taking care of Gershwin's ostinato harmonic interest. Evans joined the pattern in his own adroit way, and Motian was engagingly bustling on brushes, the cross-rhythms between bass and piano working well. The ending simulated the aural and structural equivalent of the pop fade, a recording trick that Riverside never exploited with Evans. Israels remembers improving the "evaporating" effect by putting the ostinato into a kind of 5/8 time.

The tone of *Moonbeams* was set by the Tadd Dameron classic "If You Could See Me Now," which Evans had played recently under the composer's direction on *The Magic Touch*. On the earlier recording he had little to do in a big-band context, but here he expanded the number into a macrocosm of pianistic and chamber-music subtleties. The tracks varied subtly in intensity from the gossamer "In Love in Vain"—with Paul Motian at his most fragile and sensitive—to the brief but concentrated "I Fall in Love Too Easily," with its matchless patch of block chording, all ten fingers in harness.

Moonbeams contained some of the group's most introspective playing, including half a dozen standards epitomizing the Bill Evans ballad conception, each one the equivalent of a classical masterpiece. Perhaps "Polka Dots and Moonbeams" most invited the label "cocktail music," for there was a feeling in some quarters that Evans was losing touch with the essential spirit of jazz. Writing in *Down Beat* the following year, John S. Wilson referred to "the pall of sound that Evans can spread with his own trio." His review of *Moonbeams* represented one widely held opinion of the pianist's sound-world: "Evans' brooding, mulling approach to his piano solos marks him as one of the rare romanticists in latter-day jazz. Playing with his trio, he seems able to shut himself off from the world around him and to move into a twilit haven where he can drift along in what seems to be a semi-comatose state as he fingers his way through long, contemplative passages."9

What music, though, qualifies as jazz? Evans's view was clear, and he spoke eloquently on the matter while chatting to his brother Harry on *The Universal Mind of Bill Evans*. Lucid as ever, he referred to the lost art of improvisation in classical music, calling *that* jazz, and its proponents jazzmen, because of their ability to play music "of the moment." In this respect, Evans had clearly not lost touch with the spirit of jazz.

In 1965, on his first visit to England, he defined the term to Les Tomkins: "Jazz is a 'how' to me. It's performing without any really set basis for the lines and the content as such emotionally or, specifically, musically. And if you sit down and contemplate what you're going to do, and take five hours to write five minutes of music, then it's composed music. Therefore I would put it in the classical or serious, whatever you want to call it, written-music category. So there's composed music and there's jazz. And to me anybody that makes music using the process that we are used to using in jazz, is playing jazz."10

Many qualities distinguish these performances from cocktail music. One could cite intensity, a sense of form, unsentimental harmony, and the molding of the performance into a "presence"; there is the depth of feeling, the fact that a thinking mind is at work, plus the chamber-music interplay within the group. Then there is the precision and tautness of rhythm in the fingers. Although the music could serve as background—so could a Mozart sonata—it is played as though it is *meant* to be listened to.

ɕ ɕ ɕ

By this time in his early thirties, Evans had so far produced just a handful of tunes that would endure in his programs to come: "Five," "Waltz for Debby," "Peri's Scope," and the gentle waltz "Very Early," written in college and recorded for the first time on *Moonbeams*. But after the demise of the First Trio and the consequent performing void, the pianist's imagination was stimulated into a phase of more intensive composition than ever before. The originals started to come in rapid succession, and they began to feature more and more in his sets.

One of the Riverside sessions was devoted entirely to five recent compositions, the trio not only coping well but professionally relishing the challenge of this unfamiliar material. They had done "Re: Person I Knew" before, at least, and it received a more thorough exploration than on the recent *Camera Three* program, the range of tonal nuances on the statement alone worthy of the finest classical artist. The artifice and single point of the composition lay in its inward-turning chordal structure, varied harmonic tensions being set up as the sequence changed against a bass pedal. Evans said, "I'm using the insides of sounds to move around in a very subtle way which, I think, ends up being inevitable. I feel it's the only solution to that particular problem that I presented myself."[11] Using the song as a set opener in clubs, he would leave it hanging in the air, a gentle way of easing in the listener. The intriguing title was an anagram of the name of his Riverside producer and friend, Orrin Keepnews; Bill loved that kind of puzzle.

Evans's compositional prowess conceals his art; only an examination of the lead sheets reveals the subtleties involved in these pieces. As might be expected, they are utterly logical. Sections of material are juxtaposed at shifted levels, but so organized that the return home feels completely natural. Chords change frequently except in middle sections, which tend to rest on pedal notes by way of "structural" relief. Evans took this central, pivotal idea straight from the compositions of Earl Zindars, specifically "Elsa" and "How My Heart Sings." For "34 Skidoo" he also adopted Zindars's idea of changing the time signature from three-time to four-time on the bridge. The title has its origins in teenage "bobby-soxer" nonsense.

Evans always carried a small, six-stave composer's notebook in his jacket pocket for writing out tunes, making notes, writing set lists, and general doodling. A new tune was as likely to well up inside his imagination and be set down on the New York subway as it was at a piano. "Show-Type Tune" was a case in point: "Songs usually required a lot of work later at the piano," he said, "but this one came out nearly complete. I still have a lot in those books that I should go back to. I read somewhere that Gershwin had to write twelve bad tunes to get a good one. That gives me confidence."[12]

During this time of concentrated composition, Evans scribbled constantly in these manuscript books. His tunes were firmly rooted in the tradition of popular American song, but with a new kind of constructive sophistication and modulatory flair. His knowledge of the musical literature—all types, from a variety of cultures—was considerable, and he drew from this inheritance, applying himself as carefully and assiduously to his composition as he did to his playing. Sometimes the melody would come first ("Waltz for

Earl Zindars, whose compositions held a special place in
Evans's repertoire.
Courtesy of Earl Zindars

Debby"), sometimes the harmony ("Time Remembered"). Whatever the
individual voicings employed in his performances, only standard chord symbols were used in the guides.

At home he kept his famous "cardboard box," containing all the tunes
that people sent him for consideration. Earl Zindars once inquired about a
couple of his tunes, asking Evans whether he had by chance mislaid them.
"No, I've got 'em," he replied. "They're in my cardboard box at home."

Dipping into *Moonbeams* and *How My Heart Sings* we witness a certain Evans-trio concept and sound of the moment. Judging from the joyful
spring of "Show-Type Tune" and the dug-in "I Should Care," it may be safely
said that the Bill Evans Trio was back on the playing scene.

CHAPTER **12** Conversations with Myself

Oh no... not this one. This is the one that could break my heart.
—Helen Keane, just before taking on the management of Bill Evans

Evans now embarked on a long period of concentrated recording. As Orrin Keepnews, chronicler of the Riverside years, says: "Between April and August 1962, the traditionally reluctant Evans entered three different studios on a total of eight occasions and recorded the equivalent of four and a half albums. One key factor in this spurt was undoubtedly his narcotics dependency and consequent financial needs."[1] Were it not for the pianist's extremity, it is doubtful whether some of these albums would ever have been conceived, let alone achieved. Riverside's trust in its artist was unwavering, a faith in the knowledge that he would both deliver the goods and repay the advances: he came through on both counts. Gene Lees, who was like a brother to him at this time, has graphically detailed his situation: "In that summer of 1962 I found Bill's life and career in hideous disarray."[2]

While enduring such a private hell, Evans continued to play, occasionally even approaching his best form. He had already surprised his producer by going into the studio for the recent trio recordings. Now his ideas were for projects in other forms, beginning with a quintet album to be called *Interplay*. Riverside welcomed the chance to feature him as leader of a larger group with a star cast, and it was good for Evans too.

The pianist's first choice for trumpet, Art Farmer, was unavailable, but Freddie Hubbard did lovely things with popular songs from the 1930s that were largely unfamiliar to his generation. The idea of a guitar as a second frontline "horn" was an inspired notion from the leader—air and light were thus admitted into the ensemble—and, after *Undercurrent*, the choice naturally fell on Jim Hall. Percy Heath and Philly Joe Jones completed the lineup.

131

With guitarist Jim Hall, left, and drummer Philly Joe Jones on one of the 1962
quintet sessions for Riverside.
Steve Schapiro, courtesy of Fantasy, Inc.

The title tune, named by Orrin Keepnews and subtitled "Blues—F
minor," was an Evans original, a gently bucking line over a stealthy, stepwise
background in tenths. Each player responded to and worked off the others in
a classically integrated performance.

Evans gave careful thought to the group presentation of the themes.
The moodily reflective "When You Wish upon a Star" was an intriguing
example, the trumpet in delicately balanced counterpoint to the guitar
melody. This ballad treatment was cast in the key of E, rare in jazz. Evans
always liked to try new keys, convinced, as are many musicians, that individual characters and colors are integrally associated with each. Besides, it can
only be refreshing to get away from the flat-key area of most jams.

In these settings Evans displayed fresh facets of his talent. He fulfilled his
bandleader's role with skill, organized a well-balanced sprinkling of links and
codas, and matched the soloing with a "horn-voice" of his own. His solos were
linear, alive, and inventive, with a minimum of chording, and in a predominantly simple harmonic language—texturally quite different from his trio work.

댜 댜 댜

Earlier, the Bill Evans Trio had played the Hickory House for the whole
of May. On the bandstand Chuck Israels was very conscious of his position in

the wake of Scott LaFaro. He had no intention of emulating the former bass player's style, but it was inevitable that the public saw him with LaFaro in mind. During this trying time for him, the new group had only slowly come together in the club.

At the end of the run, and coinciding with a month off club work, Israels had his bass overhauled. For the trio's reopening at the Vanguard in July 1962 he had resettled mentally, technically, and musically. The group took on a new spirit. Evans remembered the impact of the new Israels: "Opening night at the Vanguard ... well, it's difficult to describe the amount of difference that we all immediately felt as a result of his ability to play within the group with such a natural flow. Now I have no apprehension about the ability of the group to develop in its own direction and no hesitation about performing for anyone anywhere."[3]

Toward the end of that run the world turned for a young pianist and Bill Evans enthusiast from Wisconsin named Warren Bernhardt. He had just returned to New York after playing with the Paul Winter Sextet in South America, an extended trip on which Gene Lees had been tour manager. Lees had written English lyrics to a number of Antonio Carlos Jobim's songs, including "Corcovado"—or, in Lees's version, "Quiet Nights of Quiet Stars." In New York that fall, Lees sang on the demo of that song, with Jobim on guitar and Evans on piano.

In South America, Lees and Bernhardt had listened a lot to Bill's recordings. Once back in New York, the lyricist, already a close friend and professional colleague of Evans's, introduced the younger pianist to the master over breakfast at the Olympia, a luncheonette at 107th and Broadway. A lasting friendship developed. Bernhardt has vivid and fond memories of meeting Evans that day:

> I loved him and his gentle nature immediately. I was also impressed with how big he was. His photos had not always shown that he was a man of fairly large stature. After we ate we then went over to Bill's place, which was rather dirty and messy. It was there that I first met [Evans's new girlfriend] Ellaine and their skinny little pussycat named Harmony. I remember that the kitchen was piled to the ceiling with old newspapers and a narrow path had been left open to the sink and refrigerator. Quite a bizarre scene, but Bill had a beautiful, medium-sized Knabe grand in the living room, which I was afraid to touch with him there. Bill did not play that day, but he did invite me down to the Vanguard that very evening, where he was performing with Paul Motian and Chuck Israels.
>
> I went to the Vanguard only to find that it was apparently sold out, with no room for me. Just as I was leaving, Max Gordon, the owner, came up to me and asked if I was Warren Bernhardt, and [said] that Bill had reserved a seat for me. And what a seat it was! It was magical. Right at Bill's right hand, no more than three feet from

him was the first empty seat on the bandstand end of a long bench which ran along the angled wall in that great basement. A spotlight seemed to shine down on that empty seat, and at that moment my life changed forever. To me, being there at his side, in that presence, was the most beautiful moment in my life, the sound the greatest thing I had ever heard (except perhaps that of certain recordings of Rachmaninoff playing his own compositions, which had moved me deeply as a small child).

We spent the breaks together, smoking cigarettes and talking about music. I was in heaven. Bill wrote out some changes on a couple of Village Vanguard folding table cards during his break. What a generous and loving thing for a busy man to do for a young fan, a kid he had only met that day! He even meticulously drew out the ledger lines on the blank cards.

On that night of August 11, 1962, one of the tunes Evans wrote out between sets was "Waltz for Debby." Whenever he wrote down this melody, he spelt *Waltze* with an *e*. Warren Bernhardt's copy shows a charming variant of the melody at the end of the bridge. Another (two-handed) version, written later for Helen Keane's ten-year-old son Christopher, contained some rich inner parts specially designed for small hands. Bernhardt goes on: "I soon became friends with Chuck Israels, and we began to hang out at his place, where he showed me Bill's bass book, which I copied immediately so that I could begin to study Bill's music from the source. The tunes were entered into this volume quite simply. Everything was very straightforward and was written in an exceptionally clear system of notation. There was never any doubt or confusion as to what was intended, harmonically or rhythmically. Some passing tones were notated, but no melodies were written down—after all, this was for the bassist in the trio."

After step-by-step progress up the ladder of fame, at a pace befitting an artist of such diligent application, Evans was finally voted into top place in the piano category by the *Down Beat* critics and into second place (behind Oscar Peterson) by the magazine's readers. Creed Taylor, now at Verve Records, was openly trying to recruit Evans; he wanted the pianist to record with Shelly Manne. Taylor remembered the phenomenal success that Manne, André Previn, and Leroy Vinnegar had made out of *My Fair Lady* in 1956. Their disc of that show was the first jazz album to sell a million, taking the message to thousands who had never previously been attracted to jazz; word had spread, and it had become fashionable to own the album.

Seven years later a show was coming to Broadway that already had more than a million dollars worth of presales. It was called *Mr. President*, the music was by Irving Berlin, and many top names were involved in the production. Even though the show had not yet opened, Verve sent the complete score on a Sunday morning to Evans, who was to go into the studio with it on Monday

During a break at the Vanguard, Bill wrote out one of his tunes on a club menu specially for the young pianist Warren Bernhardt, whom he had only met that day.
Courtesy of Warren Bernhardt

night. Ruefully he commented: "So I spent I guess almost damn near twenty-four hours straight, working over this music, to restructure it—how we could approach it, rewriting the harmonies, etc. I really worked hard on it. Well, before going into the studio, Creed called me..."[4]

The news was bad: the show was going to bomb, and there was no sense in going ahead with this material. Evans's retrospective view—that it is in any case a mistake to try and emulate such history-making records as *My Fair Lady*—was all too accurate; Manne's group had in fact tried several successors themselves, all of which had flopped in varying degrees.

Shelly Manne and his Men, another lineup altogether, were in town for a Village Vanguard run, sharing the billing with Evans, so the producer set up a recording date for Manne, Evans, and the Manne group's bass player, Monty Budwig. They went ahead with a revised program. On this Verve album, *Empathy*, recorded in August 1962, Evans, playing by courtesy of Riverside, had equal billing with Shelly Manne.

A couple of numbers from the flopped *Mr. President* survived onto the disc: "The Washington Twist," a jaunty blues in C, and "Let's Go Back to the Waltz," a lovely tune in the classic Berlin mold. The longest excursion took place on Rodgers and Hart's "With a Song in My Heart," whose cheeky, lightweight chording recalled some of the delicacy of *Explorations*. All part of the fun was a self-contained "Loony Tunes" freak-out from piano and drums, a music-hall routine incorporating a mock-serious tone-row interpretation in wide-spanned octaves.

On this one-off album, the sound of these players refocuses our attention upon the unique flavor of Evans's own trio, its homogeneity in particular. There, the musical intention was integrated by a consistency of approach, developed and sustained over a period of time. On *Empathy*, in contrast, Evans was having a night out and enjoying the change. Shelly Manne, too, had a ball, interacting constantly and prompting Evans into more clipped exchanges than usual, while Monty Budwig lent clean, rich-toned support.

⊂⊱ ⊂⊱ ⊂⊱

At Verve, Evans was recorded by Rudy Van Gelder, widely regarded as one of the best recording engineers on the jazz scene. The results cannot go without comment. Van Gelder's piano sound was curiously dry and boxy, seeming to extract all life, warmth, and bloom, leaving only an anonymous residue. As far as touch was concerned, all pianists were made to sound like clones under this treatment. This distinctive sound, as imposed upon Evans, had first been in evidence on those Savoy and Prestige albums in 1957 and reappeared on several Verve recordings to come. The treatment was scandalous, as no jazz pianist graded his sound more finely and cared more passionately about tone quality than Evans. He had it within his imagination and expressive technique to make a honky-tonk sing, but he was powerless over his engineer.

How could he tolerate such a travesty of his unique sound? My guess is that he felt it was not his business, trusting the sound department to do its job as he would do his. One of the many things that Creed Taylor disliked about the Verve product he took over from Norman Granz was the sound mixing, including that dead piano sound; he was never able to change it on all those records made at Englewood Cliffs.

After the *Interplay* sessions in July, Evans approached Orrin Keepnews with another quintet proposal, this time having under his arm a whole sheaf of his own compositions—enough for an entire album. It was obvious that he was pushing hard for all the cash he could get. (Loan sharks threatened to break his fingers.) Keepnews suspected that Evans's music publisher would pay him only if his pieces were scheduled for recording. Feeling a bit misused, he decided to go ahead anyway, saying later, "I justified my actions this time on both humanitarian and practical grounds: I found it impossible to turn down urgent financial requests from a man who was both a major creative artist and my friend."[5]

Evans felt that his new material best suited the tenor saxophone, and Zoot Sims was booked. Jim Hall and Philly Joe Jones were retained from the *Interplay* lineup, and Percy Heath, who was away with the Modern Jazz Quartet, was replaced by Ron Carter. So the day after *Empathy*, Evans was back with Riverside at Tommy Nola's Penthouse Studio. The tracks were eventually issued on the double LP *The "Interplay" Sessions*, the CD version of which became *Loose Bloose*. The long hours were fraught with difficulty, tempers were frayed, and the engineer was having problems. Extra rehearsal or studio time was not available in those Riverside days, and this ambitious music turned out to be a far cry from the standards of the earlier *Interplay* program.

The title tune, "Loose Bloose," was a kind of "Interplay" Mark II, the melody more fragmented yet wider flung; it is less a tune than a collection of jagged motifs, ever expanding in range. For soloing purposes, Evans took in four or five sets of new blues changes, written out for the musicians to choose. Zoot Sims was not interested, Jim Hall had a go, but Ron Carter—at twenty-five, easily the youngest of the group—was keenest to accept the challenge.

On "Fudgesickle Built for Four," named for a popular ice cream–on–a–stick treat, the voices entered fugally in the baroque manner. Two more tunes were wrapped on this first day. The mellow lyricism of "Time Remembered" evoked a warm response from Sims, and of the seven originals it became the only one to survive as part of Evans's regular repertoire. The catchy, Latin-flavored "Funkallero" bore more than a passing resemblance to Bud Powell's "Un Poco Loco." The pianist had first come up with it during his early New York days. "I was getting into kind of a swing thing," he said, "and this line just naturally came out of that feeling. It's a natural vehicle for blowing."[6]

Bill's partner, Ellaine, while the couple stayed with Brian Hennessey in England, 1972. Bill and Ellaine loved animals, especially cats, and later had two Siamese of their own in New York.

Courtesy of Brian Hennessey

The second day began with "My Bells," the essential harmonic ingredient of which was the interval of the fourth; most of the chords were built up with a pile of fourths (with the occasional third) from the bass, as in Evans's voicing of the responses in "So What" on *Kind of Blue*. Much of the harmony of "My Bells" (in the key of B major) progressed in parallel diatonic motion, as may be heard in the works of Ravel and Debussy. Problems in recording arose due to the complexities of the time divisions and uneven section lengths; these were ultimately self-defeating because the musicians were too busy counting to make music. The piece worked better in later renderings when it was "ironed out" into a single pulse. At the pianist's request, Gene Lees wrote a lyric for the melody in this format—one of his three lyrics to Bill Evans tunes. (The others were "Waltz for Debby" and "Turn Out the Stars.") Lees and Evans made a demo of "My Bells" for Howard Richmond of TRO, the publishing company with whom they both had writing contracts.

The appealing "There Came You" and the convoluted "Fun Ride" remained to be done. Both had quick-changing chords ranging through keys far and wide, and both were stillborn in the pianist's repertoire. That was a pity in the case of "There Came You," which makes a satisfying ballad vehicle; Evans was proud that it contained a lot of Duke Ellington. As Warren Bernhardt says, the title referred to Ellaine: "This song is actually about that first moment he laid eyes on her; they fell immediately in love." She wrote a lyric (originally "Then Came You"), and at some point Evans sent it with a batch of songs to Tony Bennett.

The quick "Fun Ride"—which Evans declared that even he could hardly play—was as intricate as any bebop tune and had a chord sequence to match. Listening to Evans's three solo choruses one can imagine the concentration on Jim Hall's brow as he quietly kept track of the changes. "Bill really dug the piece," said Bernhardt, "especially the way that a pianist makes use of the two thumbs as a 'third hand' when executing the opening passages." Bill admired the way Warren played it and urged him to record it, as well as "My Bells" and "There Came You."

In due course, Evans turned his attention to the unedited tapes. At the time, he was staying with Bernhardt, who recalls:

> One day, he suggested that I accompany him to Riverside, as he had to listen to some recent tapes and decide what to do with them. The sessions turned out to be the ones with Zoot Sims. Bill and I and Ray Fowler, the Riverside engineer, spent several hours listening to them together, and I remember that what we heard was not to Bill's liking. He got more and more depressed as we went further into the takes. Finally, as we were leaving the building, he said something like, "God, I hope they never release those tapes after I die!" He was especially unhappy that things had not gone smoother on "My Bells" and "There Came You." I know how much he loved those songs.

Nevertheless, he did sanction an edited version of "Loose Bloose" that day, and it was included on the double album *Peace Piece and Other Pieces* in 1975. The remaining tapes eventually found their way to the Fantasy jazz record complex in Berkeley, California; they were released on *The "Interplay" Sessions* in 1982. Sometimes, having vetoed the release of material at the time of its execution, Evans later saw it in a clearer light and eased his view. Orrin Keepnews, who knew this better than anybody, is especially to be applauded for making available rare recordings of four of Bill's originals: "Loose Bloose," "There Came You," "Fudgesickle Built for Four," and "Fun Ride." Evans may have been looking for money, but he cut no corners in writing and preparing the material for this (almost lost) disc.

During the autumn of 1962 Evans continued to play gigs in New York. The bassist Hal Gaylor stood in for a long trio run at the Hickory House. Another engagement was at the Village Vanguard (fast becoming a regular club fixture), with Chuck Israels back in the group. Gene Lees observed: "During ten weeks at the Hickory House, the thing just wasn't happening for the trio. But suddenly, during the Village Vanguard engagement, it began. The change is startling, reflected even in Evans' appearance and morale. A certain wistful lethargy that had crept into his playing is gone. His ballads are as extraordinarily evocative and lovely as they were in LaFaro's time, and his up-tempo things seem—to me, at least—even stronger than before."[7]

Lees went on to extol the playing of Chuck Israels, who in Spoleto, Italy, had acquired an old, battered, but superb, Italian bass. It was a period of flux for the trio, with Israels away on various jobs, but Evans was in such good form during this Vanguard run that Lees took Helen Keane to hear him, urging her to become the pianist's manager.

⊂⊧ ⊂⊧ ⊂⊧

The story of Helen Keane's achievements is one of the most remarkable in show business. Starting in the fifties as a seventeen-year-old secretary for the booking agency Music Corporation of America, she gradually made her way to the top of her profession, becoming by turns the first female agent, manager, and producer. An early flirtation with acting contributed to her empathy for the life of the performer, as well as her understanding of the elations and disappointments that result from the artistic temperament.

This ability to work in emotional harness with a few chosen artists, combined with shrewd handling of the practicalities, accounted for her rise. While still an agent, she set Harry Belafonte on course, by putting him into the Blue Angel and the Village Vanguard, singing the folk songs he wanted to sing. She joined CBS Television as director of variety casting before running her own self-built management company from her Manhattan apartment. The moment she heard Evans at the Vanguard, she knew she had to look after him. "Bill and I met and liked each other immediately," she said. Fortunately, her business was in reasonable shape: "I was able to give the dedication and commitment to Bill and build him without starving to death."[8]

Gene Lees was instrumental, in a practical sense, in allowing her to take over. By dint of a union mistake, Evans was currently under simultaneous contracts with two managers (Bert Block and the unsympathetic Joe Glaser), but Lees succeeded in getting both pacts invalidated. Thus Helen Keane became Bill Evans's new personal manager, a position that she faithfully retained to the end, eighteen years later. With his recording contract at Riverside about to be terminated and the new one with Verve beginning, she was able to negotiate terms and collaborate on projects with Creed Taylor. The pianist's morale received a huge boost.

The move to Verve happened around the beginning of 1963, although a couple of final Riverside projects were still in the pipeline, as specified in that company's departure contract. For the first of these, Orrin Keepnews opted for a solo session, knowing that it would be his last in the studio with Evans. "The split with Bill had been totally mutual," he mused. "He and his manager were still my friends; it was all so damn *reasonable* that I found it quite distressing that this was to be my last view from the control room of Bill Evans at work."9

The result was *The Solo Session (Volumes 1 and 2)*, recorded in January 1963. It could be regarded as another shot at the abandoned solo attempt of the previous year, but whereas the earlier session held an air of abstraction, with periodic lapses in focus, now there was a concentration of purpose. Evans challenged himself in every bar, always experimental, never obvious.

We are invited into the artist's workshop, to survey the tools of his trade, piles of sketches, scattered maquettes. Everything has a raw, unfinished aspect; and there is much craziness besides. An Aladdin's cave unfolds before us. We witness, for instance, the intellectual and digital coordination required to improvise exclusively in tenths, a self-imposed discipline still more impressive than that required for octaves. There was no let up in the creative strife, the pushing of the imagination to the edge. Ideas splintered from his imagination and on several tracks he was at the height of his intellectual powers.

The producer saw the choice of repertoire—particularly the song titles themselves—as pointedly gloomy. Certainly, Evans was guilt-ridden, sick at heart, and furious with himself for getting ensnared in the consequences of heroin. Consciously or not, he set out with "Why Was I Born?" (unfinished and unissued), followed immediately by "What Kind of Fool Am I?" and, later, "Everything Happens to Me."

Both pianist and producer were unhappy with the evening's work, as were Gene Lees and Helen Keane, and the material, quite unlike anything else Evans did, was set aside and forgotten. When Orrin Keepnews came to reconsider it during a major review of unreleased Riverside tapes in 1984, however, he had no hesitation in putting it out posthumously as part of *The Complete Riverside Recordings*.

Meanwhile, over at Verve Records, a young vibraphone player from Los Angeles, trying his luck in New York as a professional arranger, had just been taken on as a regular chart contributor. Gary McFarland had met Evans when a student at Lenox in 1959. While planning an album of his own compositions, he ran into the pianist again and plucked up the courage to invite him onto it.

From the moment that Evans agreed to be special guest soloist, the program of *The Gary McFarland Orchestra* was built around his special magic. The orchestra was a lightweight ensemble ideally suited to the attractive material. Affectionately, McFarland emulated that Evans trademark, the quarter-note triplet, on unison pizzicato strings. The pianist had always tended to work well with vibraphonists, as his records with Eddie Costa, Dave Pike, and now McFarland showed. Here his touch was delicate, sparkling, and mostly decorative in character. On the joyously swinging "Misplaced Cowpoke" he left space for the supremely satisfying rhythm unit of Richard Davis and Ed Shaughnessy, the resilience and resonance of Davis (with his attractive high register twang) combining thrillingly with the big-band drive of Shaughnessy. This was the earthiest track, Jim Hall bluesy on electric guitar, Evans matching him with some fine licks of his own.

⫷ ⫷ ⫷

For his next album, the first for Verve exclusively under his own name, Evans planned to switch direction again, by overdubbing himself playing solo piano. This recording technique had been around for some time, even in the classical world—Jascha Heifetz, for example, playing both solo parts in his 1946 recording of Bach's Double Violin Concerto. On the popular scene the practice became widespread, but jazz musicians generally viewed it with suspicion. Then Lennie Tristano, controversial as always, made his first attempt on *Ju-Ju* in 1951, and in the summer of 1955 he made an album for Atlantic called *Lines*, on which he used multitracking and speeded-up tape. "Turkish Mambo" from this album, with its extension into triple-tracking, was technically, though not musically, the precursor of Evans's new recording, *Conversations with Myself*.

Like Tristano, Evans had no qualms about multitracking, and he threw light on his forthcoming album in the sleeve note that he was encouraged to write by Gene Lees and Helen Keane:

> Until the evolution of jazz group improvisation the history of Western music, or music as we know it outside of jazz, represents the reflection of one psyche. For the first time in a music of Western origin, jazz group improvisation represents the very provocative revelation of two, three, four, or five minds responding simultaneously to each other in a unified coherent performance.
>
> I remember that in recording the selections, as I listened to the first track while playing the second, and the first two while playing the third, the process

involved was an artificial duplication of simultaneous performance in that each track represented a musical mind responding to another musical mind or minds. The argument that the same mind was involved in all three performances could be advanced, but I feel that this is not quite true. The functions of each track are different, and as one in speech feels a different state of mind making statements than in responding to statements or commenting in the exchange involved in the first two; so I feel that the music here has more the quality of a "trio" than a solo effort.

Another condition to be considered is the fact that I know my musical techniques more thoroughly than any other person, so that, it seems to me, I am equipped to respond to my previous musical statements with the most accuracy and clarity.[10]

One can only imagine the technical problems facing the team on this project, but by the end of the first day, February 6, 1963, Evans had managed to complete one number, an original composition called "N.Y.C.'s No Lark." The intriguing title turned out to be another of his anagrams, this time in tribute to his good friend and influence, the pianist Sonny Clark, who had died on January 13. The tempo was slow, the progress inexorable, and the mood brooding, the massive climax carrying its heartfelt personal message.

A pattern of procedure was set, and on the second day several tracks were accomplished in triplicate. On the previous month's solo date, "How About You?" had entered a scintillating groove, a feeling that was maintained on the new "trio" version. The track was reissued in a later Verve compilation called *The Best of Bill Evans,* for which Helen Keane insisted on a remix. Closer to Evans's original conception, the new sound balance differentiated more between track levels, giving a clearer, less blended texture.

Evans used the overdubbing concept as a creative force, the three "voices" operating at different dynamic levels, initiated by his touch, and closely controlled by Creed Taylor's chosen engineer, Ray Hall. Often, a harmonic track functioned like a watercolorist's background plane, a subdued level upon which lead voices could "perform" in highlighted tone. These might be improvised melodic lines, or fragmentary comments etched in crystal octaves. Sometimes a walking bass took over a chorus or two. The roles were also exchanged, the harmonic layer, perhaps, turning up in a different voice later on. In this regard, Evans achieved a feat of memory that took in the overall view. He even managed to breathe in unison with himself, as in the uncanny, threefold-synchronized phrasing of "A Sleepin' Bee."

In the triplicate setup Evans saw a unique opportunity to indulge his admiration for Thelonious Monk, including three of his tunes. The construction of "Blue Monk," for instance, lent itself well to the kind of imitative treatment that was to hand. The composer's spirit also pervaded Evans's rendering of "Bemsha Swing," written jointly by Monk and Denzil Best, whom

Evans considered to be an ideal trio drummer. Evans chose not to issue this track originally, finding it a little rough, but Helen Keane liked it and it appeared for the first time on *The Best of Bill Evans*. Many years later, Evans conceded that it contained some interesting things. The other Monk composition here, "'Round About Midnight," came over with particular clarity, a rich tapestry seemingly reconstructed by the interweaving of its constituents. A great deal of this performance was off the beat, one passage being entirely so in all three parts: yet the rhythm could not be more precisely executed.

A number of tunes started with brief atmospheric introductions, colored by delicate, pointillistic rippling. This was Evans the orchestrater at work, thinking perhaps of the pianissimo flutes, clarinets, and harps of dawn in Ravel's "Daphnis and Chloe." A good example was the ruminatory love theme from Alex North's score to *Spartacus*, the 1960 Stanley Kubrick block-buster that Bill had seen with Scott LaFaro. At the emotional major-key release the idea was expanded into further realms of decoration by way of a reiterated, single-note pulsation. Evans made a half-dozen or so versions of the foundation track before he was satisfied, aware of how much the other tracks depended on it. After the animated, moderate four of the main body, there came the glory of the set, a restrained coda of compelling radiance.

Evans was using Glenn Gould's cherished Steinway, an instrument upon which much attention had been lavished by its makers, and the one that Gould used exclusively after 1960. In Evans's hands (as in Gould's) the instrument exuded quality, sounding rich and alive in spite of poor tuning. Its characteristics were enhanced by the warm acoustics of Webster Hall, the sound reflecting from the wooden surfaces and revolving chandelier of the old dance venue. Gould—himself a connoisseur of Evans's work—finished recording the Bach D major Partita on it soon after Bill's recording, but at the old CBS 30th Street Studio, a mile or so uptown.

This monumental venture was a feat of endurance from the ailing pianist. He began to suffer from heroin withdrawal during the sessions, but he insisted on completing the job. Helen Keane and Gene Lees, deferring to his resolve, turned the lights down low and lent their heartfelt encouragement.

Although some listeners resist what they consider to be overkill, preferring Evans to communicate directly with them rather than with himself, it remains a work of staggering resource and beauty, appreciated especially (but not only) by professional pianists. Early the following year, the album brought Evans his first Grammy Award, and Britain's *Melody Maker* voted it jazz record of the year for 1964.

CHAPTER **13** An American in Europe

It was outdoors, rainy and damp, the piano was rotten and for the first number, photographers were all over the stage, between my legs, under the piano, it was ridiculous.

— *Chuck Israels*

The extreme turmoil of Evans's life in the early 1960s was reflected in the diversity of his playing, as his financial needs led to his most concentrated period in the studios under his own name. Fortunately, he could present himself in a variety of formats, seemingly able to face most challenges with ease. In the past year alone he had coped with solo piano (including himself in triplicate), duo with guitar, two trio lineups, and two quintets, as well as small and big bands. He was even shortly to flirt with the glittering, if shallow, role of Hollywood-style star pianist.

As if all that were not enough, he played one-handed throughout a week's booking at the Vanguard, having numbed his right arm with a heroin needle. With his left hand and some virtuoso pedaling, he was able to maintain harmonic interest in support of treble lines. In morbid fascination, pianists dropped by to witness this phenomenon. Bassist Bill Crow, who regrets passing up a chance to play with the trio for a week in Pittsburgh at that time, refines the story: "He would dangle the dead hand over the keyboard and drop his forefinger on the keys, using the weight of the hand to depress them. Everything else was played with the left hand, and if you looked away you couldn't tell anything was wrong."[1] It is easy to imagine Evans (who was in any case left-handed) grappling keenly with this intellectual and physical problem.

Considering that Evans had just signed a new recording contract, 1963 was sparse in the studio—or perhaps it only seemed so after the previous year's industry. *Conversations with Myself* had been nothing if not enterprising, but ambition—Creed Taylor's, for he would make Evans a star—took on a new flavor entirely with the next MGM-Verve project, an album of popular tunes in smoothly romantic and openly commercial settings.

Most musicians will play anything for a price, but whether they would readily attach their names is another matter. Evans seriously considered using his Russian name for this album. In the event it was billed as *Bill Evans, His Piano and Orchestra, Play Theme from The V.I.P.s and Other Great Songs*. For Claus Ogerman, the uncredited arranger and conductor, it was a typical commission of the sixties, reflecting the general flavor and Latin beat of his settings for the guitarist and composer Antonio Carlos Jobim.

The ingredients of Ogerman's arranging style were simple, and he deployed them skillfully. A vibraphone might hover, lending a gentle background wash; succinct motives were given to the bass clarinet; and he had a winning way with a silky, unison violin line. Emerging from these settings, the Evans touch may be recognized by its voicing and weighting of tone, or by its classical, inner-part figuration. Pianist and arranger got together for an original F minor blues called "Hollywood" (reminiscent of "Interplay"), the only track allowed to run more than three minutes.

Of the rest, many were the previous or current year's film and TV themes, and all seem to have been designed as potential singles. (To fit the three-minute maximum, "On Green Dolphin Street" had its first eight-bar section cut out on the reprise.) Perhaps Creed Taylor was looking for follow-ups to Jimmy Smith's best-selling single "Walk on the Wild Side" (a tune also included here). It was all very easygoing, and the pianist was both philosophical and realistic: "As long as I know where I'm at, know that it's commercial, I'm okay. If I didn't know I'd be very worried! If this record could have done something for widening my audience, getting better distribution for my other records, I'm all for it. Because it's a cold, hard business. Now, even my jazz records, like, say *Conversations*, go fine in places where you will find no other jazz records—because of *this* record."[2]

⊂⊱ ⊂⊱ ⊂⊱

During the late 1940s, when Evans was a student in Louisiana, many young English jazz musicians worked the ocean liners to and from New York, drawn like moths to the beacon of bebop. One such musician was a tenor saxophonist named Ronnie Scott, who, bowled over by the proliferation of New York clubs, determined to start up one of his own in London. It took a while, but in 1959 Ronnie Scott's, destined to become one of the great jazz clubs of the world, began life humbly in a Soho basement. During the

first year, West Coast drummer Shelly Manne dropped in, and Scott maintained that Manne opened his own club in Hollywood soon after as a direct
response to the atmosphere at "Ronnie's."

That club was Shelly's Manne Hole, and Bill Evans spent all of May
1963 there, beginning in a duo with his old bass-playing friend Red Mitchell.
Chuck Israels was on tour with "The Midgets of Jazz"—Ben Riley's name for
the Paul Winter group—but was able to wind it up in Denver and replace
Mitchell for the last two weeks at the Manne Hole. Shelly Manne himself sat
in from time to time—after all, it was his club. Israels said:

> After a few nights I got to talking with many of the Hollywood musicians who were
> coming in to hear us and I paid particular attention to the pianist, Clare Fischer,
> who kept insisting that the dapper, elegantly bearded man, whom I had seen listen-
> ing intently to Bill's piano playing, was the most sensitive possible drummer for us to
> have and that I should persuade Bill to invite him to sit in. To say that that first expe-
> rience of playing with Larry Bunker was a revelation would only be half the story....
> I smiled and Bill grinned broadly and dug in to play all the more and Larry was
> hired on the spot to finish out the job with us. The following week, Wally Heider
> came in to record the group for Riverside.[3]

Thus was fulfilled the one remaining project on the Evans-Riverside
books. Both the pianist and his producer of almost seven years, Orrin Keepnews, wanted their final collaboration to be a live recording with the working
trio, a logical follow-up to the 1961 Village Vanguard dates with LaFaro and
Motian. But when the time came, Keepnews was disbanding his ailing company in New York and was unable to get out to Hollywood. The sessions,
issued as *Bill Evans Trio at Shelly's Manne Hole* and *Time Remembered*, were
supervised by Los Angeles–based Richard Bock.

We have Israels's word for it that the events of those two evenings are
accurately represented on the records. "You can hear Larry's hands through
the wires on the brushes," he said, "feel the exact weight of his foot on the
bass drum and identify the timbre of each cymbal and tom-tom. The sound
of the bass, too, is faithfully preserved. That was just before jazz bassists
almost universally switched over to the metal strings most symphony players
had used for years."[4]

The empathy between Israels and Evans was evident in these fine performances. Together with Larry Bunker they reveled in creative interplay
and were obviously at home in the congenial surroundings of this intimate
club, to date the pianist's second-favorite to the Village Vanguard. Israels was
more relaxed than on the studio sessions of a year ago, swinging notably on
his own "Blues in F," and Bunker was clearly relishing a break from his habit-

ual studio round, contributing a continuous web of sympathy and propulsion. There was the feeling that the trio was among friends, unpressurized to strive against any odds—for the odds were, indeed, stacked in their favor. Evans had at his disposal a baby grand, which, though thin and wiry on top, was capable in his hands of a pellucid middle-range tone.

Evans had brought new material, and his colleagues were thrown in at the deep end and left to surface as best they might, always to be the pianist's way of working. Another surprise was his harmonic rethinking of "Lover Man," the middle eight of which was reconstructed outright. The pianist's motivation was sound, the usual chords being vapid at ballad tempo. He felt a need for a more densely changing (and deeper) key exploration by way of central contrast. His solution satisfied in a formal sense, as well as providing a firmer, yet more variegated foundation for fantasy.

"Time Remembered," the only Evans original issued from these evenings, received its first trio exposition on disc. The piece's harmonic structure is notable for studiously avoiding the dominant seventh. As a result, a modal feeling permeates the timeless progression of its predominantly minor sevenths. In this performance the floating chords at the end of the piano solo spilled gently and seamlessly over the beginning of the bass solo, the overlapping another feature of the chamber approach, the desire to get away from a "blowing list." That three-way discourse, highly developed in the First Trio, was now operating more naturally, less self-consciously, the result arguably a more convincing vindication of the Evans "creed of interplay."

The traditional night off was Monday, but Shelly asked Bill to take Tuesdays off instead so that the local musicians could hear him. Israels told me: "I saw most every California musician that I had heard of in the club during that engagement, some of them (like Terry Trotter and Bill Goodwin) almost every night." Goodwin himself recalled Evans's condition: "He wasn't in very good shape, physically. That was when I first met him, and he was beautiful—a wonderful guy. It was really incongruous that he could be so messed up and yet be such a normal, regular person."[5]

Like Dave Jones before him, the engineer Wally Heider captured the trio, and the ambience of the club, to perfection. (Ironically, the club was eventually forced to move, as the sound of the heavier electric bands began spilling through into the echo chamber of Heider's own recording studio next door.) These recordings formed a fitting farewell for Evans and Orrin Keepnews at Riverside, one of the great recording partnerships in jazz. Though they bid adieu professionally, Orrin continued to follow Bill's career avidly, and they remained friends until the end. Evans later reflected on the value of small record companies at the start of an artist's career: "You need those companies; actually jazz needs those companies because, until you establish yourself, [they] offer an entrance way....To sign a standard union contract for scale, with Riverside, for two records, was to me the biggest thrill that could happen at that time....I never got a royalty statement, not even as by law every three months—never saw one, never expected one—didn't care really, because at that point you want to get your records out there. So it works for both."[6]

Late in 1963, Bill Grauer, in charge of business at Riverside, died of a heart attack. Evans had had little to do with him but had always found him rather a rough character. The pianist's sense of black humor prompted him to observe: "I figure he must have died in self-defense."[7] The company had been sliding steadily toward bankruptcy, and finally folded in mid-1964.

⊂Ε ⊂Ε ⊂Ε

Evans kept a meticulous tally of his debts, and with the help of a very large advance from Verve—probably for *The V.I.P.s*—he paid off as many as he could. He was still in trouble, though. Mundell Lowe, then living a few streets away, received a call from him one night: Bill was sick, and he and Ellaine were being evicted from their 106th Street apartment. They were out on the street with their furniture around them. Lowe called John Gensel, a minister. "He was kind of the friend of the jazz musicians," he recalled, "and we went up and tried to help Bill get situated. Most of the furniture we couldn't do anything with, but we took Bill and his wife down to a hotel and checked them in, paid their bill for a couple of days."[8]

Bill and Ellaine were never legally married, but they were in every other respect man and wife. Neurotic as she was, she was nevertheless able to look after his everyday needs. Ellaine doted on Bill and his music, and he, in turn, sympathized with her mental problems. She, too, was a heroin addict. At the time, Ellaine meant everything to Bill and was the only person with whom he found genuine comfort. Evans knew that he had to escape the clutches of heroin, and that he must get away from his regular haunts to do so. The eviction reinforced his resolve to clean up. Abandoning the apartment with his Knabe grand piano, he again sought refuge at his parents' home in Florida. On these sojourns he always put on weight, a healthy outcome in his case. It is unlikely that his parents suspected his addiction; hepatitis had afflicted their son for as long as they could remember. It was all the more tragic for Evans that, medically, the combination of hepatitis and heroin contributed to his torment.

One night that summer, Paul Winter's group played at Daytona Beach. Evans was eager to meet the flutist in the band, Jeremy Steig, whose debut album, *Flute Fever*, had impressed him. Bill's friend Warren Bernhardt was the pianist in the group. "Bill showed up backstage quite unexpectedly," Warren told me,

> looking much healthier, with a beard, a suntan, and dressed in jeans and a big flannel plaid shirt. He was in high spirits, and it was so great to see him once more. Ellaine was a waitress at a fried chicken joint over by the ocean, Bill was not working at all, and they were both taking time away from New York and had gotten off of all drugs. They looked great (compared to what I had seen earlier up at Bill's pad, when Ellaine looked like she had been in a concentration camp and Bill had tracks all over his hands, et cetera), and seemed to really be enjoying themselves down there.
>
> Bill's mother was very sweet and kind to them, as well as to me and Jeremy. His father was suffering from the aftereffects of a stroke, I seem to recall, and lived in his pajamas in the house, never venturing out for long. There was a spinet piano there, and the next day we ended up playing four hands together—the first of many wonderful sessions at which we shared the keyboard.
>
> Bill invited me to stay on in Florida so that we could spend some time together. I took an inexpensive room at a motel right on the ocean, a couple of blocks from Harry's house. I am to this day so very happy that I did this, for those times together were really the best times we ever shared. Bill introduced me to the Bach two- and three-part *Inventions*, which he loved dearly and sight-read almost to perfection. We marveled at their architecture and mathematical purity. He was convinced that the *Inventions* were the perfect exercises for a pianist, not too difficult, but each one a finger-bender and a gem.
>
> We also spent time together just hanging out. We played miniature golf, drove golf balls, went bowling, shot pool, played billiards, went to the beach and drove around Florida for hours at a time. We even went to the drive-in movies one evening, arriving at the theater early to watch the sunset; and then we watched *Spartacus*, which he loved. He wanted to hear the love theme.

Evans had to return to New York, but he had nowhere to live and was afraid of returning to his old ways. Bernhardt, who did not use drugs, offered him the use of his apartment near the Hudson River, and Evans stayed for about two months. Ellaine remained in Florida; for a while both she and Bill, living in "clean" environments, stayed off drugs.

During the daytime, the two pianists played four-hand pieces and arrangements on Bernhardt's Steinway: the Mozart and Beethoven symphonies (Evans adored the *Jupiter* of Mozart), the Mozart four-hand duets, and Rachmaninoff's Second Symphony. Evans did not consider himself to be a classical pianist in spite of his thorough training and graduation in that field. Since leaving Southeastern, he had never dedicated himself to the technique or the repertoire, but he did have a deep love for it and played the music of the masters constantly for pleasure.

Warren recalled these sessions:

We continued our "lessons," which were not lessons at all, but consisted of Bill sitting across from me at the couch listening to me play, quietly offering suggestions from time to time. He would never show me anything, like his voicings, which everyone wanted to steal from him. He did show me an approach to harmonic textures which I use to this day, and I spent many hours looking over his shoulder or sitting next to him while he practiced.

I never heard him make a harmonic mistake. Never. He organized his materials and chose his harmonic palette with complete mastery. He could play any of the tunes in his book in any of the twelve keys. He often practiced this way, moving around in the strangest, most awful keys without any apparent difficulty. It was frightening. Sometimes he would search for weeks, even months, for the right keys to use with the trio. More than anything else, his concentration and unswerving focus on his art were the most amazing and inspiring phenomena to me. I remember that quite a few great musicians came to the apartment while Bill was there, to see him and hang out with him—and some younger, lesser-known ones, too.

Meanwhile, Gene Lees had taken over a basement apartment on West End Avenue. Bill moved in there for a while, and he and Gene wrote "Turn Out the Stars." Lees recalls: "I got the idea from the title of an old movie I saw listed in TV Guide (it was called 'Turn Off the Moon' but 'off' is an unattractive word to sing and the moon seemed pedestrian), and I suggested the altered title to Bill late that night when he got home from work at the Vanguard. He developed the dark (and very hard to sing) melody from the phrase in the next day or so and I completed the lyric in an evening or two while, as I recall, he was still at work at the Vanguard."[9]

In due course, circumstances enabled Bill and Ellaine to move out to Riverdale in the Bronx. A Chickering grand belonging to her family was installed in their seventh-floor apartment. Although, at five-foot-three or so, it tailed off a little in the bass, it was a lovely instrument dating from a period in the 1920s and 1930s, when Chickerings were at their best.

⊆Ƒ ⊆Ƒ ⊆Ƒ

Chuck Israels and Larry Bunker took time off for a few months, and Evans re-formed his trio, teaming up again with Paul Motian and a new bassist, Gary Peacock. Peacock had recently moved from Los Angeles, where he had been working with pianists Clare Fischer and Paul Bley. It was at this time that Evans signed an exclusive, long-term agreement with Max Gordon at the Village Vanguard, establishing his trio as the house band and affording him singular security for a jazz musician. For a long period at the end of 1963, he was nightly in residence at the club. Whitney Balliett wrote of the trio: "On the basis of its showing one night recently, it is an intense, welling-up group...."

The bass player Gary
Peacock joined the trio
briefly in 1963.
Leo Tanner / The Jazz Image

Evans, more of a ghostly figure than ever, seems freer and has perhaps found
the median between his Werther musings and open, selfless playing."[10]

The group played dates in Toronto and Montreal and spent two weeks
at the Jazz Workshop in Boston. The pianist Hal Galper, who heard every set,
recalls that the fourth and fifth fingers of Bill's right hand were paralyzed—a
vestige of his needle injury—but that he played without a single mistake. In
the audience one night was the eighteen-year-old Keith Jarrett, on tour with
one of his first bands; he had heard few pianists live at that time, and the
Evans performance must have fired his imagination, not least for its group
interplay. At the end of that run, on the last set only, Evans retired sick—he
was often sick, but rarely retired—and Galper stood in.

In December 1963, Evans, Peacock, and Motian went into the studio to
make *Trio 64* for Verve. The new collaboration illustrated how colleagues
could ease Evans into new directions. The restless Peacock alternated hyper-
activity and repose, his thoughts emerging in brief flurries arrested by longer
ringing tones. This rubbed off on Evans, who was encouraged to think in
short phrases that were then further clipped into sharp silences; as a result,

he was somehow trapped in the rhythm, unable to get any kind of a line flowing. It was as if Peacock, while spurring Evans into penetrating bursts of thought, at the same time shattered his sense of continuity. The peculiarly bumpy approach of Paul Motian only enhanced the fragmentary impression.

With the material condensed and the nervous energy at a peak, the tracks were inevitably brief, around four minutes each. Hal Galper remembers that in Boston, too, the tunes were short—as many as fifteen a set—the players unable to sustain such concentration for longer on any one tune. The pianist tended to launch the bass solos sharply, in striking contrast to the overlapping of such joins with Israels and Bunker.

"Little Lulu," the girl with corkscrew curls, was introduced into the list of lightweights in Evans's repertoire. Another character, recruited on *The Solo Session*, made his seasonal appearance in "Santa Claus Is Coming to Town." These two sets of gossamer wings were mounted to perfection, but some other choices were odd: playing "Always" and "I'll See You Again," Evans confirmed that he could make a convincing statement out of any material but, in these two cases, added little. Nevertheless, Evans and Peacock satisfyingly amalgamated their sound, the bass actively underpinning, the piano nestling in its reverberating overtones.

Here was a new Evans, catalyzed into creating by spasm. The resultant impression was of a quite fresh language or style, explosively rhythmic rather than harmonic, and rich in potential. This promise was never to be fulfilled, though, as Peacock took a detour into what Evans called a "dietary and spiritual trip." Bill remained a great fan of Gary Peacock, admiring his freedom over the form. He thought him a rare talent, finding him less melodic than Scott LaFaro but just as creative.

On the production side, Creed Taylor was losing patience, and with *Trio 64* Helen Keane began to feel her way into the role, revealing quite a talent in the process. For all that, the album was prepared hurriedly and did not truly represent what the artists had achieved elsewhere. It was Paul Motian's last recorded appearance with Evans before pursuing his own career: in so doing, he developed in more avant-garde contexts the freedom that he had experienced with the trio.

⋐ ⋐ ⋐

In 1961 Metro-Goldwyn-Mayer had purchased Verve Records from Norman Granz. Creed Taylor became the new executive director, and made a number of crucial policy decisions, including the sacking of the majority of Verve's contract artists. One of a handful to survive was Stan

Getz, who had been recording for the company since 1952. Taylor aimed to reach the largest possible audience through jazz, and he succeeded; Stan Getz, for example, soon wooed the public with his smooth bossa nova explorations—not to say hits—with Charlie Byrd, Astrud Gilberto, and others. It seemed inevitable in 1964 that Taylor should team up his star tenor player with Bill Evans; with Evans still fresh from his Grammy Award, the pairing promised commercial success.

Rudy Van Gelder had finally abandoned his career of optometry and had built a new studio at Englewood Cliffs, New Jersey. In early May, Evans spent two days there recording with Stan Getz and the drummer Elvin Jones; Richard Davis and Ron Carter shared the bass spot. This collaboration of mixed fortunes was issued as *Stan Getz and Bill Evans*. To be sure, Getz was alternately ravishing and ebullient, but Evans seemed curiously empty of ideas when up-tempo, resorting a couple of times to his "dribbling" cliché (four or so quick notes, rising by semitone, in groups syncopated across the beat), a sure sign of unease. On "My Heart Stood Still," the drummer seemed to be powerhousing a big band that was not there. For a track like this, Richard Palmer is right to suggest that McCoy Tyner would have been a more successful choice as pianist for the date.

Getz seduced "But Beautiful" through Bill's characteristic key-cycle of thirds, and "Funkallero" (from *Loose Bloose*) proved itself a fine blowing vehicle, but the group was not settled, and Evans exhibited a sense of rhythmic strain on "Night and Day." This and other tracks were subjected to the almost obligatory Verve fade. As for "The Carpetbaggers," Bill may well have thought to himself, *I can't believe I'm actually doing this!* as he continued, robotlike, to put down beats two and three . . .

Equal in curiosity value is the WNEW theme song, meriting just one chorus each of piano and saxophone and playing out in under three minutes. Ah, but of course: another potential hit single for the flip side of "The Carpetbaggers"! On the original LP, snatches of "Dark Eyes" formed a mad postscript, a mutual flashback to teenage dance-band days complete with flatulent vibrato and pummeling stride; Getz yells, "You forgot the arrangement!" The writer Barry Kernfeld reminded me of the circumstances: "In what was meant to be a private joke at the end of the session, Getz recorded a parody of 'Dark Eyes' in which he exaggerated the crassest elements of tenor saxophonist Charlie Ventura's raspy style; the Verve company released this recording, to Getz's embarrassment and fury, but Getz managed to have the Ventura send-up deleted from reissues."

Evans summed up the star-crossed nature of the session much later:

"Both Stan and I had a mutual desire to do a record together but when it was over, we both felt that we had not got to the level we wanted. Stan had a clause in his contract that would prevent the release of anything that he did not approve and so the record was not issued. However, later, Verve released it without approval. I am not so unhappy about it now but this is the sort of thing that record companies do without reference to the artists involved."[11]

In fact, Evans had the same clause in his contract, and both players had the same lawyer. Artists and management alike were unhappy with these tapes, but it would have cost $10,000 to get an injunction. Resigned and angry, Helen Keane and her pianist let the recording come out in 1974.

ᒧ ᒧ ᒧ

The National Association of Recording Arts and Sciences (N.A.R.A.S.) had bestowed its Grammy Award upon *Conversations with Myself* as the best instrumental jazz LP (soloist or small group) of 1963. Initially thunderstruck by the news, Evans remained elated about it.

On May 12, 1964, he was obliged to attend the annual dinner and awards ceremony at New York's Waldorf-Astoria, an undertaking that quickly assumed comic dimensions. Now that Evans finally had something to smile about, he managed to break a front tooth; then, having no tuxedo for the banquet, he was rescued, after a fashion, by his good friends Gene Lees and Warren Bernhardt. Bernhardt recalled: "I had my father's old tux stashed away in a closet. Gene Lees came over and he and I tried to make this old garment fit Bill. He was roughly the correct height, but we had to use safety pins all over the inside of the jacket and the trousers to make an approximate fit for the at-the-time slender Bill. It was a humorous scene while we worked away like bad tailors with Bill standing there patiently."

Evidently the results were not up to scratch; as Gene Lees tells it, Bill eventually received his award in a blazer of Woody Herman's that was being stored at Lees's apartment. Honored to have the garment on loan, he continued wearing it nightly to a Vanguard engagement.

ᒧ ᒧ ᒧ

Evans immediately rejoined Israels and Bunker for a week's engagement at a lovely waterfront jazz club called the Trident—now long gone—in Sausalito, California. Verve did some taping, then used the fruits to exploit its artist once again. Without warning or consultation, an LP of tracks from that week materialized in the early seventies as *The Bill Evans Trio "Live."* Evans thought the recording far below standard, but the release was a fait accompli.

He barely prevented a second album from appearing, and that only because Leonard Feather called to chat about the liner notes.

It fell to Helen Keane to battle for artistic values against the commercial instincts of certain record companies. Without her there, ever-present to "hold his hand" and supervise these matters, Evans would have lost all authority over his releases. Meanwhile, the Trident recording had slipped through the net. Despite his reservations about the playing, it remains an interesting document of a typical club evening of the time. "What Kind of Fool Am I?" furnishes an early example of a new ploy to finish out a number, a procedure that Evans's trios were to use again and again: toward the end the bass and drums drop out as the pianist takes the tempo by the scruff of the neck, beating it into ad lib submission for a last solo run-through into the final flourish.

⊂⊧ ⊂⊧ ⊂⊧

For the late summer of 1964, Helen Keane organized a first tour of Europe for the Bill Evans Trio (with Israels and Bunker). The drummer gave up lucrative work in the Los Angeles studios to play with his favorite pianist, justifying his decision on strictly musical grounds: "I've been listening to almost no one else in the last five years. His are the records that are always on my phonograph."[12]

The trio was booked throughout August into venues in Belgium, France, Italy, Holland, and Scandinavia, opening in the rain-soaked Belgian village of Comblain-la-Tour in the Ardennes Mountains near Liége. Here, in a football field, with imported stage, chairs, and tents, Belgium's five-year-old Festival International de Jazz took place. The event had previously been criticized for cramming in too many groups at the expense of quality, but the Bill Evans Trio, following the Johnny Dankworth big band, played to an attentive and appreciative audience.

Their Stockholm sojourn centered around two weeks at the Club Gyllene Cirkeln, or Golden Circle, where the renowned Swedish baritone saxophonist Lars Gullin joined them for some standards. Ten years earlier he had been the first European to win an American jazz poll, as the *Down Beat* critics' choice for New Star on baritone sax in 1954. He was not on form for this engagement, though, and the musicians struggled to find rapport. Part of the trouble may have been the Evans group's bent for functioning as a self-contained unit rather than as a supportive straight-blowing rhythm section.

At the club Evans was thrilled to be playing on a remarkable instrument—a ten-foot concert grand, designed and constructed by George Bolin, master cabinetmaker to the Royal Swedish Court. Of three such instruments

The Second Trio, with bassist Chuck Israels and drummer Larry Bunker, in Copenhagen, August 1964. It was Evans's first visit to Europe.

Jan Persson

in existence, one was in New York, on exhibition at the Swedish embassy. Arrangements were made to move it into the Café Au Go Go for Evans's forthcoming engagement there. The pianist was even offered this instrument as a gift, but, daunted by the legal aspect and its attendant paperwork, he declined.

"It is a marvelous instrument," he said. "Probably the first basic advance in piano building in some 150 years. The metal frame and strings are suspended and attached to the wooden frame by inverted screws, and the sound gets a kind of airy, free feeling that I haven't found in any other piano. Before this, Bolin was famous as a guitar maker—he made instruments for Segovia and people like that. To build an instrument like this, a man has to be as much of a genius as a great musician."[13]

While in Stockholm the trio performed "My Foolish Heart" for television, a recording that has been issued on the Green Line video *Bill Evans in*

Europe, as well as the Moon Records CD *Emily.* They played it, as always, in
the key of A, rare in jazz. It was mesmerizing, the pianist's long melody notes
ringing out like bells, the touched-in harmonies beneath dissolving one into
the other so that the main note itself seemed to change color as it faded.

Bill met the twenty-six-year-old Swedish singer and actress Monica
Zetterlund, who had been a fan of his for some time. She had made an EP
recording of "Waltz for Debby" with a Swedish text entitled "Monicas Vals,"
and Evans was bowled over by it. Helen Keane set up a record date for the
end of the tour, and during the trio's packed booking at the Golden Circle,
Evans spent time at Zetterlund's island villa, working on their program for
the disc and a forthcoming radio broadcast. Included in the latter was
"Corcovado," the bossa nova tune for which Bill and Gene Lees had made
the demo. One other item preserved on tape (but not broadcast) was Evans's
vocal rendering, in his nasal New Jersey twang, of "Santa Claus Is Coming to
Town."

The singer and the trio went into the studio for Philips to make the
album *Waltz for Debby,* an intriguing sidestep of artistry in the course of the
trio's career. Zetterlund had a purity of almost vibratoless line, shading subtly
into warmth out of a cool innocence. Her delicate floating over and around
the beat of "Waltz for Debby" left no doubt why Evans had been captivated,
and her talent and taste had a distinct effect on his own playing. Also outstanding was "Some Other Time," with Evans making the most of another
fine instrument, almost certainly a Steinway, prolonging the mood with
beautiful sound, the content pared down to almost nothing. Seldom had he
been so relaxed. In his "Lucky to Be Me" solo, myriad gradations of tone and
timing, emphasis and release were organized into a living whole, like sculpting sound out of the air.

⋐ ⋐ ⋐

Back in Greenwich Village, the trio played the Café Au Go Go for six
weeks. Its owner, Howard Solomon, had a policy of mixing his acts, and
Evans was delighted to find himself opposite such then-unknown comics as
Richard Pryor and George Carlin. Nat Hentoff was there and had this to say:
"His narrow back hunched over the piano, Evans, after a few minutes, gives
the impression of having entered the instrument. The body we see is simply a
husk waiting to be filled again when the set is over. It is the distilled quality of
Evans' intensity that I am trying to convey.... Those who complain that
Evans is too removed from his audience, that he makes no overt signs to draw
them into his music, are simply not willing to give that music at least a tithe

Copenhagen, August 1964. Bill wrote tunes on the subway and in the waiting room, as well as at the piano.

Jan Persson

of the concentration Evans does. Communication is there, and don't shoot the piano player if you're blocked."[14]

The George Bolin piano was duly in place for this run, as Warren Bernhardt has every reason to remember: "Once, Bill was ill, and Gene Lees called me at the last minute, all excited, and asked if I could sub for him at the Café Au Go Go, with Chuck Israels and Larry Bunker. Of course I was terrified, but I made the gig, for better or for worse—mostly the latter, because we were unrehearsed and I was terribly nervous and quite unprepared to sit in that 'hot seat' at that huge piano." Israels remembers that the gig extended beyond the time that Larry Bunker was able to stay in New York, and Israels and Evans worked for two weeks with guitarist Jim Hall instead of a drummer. "It was heaven," he said, "and I wish it had continued and been recorded."

Evans thought that his next record was essential to his canon. After exactly two years with Verve he needed to exhibit the essence of his work, his current trio's continuation on the original course set by LaFaro and Motian. On *Trio '65*, made in February 1965 with Chuck Israels and Larry Bunker, there was one musical trait retained from the Gary Peacock period: the short, clipped phrase when chording. But now it was subsumed into an overall line, Israels able to keep the end of the phrase in view and Bunker's brisk support continuously propelling the music forward.

One number was new to the trio's book: the latest Leslie Bricusse–Anthony Newley hit, "Who Can I Turn To?" This kind of showtune satisfied Evans's sense of form, its solid, thirty-two-bar construction harnessing melody and harmony toward a heart-filling climax. A pianist opens himself to sentimental temptation with such material, but Evans knew that the pedigree of his musical language would guarantee the integrity of his performance.

The album, though—in spite of some fine block chorded sections and exemplary all-around execution—smacks of a clinical documentary. The earlier trio recordings of most of these numbers had been more inspired, and both pianist and manager knew that the sessions had not gone well. The album seems to say, *Here is the point we have reached, and this is just for the record.*

For years in the *Down Beat* polls—those comparative assessments that for some reason dog the art of jazz—the magazine's readers had been lagging behind the critics in their support for Evans, but in 1964 they at last caught up, and both factions cast him into first place. Over the ensuing years he would hover near the summit in both polls.

But he still had his detractors. The former *New York Times* critic John S. Wilson had for some time been smoldering in the pages of *Down Beat*. He seized on *Trio '65* to launch his attack:

> The more I hear of Evans, the more I become convinced that the propagation of the Evans mystique must be one of the major con jobs of recent years. Evans' performances—and this one is fairly representative—are clean and polished, but they neither seize nor hold the attention; not mine, anyhow. There is a self-effacing quality about Evans' playing that makes the whole thing slip away from a listener so that steady listening has to be a deliberate, directed effort. This is great jazz? It's more like superior background music, music that forms a pleasant atmospheric setting but does not distract. There's nothing wrong with this sort of music, and Evans does it very well. But it scarcely seems the thing that jazz cults are based on. Still, Evans has managed to do it.[15]

Some lively correspondence ensued—quite a bit of it supporting Wilson—with one reader dismissing all Bill Evans lovers as a bunch of tin-eared idiots.

⊂⊱ ⊂⊱ ⊂⊱

Hot on the heels of its first European tour, the same Bill Evans Trio embarked on another. This time the group was broadcast from the Maison de l'ORTF in Paris, the first in a line of recordings over the years from Radio France. The performance given on February 13, 1965, has been released as *How Deep Is the Ocean?* and as *Paris 1965*, typical examples of a whole string of poor quality bootleg Bill Evans issues emanating from Europe. A couple of tracks have been mutilated to eliminate radio announcements, and much of the printed information is glaringly incorrect. The playing itself, though fascinating to the Evans enthusiast, would not have been likely to receive approval for release by Evans. A live broadcast is one thing (the artist tacitly endures that momentary peril), but the gratuitous circulation of substandard performances is quite another. There are, of course, honorable and wise persons in the business (Orrin Keepnews and Helen Keane spring to mind) who would put out posthumous tapes only with the deepest consideration and concrete musical reasons.

Evans may not have sanctioned the issue of these performances, but he does sound happy to be playing on this occasion, and one track is exceptional. Only an artist who felt at home in the venue and comfortable with his audience would take "Some Other Time" quite as slow as this. The indulgence in extreme tempo was reflected in the dynamic level—at times pianissimo. This was communication by implication. A wondrous thing happened: the more densely Evans packed in harmonic "information," the softer he played it and the more expressive it became. Another jazz pianist who really cared about his sound was George Shearing, and Evans valued his quality of touch, especially in pianissimo: "I learned a great lesson listening to George Shearing play 'Tenderly' one night at The Embers in New York. He managed to keep that club quiet—no mean achievement."[16]

For this tour Chuck Israels had acquired a set of metal strings, and he played with a new confidence, especially in the higher register. With Israels aloft and in duet with Evans's right-hand lines, an exciting counterpoint resulted, something that had been on the cards ever since the bassist had joined the group. Suddenly he was transformed into a linchpin—and more surprisingly, perhaps, a devotee of the limelight.

The French capital was to become one of the pianist's favorite places to play, and over the next fifteen years he nurtured a special rapport with his audience there. His refined art, alert with detailed nuance, appealed to Parisians' sophisticated taste. In fact, he was delighted with his European listeners generally. "Wherever we go the audiences have been superb," he told Val Wilmer a little later. "It's very rare to be able to play ballads on a Saturday night, for example. In New York it's so noisy that we have to stick more or less to the swinging things."[17]

One other inferior recording from the tour must be mentioned: a Unique Jazz LP, also containing later material, called *Two Super Bill Evans Trios*. Evans showed his disgust with a piano that was best forgotten, nailing home a string of consecutive sevenths at one point and ramming down the two-note start to "Nardis" in deliberately "split" semitones, as if to say, *What's the difference?* More exasperated by the minute, he was clearly giving up on the situation and handing the show over to his colleagues. In the end, Chuck Israels carried the evening. The road can be tough.

⋲ ⋲ ⋲

For many decades the transatlantic traffic of jazz musicians suffered at the hands of politicians. Not until 1965, after a history of restrictions and exchange agreements, was the gate fully opened for all-American bands to play in Britain. In March of that year the Bill Evans Trio became the first such group to play at Ronnie Scott's jazz club, and for the pianist's British followers it was a momentous visit.

For a television preview, the trio was joined by Ronnie Scott on tenor sax (sounding for all the world like Stan Getz) for a run-through of "My Foolish Heart." But Evans's visit to the club gave cause for concern in the Scott camp: in anticipation of the master's touch, the condition of the house piano came under scrutiny and was deemed unfit, calling for drastic action. Scott told Les Tomkins:

> We had a piano in the club which was okay, but it wasn't the kind of thing Bill Evans would be very taken with. I mean, I'm sure he could have worked on it, but we wanted the best we could possibly get. So we arranged with a firm in Covent Garden to hire us a good grand piano; they would bring it in on the Monday that Bill was due to start. We sold our existing piano, and it was taken away on Sunday, after the week at the club.
>
> There was the club, then, with no piano. And the guy whom we were hiring the grand from came down to the club in Gerrard Street, and decided that he wasn't going to hire it to us after all. It was a difficult stairway to get down with a grand—if you remember those wooden stairs outside—and then getting it round a corner into the club wouldn't be easy. He didn't realise it was a jazz club, and he had visions of girls dancing on the piano, people pouring beer into it, and that kind of thing.
>
> So we went to Steinway's, I remember, to hire one; they had a place in Marble Arch, run by this German lady. And she had no grand pianos she could hire us, but she did have an upright. I said: "You can't have Bill Evans playing an upright piano." She said: "Vy not? He can see der boys over der top."
>
> Eventually what happened was that Alan Clare helped us out; he knew someone who had a good piano, and was prepared to lend it, or hire it, to us. It was all a panic by then—and we finally got the piano in about an hour before Bill played his first set.[18]

Evans, who felt that he should have been given a Steinway all along, was still not happy—in fact, he was out of sorts generally, as the English fan and pianist Michael Garrick found out when he spent a memorable day with Evans:

> "I had discovered," said Garrick, "that Bill was taking his interval victuals at a spaghetti house on the corner, and plucked up the courage to approach him to say how much I liked his playing. He was on his own, morose and depressed, but more than that I was surprised how ready he was to talk about it—and in colourful language—to a complete stranger. It was years later that Brian Hennessey told me he was heavily on drugs.
>
> "Anyway, I asked him if he could possibly fit in a piano lesson. He agreed to a listen, and we met up at Weekes' Studios in Hanover Street—it was like a rabbit warren, full of operatic singers and piano students. He was complimentary about a piece of mine, but would go into no detail about the aspect that fascinated all of us pianists at the time—his 'floating' left-hand voicings. I'd heard him at the Marquee the previous Sunday, and was entranced with a new composition, 'Time Remembered,' particularly the 'middle' section—bars 17 to 20.
>
> "'Diminished relationship,' he said curtly. I begged him for a copy.
>
> "'I'll write it out for you and leave it at the club,' he said.
>
> "We had to leave, since he needed to get to Highgate Village to see his lady, Ellaine, who he said was there in a nursing home. I offered him a lift. Going up a steep hill, the road narrowed quite suddenly, and we found ourselves head-on to a fast descending (and bouncing) tipper lorry full of builders' rubbish. To my horror, a house brick leapt off it and, with an almighty smack, hit the windscreen full in front of Bill's head.
>
> "'Christ, this is it,' I thought. The windscreen didn't even crack.
>
> "'That was close,' murmured Bill. Had that brick gone through—at that speed—it could have killed him."

In the basement of 39 Gerrard Street—referred to nostalgically, by those who knew it, as the "Old Place," and now swallowed up by Chinatown—the Bill Evans Trio played to packed and mesmerized houses. "There is a table at the club," Ronnie announced, "which overlooks the keyboard of the piano, and for the month of March we are reserving it solely for pianists. The table is crowded every night."[19]

The critics for *Melody Maker* had just voted Evans into first place in their jazz piano poll. Such critical reaction was based on his recordings, but there is nothing like hearing the real thing. Today it is easy to forget the impact of this new voice whenever he went to a new place. The pianist John Horler recalls his first experience of the Evans sound: "I remember being at the bar at Ronnie Scott's with my back to the bandstand when I heard these chords being played very quietly on the piano. The impact was as great as if you'd suddenly heard the Count Basie band in full cry! I turned around, and Bill Evans was sitting at the piano ready to start his first set."

To British jazz fans, used to a wilder aspect, the physical appearance of the three trio members was arresting. Studious and sober, neatly dressed in suits and sporting cropped Ivy League hairstyles, they took the stand exuding quiet confidence and self-control; such qualities permeated their music making, defining but not stifling their inner passion and lyricism. They brought for the first time into an English jazz club a sophistication, an aura of gentility that, without being precious, elevated jazz onto a more rarified plane. With immense care they shaped their phrases, molded their corporate sound. Audiences were captured by their dedication, concentration, and hushed intensity, the trio's own sense of wonderment at the beauty they had discovered communicating tangibly to those who would receive it.

After each number, Evans nodded curtly, almost apologetically, to the audience, his thoughts already on the next song. This was the least showy man in the business. "I have always been basically introspective," he said. "I was very serious as a kid. My brother and I would get taken to a circus and he'd kill himself laughing. But I would sit there completely expressionless. Yet I would be enjoying it tremendously."[20]

Besides the four-week residency at Ronnie's, the group had several other engagements to fulfill, including the filming of two sets for BBC Television's *Jazz 625* series. These sessions, presented by Humphrey Lyttelton, were reissued in 1996 by Pearson New Entertainment as *Bill Evans Trio (Episodes 1 and 2)*. In the formal atmosphere of London's Cine-Tele Sound Studios the immaculate presentation was like another installment of *Trio '65*, the current, state-of-the-art trio showing off its wares in a well-oiled routine.

Once warmed up, though, Evans played superbly, the high spots being "Someday My Prince Will Come"—pushing hard all the way and erupting into a scurrying moto perpetuo, all tortured shape and meaning—and near-perfect renderings of "How Deep Is the Ocean?" and "Come Rain or Come Shine," which exhibited outstanding group rapport and exemplary block chording. At the end of episode 2, the play-out, "Five," is preserved intact. The pianist had devised a format that incorporated his own tune, Sonny Rollins's "Oleo," and elements of the old "52nd Street Theme," a common sign-off property of bop bands in the forties.

Evans had a habit of bringing onto the bandstand a penciled list of tunes for the set, and we see it here in the shape of a three-by-five notepad sitting on the wrestplank of the Steinway (sometimes he would prop it up vertically between the pins). Only he had this information, leaving his sidemen guessing as to the next tune. This was not usually a problem, for his habit by this time was to ease into a number with a free solo introduction; just this

During rehearsal for BBC Television's *Jazz 625* series, London, 1965.
David Redfern

once, though, he went straight into "Nardis" cold, and Chuck Israels barely
made it to the fingerboard for his third-beat entry.

These videos enable us to observe a few aspects of Evans's physical
approach to playing. Quality of tone was produced by armweight, fingers
were naturally bent for maximum articulation, forearms horizontal for greatest ease of lateral movement. The trunk, shoulders, arms, and wrists all functioned together as an ever-adapting set of shock absorbers behind the finger-
tip action. When block chording, his left hand looked as though it was cush-
ioning the rhythms of the right. The head moved in sympathy with those
rhythms, merely as a reflex action; this served no purpose but confirmed that
all body components were colluding smoothly in a state of balance.

The fact that he ended up hunched over the keyboard could be taken as a good sign—the natural force of gravity was being tapped. He started each number seated relatively upright; gradually, as the music developed, gravity took over. The lower the head fell the better Evans played. Finally, his open mouth showed that he was breathing freely—and only then would the music do likewise.

Peter Clayton once put it to Evans that he seemed to be trying to think his ideas straight onto the keys. Evans, as puzzled as anyone, tried to explain: "I don't know why that is, but it's not just a mannerism or a fault of posture; it is, as you say, something to do with my thinking and concentration. I feel somehow that my head, at a certain angle in relationship to the piano, in relationship to my hands, seems to have a greater collective thought potential—something like that."[21]

Evans felt very comfortable performing for television. The studio audience (including jazz critic Charles Fox) appeared stunned into an awesome respect, none more so than the actor John LeMesurier, who was sitting on the front row and who could frequently be found at Ronnie's during Evans's visits. The comedian Spike Milligan was another who frequently went to hear him, as did Dudley Moore.

I was a music student in London at the time, and I too heard the trio at Ronnie's. Nineteen years old, I was already a fan of some five years' standing. As a student of classical music, the construction and procedures of jazz being still a mystery to me, I did not fully understand what I heard, but I knew from my handful of Evans recordings what magic to expect. I was not disappointed, and, already hooked on disc, I now determined to catch Bill Evans live wherever I could.

CHAPTER **14** A Simple Matter of
Conviction

I believe that all people are in possession of what might be called a "universal musical mind."

— *Bill Evans*

The trio returned to America, almost immediately flying west to revisit Shelly's Manne Hole, then on to a six-week run at the Trident in Sausalito. Evans wanted to sort out some new repertoire, but halfway into the engagement, drug-induced illness struck again. He was hospitalized, diagnosed as suffering from, among other things, malnutrition. Two weeks at the Plugged Nickel in Chicago, booked well in advance, had to be canceled, Jon Hendricks stepping in at the last minute. This incident prompted Larry Bunker to quit the trio.

Meanwhile, in New York, an exciting project was under way as the next Bill Evans offering from Verve. Both Evans and Creed Taylor were keen on presenting a variety of musical contexts to the record-buying public, and the new recording, *Bill Evans Trio with Symphony Orchestra*, was to include some reworking of European classical repertoire. The settings were entrusted to Claus Ogerman, who had already provided the backings on *The V.I.P.s*.

Since arriving in New York in 1959, the Silesian-born composer, arranger, and pianist had earned a living as a commercial arranger, eventually accumulating scores of albums to his credit in the jazz, pop, and R&B fields. These included many arrangements for Antonio Carlos Jobim and sessions with Oscar Peterson, Stan Getz, and Wes Montgomery. Later, through the 1970s, he would tackle more extended jazz compositions, including a further collaboration with Evans (*Symbiosis*).

Two of Evans's compositions, "Time Remembered" and "My Bells," were included on *Symphony Orchestra*, and some of the other repertoire would have been familiar to him: "Prelude" was Piano Prelude in D♭, Op. 11, No. 15, written in 1895 by the Russian composer Alexander Scriabin, a kindred spirit into whose large body of piano works Bill had dipped his fingers over the years, while "Granados" was based on "The Maiden and the Nightingale," from a set of seven piano pieces called *Goyescas* by the Spanish composer Enrique Granados. "Elegia," though, was quite new to Evans, being the second movement of Claus Ogerman's Concerto for Orchestra and Jazz Piano, here receiving its recorded première.

Some composers survive "treatment" better than others. The works of J. S. Bach, for instance, will withstand a good deal of rough and tumble; "Valse" was a version of the Siciliano from the Second Flute Sonata. By way of smoky atmosphere, Ogerman devised a brief but delicious play-in and play-out tag. On the other hand, Gabriel Fauré's short orchestral piece "Pavane" fares less well—there is such a quiet perfection about this French master's music that it seems a sacrilege to tamper with any detail.

"Blue Interlude" had a tantalizing genesis. Bill explained: "For the Chopin track…I owe a debt to Gil Evans for the idea. We were supposed to do a record together, in fact they had already made the album cover. One of the ideas on the album was to do the Chopin C minor Prelude. It lends itself well to a blues kind of feeling."[1] The collaboration, Gil Evans's first project for Verve, was even advertised in *Down Beat* in June 1962, but it sadly did not materialize.

Although the production credit on the new record went to Creed Taylor, Helen Keane was equally active in the role of evaluating solos, checking balance, and choosing the takes. Initially, Gene Lees gave the album a negative review, but, as he told me, "A year later, as I was listening to it again, I forgot where the splices were, overlooked the dodgy intonation of the woodwinds, and wrote another review, recanting the first. For all its flaws, including that rain-barrel piano sound, and the sloppy orchestral performance in places, it's quite lovely."

Some regarded it as a "stunt" record, many of Evans's discerning fans reacting with a mixture of puzzlement and dismissal. The composer Richard Rodney Bennett said to me at the time, "He doesn't need to do that sort of thing." I, too, felt uneasy about Evans's motivation, the lush, soft settings hard to reconcile with the purposeful element in his character. On the other hand, the composer Johnny Mandel liked it a lot, and singer Tony Bennett declared it one of his all-time favorite albums.

Opinion is similarly divided on Creed Taylor's work. Gene Lees, who attended most of Taylor's sessions with Evans, usually manages to see his endeavors in a positive light, finding him an astute and creative producer.

Barry Kernfeld, in contrast, regards Taylor's commercial aims as misguided and holds him responsible for creating "jazz fluff." Gary Giddins, too, attacks Taylor's commercial approach. In fact, the producer and his assistant Claus Ogerman were trying to reach as many people as possible through their jazz-oriented recordings, but my own feeling is that, for all the incidental beauties, the jazz-oriented settings do nothing to improve the originals.

In musical importance the disc sits outside the main Evans canon, unlike *Conversations with Myself,* surely the best of the Evans-Taylor collaborations; it is no coincidence that the idea for *Conversations* came entirely from the pianist.

⋹ ⋹ ⋹

At the end of October 1965, between sessions on the *Symphony Orchestra* project, Evans revisited Europe and Scandinavia, playing largely with non-American rhythm sections. The exception was a reunion with Lee Konitz, with the support of drummer Alan Dawson. Konitz had been especially popular in Germany for some years. Dawson, Konitz, and Evans were just three of an impressive lineup of American jazzmen in George Wein's "best of Newport" tour, which played the second Berlin Jazz Festival and an additional seven-day itinerary. Completing the quartet on bass was a nineteen-year-old Dane, Niels-Henning Ørsted Pedersen, who received resounding acclaim for his contributions.

The quartet aired its program for the week, including an engagement in Berlin's Philharmonic Hall on October 29. The constantly engaging Dawson, hot from Jaki Byard's combo, supplied an attractive bouncy feel willingly adopted by Evans. Some numbers appeared initially on the bootleg LPs, *Lennie Tristano Solo in Europe...* and *Lee Konitz, Chet Baker, Keith Jarrett Quintet,* then subsequently on *Together Again* from Moon Records.

The next day, an event advertised as the Battle of the Pianists began with a "relay-blues" in C, the successive entrances of Earl Hines, Teddy Wilson, John Lewis, Lennie Tristano, Bill Evans, and Jaki Byard being announced by the festival producer, Joachim-Ernst Berendt. Evans was introduced as the "Chopin of jazz piano" (Berendt has elsewhere, justifiably, likened Bill's touch to Artur Rubinstein's). This item and two trio tracks by Evans were issued in 1990 on the Italian Philology label under the title *Piano Summit.*

The day after Berlin, the "package" went to Copenhagen. Here, at the Tivoli Gardens, Ørsted Pedersen was on familiar ground, the stage being within walking distance of the Jazzhus Montmartre, where he had been house bassist for three years. Lee Konitz, after two opening numbers with bass and drums only, turned to the microphone to say: "If Bill Evans is within shouting distance, maybe he would come out here and join us for a tune." Evans duly appeared, looking sullen, gaunt, and hollow-cheeked. As he hunched over the piano (a local Hornung & Møller) he appeared old for his thirty-six years. Even so, he was able to rise artistically above an apparent indifference to the situation.

Evans's moodiness intensified a day or two later at Stockholm's ice stadium, where the piano was atrocious. Normally at one with his instrument, Evans waged war with this specimen, following a sledgehammer blow to the bass at the end of "Detour Ahead" with a crudely striding-out "Come Rain or Come Shine" (both unissued). As part of the package, the quartet joined in the Second Paris Jazz Festival, broadcasting the next day from the Salle Pleyel.

The trio then split up and Evans returned to Stockholm, beginning two weeks at what had become, in barely a year, a kind of home-away-from-home: the Golden Circle Club. He settled in with the bassist Palle Danielsson and the drummer Rune Carlsson, both Swedish. Two half-hour sets from the second week of this engagement appeared in 1991 on the Royal Jazz CD *Stockholm 1965*. The issue is more than a semitone sharp, which affects tempos considerably and gives a misleading impression. This recording reflects a common flaw in live recordings. Collectors routinely circulate private tapings that have been copied and recopied on all manner of machines to the detriment of accuracy—I have heard tapes whose pitch is a minor third sharp—and often those tapes are put out onto the market by indiscriminate record companies. As a document *Stockholm* proved that Evans really did go to work—and hard—every night during a run. He also played in a different way with unfamiliar sidemen, the fresh and more open situation (compared to his own trio) propelling him into more direct statements. The record is a salutatory reminder of all the evenings that disappeared into thin air by the hundred.

Evans's popularity in Sweden was reflected in film director Bo Widerberg's choice of "Peace Piece" for the soundtrack of his latest film, *Kärlek 65* (Love 65). The following year some of Evans's music was used on the short Danish film *Signalet*, directed by Ole Gammeltoft.

Evans finished the tour in Denmark, where he and Ørsted Pedersen were joined by the young Danish drummer Alex Riel for a concert in Holbæk on November 28. Danmarks Radio broadcast the concert, as well as a continuous solo medley from the Radiohuset in Copenhagen, including a lively but beautifully controlled "My Funny Valentine" in the vein of Evans's classic recording with Jim Hall.

⊂⊱ ⊂⊱ ⊂⊱

Evans's gift for clarity extended into the written word. He frequently annotated his own records and contributed liner notes to other musicians' albums as well, including Columbia's *Monk* and Riverside's *Soulmates*, with Ben Webster and Joe Zawinul. On *Soulmates*, Evans pointed to the "fortunate historical coincidence" by which the emergence of sound recording enabled jazz improvisation to be preserved, standard systems of musical notation being inadequate to reflect the nuances of the individual performer.

He wrote an introductory note to *Contemporary Piano Styles*, volume 4 of John Mehegan's treatise *Jazz Improvisation*. Mehegan considered Evans's own contribution to the genre, including a complete transcription of "Peri's Scope" from *Portrait in Jazz*. When Evans received his complimentary copy from the publisher, he gave it on the spot to his pupil (and later friend) Andy LaVerne, who was having his first lesson at the time. Andy remembers how pleased Bill was to find some of his own left-hand voicings set out in Mehegan's study.

The publication of Evans's compositions has a convoluted history; over the years, particularly in Japan, transcription of his compositions and improvisations has become quite an industry. His first tunes had been acquired in 1962 by a company called Acorn, later dissolved and absorbed into Folkways Music, both houses existing under the umbrella of The Richmond Organization (TRO). In the years immediately following, TRO was engaged in producing the first book of Bill Evans compositions, *Bill Evans Piano Solos*. It was not related to any recording, although the printed versions (which he wrote out himself) came close to his playing of "Waltz for Debby" on *New Jazz Conceptions* and "Very Early" on *Moonbeams*. The folio, which came out in November 1965 under the imprint of Acorn Music Corporation, has been followed over the years by several further volumes, printed and reprinted under the assiduous eye of Judy Bell at TRO.

Earlier that year, another company, Ludlow Music (also owned by TRO), entered the picture. Judy Bell details the terms of Evans's new contract with them: "On May 14, 1965, Bill entered into a contract which was for a three-year period, during which time he was to write a minimum of three 'units' per year. A full unit consisted of one composition which was also commercially recorded by Bill. A half-unit would comprise just the manuscript, consisting of melody with full harmonization. Bill also received advance payments in certain preset amounts. Also, if he happened to write more than fifteen tunes over the three-year period (which I don't think he did) he would get another payment." In 1997 TRO produced the *Bill Evans Fake Book*, a complete collection of his compositions, including seven unrecorded and previously unknown numbers written under the Ludlow contract. One of them, "Bill's Belle," is a beauty.

⊑⋢ ⊑⋢ ⊑⋢

In February 1966, Evans's father died, after a series of strokes, and Bill flew straight down to Florida. Meanwhile, in New York, Helen Keane was working hard organizing some one-off appearances for her pianist. The first of these was a television presentation of some of the *Symphony Orchestra* material—the Chopin, the Scriabin, and the two Evans numbers—along with a couple of trio-only numbers. Larry Bunker had left, and Arnold Wise, an Englishman from Golders Green and an old friend, had joined the trio; he was to stay for a year or so, returning later for another stint.

Just three days later, Evans made his New York concert debut—though he had been playing the club circuit in that city for a decade. The billing for the Town Hall appearance read: "Helen Keane presents Bill Evans—Solo, Trio & With Orchestra." The star-studded big band led by Al Cohn, which joined in the second half, borrowed a number of players, including Bill Berry, Bob Brookmeyer, Jerry Dodgion, and Eddie Daniels, from the newly formed once-a-week rehearsal band known as the Thad Jones–Mel Lewis Orchestra. Ernie Royal and Clark Terry played, too. Al Cohn had included "Funkallero" and "Waltz for Debby" among his arrangements for the occasion, all the numbers being linked by either woodwind or piano, forming a continuous suite, and featuring Evans as one of several soloists. Helen Keane recalls that Evans did not play his best. Two albums were planned by Verve, but it was decided not to use the big-band material. Only the first half of the concert was issued, as *Bill Evans at Town Hall, Volume 1*.

After the death of his father, Evans had composed—or, rather, assembled—a requiem for solo piano, "In Memory of His Father, Harry L. Evans, 1891–1966," consisting of four sections and drawing on some earlier material. "Prologue" (shades of Satie and Debussy) was new, but the closing "Epilogue" was the one that had finished each side of the *Everybody Digs* LP. The lengthy central portion consisted of improvisations on an extended and elaborated version of "Re: Person I Knew" (now called "Storyline"), which led into the first exposure of "Turn Out the Stars," written some time previously by Evans with Gene Lees. (Contrary to some documentation, its actual composition was unconnected with the death of Bill's father.) The song remains one of the pianist's finest compositions and carries a full, somber lyric from Lees. Although this whole suite was a one-off performance (or almost—Evans repeated it for television in 1968 in memory of Robert

Kennedy), "Turn Out the Stars" was to endure and become arguably Evans's second-greatest classic after "Waltz For Debby." To assist Gene Lees in writing the lyric, Evans asked Warren Bernhardt to record a precise melodic performance from a manuscript copy of the tune, written out by Bill specially for the purpose. Typically, he had misgivings about the tune and attached a note encouraging Lees's free and poetic response regarding such matters as the adjustment of syllables and rhythmic phrasing. Gene knew Bill well enough to accept the invitation to change, and his lyric did succeed in freeing a certain squareness in the given melody.

One other original tune, "One for Helen," was aired that evening at Town Hall, and I have it from Helen Keane that it was not originally entitled "My Lover's Kiss," as has been stated elsewhere.

Arnie Wise had quickly absorbed the Evans book on recent club dates, as witness the immaculate ensemble at the end of "I Should Care." Chuck Israels valued his contribution highly: "He's like a catalytic drummer, instigating nothing but taking everything in his musical surroundings and gluing it together, melding the elements."

Bill Evans at Town Hall marked Israels's last recorded appearance as a regular member of the Bill Evans Trio. He wanted to stay in one place and pursue his studies in arranging and composition, and he was finding the pianist's drug use increasingly hard to tolerate. It was not quite adieu, though; they would collaborate again in the mid-seventies when Israels became director of the National Jazz Ensemble. The lyrical rapport built up between these artists in four and a half years on the road and in the studio was astonishing. Equally remarkable to observe is the bass player's own development from the shy and hesitant contributor to *Nirvana* to the assured bearer of the demanding chamber role in one of jazz's greatest piano trios. He was able to complement and enhance the tenet at the heart of Bill Evans's vision—to sing above all.

ᗴ ᗴ ᗴ

Evans had by this juncture created an entirely individual harmonic language as estimable in its thoroughness of working as those of, say, Gershwin, Messiaen, or the neoclassical Stravinsky. It was based on the tonal system of the popular song and had evolved at its own painstakingly slow pace, its creator never in a hurry to leap ahead, always content to add voicings and intensify harmony step by step, consolidating all the way.

It was a craft of distinction; because he selected the notes of a chord with extra care he could heighten expressiveness by playing fewer of them, his thoroughly grounded knowledge enabling him to make quite original substitutions. As each new element of his vocabulary became assimilated into general use, so the ground was laid for the next, and thus his own successive brands of piquancy came alive. This essentially harmonic world was enhanced by inner and outer moving parts, comments and colorings: a note that began life as a chromatic passing note might be transferred into the chord itself, which then emerged as a fresh voicing. The evolution spanned his whole life and was continuing to develop at his death.

In parallel with the choice of notes was the rhythmic variety into which they were cast, an acuity which had been sharpened early on, during his first excursions with George Russell. In trying to describe some of his rhythmic approaches in the trio, Evans likened the placement of his chords to shadow lettering, in which the shadows rather than the letters are drawn, yet the observer is always conscious only of the letters themselves. He was fascinated by disguise, surprise, and asymmetry; asymmetry, in fact—in the form of displacement—almost developed into an occupational hazard. Phrases fell according to their content rather than the position of the bar line. Evans referred to an "internalized" beat or pulse, *around* which the trio played, avoiding the obvious and the explicit. As for cross-rhythms, he had always been at home in two meters at once, leaning fearlessly into the one he was engaged upon. A further subtle dimension in his playing, extra to written time-divisions, is all but beyond description: an impulsive motion that can only be likened to the timing of a great actor or comedian. In ballads especially, this sense was indispensable to their strength.

⊂⊱ ⊂⊱ ⊂⊱

For some four years, one of the pianist's regular fans had been an optical physicist and amateur pianist named Mike Harris. His discovery of Evans, like so many other people's, was a revelation, and he recounted it to Doug Ramsey thus: "One afternoon, I was driving into New York on the Cross County Parkway and listening to Billy Taylor's program on WLIB-AM. He played 'Waltz for Debby,' and I said, 'What the hell is that?' I drove immediately to a record store and bought everything of Bill's I could find, which were his first four albums.... I said, 'Okay, that's it. It's not going to get any better than that.' "[2]

Harris and his wife, Evelyn, quickly became regulars at the Village Vanguard and Evans's other venues, their high regard for his music making soon turning into an obsession. Harris was troubled by the obvious fact that this remarkable playing was vanishing into thin air on a nightly basis, so one evening, taking the law (and musical posterity) into his own hands, he brought a small rented Uher tape recorder and RCA microphone into the club. Max Gordon, the owner, turned a noncommittal eye to this, the first of countless Harris eavesdroppings spread over fourteen years. Evans himself appeared not to notice. "Sometimes I wondered if he knew we were taping him," Harris recalls. "We'd be there often with this rather large bag, sitting right up front. But most likely, he didn't."[3] Orrin Keepnews has likened Harris's activities to those of Dean Benedetti on behalf of Charlie Parker. The full story is told in the booklet to the eight-CD boxed set *The Secret Sessions*, produced by Keepnews and released on Milestone in 1996.

In March 1966, after playing at the Jazz Workshop in Boston, the Bill Evans Trio settled into the Village Vanguard. Arnie Wise was now at the drums, and the bass player was Teddy Kotick, who had played with Evans from time to time since making *New Jazz Conceptions*. He was reportedly shy of soloing, but Evans encouraged him fully, and the bassist took many spots during this run at the club. Both of Bill's recent compositions, "One for Helen" and "Turn Out the Stars," were on the nightly set lists, and they appear among the opening tracks of *The Secret Sessions*.

Also at the Vanguard every night was a twenty-one-year-old bass player from Puerto Rico named Eddie Gomez, playing opposite the trio in a tryout Gerry Mulligan group. For some time, Gomez had nurtured a desire to play with Evans, and the booking was no accident. He knew that Chuck Israels was leaving the trio, and he had arranged to be in the Mulligan group so that the pianist could hear him in action. Evans invited Gomez to sit in. It does not take long to recognize talent and potential, and Bill straightaway instructed Helen Keane to hire him. She well remembers her phone call to Eddie: "He was utterly speechless." Never was there a more willing catch.

ᴇᴋ ᴇᴋ ᴇᴋ

Eddie Gomez was born in 1944 into a nonmusical family in Santurce, the heart of San Juan, the capital of Puerto Rico. From the age of one he was raised in New York City. His heart was set on the cello, but the instincts of his grade school teacher steered him firmly toward a half-size double bass when he was twelve years old. Two years later Gomez was already studying with the most famous double bass teacher and maestro to the classical world, Fred Zimmerman, whose glowing, Pablo Casals–like sound influenced him greatly. So, too, at that time, did the warmth and individuality of Paul Chambers.

Already precocious on his instrument and with his roots firmly in jazz, Gomez entered Marshall Brown's Newport Festival Youth Band. Brown, a

Eddie Gomez, Ronnie Scott's club, London, January 30, 1972.
Val Wilmer

trombonist and an innovator for jazz youth, said of the audition: "He was totally confident. He used rather unorthodox fingering, but who cared. He was swinging already, and his time was *great!* . . . When I broke up the band in 1960, he was then technically one of the better bass players in town, and he was only sixteen. The only thing was, nobody knew it except me, but I knew it was just a question of time before Bill Evans found him. He's like another Jimmy Blanton."[4]

Charles Mingus and Ray Brown made an early impression on Gomez, but it was Scott LaFaro, and his role in the Bill Evans Trio, that became his greatest influence, to the extent that Gomez named his first son Scottie. A two-year stint with Marian McPartland's Trio lasted until his discovery by Evans. He had played with Jim Hall, Miles Davis, and Jeremy Steig and had embraced the free jazz scene, too, recording with Paul Bley.

Gomez was initiated into the trio on a two-week gig at Chicago's London House, with Joe Hunt on drums. They played Shelly's Manne Hole, Stanford University, and San Francisco's "Both/And" club, a small neighborhood venue that was attracting top artists. Gomez recalled his fledgling position: "When I joined Bill, in 1966, I was twenty-one, a very raw kind of talent. I had no idea what any of that really was. I was really just mostly scared and concerned about replacing this wonderful innovator Scott LaFaro, and how I would fit in."[5]

Immediately evident was Gomez's willingness to leap into the spotlight on a solo; he did not climb into the high register but jumped straight there. It was equally clear that there were going to be a lot of notes. Evans had told Marian McPartland: "I'm looking forward to having a long-term development with Eddie. Having him is a tremendous thing for me. At this point I don't know what we're going to get into.... He's just bubbling over, and his ideas come pouring out. He has that same sort of quality that Scott had when I first heard him—he wanted to say so much, he almost played twelve solos at one time. When he reined in was when he really started communicating."[6]

A busy summer ensued, with appearances in Riverside in New Jersey, and at the Museum of Modern Art in New York. Then there was Lennie's-on-the-Turnpike just outside Boston, Lennie Sogoloff's establishment near West Peabody, highly regarded by players for its strict preservation of a good listening atmosphere. A stint at the Vanguard, with Arnie Wise at the drums, is partially preserved on *The Secret Sessions*, marking the ebullient Gomez's first appearance on record with the trio.

ᏋᏋ ᏋᏋ ᏋᏋ

At this time, guitarist Jim Hall resumed his jazz activity after recovering from illness. He teamed up again with Evans for the first of two discs the pianist was contracted to make that year for Verve. On *Intermodulation* the textural and creative amalgam of their earlier *Undercurrent* was perpetuated, the complementary interweaving of solo and supporting roles again done to perfection. Evans recalled: "I loved working with Jim Hall. The wonderful thing about him is that he is like a whole rhythm section. There is one track called 'Jazz Samba.' We could not have got the same result with a full rhythm section. It's hard to get that buoyant moving feeling."[7]

Evans's new masterpiece, "Turn Out the Stars," revealed its constructional qualities more readily in this more formal studio presentation, although it was no less lyrical for that. Its long-spun line makes a satisfying arch of melody, each bar leading us on a modulatory journey away from home; this takes in a two-level pedal-point in the bridge (via Earl Zindars, through Bill's "Walkin' Up") before the loop is joined. Although the harmonic span is a wide one, it never feels uncomfortable, such is the logic of each step. In this performance, as the players were drawn deeper into the inexorable advance, so the tempo wound down into an ever-slower-motion vortex.

The delight for the listener throughout the record is the privilege of sitting in on two supreme artists playing for pleasure—a winning formula.

⊂⊦ ⊂⊦ ⊂⊦

In early autumn 1966, in a studio on New York's East Side, Evans made an educational video for Rhapsody Films, projecting some of his thoughts about the nature, and the teaching, of jazz. The idea developed out of an NET television program on which he had played and discussed his musical background with his brother. The two had watched all the available teaching films and decided that they could supply a crucial omission: "They didn't touch the subject," Bill said. "We tried to go into the psychological things you have to go through to master this nebulous craft; not to put it in terms that were so theoretical."[8]

On the new video, called *The Universal Mind of Bill Evans*, Harry played a pivotal role by engaging Bill in conversation in various fields. The video opens with a remarkable montage sequence, put together and edited by Helen Keane. Over still photos and the opening bars of the "*Spartacus* Love Theme" from *Conversations with Myself*, Evans intones the following credo:

> I believe that all people are in possession of what might be called a "universal musical mind." All true music speaks with this universal mind—to the universal mind in all people. The understanding that results will vary only insofar as people have or have not been conditioned to the various styles of music in which the universal mind speaks.
>
> Consequently, often some effort and exposure is necessary in order to understand some of the music coming from a different period, or a different culture than that to which the listener has been conditioned.
>
> I do not agree that the layman's opinion is less of a valid judgment of music than that of the professional musician. In fact, I would often rely more on the judgment of a sensitive layman than that of a professional, since the professional, because of his constant involvement with the mechanics of music, must fight to preserve the naïveté that the layman already possesses.[9]

After the opening credits, the comedian, songwriter, and pianist Steve Allen comes on to introduce what follows. He had already given Evans airtime on his show—a rare television showcase for jazz artists—and would do so again. In due course, Allen offers a comparison between music and mathematics, equating the music of Trini Lopez or the Beach Boys with simple arithmetic and that of Evans with trigonometry or calculus. As far as it goes this is fair enough, but Evans would not have approved it as a final assessment, conscious as he was that his sophistication was only a tool toward a poetic end.

Evans reflects on his entry into jazz:

> It's obvious now that jazz is the most central and important thing in my life. Yet I never knew that. I was involved with jazz, but I went to college—I got a teacher's degree because I thought I might teach—but when the moment came, bang! I went out into jazz. It was so much a part of my inner life, and I didn't realize it. It's like, you ask a kid what do you want to be when you grow up? Well I would have said anything, because I didn't really know, and I don't think many children do. But I just became so involved with jazz…it just pulled me here, pulled me there, and finally it revealed itself as the most important thing in my life.
>
> I don't consider myself as talented as many people. But in some ways that was an advantage because I didn't have a great facility immediately—so I had to be more analytical, and in a way this forced me to build something….
>
> I think most people just don't realize the immensity of the problem, and either because they can't conquer it immediately think that they haven't got the ability, or they're so impatient to conquer it that they never do see it through. But if you do understand the problem, I think then you can enjoy your whole trip through.[10]

There follows a discussion of his experience of teaching at Music Inn in 1959. His clear attitude to the learning process has been confirmed by numerous accounts. His brother, for instance, recalled a visit Bill once made down to Harry's home in Baton Rouge: "I hadn't seen you in three years, and told the musicians in town, Bill's coming down. Boy, am I going to learn this week. And you came down and spent a week with me, and I said, 'Bill, show me those changes and harmonics [sic].' And this went on for three days, and you didn't move from the couch to show me, and about the fourth day I said, 'Bill, will you please show me,' and you walked over to the piano and said, 'Well, I don't want to deprive you of the pleasure of finding this out for yourself, and for that reason I'm not going to show you a thing. If you sit at the keyboard and get into it yourself, it'll be a marvelous experience.'"[11]

Harry Evans's playing possessed many features in common with that of his brother: for him, too, the exploration of tonal nuance was central to the touch. The brothers shared an introspection on ballads, as well as a feeling for mood and atmosphere, and sensitivity to the overall group sound; Harry's ballads would periodically erupt into fascinating cascades, with lightning, intricate twists. In addition to his full-time teaching post, he often played

three or four gigs a week—leading, as he put it, a Jekyll-and-Hyde existence
as educator by day, jazz musician by night.

⋐⋑ ⋐⋑ ⋐⋑

On October 11, 1966, a recording session for trio was set up by Creed
Taylor at Rudy Van Gelder's studio in Englewood Cliffs. Shelly Manne flew
in from Los Angeles just for the opportunity to play with Bill. *A Simple
Matter of Conviction* was Evans's and Gomez's first recording together, and
both were on edge. The pianist exhibited an uncharacteristic proportion of
slips generally, and the bassist sounded conscious, as he readily admitted, of
being in over his head. A lot of the time, the two were so hyped up with nervous energy that Shelly Manne, who made no concessions, had his work cut
out to hold them down to his beat. This was not an integrated trio but three
personalities striving for rapport. Bill had been writing furiously, and a great
deal of material was covered in the one day.

He sounded tired (on the fourth take) returning to the melody of "Only
Child," the most tuneful of four originals receiving formal airings. The title-
track was a 3/4 minor blues, a sort of invitation to the album.

"Unless It's You" was originally called "Orbit," a more descriptive title of
its overlapping ellipses, but in contrast to "Turn Out the Stars," the motion
was inexorably upward. As with many of Evans's tunes, the interest was
mostly harmonic, the top line consisting of a constantly repeated germ cell,
the significance of almost every note dependent on its attached harmony. Of
his own pieces, Evans and the trio were to find it one of the most difficult,
along with "One for Helen," "Walkin' Up" and, later, "Twelve Tone Tune."

"These Things Called Changes" was a deliberately jagged chord
sequence that evolved out of "What Is This Thing Called Love?" whose chord
changes had themselves been recently refurbished by Evans. Eliot Zigmund,
a later colleague, recalled that for many years there existed on the circuit two
ways of playing a tune: with the standard chord changes, or with Bill's
changes. "Pianists were constantly trying to figure out—transcribe—his
changes," Zigmund said. "They were trading chord sheets back and forth."[12]
"These Things Called Changes" might have been designed to floor the most
confident auditioner, but Eddie Gomez already had the job and took a fear-
less solo to prove it.

Evans took on board the energy exuded by Gomez, who put together
his best solo on "My Melancholy Baby," delivered by Evans in the same
tempo, key, and feel as on his recent European tour with Lee Konitz. The
small but dynamic Gomez displayed some of the elements of his artistry:

technical brilliance, cellolike clarity of tone, and hints of healthy aggression mixed with an extroverted lyricism. The whole enterprise was almost fever-ish—there was nothing approaching a ballad—and Evans's excitement at being on the edge of something new and challenging was manifest.

The pianist had embarked on the longest musical relationship of his career, for Eddie Gomez would remain in the trio for eleven years.

CHAPTER **15** Quiet Now

One time there was a kid lying under the piano—the best seat in the house!
—Marty Morell

In October 1966, after a Village Vanguard engagement (with Arnie Wise at the drums), Evans took his new bass player to Scandinavia. They were joined in Copenhagen by the drummer Alex Riel, who had played with Bill the previous year and who since had spent a semester at Berklee in Boston, studying with Alan Dawson. Riel, who had just been voted Danish Musician of the Year, had, with Ørsted Pedersen and the pianist Kenny Drew, a regular trio that accompanied all the great American guests at the Jazzhus Montmartre.

Among the Bill Evans Trio's engagements was a charity show for the Danish Red Cross at the Royal Theatre, with Monica Zetterlund as guest. The evening was televised, and six numbers from the trio appeared on an Italian bootleg CD, *Bill Evans Trio,* in the Green Line series Tempo di Jazz. Already notable was Eddie Gomez's willingness to carry the weight of each performance from his central position, standing as he always did between the pianist and the drummer. He seemed intent on picking up where Scott LaFaro had left off, but with a harder bite into the string. The moment a piano solo began he was active underneath, pursuing the group's chamber music concept. His energy was such that Evans was in no mood for sustaining ballads, even "Detour Ahead"—with its central, doubled-rate chord sequence—emerging as a hard swinger.

A few days later, they were in Norway, their performance at the Munch Museum in Oslo being filmed by the Norwegian Broadcasting Company. A video of this show, entitled *Bill Evans Trio in Oslo,* has been issued by KJazz. Beneath Edvard Munch's vast canvas *The Researchers,* the trio gave a stunning, swinging set, Evans's head going down early for more focused listening

Copenhagen, October 25, 1966: rehearsing with Monica Zetterlund for Danish television.

Jan Persson

on the clear-toned Steinway. Playing right on top of the bass beat, he produced some concentrated passages of invention, the ideas flowing easily.

His big problem was that he lacked a permanent drummer. Arnie Wise was playing most of the Stateside dates but disliked travel and remained uncommitted to the job. His musical commitment, though, is preserved on *The Secret Sessions,* in particular on two creative sets at the Vanguard in November, during which pianist and drummer effectively parried each other's variety and punch. There also may be heard Evans's first recorded versions of three recent movie hits: Johnny Mandel's "Emily" from *The Americanization of Emily,* André and Dory Previn's "You're Gonna Hear from Me" from *Inside Daisy Clover,* and Burt Bacharach's "Alfie" from the British film of that name. The young actor Michael Caine had just made a name in *Alfie*, and for several years, as a hushed centerpiece in sets, the title song was especially appreciated by Evans's London fans. Typically he underpinned it with strongly adapted chord changes.

Early in 1967, the drummer Joe Hunt, stalwart of groups led by Stan Getz and George Russell, spent some four months with the trio, his progression from gentle nurturing to outgoing response over that period well documented on *The Secret Sessions*. Between regular Vanguard appearances this group went on the road, ranging from Shelly's Manne Hole on the West Coast to the Town Tavern in Toronto. In that city Evans often did interviews on Ted O'Reilly's daily radio presentation *The Jazz Scene* at CJRT. His clarity as a thinker and speaker was widely respected, and he was invited to seminars and conventions to discuss such topics as the future of jazz with top critics and writers like Gene Lees, Ralph Gleason, or Leonard Feather. One such meeting was in Berkeley as part of the University of California's Jazz '67 festival weekend. Later in the year Evans played at the Los Angeles Jazz Festival, where a distinguished band was fronted by Gary McFarland, the pianist joining him for "Reflections in the Park" and "Misplaced Cowpoke" from their 1963 album *The Gary McFarland Orchestra*.

In May, Evans invited his all-time favorite drummer, Philly Joe Jones, to join the trio. This group also traveled the familiar circuit, from San Francisco to Boston. In Rhode Island the fourteenth annual Newport gathering (the wettest ever) was followed by three nights at the Kings and Queens club in Providence. Evans also played at Carleton University in Ottawa for the first time, a booking that led to several autumn appearances at nearby Camp Fortune's open-air venue.

Home base, however, was still the Village Vanguard, and the group's playing there, over the six months when Jones and Gomez were aboard, is well documented both on a double LP called *California Here I Come* and on *The Secret Sessions*, which contains cuts from several dates. In *The Secret Sessions* recordings Evans refreshed several rarely heard numbers from his past ("Easy Living," for example—much looser than on *New Jazz Conceptions*) and proffered his only recording of Sonny Rollins's "Airegin," the second eight delivered in two-part counterpoint with the help of a judiciously prodding left thumb. Evans liked Philly Joe Jones for his bustling drive and willingness to push ahead on fast numbers. Although both drummer and pianist were playing with abandon on those nights surreptitiously captured by Mike Harris, they drew in the reins somewhat for the Verve microphones and *California Here I Come*. The professional pianist learns to adapt to the instrument he is given. The grainy piano at the Vanguard, though sturdy and serviceable, was rather worn and sour—one factor dictating Evans's avoidance of the ballads at which he excelled. The youthful energy of Eddie Gomez and the exuberance of Philly Joe Jones were further injunctions to keep things swingingly on the move.

A decade had gone by since Evans had recorded "Gone with the Wind" with Tony Scott on *A Day in New York,* and this Vanguard performance gives pause for a revealing comparison. As might be expected from his artistic philosophy, many factors remained constant: procedures of invention, a certain relationship between the given song and its decoration, a general mastery of the keyboard. In the intervening years, though, Evans had grown into a world of freedom, manifesting itself both in the field of harmony—now developed into a kind of open-ended commodity that could embrace situations at will—and a world of rhythm, liberated into a fluidity that would not have been possible in the mid-fifties. Whereas the framework of the earlier blowing version seemed to strait-jacket the playing, it now functioned as a point of departure, as witnessed by the free-wheeling fours between piano and drums. The liberation was hard-won but all the more genuine for that.

All jazz musicians enjoy swapping eights and fours, but on "Wrap Your Troubles in Dreams" Evans and Jones took the pattern to its sparring limit by adding twos and then ones. This drummer's relationship to Evans was like no one else's, fully complementary without for one moment compromising his own character. Evans introduced a neat touch at the end of "On Green Dolphin Street," shifting the key up a third, but only at the last minute, halfway through the out chorus. Thus elevated, the piece seemed to go out on a "high." One more Evans original made an appearance here, the directly appealing and provisionally titled "G Waltz." As Brian Hennessey said, Gomez would first have known about it one night when receiving "the customary communication from the Evans pocket notebook." At the time, Evans felt the music was not strong enough for release, and the results emerged only posthumously in 1982.

Ever since Gomez had joined, all Bill's numbers, regardless of individual character, had been taken by the scruff of the neck and given a good shaking down. The pianist had high hopes for this particular trio, but for nonmusical reasons Philly Joe Jones was obliged to leave it. One of their last engagements was at Baker's Club in Detroit.

⊂⊱ ⊂⊱ ⊂⊱

In August 1967 Evans returned to Webster Hall to have another try at an overdubbed album for Verve. Although *Conversations with Myself* was generally regarded as a masterpiece, Evans was unhappy about its over-crowding of textures, and on *Further Conversations with Myself,* he decided to pare down from three channels to two. It was Evans's first record to be officially produced by his manager Helen Keane, who had been learning on the job with Creed Taylor. Both Taylor and Evans were beginning to rely upon her input. In effect, she had been producing Bill's records for some time. As she recalls, "Creed Taylor began asking me, 'What do you think of that tune?' and 'Why don't you talk to Bill about such and such?' After a while he said, 'You know, Helen, you are producing these dates.'"[1]

Taylor was moving on to form a label of his own, CTI, and that summer he issued Helen Keane a contract under which she would succeed him as Bill's producer for Verve, a gesture that afforded her great satisfaction. Very few managers had Helen Keane's qualities of musical judgment, and she was able to maintain this dual role to the end. "I love that maybe best of any-thing," she said. "The ideal way to function as a manager is to be the pro-ducer. They are two separate functions, but the manager really knows more about the artist than anyone else — his or her creativity, life, habits, how disci-plined or undisciplined they are when they work, what music they like best, how they choose their material, how they like to record. Therefore the man-ager can obviously be the best producer."[2]

Further Conversations opens with the arresting beauty of that new title in the Evans book, Johnny Mandel's "Emily," a fresh bloom that was to become a great favorite. The same composer's Academy Award–winning "The Shadow of Your Smile," from the 1965 film *The Sandpiper,* received a probing performance, one of the most concentrated of Evans's career, devel-oping with increasing insistence and relentless pace until finally, for the last chorus, he was forced to apply the brakes; the emotional range ran the gamut from serenity almost to anger. His two fluffy characters from *Trio '64* reap-peared — Santa Claus still practicing his Alberti bass, and Little Lulu bowing out in a protracted series of surprise codettas, the mischievous cartoon kid finally quitting the stage with an engaging twinkle.

By contrast, a stark emotional directness was brought to Denny Zeitlin's fine tune "Quiet Now," another Evans mainstay-in-the-making. Zeitlin, a pianist-composer (and psychiatrist) from Chicago, was a one-time pupil of George Russell. Also influenced by Evans, he had a trio with Charlie Haden on bass and Jerry Granelli on drums. Evans had first heard him as the pianist on Jeremy Steig's *Flute Fever.* While holding down a Monday night gig at the Trident in Sausalito, Zeitlin had recorded "Quiet Now" — Evans's introduc-tion to the tune.

Finally, a new Evans original, "Funny Man," was recorded for the first time. What a Broadway blockbuster of a finale this underrated tune, with its heart-stopping modulation, would have made. Such success would have pleased its composer, but he never would have thought to push for it.

Further Conversations was nominated for a Grammy.

⊂≣ ⊂≣ ⊂≣

That autumn Arnie Wise rejoined the trio for about six months and was persuaded by Evans to cross the Atlantic for an engagement at Ronnie Scott's. The club had just moved into more spacious premises in Frith Street, a few streets away from the original establishment. While in London, the group stood in for the indisposed Teddy Wilson and Albert Nicholas at London's Jazz Expo '67, an event that tied in with George Wein's Newport Jazz Festival in Europe. But at the Odeon in Hammersmith, the substitute group did not go down well with the more traditionalist fans. On the same trip were concerts in Italy at the Bologna Festival and in Switzerland at the Lugano Festival. Evans was including "Yesterdays" in his sets at this time, and a performance of it was televised from Lugano.

This trio played two engagements at the Vanguard in the new year. With some tracks from the first of these, along with half a dozen earlier dates, *The Secret Sessions* helps to preserve the scintillating and integrated trio work of Arnie Wise, one of the forgotten talents. At the second engagement they were filmed by Leland Wyler for *Camera Three* as part of a seventeen-minute portrait entitled "Bill Evans." They played Shelly's Manne Hole and the Both/And on the West Coast, Sammy Mitchell reporting on Wise's contribution at the Both/And: "His light cymbal work was the ideal goad to Evans's sometimes ethereal piano, and he had a smart snap when the pace grew heated."[3] They went on to the Top of the Gate for the whole of March.

Later, yet another edition of the Bill Evans Trio was filmed for the TV series *Dial M for Music*. This time the drummer was Jack DeJohnette, a recent arrival in New York from Chicago who had been doing great things with the Charles Lloyd quartet and who was recommended by Eddie Gomez. The program included Evans playing solo over two prerecorded tracks of "Emily" to demonstrate the overdubbing technique used on the *Conversations* albums.

In early June 1968, this new group—there seemed to be a different trio every few months—played at the Top of the Gate. They then embarked for Europe, appearing at the fashionable Swiss health resort of Montreux, host to a well-established classical music festival and now graced with its own one-year-old jazz event. Gene Lees, with local businessman Claude Nobs,

At the Montreux Jazz Festival, Switzerland 1968, with bassist Eddie Gomez and drummer Jack DeJohnette.

Jan Persson

arranged for the trio to perform there as one of the headliners in the festival's second year.

For the planned album, *At the Montreux Jazz Festival*, Helen Keane's role in production was all-embracing, from front-of-house to tape. This was yet another Evans, already energized by Gomez and now responding to Jack DeJohnette's open-ended conception. Evans said, "With Charles, Jack was playing an all-out freestyle, and many people really wondered how I even could conceive of selecting him to come with the group. But Jack is very intelligent, [and] has wide scope musically. He's been fitting in beautifully and has a tremendous creative mind. He has something else going that fits that no other drummer would conceive of."[4]

DeJohnette had learned the piano before the drums, and during their preparations in Montreux he was to be observed showing Evans the chords to "Here's That Rainy Day," a tune that Bill recorded later in the year. Indeed, Jack had been well established as a pianist in his hometown of Chicago before hitting New York as *the* new drummer on the scene. Evans, clinging to the spirit of his recent trio with Philly Joe Jones, was in good mental condition for working within a freer context than usual, and he incorporated the young DeJohnette's approach with ease.

The rapid-fire opener, "One for Helen" (from Bill's Town Hall debut), exhibited the essential ingredients of this thrilling group: the wound-up Evans, the percussive rhythmic force of Gomez, and DeJohnette's inspired coloration and lethal drive. Recovering from the onslaught of the first two numbers, we may catch our breath with DeJohnette's living, whispering brushes on "Mother of Earl" and reflect on a new quality evident in the music making, a heightened, all-around commitment to the due meaning of every note—nothing wasted, nothing routine.

The album won Evans his second Grammy Award (for best instrumental jazz performance, small group). There had been skeptics at MGM/Verve when Helen Keane stepped into Creed Taylor's producing shoes, but they were mollified when *Further Conversations with Myself* was nominated at N.A.R.A.S. and then the Montreux album won. It was the first of seven winners that Bill and Helen would have together.

To those concerned with music as art rather than as money-spinner, though, the Grammy winners' *Best on Record* TV broadcast left much to be desired. On behalf of those winners from both the classical and jazz sections who were not invited to perform, Evans wrote to *Down Beat* columnist Leonard Feather, recently elected secretary of the academy's Los Angeles branch, to express his anger. "I was under the impression," he complained, "that N.A.R.A.S. was trying to build a meaningful award, but apparently they gave way to the wishes of the network or sponsor."[5] Feather replied to the effect that the academy had been caught between art and TV ratings.

A week after Montreux, the trio played to a studio audience in Hilversum, the radio capital of Holland. The formality of the radio station atmosphere was a jarring change from the free-and-easy festival event, but it is a tribute to the commitment of the artists and the discernment of both audiences that great music was made and appreciated on each occasion.

They went on to play four weeks at Ronnie Scott's in London, Brian Priestley beginning his review with the piquant observation: "When Bill Evans is in town, one goes not to listen so much as to worship."[6] It was at this stage in the trio's evolution that performances of "Nardis" began to assume marathon proportions: twenty-minute interpretations were a nightly event, centered around Jack DeJohnette's thrilling solo and usually ending the second of the three evening sets when the place was packed. Evans always spoke highly of his new drummer in interviews. "As a matter of fact," he said, "he's getting me off my musical ass."[7]

Another nightly feature that emerged was Eddie Gomez's virtuoso spot on "Embraceable You," Evans merely touching in the bare bones by way of charting progress. On his fifty-year-old, machine-made bass, Gomez carried the whole song. The performance switched in and out of two tempi, both in 4/4; a half-note in the slower tempo was equivalent to three quarter-notes in the faster. To put it another way, dividing the slower tempo's minim into a triplet of crotchets and adding one would give four beats, or one bar, in the new tempo. Additionally, key changes from G to C and back again coincided with these speed changes. This was the cunning framework, but the execution was carried off with evident spontaneity, leaving me, at any rate, reeling and thinking, *How on earth did they get that together?*

Yet another "trick" (as Bill would delight in calling it) taken on board that year was the alternation of 3/4 and 4/4 time signatures, per chorus, on "Someday My Prince Will Come." In his rollicking performances of this number, Evans took a leaf out of DeJohnette's book, deliberately playing his rapid, scurrying runs in free time.

These numbers, in their new guises, had been included on the Montreux album. Evans delighted in showing off his two colleagues, Gomez's feature on "Embraceable You" nicely balancing DeJohnette's on "Nardis." With the insertion of his own solo spot on "I Loves You, Porgy," the leader was extracting maximum variety from his trio's sets.

In those days Eddie Gomez in full flight was one of the great phenomena in jazz. With his newly developed strength, and with confidence born of a good year and a half in the trio, he was being given generous solo space. A powerhouse of dynamism, he consistently galvanized whole sets. He was the master of all his pianist's unusual sequences, and no tempo seemed too daunting for his lightning finger coordination, a scurrying activity that constantly enlivened his solos. It alternated with a lyrical invention, sometimes harmonized, as with LaFaro, guitarist-fashion across the strings. Occasionally the phrasing would be punctuated by a plunge to the depths, the instrument punished by a great slapping, as if to clear the air for the next assault on the peaks. This blatant exhibition of string vibrating on fingerboard characterized, to an exaggerated degree, all his playing, and contributed to his rhythmic power.

The supporting group at Ronnie Scott's included Dave Holland on bass. One evening in mid-July, Miles Davis took everyone by surprise by dropping into the club. As a result of what he heard that night, both Holland and DeJohnette were invited into the trumpeter's band. By the end of November, DeJohnette had already recorded some music with Miles that would appear on *Directions*, and in due course he would join him for an extended period. Without the call from Davis, DeJohnette would undoubtedly have stayed with Evans longer; Miles Davis was the only musician at the time capable of enticing the drummer away from Bill's trio. Having himself been with Davis a decade earlier, Evans ruefully had to admit that he was in no position to argue.

ᒧ ᒧ ᒧ

When recording *Further Conversations with Myself,* Evans had said that he would not be surprised if his next studio album turned out to be a solo effort. And so, with *Alone,* the paring down was complete. We are fortunate to have the pianist's own thoughts on the album cover:

> Perhaps the hours of greatest pleasure in my life have come about as a result of the capacity of the piano to be in itself a complete expressive musical medium. In retrospect, I think that these countless hours of aloneness with music unified the directive energy of my life. At those times when I have achieved this sense of oneness while playing alone, the many technical or analytic aspects of the music happened of themselves with positive rightness which always served to remind me that to understand music most profoundly one only has to be listening well. Perhaps it is a peculiarity of mine that despite the fact that I am a professional performer, it is true that I have always preferred playing without an audience. This has nothing to do with my desire to communicate or not, but [is] rather I think just a problem of personal self-consciousness which had to be conquered through discipline and concentration.[8]

His playing on the album conveyed a feeling of unaffected nobility. Evans made no special effort to produce beautiful tone, but did so anyway—it was simply the way he played. There was much oscillation between keys a major third apart, except on the superbly paced "Never Let Me Go," which built and arched consistently in one tonality and unified mood. There are two "bonus" tracks on the CD release, chips off the workbench block that Evans would surely not have wanted to be issued—witness the disdain with which he casually finger-flicked the endings away, as if to say: *No good, forget that one!*

This LP won him his third Grammy award.

ᒧ ᒧ ᒧ

That fall, Evans used two other drummers for his engagements. The brief contribution of one of them, John Dentz, has been captured on *The Secret Sessions.* Then Gomez, who had introduced Jack DeJohnette to Evans, did the same with Marty Morell, who settled in with the trio for a month at the Top of the Gate. This particular group departed for Raleigh, North Carolina, to a thriving suburban outpost called the Frog and Nightgown.

Drummer Marty Morell stayed with the trio from 1968 to 1974.
Lee Tanner

Morell also joined the trio on another installment of NBC's *Camera Three*, Evans's third appearance on that program. On an unaccompanied "I Loves You, Porgy," the TV direction mixed to a remarkable overhead shot for the second bridge, by which time Evans had his head well down in absorption, resembling nothing so much from this angle as a praying mantis at the keyboard, his gaunt arms and legs seeming to elongate the strings.

The flutist Jeremy Steig, whom Evans had met in Florida with Warren Bernhardt, was guesting on the program and joined the trio in the "*Spartacus* Love Theme." This was kept short, to leave as much room as possible for the mainstay of the show—a "working session" in front of the audience, in which Evans analyzed the built-in structure of "So What" and the quartet's subsequent approach to the song.

His lucidity served him well here, and at the keyboard he was able to explain, in layman's terms, the nature of the raw material:

I'm going to lay out a routine of how we can handle this form to make a balanced and well-shaped performance for the guys. Say, first, let's put something in front—a preparation or an introduction. Let's make that entirely free, just whatever we get into; start without too much tension, and let's build the tension until we get up to a point where we can just more or less relax it quickly down into whenever Eddie wants to give that first statement. Then, after the thematic chorus, Jeremy, you play two choruses but don't build too much; I'll play a linear obbligato behind you for one chorus, and maybe some chord things for another chorus. Then I'll improvise alone with the rhythm section for two choruses; then you improvise and build as much as you want for a couple of choruses. Then Eddie, you can play a chorus, leading back finally into the theme again. We'll take the theme out one chorus, and then just extend it with the same motion beyond the out-chorus until it just goes out with that motion.[9]

This, with extra solo choruses all round, was how the piece was performed by these artists on Bill's next record for Verve, *What's New*, made early in 1969. In general, the traditional nature of the Evans approach acted as both anchor and foil to Steig's turbulence.

Jeremy Steig comes from a highly artistic family and has illustrated his own record covers. He admits that his imaginative innovations in sound came about at least partly as the result of a motorcycle accident in 1962 that paralyzed the left side of his face, affecting his hearing. He was a leader in the jazz-rock field with his own recently formed group Jeremy and the Satyrs, in which, incidentally, Eddie Gomez played.

Late in 1968 Steig lived in the Village and sat in on frequent late sets with Evans's trio at the Vanguard and the Top of the Gate. Warren Bernhardt told me of those occasions: "Many times Bill had Jeremy (and myself, too) sit in at the Vanguard. We used to play the last set for him. Sometimes he would listen to us, other times he would disappear quietly while we played—he called this doing his 'phantom' bit." It was actually Philly Joe Jones who first called Bill "The Phantom." Anyone wanting a quick word after a set had a problem—he just vanished.

Marty Morell was proving himself to be an alert, clean, and straight-ahead drummer, as can be heard on a handful of tracks from this era on *The Secret Sessions*. He was to stay with the trio for more than six years, resulting in the longest period of stable personnel that Evans ever had. Gomez and Morell were the same age, the thirty-nine-year-old Evans giving them fifteen years apiece. The pianist's commitment to music would not admit the notion of fading energy, but his young colleagues infused him with new spirit nevertheless.

Age aside, Evans was happy with his newfound percussionist, and the trio did further spells at the Top of the Gate, a room upstairs at the Village

Gate that booked mostly pianists. The Top of the Gate was fast becoming second in frequency only to the Vanguard in Bill's New York diary. Around this time George Wein initiated a Sunday-night jazz series at the Fillmore East—predominantly a rock, blues, and pop venue—and the trio with Jeremy Steig featured in the second of these events. It was a bad time for jazz, though, and attendance was poor, the concerts fizzling out early in the series.

On March 12, 1969, Evans donned tuxedo and black tie and went to the Hotel Astor in New York to receive his Grammy Award for the Montreux album. For a year or so now he had been maintaining that physical aspect observed at first hand by Gene Lees, who in Montreux had found him "relaxed, tanned, and in a better frame of mind than at any time in the many years I've known him."[10] Later in 1969, Evans's picture on the cover of *Down Beat* would present him in his most positive mien to date, a portrait of the artist seemingly, for that moment, in control of his life.

ᴄᴌ ᴄᴌ ᴄᴌ

The Atlantic crossing was now becoming routine, and the trio went to Holland to make two recordings at the Vara-studio in Hilversum. For one they improvised on the Claus Ogerman scores of "Granados" and "Pavane" with the Metropole Symphony Orchestra, conducted by Dolf van der Linden; for the other the trio recorded fourteen numbers, including a rarity for Bill, Duke Ellington's "I Let a Song Go Out of My Heart." A friend sent me a tape of this session, which was aired again recently by Dutch radio. The group was in top form and very well recorded; like many European radio tapings the session would make a fine CD.

In May, at Ray Iverson's Senate Lounge in Denver, the trio received an enthusiastic response from the packed clientele. Back in Manhattan, they went on the *Steve Allen Show*. Thriving, working musicians, they jetted back and forth, fitting in the opening night at Newport (Jeremy Steig sitting in) between some of the regular West Coast clubs like the Manne Hole and San Francisco's Jazz Workshop.

In July they appeared at the inaugural Pescara Jazz Festival on Italy's Adriatic coast. Unlike the Montreux performance a year earlier, this program was officially recorded by radio only, with no thought of release on disc. The fact that the bulk of the music came out on two records "made by a legit company" (as the pianist once put it in an interview—the label was Joker in Japan) did nothing to appease his, or Helen Keane's, indignation. Nevertheless, on these issues—*Piano Perspective* and *Autumn Leaves*—there are some fine tracks.

Any one of four consecutive tunes on *Autumn Leaves*, starting with

"Emily," would stand alone as a first-class example of the pianist at work with his own group. In fact, there were many hundreds of such performances. Taking a typical club night of three sets of, say, six numbers each, one can begin to do the sums. Many playings fell short of this Plimsoll line—the best musicians are only human—and, conversely, some performances were truly outstanding, but on this particular gig (and at this period generally) things were nicely over par.

Something the pianist said on the video with his brother is revealing here. Remarking on Bill's professional discipline, Harry observed that he seemed to need no time in preparation or getting in the mood. Bill replied: "You learn to throw that switch. As a matter of fact, there's plenty of times when you just feel like, 'I can't possibly get up there and play.' But as soon as you get up there, when the moment comes, you have that discipline. There's a professional level of creativity that I can depend on, and which is satisfactory for public performance always. . . . But those other high levels which happen just occasionally are really thrilling. You don't know when the heck they're gonna come. There's no way to try to do it, you can't try to recapture it; all you can do is always look for it, and sometimes it happens."[11]

In the gradual development of his trio repertoire the pianist devised and maintained a format that was special to each number. "Quiet Now," in Pescara, was a case in point: for the final chorus, he commenced solo, building agitato on the bridge to the reentry of bass and drums for the last eight in tempo; a big, drawn out coda ensued. One track, "So What," is preserved only on *It Happened in . . . Pescara (1969–1989)*, a commemorative double LP on the Philology label of single tracks culled from the first twenty years of the festival.

Since joining the trio, Marty Morell had taken the lead when moving to sticks, and his sometime initiative of setting off a notch higher on the metronome produced a thrilling outcome. He was particularly good, too, at coming down to a hushed ballad level, using his brushes to telling effect, and contributing in a real way to the unique trio sound that Evans created.

The group was in peak condition, returning to New York for residencies at the usual clubs. From time to time, by way of varying these continuous spells, Evans would participate, along with other top players, in fund-raising events. These included the Midnight Concert in Harlem at the Apollo Theater (part of a campaign for a jazz center in the community) and a benefit at Town Hall for the Congregation Beth Torah of Upper Nyack, New York. In spite of the heavy schedule, Eddie Gomez was able to play occasionally elsewhere, joining Joe Henderson's quartet at the Vanguard and the Thad Jones–Mel Lewis band at the Laurel Festival.

⌐⌐ ⌐⌐ ⌐⌐

Perhaps it was the Russian strain in Evans's blood that evoked a special response from his Scandinavian followers. Along with Yugoslavia, which he visited shortly afterward, these regular northern haunts were the nearest in geography and kinship he would ever get to his motherland; his countless Russian fans were forever deprived of the chance to hear him on their own soil. Most of November 1969 was taken up with a Scandinavian tour, taking in Göteborg and Stockholm in Sweden and Århus in Denmark before moving on to an especially favorite venue, Copenhagen's Jazzhus Montmartre.

One evening there the Danish Jazz Centre made a private recording, and much later the tapes were brought to the attention of Helen Keane by Karl Knudsen and Evans's discographer, Peter H. Larsen. Permission was obtained from the Bill Evans Estate for their release on Milestone in 1987 as *Jazzhouse* and *You're Gonna Hear from Me*. Marty Morell sets the scene: "Whenever we played the Montmartre, the place was packed. It was like a special event in Copenhagen. We loved it there. Every corner that could hold a body, there was a body. One time there was a kid lying under the piano—the best seat in the house! Nobody made a sound when we played, except for the tremendous applause. It was an incredible experience."[12]

These performances were similar in feeling to those at the Village Vanguard on *California Here I Come*, representing the trio having a good time in ideal surroundings. The mood was happy-go-lucky, tempos were up, ballads moved smoothly along. Often the driving insistence of the improvising was such that the playing could well be called "hot" from the famously "cool" pianist. While on brushes, Marty Morell seemed reluctant to go along with the intensity of Evans's propulsion, but he was happy for a tandem launch when moving over to sticks. The pianist, not to put too fine a point on it, was pushing ahead like crazy, a factor that would cause discomfort to more than one colleague through the following decade.

"Stella by Starlight" came in for the two-tempo treatment around this time, but with an extra twist in the application. Both the bass and the piano solos, as well as the out chorus, underwent the gear change in midflight: that is, on the turnaround of the respective solo choruses, and at the middle eight in the out chorus. (There is another example on *The Secret Sessions* from the following February.) Then, as if to say, *That one's well and truly dealt with*, Evans left the piece largely alone till almost the end of his life.

Four days later the trio played a concert in Amsterdam, preserved on the Affinity label as *Quiet Now*. Evans eased into "Very Early" as if out of nowhere, his preparatory chords nudging upward by the semitone toward a polished presentation of the theme. With incredible ease, the trio had moved into a swinging, high gear by the third chorus. The pianist's soft-toned shadowing behind the first bass chorus is worth listening to once in isolation for its smooth, continuous cushion. Eddie Gomez recalled this sort of playing much later: "How I bathed in that glorious sound he prodded out of the piano, lost and distracted by the sheer beauty of his accompaniment during my bass solos."[13]

In December, TRO published a second book of music, *Bill Evans Plays*. This contained five transcriptions taken from the albums *A Simple Matter of Conviction* and *Bill Evans at Town Hall, Vol. 1*. Evans had great faith in the book's uncredited transcriber, Art Murphy, who went on to produce the piano solos in a posthumous volume called *Bill Evans/the 70's*. Art told me how he met Evans in 1963: "I screwed up my courage and went down to the Vanguard to see Bill, various transcriptions in hand. Gary Peacock and Paul Motian were in the band. I accosted Bill during a break and started pulling manuscript from an envelope. Bill looked horrified and tried to escape, probably thinking I was going to show him some tunes of mine and ask for his help. I quickly told him they were *his* tunes, and he relaxed and looked them over. I don't mean to imply that Bill was arrogant or inaccessible; on the contrary, I think he was extremely modest and reluctant to criticize other people's work." So it was that Evans recommended Murphy to TRO for *Bill Evans Plays*. Neither Bill nor Art was around to proof the galleys, and a few errors slipped through.

The late sixties had been lean years for jazz interest, especially in America, but Evans had managed to keep going, both on the road and in the studio. He reflected on the decade thus: "The whole rock scene pushed jazz into a corner in the sixties. Work and recording opportunities were less frequent, particularly for new talents. I was fortunate because I had obtained some recognition prior to the rock explosion, and I could never complain that I had no work."[14]

Nor was there a shortage of awards for that work. In 1967 Evans had topped Japan's *Swing Journal* readers' poll for the first time, a position he was to hold for five consecutive years. In 1968, with his group's reputation boosted by DeJohnette's presence, he won the *Down Beat* critics' poll again, as well as Great Britain's *Melody Maker* award. Then in 1969 came Scandinavia's Edison Award, and Evans's old college, Southeastern Louisiana, endowed him with its first Distinguished Alumnus Award.

Around this time, a trip to Russia was canceled at the last minute. The trio was set to depart from Kennedy Airport in New York City, but Evans was busted by airport customs and spent two or three days in jail for possession of heroin. The press reported that he canceled the trip due to political reservations. The experience had a monumental effect: soon after, he and Ellaine entered a methadone rehabilitation program.

CHAPTER **16**   Living Time

Many clubs pay more attention to their trash cans than the house piano.
— Bill Evans

A promising turning point in Evans's physical condition came at the beginning of 1970, as he sought help to end more than a decade's use of heroin. (Ironically, there was about to be a record influx of the substance onto the New York City streets.) Brian Hennessey observed: "It was probably the deep personal desire to acquire a family home away from New York and have children of his own that provided the impetus to defeat his dependency."[1]

After embarking on a methadone program at Rockefeller University he lived for several years free of heroin. The opium-based substitute slows the body down and minimizes the tormenting effect of withdrawal. It, too, can be misused, either as a substitute for heroin or in its own right; it doesn't give the same "buzz," but it is nevertheless addictive. But Evans received carefully controlled treatment. His lifestyle improved beyond recognition as a result; friends and fans observed a changed personality, almost a metamorphosis. The frequently sullen, withdrawn, and unapproachable figure of old manifested a new frankness in acknowledging the people around him. Likewise on the bandstand, that apparent indifference to audience presence was replaced by a smile and a nod, albeit reserved, toward the listeners' welcome.

Musically, too, he started the decade with a new departure, recording for the first time on the Fender-Rhodes electric piano. Harold Rhodes had collaborated with Leo Fender (inventor of the electric bass guitar) to create the new instrument, and manufacture had begun in 1965. From the end of 1967 onward, the electric keyboard was used in various Miles Davis groups by Herbie Hancock, Chick Corea, and Joe Zawinul, and its sound went on to become a mainstay of jazz-rock bands during the seventies.

The Fender-Rhodes is touch sensitive; the pianist can actually mold a line in a smoother way on it than on the conventional piano. There is a soft attack within each note, and the sound seems to die more slowly. Although strings are not plucked—the "strings" are in reality metal bars—one feels when playing rather as if they were; the musician feels very much in contact with the sound, and well able to manipulate it by weight. In a curious way, and at a not-too-subtle level, "shading" by touch is made easier than on what henceforth became known as the acoustic piano. Harold Rhodes said: "The ultimate vindication for a lifetime of effort spent in the development of a new musical instrument is the thrill of hearing it respond to the deft and sensitive touch of such an artist as Bill Evans."[2]

For his first album using the Fender-Rhodes (as well as the Steinway) Evans collaborated with a composer of theatrical pedigree, Michael Leonard. Helen Keane had met Leonard many years earlier at a summer musical theater, and followed a hunch in bringing them together. The MGM record that resulted, *From Left to Right*, gives pleasure from beginning to end. Evans frequently functioned on both keyboards simultaneously, his right hand on the Fender-Rhodes, his left on the Steinway. He used the Fender-Rhodes sparingly, restricting it mostly to single lines with an occasional octave reinforcement; he was wary of getting involved in harmony on the electric instrument.

Two tunes from the pen of Earl Zindars, "Soirée" and "Lullaby for Helene," lent themselves to this pure approach, the latter inspired by Earl and Anne Zindars's daughter. Bill was best man at the Zindars's wedding and became a good family friend. Occasionally he would go to their home for dinner, and Helene has a favorite memory of one of Uncle Bill's stories:

> Lying down on the sofa (as he was nearly always in poor health and needed to rest at any occasion), he started telling us some recent stories about himself. I'll never forget that special twinkle in his eye that sparkled with a combination of knowledge and childlike innocence, all at the same time. He decided to tell us the one about his "Favorite Cookies."
>
> His eyes gleaming, he sat up while beginning his story, telling us that his favorite cookies were Pepperidge Farm molasses crisp cookies—but that wasn't specific enough for him: these cookies had to be burnt around the edges, while completely without air pockets or bubbles. Further, to insure that they were indeed crisp, he would check the serial number on the package. If it was within a certain range and followed a certain "secret sequence," then (and only then) was it the right bag of cookies. Most likely improvising a little, he recounted "documented experiences" of his travelling many miles and rummaging countless shelves to find his "favorite cookies," and throwing them away if they didn't measure up to his standards.[3]

Mickey Leonard arranged a children's song of Bill's as a montage of sections in different keys. The composer described its evolution: "I had written a little tune called 'Children's Play Song' which I always felt was just a little simple nothing, but Mickey fell in love with it and wrote what was a very austere, slow version of it, because I had shown him how you'd harmonize it if you wanted to play it in a slow way. The way I conceived of it was the type of tune kids would whistle while out playing hopscotch or something. I had suggested, on hearing the take back, that playing it entirely slow was a mistake and that we should prelude it by recording children at a playground in front and back, then I'd superimpose the original version over it."[4]

A new Michel Legrand tune, "What Are You Doing the Rest of Your Life?" was given a richly romantic setting. The song became a favorite of the trio's after this recording; there is an example on *The Secret Sessions* on which Eddie Gomez is still undecided about the bass line. Then, epitomizing the flavor of the album, Leonard took Evans's electric piano solo from the first take of Luis Eça's bossa nova "The Dolphin" and added flutes and piccolo in close harmony over held strings. Both versions were offered, side by side.

The aim of *From Left to Right* was far removed from the continuing work of the trio. This album and the earlier *The V.I.P.s* are the only Bill Evans records to be filed appropriately under "easy listening" at your local record store. The trio then spent three days in Copenhagen collaborating with the Royal Danish Symphony Orchestra and the Danish Radio Big Band in some arrangements by that country's trumpeter and composer, Palle Mikkelborg. For a television program called *Speak Low*, Mikkelborg made a continuous suite from Evans material, including "Time Remembered," "My Bells," and "Waltz for Debby." "Waltz" came in two settings that delighted Evans, one broodingly romantic, the other delicately embellished with sweet-and-sour fragments from woodwind and strings.

ᗾ ᗾ ᗾ

The trio was invited to make its second appearance at the Montreux Jazz Festival. Again, Géo Voumard introduced them to the eager audience, recalling one particular Saturday almost two years ago to the day, when an unforgettable moment of "sensibilité, intelligence, et musicalité" had taken place. He hoped, courtesy of the three musicians, that the audience would relive that experience. He need not have worried. The atmosphere was, if possible, even more electric than before, the crowd rowdier, but no less appreciative; and little wonder, for the performance was sensational.

Evans recalled:

We had a good reception on our first visit to Montreux in 1968 but this evening surpassed it. Enthusiasm is infectious although the artist never really believes that the one specific performance to which an audience responds is really that much better than a hundred others.

We have noticed that our audiences seem to be getting younger and this gives me new impetus. If we were just getting half a dozen drunks every night, I would have to think seriously about continuing in this business. But at the moment, I am heartened by the audience interest. Jazz will never be a mass appeal music but there is nothing more that I can give an audience than I give myself. I'm not trying to be abstract or esoterical. I'm just trying to play my conception of music, and I have to direct myself to that rather than the audience because I'm the only one who can tell if I'm achieving the objective. When an audience responds with applause, it can give real impetus, but if I had a choice, I'd prefer no expression of enthusiasm as, to me, it can be a distraction.[5]

That the audience should be so responsive to an artist who is not in any way pandering to them says much for that particular public's taste, as well as for Evans's ability to communicate. The trio's two sets that night were taped by Radio Suisse Romande. The one released, as *Montreux II*, is on Creed Taylor's CTI label.

Evans had hardly played for several weeks, but you would never know it. The introduction recently created for "Very Early" brooded with menace, Eddie Gomez moving quickly from his first note; Marty Morell joined, and the trio was instantly in a working groove, swinging hard. For contrast, "Alfie" formed the archetypal Evans showcase-ballad, rapt and concentrated. The rest of the set was cumulative in excitement and quality, the strength and resilience of the pianist's fingerwork remarkable. Since 1965 Johnny Carisi's "Israel" had brought out the best in Evans, and this pummeling version drove hell for leather. "I Hear a Rhapsody" followed, by contrast, panting in its wake, Evans miraculously "chording" a skeleton of the melody, two-fisted, in his solo. There was an unimportant but nice personal touch, which would become routine, introduced here on a rare revival of "Peri's Scope" — a slow (timeless) glissando the length of the keyboard, first down and then back up, setting up the drum break.

With the early seventies came the advent of double–bass pickup technology, and Eddie Gomez took full advantage of the resulting immediacy of sound. For one thing, he tried out more harmonics than usual, half stopping the string, newly confident that the effect would be heard. A rising sequence of fourths in the bass line of "How My Heart Sings," in accord with the tuning of the instrument, lent itself ideally to this procedure.

A few days later, the trio was again in fine form for the Kongsberg Jazz Festival in Norway. According to Peter Larsen, it was most likely in that month of June that the trio visited the city of Villingen in the Black Forest, where Hans Georg Brunner-Schwer had built a state-of-the-art studio. Recordings made there came to be marketed on the Musik Produktion Schwarzwald label (MPS); that was where, during the sixties, Oscar Peterson had made, by his own estimate, some of his finest records. "Turn Out the Stars" was one track recorded privately in that studio by the Bill Evans Trio and included on an MPS promotional record.

Back in New York, the trio slotted in to the steady club work upon which it could rely, spending the whole of July, for example, at the Top of the Gate restaurant. The *New Yorker* magazine's nightlife listing for this engagement followed typical editorial style: "Bill Evans' refulgent trio plays for cocktails and dining."[6] As an Englishman visiting New York during the seventies, I was always astounded at the incongruity of the nightly role played in that city by some of the great names in jazz, pianists in particular. Making a point once of seeking out Jimmy Rowles at his regular club, Bradley's, and anticipating some first-class listening pleasure, I was dismayed to find his efforts all but drowned by the general clatter of bar and restaurant business. Of the professional piano soloist Evans said: "It is sad that this great tradition in jazz is in danger of extinction because of the prevalent public attitude relegating a single pianist to background for conversation or dinner."[7]

The trio's autumn schedule brought some fresh venues and occasions. In California, as part of the Monterey Jazz Festival in September, they were broadcast by KJAZ, teaming up with the fifty-two-piece Oakland Youth Chamber Orchestra in three of Claus Ogerman's *Symphony Orchestra* scores. Then, at Seattle's Northwest Jazz Spectacular, Evans participated in a piano workshop with the fast-rising pianists Herbie Hancock, Keith Jarrett, and Joe Zawinul. At the Center Arena the trio survived colored lighting changes during the evening set that they shared with the quintets of Herbie Hancock and Miles Davis. Evans hated the visual distraction, and he and Morell appeared bored, leaving it to the inspired Eddie Gomez to carry the spot.

In November the trio was in Chicago, recording a half-hour set for television. The film was made for use in Los Angeles and was later relayed from the Homewood Theatre in Hollywood under the title *Jazz Sounds and a Cool Groove*. Mundell Lowe, the guitarist who had "discovered" Evans, was then music supervisor at Homewood. The Evans set was issued as *Homewood* on Red Bird Records, a rare pressing indeed. Playing a fine Baldwin piano, Evans presented a clear-cut, hard-driving set, but with theme statements spaciously delivered as if for maximum clarity on the inferior sound of television. His uncharacteristic but effective solo on "So What" conjured up, for a startling moment, shades of McCoy Tyner.

The trio ended the year with a five-week stay at the Top of the Gate, Lee Konitz sitting in frequently.

⋐ ⋐ ⋐

At the start of 1971 Evans signed with Columbia, a childhood dream come true. Although the offer was good, it turned out to be a short association. The company's president, Clive Davis, another of the corporate producers, was eager for Evans to record a jazz-rock fusion album, but the pianist had other ideas, as did Eddie Gomez, who recalls:

> Columbia had a brainstorm…to do an album with Bill playing acoustic and electric piano, and me playing acoustic and electric bass. They rented me one for a few months and finally came the day that we were recording in the studio, and the thing was just a harrowing experience. I'd practiced a little bit but it was not for me, as the song goes. It was a disaster really, because of my playing. So anyway they switched it over to a trio album and we recorded *The Bill Evans Album* on Columbia, which won a Grammy. I feel responsible, just for having been such a god-awful electric bass player. So…I didn't end up playing bass guitar on that album. That idea was deep-sixed. I am going on record here by saying that I am not on record playing the electric bass![8]

Evans did stick with the Fender-Rhodes, though, alternating and combining it with the Steinway, as on *From Left to Right*. He gave some of his views on pianos in general to Brian Hennessey:

> I've been happy to use the Fender-Rhodes to add a little color to certain performances but only as an adjunct. No electric instrument can begin to compare with the quality and resources of a good acoustic piano. Of course, many clubs pay more attention to their trash cans than the house piano but I've been lucky in this respect and most of the instruments I use are acceptable though not always in tune. It also takes a couple of nights to adjust to a different instrument. You can reduce the risks I suppose by carrying your own keyboard with you but that's not for me. What I really like is to follow Oscar into a club. They ship in a new Bösendorfer for him and sometimes they forget to collect it until I have been through. That's a thrill for me and those nine extra bass notes under the flap on the big Bösendorfer are just out of this world.[9]

Certain pianists have endorsed certain makes of instrument: for instance, Oscar Peterson the Bösendorfer (and earlier the Baldwin); Glenn Gould, McCoy Tyner, and Keith Jarrett the Steinway; Sviatoslav Richter the Yamaha; and Erroll Garner and Dave Brubeck the Baldwin. In due course, Bill Evans, too, would become a Baldwin artist.

One time he wanted to rent a Fender-Rhodes 88, the one with the longer keyboard. "I went to a store," he told Jim Aikin, "and went up to the loft where they keep them, and I tried perhaps twenty of them, and not one was good. Not one. They were so beat up and noisy, with pedal noise and so forth, and actions beat all to hell. So I suggested that they keep at least one for people who are not going to use it as a pounding board, for pianists that would play it like a piano. And they didn't go for the idea. I don't know why, because the rental for that one week probably would have damn near paid for it at their rates, you know?"[10]

On the new record, *The Bill Evans Album*, all seven numbers were written by Evans, four of them new. (The trio also tackled his difficult "Fun Ride" but it was not issued.) "The Two Lonely People" must be his longest tune. Gene Lees has described how he likes to put words to music, whereas Evans liked to fit his music to a given text. Carol Hall had done the former when she added words to "Very Early," but for this new song she wrote a poignant verse narrative, originally called "The Man and the Woman," and sent it to Evans, who said: "It was an unusual lyric, and it gave the form to the piece; consequently the form is not just standard. It so happens that I can write quite easily to a lyric, so this melody came very quickly."[11] The tune was nothing if not unified, and it seemed to spin an endless yarn. It took its due place in the pianist's slowly changing repertoire.

"Sugar Plum" did likewise. The lyrical connection here was surely unique: the songwriter, manager, and producer John Court (who, incidentally, managed Jeremy Steig's band, the Satyrs, as well as Warren Bernhardt) became obsessed with an improvised fragment of Bill's from "Angel Face" on *Intermodulation* and created a lyric to accommodate several repetitions of the theme, thus delivering the pianist of a "freebie" original for (and from) his repertoire. Evans was delighted with Court's idea and even made constructive suggestions for improving the lyric. In the original lazy ballad tempo on *Intermodulation*, the section in question had occupied four bars, but it was now made to span the eight-bar improvising "chunk." Each time, the key went down a fifth, so that eventually (in ninety-six bars) a full cycle of keys was completed and could be recommenced. Evans's writing contract with TRO had expired, so some of his new tunes started to go into a Fantasy company called Orpheum Music, but "Sugar Plum," with its complex derivations, ended up with a company called Pennywhistle Music.

In a nutshell, a "twelve-note row" was the working ingredient of a group of composers led by Arnold Schoenberg, who saw it as a logical way out of a musical dilemma in the early years of the twentieth century. "Twelve Tone Tune," the third newcomer from Evans, was a fine instance of his ability to reach his public through, or in spite of, his intellect. In time-honored fashion the twelve notes of his chosen row were strung out one by one, the recurrence of any note being traditionally disallowed until they are all used up. By doing this three times in succession he arrived at his "tune," which was then, of course, thirty-six notes long (octave displacement *is* allowed, so there was scope for contour). Here, however, he ended his twelve-tone gambit, proceeding to clothe the line with diatonic harmony. As he pointed out, twelve-tone music (as a pervasive operating language) was incompatible with the art of improvising.

The final debut was made by "Comrade Conrad," a tune that grew out of a jingle Evans had written for Crest toothpaste. The trio had tried it once or twice on gigs, but it had never quite worked out, although Evans always had a feeling that it could. It acquired its name when he dedicated it to a friend in San Francisco, Conrad Mendenhall, who was killed in a car crash; Evans had from time to time used his houseboat as a refuge. Like "Sugar Plum," the song pursued a cycle of fifths, but this time upward. The pianist completed his formal plan by alternating sections in 4/4 and 3/4.

The Bill Evans Album was an enterprise of diligence and serious intent, though the musicians were still enjoying themselves, as the frequent foot-tapping testifies; tempi were held steady and the material was challenging to players and listeners alike. The album brought Evans twin triumphs, his fourth and fifth Grammy wins in two categories—best jazz performance by a soloist and by a group.

Soon after this, *Voice of America* broadcast the trio from New York's newly refurbished and air-conditioned Town Hall, the occasion being a "Piano Party," one of a set of six Connoisseur Concerts produced by Willis Conover. Evans hosted a memorable evening with a panoply of talent including Cecil Taylor, Mary Lou Williams, Teddy Wilson, and the Billy Taylor Trio.

Trude Heller's club in Greenwich Village provided the Bill Evans Trio with work for the summer. Part of the time, Blossom Dearie performed opposite with her trio, a shared billing that would be repeated more than once at Ronnie Scott's in London.

In September, Evans was one of fifty-five artists chosen to perform at the opening of the John F. Kennedy Center for the Performing Arts in Washington, D.C. These founding artists received a marble replica of the center and had their names inscribed on a plaque mounted on the building. Evans went on to play in further jazz events produced by Willis Conover for the center's opening season.

⊂⋵ ⊂⋵ ⊂⋵

The trio began 1972 with a huge tour of Europe, taking in England, France, Germany, Holland, and Italy. On January 3, the group began a four-week residency at Ronnie Scott's, London. Brian Hennessey, Evans's English friend, remembers that period well:

> It was on this engagement that Bill and Ellaine stayed at our home in Stoke Poges, some thirty miles from London. At the time, we owned a cottage and small converted stables which had originally been part of the estate where Gray wrote his Elegy. Builders were doing major repairs in the cottage, and we moved Bill and Ellaine into a downstairs room in the stable block which originally had been a bedroom and playroom for our two children. They were about ten years and eight, and attending the local school. We had some concern that the disruptions would be rather disturbing for our guests, but it was soon clear that Bill was enthusiastically absorbing the everyday pressures and pleasures of family life, something he had not experienced since his childhood. At this time he had been free of narcotics for just over two years and had put on a little too much weight.
>
> There was one further thing bothering me, and that was the appalling state of his teeth. When talking to him about it he explained that dentistry in the U.S. was expensive and he could not afford it. He also knew that his teeth had deteriorated beyond repair and a visit to a dentist would involve total extraction and, he suspected, a great deal of blood and pain. Fortunately, a good friend of mine was a dental surgeon with a practice nearby; through me, he had listened to Bill's recordings, and, while not a natural jazz fan, he had become increasingly responsive to Bill's music. I therefore invited him round for Sunday lunch to meet Mr. Evans and Ellaine, and explained my desire to get his help in improving Bill's bite. They got on well, and some appointments were made; no money changed hands.
>
> I had arranged for a chauffeur-driven limousine to be available to him throughout his stay. (As I was the managing director of a major vehicle rental company in London, this was not as generous as it seems.) Bill was obliged to utilize the service when returning from Ronnie Scott's at 3 A.M. to Stoke Poges, but he refused to put the chauffeur to any trouble when traveling into London for the gig. My wife would sometimes give him a lift to Slough station for the London train, and I helped out too if I was home. On some occasions he caught the bus from the village to Slough.
>
> So, Bill's day would go something like this: he would get home by car at about 4 A.M. after Ronnie Scott's, and go to bed. At 8 A.M. the workmen would start the Third World War, and Bill might get up for a cup of coffee around ten o'clock. No complaints from him; he would read, watch television or maybe write a little music. Although we had a baby grand piano at the time, Bill rarely played it during his stay. Sometimes he would take advantage of the fact that my wife was using a vacuum cleaner, and play a few things on the piano—hoping they would be drowned out by the electric motor.
>
> At two o'clock most weekdays we had an appointment with the dentist, who was only able to extract two or three teeth a session before the bleeding gums and general level of pain became too great to continue. Bill would return home at around four, and then walk to the village school to meet our two children and walk home with them. He loved to sit down with them at tea-time and discuss whatever topics they had on their minds. On Sunday evenings, his night off, he insisted that my wife and I should go out while he "baby-sat" for us.

Ronnie Scott's club, London, January 30, 1972.
Val Wilmer

My children did not, of course, show the reverence for Bill that I did; they merely treated him as a friendly guest who could tell good stories. Bill clearly loved being treated as "normal," and showed his affection for children. In fact, this period may well have prompted his rather naive conclusion that his life would be finally sorted out by having a family of his own. At around six he would get ready for work, and depart for London at about seven.

Despite the considerable pain suffered from the dentistry, he never once complained seriously, nor missed a night at Ronnie Scott's. By the end of the last week of his engagement he was wearing a full set of temporary dentures. An example of his humor followed later when there appeared on the rear cover of *The Bill Evans Album* a small photograph showing his new teeth rather prominently. He sent a copy of the album to the dentist, saying how appreciative he was of his work, and how he had decided to feature it on the album cover.

At this time Ronnie Scott had a Petrof grand installed in the club. One night its tuning was unbelievably bad, and Ronnie himself could be seen desperately trying to remedy the situation. Unfortunately, he succeeded only in compounding the metal madness. Still, Evans soldiered on stoically.

He generally adopted a philosophical approach toward pianos and their problems. He shrugged and settled for "I'll get along with it." Like the heckled sportsman, the artist must get on with the job.

⟨⟨ ⟨⟨ ⟨⟨

After the London stint, the trio returned to Paris and the broadcasting house where they had played so memorably in 1965. The full evening's program was issued in 1988 on two LPs, *Live in Paris 1972, Vols. 1 & 2*, on the France's Concert label. This two-part concert had a curiously routine character, rather as though the musicians were on physical and emotional automatic pilot, though Eddie Gomez continued to respond imaginatively to his new bass pickup.

Evans himself settled for long stretches of meager invention, stringing together stock phrases and motives. Perhaps he was working away diligently as usual, but the elements were not coming together into an exciting whole. He admitted that he was in a period of nonprogression, and it gnawed at him. The methadone he was taking, with its sedative effect, may have been a contributing factor. Theoretically, especially for such a sensitive pianist, the setup was ideal. As he remarked to François Postif in *Jazz Hot*, "The piano was exceptional...excellent acoustics...all the conditions were combined to satisfy my ear; that's how I let myself go and played on the sound more than I'm used to."[12] Ultimately though, the spark, the involvement, and the drama failed to materialize.

Evans's formal instincts led him to attach great importance to his codas, and he had always had fun devising end-tags for standards, as well as for his own pieces. "The Two Lonely People" had one such sequence, and Denny Zeitlin had supplied a nice one for "Quiet Now." The pianist sometimes exploited these wind-downs by applying an expansive rallentando. In "Turn Out the Stars," he achieved the same effect by putting the brakes on the last eight bars. His obligatory final flourish over the whole keyboard became tantalizingly delayed by this ploy and was all the more satisfying when it finally arrived.

At the beginnings of numbers, too, an interesting mannerism appeared: the embellishment of the opening note with what is technically known as a (lower) mordent, or a kind of "upside-down twiddle." This was a performing tradition emanating from baroque times by way of emphasizing a chosen note, but Evans's unobtrusive use of it was very likely unconscious—on these tracks it may be heard at the beginnings of "Waltz for Debby," "Very Early," and "Autumn Leaves."

Of the fourteen numbers that evening six were originals, another trend in the making. "I'm leaning a little heavy on original material," he said to Brian Priestley later in the year, "and I think I'll probably be emphasizing original material even more in the future. Somehow, although I don't depart from a standard form that much, the vehicles that I write lend themselves, maybe, a little better to the way the trio plays."[13]

His hands were swollen at this concert, a condition that he found somewhat embarrassing. This symptom of his liver ailment, a chronic mild hepatitis, had been developing slowly since the beginning of the sixties. "But I shouldn't complain," he said to François Postif. "Oscar Peterson has arthritis. Horace Silver has rheumatism. Both suffer. In my case, it is a kind of state which is not painful. The only cure for me is rest."[14]

In the same interview he reflected on how his finger position had changed over the years: "When I was younger, I played with flat fingers. When we possess a lot of vitality and we have a lot of energy, this method of playing permits you to use your energy effectively. As I matured technically I noticed that my fingers curled when I played.... It is a more natural position which was used by Mozart, Haydn, and especially Bach."[15]

The trio went on to Germany for another radio concert, this time for Norddeutsche Rundfunk at its broadcasting house in Hamburg, the home of Steinway & Sons. The American multiple wind player Herb Geller was scheduled to join them in the second part of the evening. Geller, like Evans and so many others, had gigged with the Jerry Wald band in New York, but he became best known for his work on the West Coast during the fifties. In the early sixties he moved to Europe, settling finally in Hamburg to compose and arrange for German radio; at the time of this meeting with Evans, he was playing in Peter Herbolzheimer's big band.

The trio arrived in the city two or three days before the concert. NDR had decided that a televised rehearsal would be good publicity, and the quartet was duly filmed at the studios, running through Geller's brooding composition "Northern Trail." Evans was quite ill at the time; looking pale and zombielike, he read through the piece with Geller playing alto flute. Two cuts and some fluctuating pitch on the surviving film are preserved on the Moon CD *Emily*, a typically careless bootleg production. (Both the year of recording and the tune title are given incorrectly.)

In the first half of the ensuing concert, the trio played much of its recent Paris repertoire, but with deeper involvement and, consequently, a more rewarding listening experience. That the French performance rather than this one is available to the record-buying public is emblematic of the vicissitudes of the recording business. For the defenseless artist, the luck of the draw determines which performances are issued posthumously, which remain on tape, which do not survive at all. In the second part of the concert, the tunes were all written by Herb Geller, and Evans sounded pleased to have an opportunity to sample some alternative fare.

⋐⋑ ⋐⋑ ⋐⋑

No sooner had they recrossed the Atlantic than the trio was headed southwestward to Texas for one of several visits to the Villager club in Dallas. One of these was attended by the pianist Peter Nero, a great fan of Evans's. The pianists shared an appreciation for the supporting house trio led by the club owner, Jac Murphy. The bass player from that group had sat in with Evans on final sets. Bill frequently took it easy at the end of a quiet evening, either playing a shorter set than usual or inviting musicians whom he knew and liked to sit in. The results were unpredictable, occasionally memorable. In any case, they varied the monotony on the road.

In March 1972 the trio was playing Shelly's Manne Hole. In the middle of the run, Manne and his men filled in for two nights while the trio flew to New York to appear at the fourteenth annual Grammy Awards, representing jazz on the show. Evans was receiving twin awards for *The Bill Evans Album*. The ceremony was presented at the Felt Forum at Madison Square Garden by N.A.R.A.S. on ABC-TV.

Returning to the West Coast, they tried out a new San Diego venue called Funky Quarters. It was a whirlwind time—there was work in Chicago (Joe Segal's Modern Jazz Showcase), a long run at the Top of the Gate, and an appearance on the *Mike Douglas Show*.

Meanwhile, a major event was brewing, George Russell presiding. From 1964 to 1969 Russell had lived in Scandinavia, teaching at Lund University in Sweden and at the Vaskilde Summer School in Denmark, rejoicing in his artistic acceptance and healthy living. On his return to America, he joined the faculty of the New England Conservatory of Music in Boston, at the invitation of Gunther Schuller, who was now president of the conservatory.

For his second Columbia date, Evans commissioned a work from Russell, who, emerging from his academic pursuits, responded with a cataclysmic score called *Living Time*, featuring the pianist on both the Steinway and Fender-Rhodes pianos. For this the composer employed a powerful studio orchestra, spanning the ages and leaning heavily toward electronics in the bass, keyboard, and guitar departments. The tuba (combined with Fender bass) was tellingly used, the brass writing keen edged. Russell avoided

George Russell in 1971, while working on Evans's commission, *Living Time*.
Courtesy of George Russell

the mellow in the orchestral forces and left the lyrical aspect to Evans's solo Steinway, which provided fleeting but significant relief.

By a curious coincidence, that idiosyncratic mordent applied by Bill as extra spice to his starting notes formed the basis of "Event IV" (out of eight), in which a feeling of drama really got under way. The idea was extended to a two-chord shake, the pianist's steely fingers leading the ensemble with percussive attack and razor-sharp time.

Twelve years had passed since Evans and Russell had collaborated on *Jazz in the Space Age*. Russell's observations made then are timeless, equally applicable to *Living Time* (the title taken from the book by the neurologist Maurice Nicoll). On the jazz music of the future he had said:

> The techniques are going to get more complex, and it will be a challenge for the composer to master the techniques and yet preserve his intuitive approach. And it will be a challenge to the improviser to master these techniques and also preserve the intuitive, earthy dignity of jazz.
>
> Specifically, it's going to be a pan-rhythmic, pan-tonal age. I think that jazz will by-pass atonality because jazz actually has roots in folk music, and folk music is scale-based music; and atonality negates the scale. I think that jazz will be intensely chromatic; but you can be chromatic and not be atonal.
>
> The answer seems to lie in pan-tonality. The basic folk nature of the scales is preserved, and yet, because you can be in any number of tonalities at once and/or

sequentially, it also creates a very chromatic kind of feeling, so that it's sort of like being atonal with a Big Bill Broonzy sound. YOU CAN RETAIN THE FUNK.[16]

The solid rock beat of "Event V" vindicated Russell's declaration with a vengeance, after which the trio unit swung into action in a straight four. Evans got down to some extended and solid modal improvisation, backed by organ and compulsive brass ostinato riffs. Eventually the solo piano persisted with a rising figure presaging an orchestral upheaval of cosmic proportions, an entry into some kind of alienation forever, and the frenetic, rapid-fire, two-chord shake had to be faded.

"Bill and I are both involved with modal music," Russell said. "But we have sort of gone off at right angles from each other over the years. Bill is more into tonal playing. I haven't stayed there; I've been working in extensions, the outer reaches of modal things. But I love and respect Bill's playing so much that I really couldn't resist the challenge. As I saw it, the task would be to create a mode that enhanced his work without inhibiting my own."[17]

Evans justified the big piano part, and Russell presided with imaginative genius over his orgasmic conception. Sensitive to Bill's fans, the composer had given him due warning that this was to be no "Waltz for Debby," but Evans had insisted that he pull no punches in the writing. Russell remarked, "Bill played like he was being pushed into some other level, hit over the head, kicked in the behind."[18] Some of the pianist's fans wrote him letters threatening never to buy another record or attend another concert if he did this sort of thing again. Nevertheless, two years later Evans presented *Living Time* at Carnegie Hall under the auspices of the New York Jazz Repertory Company.

Living Time was Evans's second and last recording for Columbia. A few years later he spoke to Len Lyons about bad deals from record companies and consequent label hopping: "You tour, but you don't get backing. They won't help out. There are no displays, no coordinated advertising. The stint I had with Columbia: I thought I'd finally arrived at a company that had the money and the interest. Clive Davis and I just didn't hit it off. I never even talked to the man, and he was already directing my career, changing me, making me 'creative,' 'communicative,' whatever."[19]

The kid from Plainfield had fulfilled his dream and recorded for Columbia, but reality fell short of the dream.

17 You've Been a
Fine Audience

*I think one of the most endearing qualities of Bill's personality was the almost childlike plea-
sure he got from the star treatment he received wherever he went.*

—*Helen Keane*

The First Trio's Village Vanguard albums had made a tremendous impact on
a young pianist and percussionist from Sheffield, England. The young man,
who had picked up the elements of music in the Black Watch military band,
was by the early sixties leading his own local jazz group. His name was Tony
Oxley, and his most celebrated and ongoing association has been with a fellow Yorkshireman, the guitarist Derek Bailey. Oxley has been called a cham-
pion of rhythmic freedom. From 1967 he became well known as the house
drummer at Ronnie Scott's in London, playing with many of the great visiting American artists.

Naturally, Bill Evans always brought his own drummer to the club, but
he was still pleased when Oxley agreed to sit in on final sets, as he had been
doing frequently since the end of 1969. On one occasion, Stan Getz was due
to follow Bill into the club; he failed to show on the first night, so Evans,
Oxley, and British bassist Ron Mathewson (who idolized Evans) did an
evening of two sets, Eddie Gomez and Marty Morell having already returned
to the States. Mathewson will never forget that night. Oxley had called him
with a nonchalant, "Fancy a gig tonight?"

"Who with?"

"Bill Evans."

"Oh, shit," muttered Mathewson, hastily packing his instrument.

For the incredulous bassist that night, Evans played a different repertoire
from his specialized fare, ensuring an easy ensemble by setting up tempos and
nodding in his colleagues. Mathewson said that Evans was in complete control

and very easy to play with. Later, just before Bill died, Oxley, Mathewson, and the English pianist Gordon Beck got together in London with Stan Sulzmann and Kenny Wheeler to make an album of Evans's compositions called *Seven Steps to Evans*. The tape was sent to Bill, and when Mike Hennessey, the producer of the album, asked what he thought of it Evans said, "Yeah, lovely album!"

"How about 'Waltz for Debby'?" Hennessey asked, referring to Gordon Beck's rapid-fire arrangement in 4/4.

"*Interesting*," came the cryptic reply. My guess is that Evans, the most open-minded of musicians (so long as quality was the first priority), would have liked it a lot, as he would Tony Oxley's menacing re-creation of "Peace Piece" on the same record. Earlier Evans had described playing with Oxley: "A British drummer, I think of exceptional creative talent, sat in last night for the last set, and I expect he'll come back and sit in again. Now just during the short time that he played—we only played four numbers, a short set— because of his different approach, things that we have been approaching from a certain viewpoint for the last three years Marty has been with me, sud-denly began to be transformed, because Tony tends to leave a lot of space."[1]

In June 1972 Tony Oxley replaced Marty Morell for a short European visit. The tour, planned for about three weeks, included several gigs in Belgium. One night Bill invited all to dinner—Ellaine, Eddie and his wife, and Tony. The surprise guest was Debby, Bill's niece and inspiration for "Waltz for Debby." She was traveling around Europe and happened to be in the right place at the right time.

The schedule included an appearance at the Ljubljana International Jazz Festival in Yugoslavia. Evans greeted his audience, "Dobar večer," apol-ogized for his lack of further Serbo-Croatian, and proceeded to announce the program item by item. Probably this guidance had been specially requested, for he rarely made such announcements; in spite of his expanded sense of communication, he preferred not to be distracted by song titles while on stage. He was conscious of a set as a musical entity, a paced pro-gram, and he paid attention not only to contrasting moods and tempos but even to key relationships. His nonverbal stance irritated some listeners and critics, notably the otherwise enthusiastic Whitney Balliett. Evans said to Mike Hennessey, "The best way I can draw people into a musical experience is to *avoid words entirely*."[2]

In Tony Oxley's memory the opening number in Ljubljana, "Very Early," was best. After that the piano monitor went dead and he could hear only Gomez. On the road, musicians often have no time for a sound check, and in large venues they find themselves spread across the stage relying on amplified feedback. From this point of view, the artist prefers the settled circumstances of a club run to a succession of one-night stands.

As often before, Evans responded positively to fresh blood. Judging from this concert, the whole tour must have been a stimulating renewal. "Nardis," from that evening, survives on *Live at the Festival,* one of those "various artists," souvenir compilations, on the German Enja label. The sleeve proclaims: "This is a documentary record of the Ljubljana Jazz Festival with the permission of the musicians." Evans's view on that "permission" was made clear in an interview with Ted O'Reilly: "There are quite a few black market records out in Europe, some of them put out by legit companies; somebody obviously sold them tapes. There's a Ljubljana, Yugoslavia Festival recording—they had no legal right to make a record out of that."[3]

This performance of "Nardis," nevertheless, was a fine one, controlled but probing, with the imaginative Oxley putting his own stamp on pace and mood. I asked him about his solo, in particular whether it was counted out. "I would describe it as an open solo," he explained. "Also, I recognize at the end of 'Nardis' a collective improvisation happening; it's a sort of colla voce treatment of the material and is an element which, if continued, would, I think, have led to a more open approach to his music." Evans was receptive to this, as his *Yeah, Tony!* at the end attests.

Evans invited Oxley to join the trio permanently, but the drummer was reluctant to spend ten months of the year on the road, based in the States. Although the freedom of Oxley's vision was readily accommodated by the Bill Evans Trio, and the position would have done much for the drummer's international reputation, the particular discipline required might have been difficult for him to sustain, and he declined.

⊂⊱ ⊂⊱ ⊂⊱

The Newport Festival came to New York for the first time that summer, and the trio, with Marty Morell, played the same set twice at Carnegie Hall on July 3, once in the afternoon and then again in the evening, both performances broadcast by Voice of America. Whitney Balliett wrote in the *New Yorker* of "six inward-looking numbers that nonetheless flashed with Evans's taste and inventiveness."[4]

The following month, the trio took part in the weekly CBC Radio series, *Showcase '72,* live from the Ontario Place Forum in Toronto: the outdoor concert stage, covered with a suspended tent roof and surrounded by grassy slopes, was built on man-made islands in the lake. In front of a large audience they performed a steady, earthbound set before joining the Ross Little Orchestra for "Blue in Green," sandwiched in the midst of a compact arrangement of "One for Helen," the latter sounding like a real classic in its low-pitched, gritty band voicings.

Toward the end of August, they returned to the Top of the Gate. The future of the whole Village Gate premises, of which the Top was a part, was in the balance for a while, but the club managed to survive to the eighties. Four numbers from the trio's final night were broadcast and televised by WNDT, and they have survived on the bootleg LP from Chazzer, *Bill Evans Trio: Rare Broadcast Material*.

For the third time in one year the trio returned to Europe, this time opposite Phil Woods and his European Rhythm Machine. As in February, two programs were played in Paris, but only one album's worth of material was issued: *Live in Paris 1972, Vol. 3*. Gordon Beck, who was playing the piano in the Phil Woods group, cherishes a personal memory—a vignette—from this date, Sunday, December 17, 1972, the last concert of the European Rhythm Machine. Like most British jazzmen of the time, he had become hooked on Evans after hearing *Sunday at the Village Vanguard*. He found himself on stage some hours before the concert with his hero and two full-size Steinways.

"Gordon! How are you doing?" greeted Bill. "What do you think of this one?" Beck tried it over and thought perhaps it spoke better in the middle than the other one.

"I think so, too," replied Evans. The matter was settled.

There was at this time an increasing temptation to view the Evans group as the Eddie Gomez Trio. During these middle years of his long tenure Gomez's role had become more and more central to the group sound, and, in terms of adventure, he had more to offer than Evans. The pianist was ringing the changes on familiar patterns rather than sounding out new ideas. At the same time, though, he was paring down notes and displaying an appealing directness of thought. The group was slick, happy, and well-oiled, but it was really Gomez who drew the ear. Evans was always generous with his colleagues in terms of space and freedom of expression, and he seemed content at this time to ride his bass player's initiative.

In an informal conversation at Ronnie Scott's in 1975, Mike Hennessey asked Evans a leading question: in view of the length of their collaboration, did it ever get to the situation where there was no longer any surprise left? Evans freely admitted there were down-cycles when they were being more professional than inspired, but he asserted that Gomez was especially resourceful in not allowing the music to become bland. The rapport within the trio was in any case complete, the jewel that was Gomez sitting in the perfect setting provided by Evans and Morell. Unfortunately, on many recordings of the time, typically this one from Paris, the effect of the bass player's aggressive exploitation of the bass pickup became exaggerated to the point of distraction. I never found it overbearing in clubs, though, where care was always taken to achieve a satisfactory balance.

⤞ ⤞ ⤞

At the beginning of 1973, Helen Keane signed Evans with Fantasy Records of California. The deal was astute, as this huge umbrella controlled, among others, the Milestone label, which had reissued many of the pianist's early Riverside recordings. Not only that, Orrin Keepnews, who had originally produced the latter, had just been appointed vice-president and director of jazz activities at Fantasy. Evans was to develop an immensely fruitful relationship with the new label.

His first recording for them emanated from the trio's New Year's tour of Japan, the first of many in a country that held Evans in the highest esteem. Helen Keane sets the scene: "We had arrived to television cameras, banners, flowers, and everything but a marching band. Everyone seemed to know who Bill was—from bellboys to waiters to giggling girls with autograph books— and, as always, he handled each situation with genuine charm. I think one of the most endearing qualities of Bill's personality was the almost childlike pleasure he got from the star treatment he received wherever he went."5

The Japanese jazz magazine *Swing Journal* held its own annual readers' poll. Each year since 1968, Evans had won the piano section, until he was toppled in 1972 by Chick Corea. The Japanese had been jazz crazy since the early sixties, and *Swing Journal* cosponsored the trio's tour, which comprised ten sellout concerts.

Evans once said that in nearly twenty years his trio might have had four rehearsals, and even those had been more like talk-throughs before concert dates involving new material for live recording. At this time the group was ripe for fresh repertoire, and it planned to air no less than six new numbers on the trip; so, to the delight of the welcoming Japanese, a rehearsal took place in the hotel at the start of the tour. The last concert, given on January 20, 1973, was issued by Fantasy as *The Tokyo Concert*.

The trio eased into the program with the first of the new numbers, "Mornin' Glory," a country hit composed and sung by Bobbie Gentry in 1968. The group played it straight, capturing and maintaining the tune's ambling spirit.

It was followed by a new favorite-to-be, "Up with the Lark," one of a handful of songs provided by Jerome Kern in 1945 for a film called *Centennial Summer*. (Another was "In Love in Vain," which Evans had played on *Moonbeams*.) The codetta played to this undemanding waltz was made up of the first few notes of the tune, but with an exploratory chord on each (an Evans trademark as far back as "Very Early"); doubtless this tag was one item on the rehearsal agenda.

Next came the alluring "Esta Tarde Vi Llover" by the Mexican composer Armando Manzanero, a song better known, with its lyric from Gene Lees, as "Yesterday I Heard the Rain"; Tony Bennett had had a hit with this one, also in 1968. The trio's approach was gentle and straightforward, lyrically endorsing their joint sonority.

In the second portion of the concert, Evans delivered yet another first: "When Autumn Comes," an evocative piece from the pen of the pianist Clare Fischer.

Then came the pièce de résistance of this tour, the newly composed "Twelve Tone Tune Two." The compositional premise was the same as its predecessor, "Twelve Tone Tune," as was the length of the sequence (twelve bars), but this time the twelve-note row was strung out five times instead of three. The resulting sixty-note line, with its frenetic rhythmic compression in the second rising phrase, challenged even the finger-flying virtuosity of Eddie Gomez. Characteristically, Evans's end flourish consisted of the notes of the basic row.

The last of these new numbers was the bassist Steve Swallow's ruminative "Hullo Bolinas," a simple tribute to the quaint seaside hamlet just north of San Francisco where he lived at the time. The tune was brought to Evans's attention by Gomez just before they set out for Japan. The trio had introduced it at the previous evening's concert, but among them they decided that it would work better as a piano solo, and it was played as such here. Along with "Mornin' Glory," it was a further nod in the direction of simple, "primary color" material, a leaning that tied in with the directness of the pianist's playing of late.

The album was nominated for a Grammy Award.

Whereas in the past Evans's need to communicate musically had been real enough, the outward signs of such contact on the podium had been notably lacking. The music on this tour, though, was presented in bolder, more appealing strokes, while being at the same time more relaxed. This was matched by a new awareness of public image. For over a year now, Evans had sported long hair and a moustache, and the choice for the trio of black tuxedos with pink frilly shirts was all part of his new character. Here was a musician who had risen painstakingly to an enviable position in the jazz world by dint of dedicated application of his musical ideals and dogged hard work. Appreciated by his public, young as well as old, the private man had the confidence to place himself boldly on stage as never before.

⋐ ⋐ ⋐

The previous autumn, Howard Rumsey had opened a new nightclub called Concerts by the Sea at Redondo Beach, California, just down the coast from his old Lighthouse Café on Hermosa Beach. On his return from Japan, Evans played at the new venue. While there, he relentlessly pursued a young woman named Nenette Zazzara. His feelings for her were tied up with his urgency to have the child that Ellaine was unable to give him. (He had considered but dismissed the notion of adoption.) Nenette's taste in music differed somewhat from Bill's, but she admired him enormously as a person. The two decided to get married.

Evans returned to New York to break the news to Ellaine, with whom he had been living for the past twelve years. She took it well at first, seeming to acquiesce. Brian Hennessey, who knew both Bill and Ellaine well, offers relevant insight into Evans's character: "Artists who show genius in one field often display ignorance in others. Bill had great integrity, and I think that when he told Ellaine, in all honesty, of his association with Nenette, he had not contemplated the question of splitting up. Bill and Ellaine had gone through some pretty sordid times together, and she treated him more as a mother does a precious son. He had always been able to confide in her with his problems and this was just another one." It may have been so to Evans, but to Ellaine, finally, it added up to a desperate scenario. After Evans had returned west she flung herself in front of a New York subway train. Helen Keane, who was a very close friend, had to identify the body. Hennessey has suggested that Ellaine's action may have been connected with her incapacity to satisfy Bill's fervent desire for a child of his own. The distraught Evans spent several weeks seeking consolation from his brother, unable to work.

⋐ ⋐ ⋐

In Evans's consistently full diary were new places to play like Gulliver's in West Paterson, New Jersey, and Diamonte's in North Hollywood. The indefatigable Helen Keane was securing her artist immediate dates in several important new venues, one of which was the remarkable Great American Music Hall in San Francisco, lovingly rebuilt after the 1906 earthquake.

In June the trio toured South America for the first time. The Buenos Aires concert was issued posthumously by Yellow Note Records as *Buenos Aires Concert 1973*, a two-LP boxed set. The audience, a little wary after the elusive opener, "Re: Person I Knew," had cemented its trust by the end of Gomez's long, lyrical, and relaxed solo on "Who Can I Turn To?" With Morell in instinctive support, Evans was spurred to turn the tempo up a notch. The stadium erupted, after which the three of them could do no wrong.

Evans was gaining inspiration from his own piece, "The Two Lonely People," this time sculpting a lovely, satisfying line in the right hand, the left giving an object lesson in rootless voicing, the prodding harmonies dripping with feeling. Most of the new tunes from the Japanese tour were in the 1973 repertoire, including the freshest interpretation of the year on "Yesterday I Heard the Rain"; but it was still classic material like "Turn Out the Stars" and "Emily" that inspired the finest invention from the pianist.

Bill married Nenette in a Lutheran church in Manhattan on August 5, 1973, the service followed by a reception at the Plaza Hotel. During the festivities he reflected for a moment on the Columbia party held there some fifteen years earlier, when he had played in the Miles Davis sextet.

ᐸᐸ ᐸᐸ ᐸᐸ

As a result of sound spillage into Wally Heider's adjacent recording studio, Shelly Manne had moved his Manne Hole club from Hollywood to the affluent Wilshire district of Los Angeles. The trio went to the new venue in November. It was considered the best jazz club in Los Angeles, but it packed up for good six months later. Manne always seemed to have trouble with his neighbors. This time he was sharing the premises with Tetou's Restaurant, which was constantly threatening to close, and Shelly suffered from nervous exhaustion through being unable to book ahead for his artists.

It was ten years since Evans had recorded at the old Manne Hole. Now, briefly, it was another club and another, fuller-toned piano. Orrin Keepnews, as vice president of Fantasy in Berkeley, was well placed to step in for Helen Keane and reprise his role as producer to the pianist. Some trio tracks came out on a collection called *From the Seventies*, and two solo tunes on another called *Eloquence*, both issued after Evans's death.

Evans's solo style was utterly different from his trio way, yet he was the master of it. On this particular night, his colleagues having left early, he was preoccupied with nudging ahead of the beat with both hands in rhythmic unison, a favorite trick of his with a firm historical pedigree; some notes were clipped, and others were simultaneously half-caught in the pedal. Both solo

Bill and Nenette's wedding, 1973.
Nenette Evans, personal collection, copyright
© Nenette Evans 1996

tunes, "When in Rome" and "It Amazes Me," were written by Cy Coleman who, like Evans, was born in 1929 from Russian immigrant parents and ran his own (albeit very different) trio.

Countless times, Evans came "home" again to the Village Vanguard. Max Gordon, the club's creator, was well qualified to assess his house pianist's progress: "Bill Evans first played at the Village Vanguard almost twenty years ago and has been coming back regularly four or five times every year. In addition to the following he has created at the Vanguard all these years, I notice now that college kids are beginning to dig him; the 'kids' who used to listen to Rock crowd the Vanguard these nights when Bill opens. He is developing a new generation of fans. Bill's music is timeless."[6]

Gordon invited Bill to select the Vanguard's new house piano; he chose a Yamaha, and, fittingly, a large photo of him was placed on the wall behind it. Evans had been impressed by a number of these instruments of late, as had his friend, Glenn Gould—the staunchest of Steinway advocates—who later fell in love with and purchased a Yamaha.

Although Evans played the Vanguard regularly, he had not recorded there officially since 1967 (*California Here I Come*, which still had not been released). For his Fantasy live recording *Since We Met*, made in January 1974, he wrote the title tune, which was dedicated to (and named by) his wife, Nenette. "Since We Met" was contained within a clear formal plan, the central section of improvisation being enclosed at either end by a frame, a gentle waltz constructed on a neat and simple idea: twelve bars, one chord per bar, each a fifth down from the previous one—a full cycle of keys as far reaching as you can get, but back to base in no time.

Additionally, every night he was playing two other numbers that were new to his repertoire and intended for the album. The first was another from the pen of Cy Coleman, the title song from his recent show *Seesaw*. Again Evans devised an immaculate setting for it, oscillating between the waltz and a hard-four presto drive. "Seesaw" was fairly soon dropped from the trio's programs, but the other new number, "Sareen Jurer" by Earl Zindars, became a group standard, played nightly in clubs for the next two or three years.

The composer's Armenian wife, Annig, who names all his tunes, explained the mysterious title to me in a letter: "Usually when Earl writes a new tune, he doesn't have a title in mind, and while he's composing the tune, picture images come to my mind. For the composition 'Sareen Jurer,' because of the beautiful flow of progressions in a downward manner, a picture came to me about the waters that descend and flow from the high mountains, after a rain or a thawing of the snow—its waterfalls and rivulets. The composition has an Armenian title (thinking of Mount Ararat): 'Sareen' (pronounced Sahreen) means 'from the mountain,' and 'Jurer' (pronounced Joorehr) means 'the waters.' Many people think that it stands for 'serene juror'—which is incorrect." Written in 1973, it was Zindars's most ambitious tune to date, intriguing for its seven-bar bridge. Additionally, Evans commenced in 4/4 and played the bridge in 3/4; knowing his fascination with structural logic, we are not surprised to find the time signatures reversed during the improvisations.

Extra takes from these Friday and Saturday night sets went into a further album, issued retrospectively, called *Re: Person I Knew*. The albums together provide an accurate representation of how this, the longest-running Bill Evans Trio, sounded during a club run. That weekend enthusiast Mike Harris was also down front as usual, operating his clandestine equipment as near to the piano and as far away from the drums as possible. One of his recordings (on *The Secret Sessions*) was a complete version of "Dolphin Dance," fulfilling the promise of an exploratory doodle preserved on *Re: Person I Knew*.

Evans reluctantly acknowledged the occasional value of audience reaction: "Typical Saturday night audiences in clubs are usually what we call the 'vegetable crowd.' I don't know why, but Saturday night audiences are harder to please than on any other night of the week, and we find ourselves sometimes working very hard just as a result of the fact that we feel there is no appreciation there, and the reason for us being there is not as strong, especially if we're not at our creative peak...so an audience can definitely, if they really respond...give you a little push."[7]

Intrusive applause rarely occurred at the end of his piano solos, so smooth was the transition into the next section. This was deliberate policy — although his ideas would be winding up logically, he always contrived simultaneously to think forward into what was to follow. By contrast, Gomez frequently placed a resounding dominant in the last bar of his own solo, firmly marking the division.

In her notes to *The Complete Fantasy Recordings* Helen Keane mentioned current "projects in the planning stages." One of these was a big orchestral date with Claus Ogerman, featuring the trio, with Evans again moving smoothly between two keyboards. For this venture, the pianist briefly departed from Fantasy, renewing his acquaintance with the German company MPS Records, for whom his trio had recorded privately a few years earlier. Gradually, during the seventies, Ogerman became less commercial, and for his third collaboration with Evans he composed a full-scale original work called *Symbiosis*. Eleven years on from *The V.I.P.s*, it was an altogether more serious affair. Symbiosis means mutual nurturing of different species, in this case the free playing of Evans and the fixed nature of the score. The pianist rose with vigor to the challenge of a variety of roles, both written and improvised, in between which the woodwind played difficult, spun out (and written out) garlands for pages at a time, sterlingly led by Phil Woods on alto saxophone.

From an ensuing European tour, two rogue CDs from EPM Records of Paris chronicle, after a fashion, some of the trio's playing. On *Live in Europe, Vols. I and II*, the trio was in good shape, stretching out and enjoying its own mutually developed brand of interaction. These were among the last engagements with Marty Morell, a circumstance that may have honed the creative edge. As on the earlier bootleg *Stockholm 1965*, though, the pitch is a semitone high, resulting in a disturbing increase in speed. Additionally, the careless nature of the assembly — it cannot really be called *editing* — makes listening an ordeal. Cut-ins and fade-outs occur at random, and solos are hacked about indiscriminately. "Some Other Time" and "Time Remembered" (both truncated) are meaninglessly glued together, titles are wrongly given, location and dates not supplied, and the sound is badly distorted.

⊏⊏ ⊏⊏ ⊏⊏

The trio was joined by Stan Getz for two summer festival appearances. The first was at the Laren International Jazz Festival in Holland, at the Singer

Concertzaal; the second, a week later, was at Jazz Middelheim (affiliated with the Flanders Festival), whose outdoor concerts took place in Den Brandt Park in the suburbs of Antwerp. In 1995 Helen Keane and her team put together a compilation from the two concerts for Milestone called *The Bill Evans Trio Featuring Stan Getz: But Beautiful*, a disc that recorded the fulfillment of the partnership that their 1964 Verve sessions had merely promised.

Getz's first number with Evans at Laren turned out to be a virtually pianoless blues. It was a long time since the two had played a program together, and they decided to rehearse on the day of the concert. They ran through the quartet numbers to be played after the initial trio spot, but when Getz came on he called a tune they had not rehearsed. Helen Keane takes up the story: "I was watching the performance on a television monitor in the audio truck and saw the angry expression on Bill's face as Stan began to play the unrehearsed 'Stan's Blues.' Bill played a little on the melody chorus, then took his hands off the keyboard and didn't play for the rest of the tune. As soon as he got Eddie Gomez's eye, Bill shook his head, meaning don't take a solo. That explains why there's no piano on 'Stan's Blues.' Bill was a gentle person, but very strong. Although he always worked well with other musicians, obviously Stan's behavior really affected him."[8]

Much the same program was played in Middelheim the following week, but without "Stan's Blues." With a frontline guest, the members of the trio sounded quite unlike the Bill Evans Trio, being forced out of their mutually evolved language and interplay into the adoption of a more generalized set of rules. Mike Hennessey put it to Evans that there might be a danger of getting too introspective in a trio format. "Yeah, a little too comfortable maybe," he replied.

> What happens when I do something like that with a front line or a couple of horns, is that I put all concept of how *we* approach music pretty much out of my head; and I say, now we're doing fundamentally a straight ahead, free-swinging date. So *I* take a different approach myself—I become more physical, more outgoing, more exuberant. So, it takes on a different character. It's something that I enjoy doing, but *all* the time I might...I don't know, I might even enjoy doing it all the time. I know that there are times when I sorely would like to just play some straight ahead stuff. We do get into it occasionally with the trio—but we're trying to present more of a variety of things.[9]

In both venues Getz and Evans came compellingly together in unaccompanied renderings of Jimmy Rowles's sinuously haunting "The Peacocks"; on the very last note the saxophonist suggested, with air fluttering through his keys, the flightless plight of the haughty birds. Getz had previously done the piece with its composer and had then introduced it to Evans.

The Middelheim concert was on August 16, and at the end Stan uttered, "Happy birthday, Bill!" (it was his forty-fourth). Jimmy Rowles relates a later occasion when Bill played "The Peacocks" at Ronnie Scott's in London: "I went in to see him and went back to his dressing room. He said, 'Oh, you just missed your song. I just got through playing it.' He stopped and looked at it and said, 'You know what, I'll play it again.' He went back out, played it again, and introduced me to the people, made me take a bow. That was very nice."[10]

ᘓ ᘓ ᘓ

After a week at Ronnie's in London the trio flew to Canada to play in a summer series created by Peter Shaw and the Canadian Broadcasting Corporation. The location was Camp Fortune, a ski resort in the Gatineau Hills just north of Ottawa. The trio had been regular visitors over the years, and in due course the tapes of their Camp Fortune performances, as well as ones given in nearby Carleton University, were acquired by Fantasy Records. Helen Keane told me that she listened to a large number of takes from both venues and from different years before settling on the program of *Blue in Green*, issued on Milestone in 1991. Most of the tracks were from the outdoor location, where, the aural evidence suggests, the keen air cleared the brain and impelled the imagination. Inspiration was high, too, on a further selection of tunes played at this venue, issued much earlier on a Can-Am Records LP called *The Canadian Concert*.

These are the last issued documents of the longest-running Bill Evans Trio (six years), and the group was captured at its absolute peak. Evans revealed a chink of light between doors that would open onto a new creative period. It was most discernible on the rarer titles of *Blue in Green*. On "If You Could See Me Now," for instance, his invention came alive, note by note (something that had not happened too often over the last few years), cliché figures were avoided altogether, and the position of every detail in the overall pattern was perfectly judged. This revival of an old tune inspired Eddie Gomez to high levels of interactive fancy, while Marty Morell was a model of supportive discretion.

Similarly, on the highly concentrated "Blue in Green," there was a sense of adventure in the choice of voicings and, equally important for Evans, the varied tone attached to them: perhaps a single note would be given more center as it stood out over a sparser harmony, while a thicker chord might spread its tone more evenly from bottom to top.

"So What" received many touches out of the usual line, some of the two-chord responses pedaled, the later bridges swathed in a Debussy-like mist. Evans embarked on a two-handed line in octaves—a throwback to the fifties. The virtuosity of his youth may have been lacking, but the ideas came thick and fast from the stimulated musician. Reminiscing with Mike Hennessey about his earlier playing, he said, "I have a record I made in a club when I was about twenty-one, a tape that was put on a vinyl disc..."

"Do you have that one?" interjected Hennessey, with suddenly rising hope, his mind racing.

"No! Nobody has that one; I don't even know if I have it. But I swear..."

"You must have it."

"...I play things on there I couldn't get near today. I mean very, very fast tempo—a lot of chord things, just goin' at it!"[11]

It was late August in the Canadian foothills, and a small space heater was set by the piano. He was still "goin' at it," but later he remarked that the fingers were reluctant to cooperate with what the brain demanded.

The insidious pressure of touring, with its consequent effect on the practicality of family life, caught up with Marty Morell. He had married a Canadian woman, and he finally left the group to settle in Toronto, an unsung stalwart of piano trio history. Especially toward the end of his tenure, he had been responsible for an exceedingly tight unit that could swing and drive relentlessly. His control of the twelve-bar sections in a number like "Twelve Tone Tune," for instance, was as snappy and precise as could be. At the same time, on ballads, he never failed to provide a listening cushion of the utmost delicacy, seeming to imbue his drums with the ability to breathe of their own volition, and always in expressive union with his leader.

CHAPTER **18**

You Must Believe in Spring

Eddie and Bill had been playing together for years, and they didn't even count it off. They would hit the first beat, I was in on the second, and we would play.

— *Bill Goodwin*

At the end of 1973, Evans and Gomez had visited Europe as a duo, playing a large part of the trio's current repertoire. The pianist had long cherished an ambition to make a duet album with his colleague, and in November 1974 the two of them went into Fantasy's California studios to that end. Evans used the Fender-Rhodes again, not just for color now, but for whole numbers.

To him, the electric piano was "kind of fun." At the same time it was, in his hands, capable of considerable expressive shading. He owned one of the original models (the smaller Fender-Rhodes, the "73") but, having a reservation about its lightness of touch, had asked Harold Rhodes to regulate it. A year hence he would start to enter the *Down Beat* electric piano polls, but somehow he never sounded completely at home on the instrument. The grand piano had developed in parallel with the European classical repertoire that was the source of Evans's dense harmonic language. Half a generation makes all the difference, and perhaps the electric keyboard's greatest exponent is Chick Corea, whose more spatial harmonies better suit the clarity of the manufactured sound.

The new album was called *Intuition,* and while recording it in Berkeley by day he played at the Great American Music Hall across the bay by night. In the studio he used a trick on the Fender-Rhodes shown to him by the engineer, Don Cody, who applied a Maestro phaser, a filter that cancels frequencies in a particular way. Evans performed two numbers in this manner on the electric piano only, the sound—swirling and eddying—given a rasping edge by the tone control. As always, Gomez played acoustic bass throughout. On his own "Show-Type Tune" and "Are You All the Things" Evans spun some of his longest lines. Aware that chording on the Fender-Rhodes invited the danger of a turgid, lumpy sound, he kept the left-hand comping spare and short.

On acoustic piano only, Evans returned to the work of Bronislau Kaper, whose film tune "On Green Dolphin Street" he had helped instigate as a repertoire classic on *Jazz Track*. His free exposition of that composer's "Invitation" was a feast of romantic pianism in the line of Chopin and Rachmaninoff.

Kaper was also the Academy Award winning composer of "Hi Lili, Hi Lo," from the 1953 MGM musical *Lili*. Bill played it here for his departed friend Ellaine, moving her favorite song up and up, "singing" through the keys, pausing longingly before taking each new step as if unable to release the pain of memory. The following year, in a rare departure from his habitually fierce self-criticism, he was heard to say what a good album this was, and it became one of the few of his own that he put on at home.

A private tape exists of the duo in the studio, testing the resilience of their particular blend of electric piano and acoustic bass. Tempos and formats were essayed, some more ambitious or successful than others. "Comrade Conrad" proved tricky, with its self-imposed framework of both key and time changes; "Gone With the Wind" was given the bar-swapping treatment in eights, fours, twos, and ones. The commitment and energy of both artists in a tryout situation was notable—they could play no other way.

⋐ ⋐ ⋐

Hard on the departure of Marty Morell, Evans was able to find a drummer sensitive to his artistry. This was the Brooklyn-based Eliot Zigmund, versatile and much in demand on the New York scene, whom Bill had first met playing at the Great American Music Hall. Zigmund told me that playing in the Evans Trio was a job he always wanted, one he knew he could do.

Born in the Bronx in 1945, Zigmund grew up in New York during the 1950s and 1960s, studying for a while at Mannes College of Music, where Evans had been a postgraduate. The drummer gained valuable trio experience with Vince Guaraldi on the West Coast before returning to New York. On *The Secret Sessions*, he can be heard swinging his way into the trio's book in January 1975 at the Vanguard before departing with them for Europe and Scandinavia.

"I remember clearly that we didn't rehearse," he related. "We started off with big concerts, no club work, which was a bit intimidating. That tour was a particularly hard one for Bill businesswise, problems with promoters and

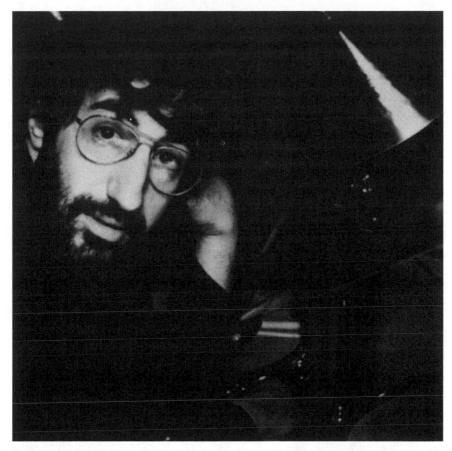

Drummer Eliot Zigmund joined the trio in 1975 and stayed for three years.
Phil Bray, courtesy of Fantasy, Inc.

pianos, et cetera—so much so that he didn't give me a commitment until we returned to the States and did some club work on the West Coast."

Their first engagement was in Switzerland at Epalinges, then a village but now a residential suburb of Lausanne and not too far from the scene of the group's previous triumphs at Montreux. The writer and producer Jean-Michel Reisser told me the story of music at Epalinges, at the same time confiding the details of widespread musical piracy of the airwaves by unscrupulous record companies:

> In 1974, Radio Suisse Romande decided to build big new studios at La Sallaz, in the eastern part of Lausanne. Pierre Grandjean and Géo Voumard were working for Radio Suisse Romande in jazz, information, and so on. The latter worked close to the mayor of Epalinges and asked if the radio station could use the new eight-hundred-seat

Maison des Spectacles there, just two kilometers away, while the new studios were being built. The mayor thought it would be good publicity for Epalinges and its new hall, so the equipment was installed, and in January 1975 music of all kinds began to be broadcast from there.

Pierre Grandjean and Géo Voumard loved jazz, and they decided to put on one or two big names such as Oscar Peterson and Bill Evans, as well as many lesser known (at that time) artists like Monty Alexander, Gary Burton, and Pat Metheny. The only condition was that each concert should be broadcast live, one transmission only. At the beginning of 1978 the new studios were finished, and everything moved out of Epalinges. So naturally the Bill Evans concert of February 6, 1975, one of the first in Epalinges, was recorded and broadcast in this way, under the supervision of Pierre Grandjean.

However, in 1990 a young cat from Radio Suisse Romande decided to put out several of these tapes, including the Bill Evans concert, as albums on the Jazz Helvet label. There were CDs of Count Basie, Muddy Waters, Charles Mingus, and Thelonious Monk. Now of course, all these artists are dead, so immediately one is suspicious. When I told Francis Paudras, who was associated with the Bill Evans estate, about the Bill Evans CD, production on Jazz Helvet was stopped within a few months. Unfortunately, however, all this material was pirated again in Italy by the Landscape label.

So this is what happens—certain radio stations cannot be trusted to honor their contracts.

Nevertheless, the Jazz Helvet issue, *Switzerland 1975*, is that rarity, a bootleg of quality. With regard to his trios generally, Evans has commented that most of the interplay (at a theoretical level, at least) takes place between piano and bass. But the character of the drummer greatly affects the individual approaches of the other two members, as well as the overall group sound. Eliot Zigmund sought to build in his own way upon the previous unit with Marty Morell while emulating somewhat DeJohnette's inclination to break up the time. Zigmund's stance was one of creativity "of the moment," and as a third equal voice. In this sense the group was returning to the tenet of the original trio at Riverside, an approach rather laid aside under the influence of Marty Morell's straight-ahead drive.

Evans always said to a colleague newly joining the group, *Feel free to do your own thing*, and by this token the previously bass-biased "Gloria's Step" now took on fresh vigor as a drum-oriented feature. Zigmund generally stimulated Evans away from his repertory of stock phrases to a high level of involvement, but without quite matching, for the time being, the conspicuous "high" attained recently in Canada.

The new trio quickly became an integrated unit, the performances fired, yet anchored, by the kaleidoscopic new drummer. Via the French city of Grenoble they arrived in Holland on February 13 for a particularly demanding day. Just as Claus Ogerman had gotten some platform mileage with Bill in the late 1960s out of his *Symphony Orchestra* arrangements, so now, from the Vara Studio in Hilversum, *Symbiosis* was broadcast by Evans and the Metropole Orchestra, conducted by Dolf van der Linden. In the evening the pianist took his trio along the road to the nearby town of Laren (at whose festival he had recently played with Stan Getz) to a favorite old haunt, Nick Vollebregt's Jazz Café, where they augmented the program with "Blue Serge" from *Intuition*.

After an appearance in Nice, they were recorded in front of an enthusiastic audience by Radio France in Marseille on February 16; some of that concert has been issued on a Zeta CD called *My Romance*. As with some other bootlegs, the pitch is approximately a semitone sharp. In that evening's fine run of numbers, delivered with punchy, concentrated energy, Eliot Zigmund's influence was paramount. It would not even occur to him to be "showy," and he resisted the indulgence of a straightforward swing, preferring to propel with an inner fund of energy; in these respects his role in the trio may be likened to that of Larry Bunker's.

By February 21 the trio was in Denmark for a radio broadcast from the Louisiana Museum of Modern Art in Elsinore. The next day, just over the water in Sweden, they were reunited with Monica Zetterlund in the Konsthallen at Lund. Material from this concert was put out in 1991 on a West Wind CD called *Bill Evans, Monica Zetterlund*. Whereas *My Romance* ran sharp, this one ran a semitone flat, with correspondingly sluggish tempos and voice distortion. Evans was playing one of the worst pianos of his career and, during the opening trio numbers, Gomez had to stop periodically to adjust the amplified bass level. With its catalog of faults, both in performance and presentation, this issue would have outraged Evans.

Joe LaBarbera, his last drummer, explains the careful planning, in collaboration with Helen Keane, that went into the pianist's recordings:

> Evans' own personal view was that, when he did a recording, he would have complete control of that recording, and he would prepare for it in such a way that his performance would be to his satisfaction. And also, he would never present four, five, six trio performances in a row. He would do a trio record, a solo record, an orchestra record, a quintet record.... He's thinking in terms of his catalog in the long term, the long view. You've got a legacy of recorded Bill Evans albums that are masterpieces. Now, all of a sudden at the tail end of it, you've got material that may be enjoyable to the fan, but in looking at Bill Evans' legacy, it doesn't fit into the picture—not the way he would want it to.[1]

꿈 꿈 꿈

For two years, Evans's erstwhile bassist Chuck Israels had been running his own National Jazz Ensemble, a band that concentrated on the re-creation of arrangements and improvisations, as recorded by artists from Jelly Roll Morton to Ornette Coleman. In doing so it played such venues as Washington's Smithsonian Institute and New York's Alice Tully Hall. Israels made a number of transcriptions of performances by his generation of the Bill Evans Trio, and in 1973 he had invited Evans to be guest soloist on his arrangements of "Nardis," "Turn Out the Stars," and "Very Early" at Tully Hall. For the same occasion he had orchestrated Evans's accompaniment to Miles Davis's solo on "All Blues" from *Kind of Blue*, which Evans then used as a springboard to a new solo.

The Israels arrangement of "Very Early" was now recorded for a Chiaroscuro collection called *The National Jazz Ensemble, Vol. 1*. It was highly effective, drawing on a sometime feature of Evans Trio performances: the juxtaposition of three and four time (although "Very Early" always stayed in 3/4 with the trio). Evans took the melody at either end, incorporating some of the double thirds printed in the sheet music folio, and negotiated the tempo and meter changes with solo links. The soloing was propelled by the sprightly drumming of Bill Goodwin.

Los Angeles–born Goodwin, a drummer with an irresistible spring in his heels, had recently become a member of the Phil Woods group. But he fitted into his schedule a brief spell in Chicago with the Bill Evans Trio. Just before, Goodwin had joined the group for a television show called *Jazz Adventures*, broadcast by WNYC from Brooklyn College. Goodwin's recollection of being thrown in at the deep end with Bill's group echoes Eliot Zigmund's and, for that matter, everyone else's:

> I called Bill and said, "Do you want to rehearse?" And he said, "No, I'm sure you've heard me a lot and you know the way I play." I allowed as how I did.
> When we got to the TV show, we didn't talk it over; we just started playing. He was playing all this stuff that I'd never heard before; in fact, the whole time I worked with him, which was a little under two weeks, I never knew the title of anything, except the tunes that I knew from before like "Five," "My Romance," "Nardis," and "Elsa"—those tunes. Eddie and Bill had been playing together for years, and they didn't even count it off. They would hit the first beat, I was in on the second, and we would play.[2]

⇇ ⇇ ⇇

It was the singer Annie Ross who told Tony Bennett that he should make a recording with Bill Evans, but as the pianist said to Len Lyons afterward: "It was one of those things that was in the air for years. I always figured that if Tony would do any of my tunes, I'd be overjoyed. In fact, he did record 'Waltz for Debby' once. Debby's my niece. I wrote that for her when she was three, and she's getting married this year. Tony and I have always had a mutual respect and a distant acquaintance with each other. It so happens that my manager and his are good friends."[3]

So indeed, Helen Keane and Jack Rollins negotiated the collaboration for Fantasy Records. Evans confessed to finding Bennett's vibrato too fast for his taste when he first heard him. "Now," he told Brian Hennessey, "I like Tony's singing. To me, he is one of those guys that keep developing—digging deeper into their resources."[4] This was a quality that Evans always admired in an artist—Duke Ellington and Miles Davis were others—and he always put his trust in late developers, realizing from his own experience the value of thorough and consistent preparation.

Anthony Benedetto was born in 1926, the son of an Italian grocer. A native New Yorker, he studied music and painting, and a drawing he did of Bill Evans adorns the cover—which he also designed—of the Fantasy trio album *Blue in Green*. Benedetto emerged from the army's entertainment branch (the Special Services that Evans and so many other fine musicians occupied) to act as master of ceremonies and sing in a Pearl Bailey revue in Greenwich Village. When Bob Hope heard him and booked him for his Paramount show, the singer decided to change his name to Tony Bennett.

His singing teacher, Miriam Speir, told him to imitate instrumentalists rather than singers, and he has modeled his performances on the jazz greats ever since. Ralph Sharon, his main musical director since 1954, always steered him toward the jazz world and encouraged him to go on the road with jazzmen in the band; huge audiences were newly exposed to the genre as a result.

Bill and Tony met in London to establish the dates and outline the music for *The Tony Bennett/Bill Evans Album*, recorded in June 1975. Most of the titles on this now classic recording were firm favorites of Evans's. The pianist, Bennett explained, would be responsible for structuring each setting: "He'd work for three or four hours on each song we did; we'd work out what tunes to do, the keys and tempos, then he'd kind of be left alone to work out a production. I used to say to Helen Keane, 'Keep the tape rolling.' I couldn't believe what he was doing, over and over again, each thing was magnificent. Then he'd turn round and say, 'I think we're ready to do one.' We did that for two or three days; we didn't have anyone in the studio except Don Cody the engineer, Helen, myself and Bill."[5]

With singer Tony Bennett at Fantasy Studios, Berkeley, California,
preparing for *The Tony Bennett/Bill Evans Album,* 1975.
Phil Bray, courtesy of Fantasy, Inc.

With a smaller quota of genius, Evans would have made a great musical
director, and in any case he was one of the most accomplished and sensitive
accompanists in the business. His backings made much use of that quietly pro-
cessional chord technique (which provided complete harmonic information
as well as pulse) that he had employed on *Undercurrent* with Jim Hall. And, of
course, there was an abundance of root chords in the absence of a bass player.
The pianist reveled in fulfilling the orchestral support to which the singer was
accustomed, and undoubtedly both were having a grand time. "It was my idea
that we make it only piano, though it kind of scared me," Bill said. "It seemed
to be the best way to get that intimate communication going. . . .

"A lot of the public wants that big sound—the studio orchestra, highly produced or over produced. So I thought we'd go all the way in the other direction, and I think it's timely because a lot of young people are looking for that personal quality."[6]

⊞ ⊞ ⊞

In July 1975 Evans was the first jazz pianist to be invited to the annual International Piano Festival and Competition at the University of Maryland. It was apt that he should be asked to advise at this particular gathering, for its sympathies were well founded in the famous Tobias Matthay approach to classical piano playing. Matthay was an English pianist and educator of German descent who founded his own school in 1900, his seminal written work being *The Act of Touch*. His approach stressed the importance of touch controlled by weight (gravity) and relaxation, essentials naturally embodied by Bill Evans. It is remarkable to ponder that this jazz pianist, by simple playing example, could have influenced the predominantly classical pianists present at this event in such matters as tonal nuance, color, and singing quality at the keyboard.

Intuition, the Evans-Gomez duet album, had been out since March, and Helen Keane arranged several European concerts in the summer for the duo. These included a further visit to the Montreux Jazz Festival, resulting in *Montreux III* for Fantasy. This time it was Claude Nobs, the founder of the festival, who welcomed the artists onto the stage. Evans turned his attention to two early John Lewis tunes—"Django," which had featured in his sideman days, and "Milano," which was new.

Also new was the beautiful song, "Minha," by the Brazilian composer Francis Hime, a tune taken up and nurtured until Evans's death. This mesmerizing creation was always played rubato throughout, a meaningful application of the old musicians' adage "once more from the top—with feeling." Lily Tomlin used this recording as the background to a sequence in her one-woman show. For these new tunes, as a safety measure in view of the potential recording, Evans had the sheet music on the stand, referring to it for the theme statements and the comping. The instrument on his right-hand side, at ninety degrees to the concert Yamaha, was actually a Fender-Rhodes, but this specimen exhibited a distressing tin-can quality.

The following day, the duo played afternoon and evening concerts at the Antibes/Juan-les-Pins Jazz Festival in the south of France, all taped by Radio France and parts of the evening performance going out on French television. Evans often threw in either a revival of an old number or something new in his sets in order to maintain freshness and a spot of color; in the

Palais de Congrès at Juan-les-Pins, "Alice in Wonderland" made such an appearance on the program. This could have been a whim or a request from the audience, perhaps from an admirer of *Sunday at the Village Vanguard*, the album on which it had appeared. The pianist was always happy to oblige in this way, as long as it was something that he played; logging it in his mind, he would engineer a slot for it in the set. Once, at Ronnie's, I asked him for "One for Helen."

"Gee, I don't know if I can remember that one—haven't played it for a while," he pondered. I was sitting in the middle, near the front, and was rewarded a few tunes later. At the end he caught my eye, half-smiled and nodded. The tune was not easy, being an eight, plus sixteen, plus ten-bar sequence, and the trio (with Gomez and Morell) had not been programming it on that visit. They played it flawlessly.

⊏⊨ ⊏⊨ ⊏⊨

On September 13, Bill and Nenette had a son, naming him Evan. The father expressed his joy to Len Lyons: "My personal life has become so happy in the last couple of years, getting a whole family thing going, buying a home, becoming a father. All of this contributes to my motivation, which is a mysterious element in anybody's life....

"I'm just feeling more alive now, alive in a broader way than just being a musician or an individual on the music scene. When you have children, it seems you're more tied to the future and to everything that's going on in the world."[7]

Soon after, in great mental shape, he played two dates at the Monterey Jazz Festival, one of the major events on the calendar. On the county fairgrounds the planned trio became a duo when Eliot Zigmund was frustrated in setting up. Later, Evans was joined by the young pianist Patrice Rushen for a rendition of "Autumn Leaves."

For the finale of the "Piano Playhouse" portion of the festival, these two pianists were augmented by John Lewis and Marian McPartland (who had earlier played individually and together) for an eight-hand rendering of "Billie's Bounce." Two full-sized Yamaha grands were in place, and the four pianists had worked out a seating choreography based on a three-chorus solo turnaround. Resplendent in red shirt and jacket, and contrasting vividly with John Lewis's black tie, Evans was evidently enjoying the special atmosphere of this novelty finale. In 1993 Storyville Records included this on a video of highlights called *Monterey Jazz Festival 75*.

The next day saw the Evans Trio reunited with the young musicians of

Bill with his mother, Mary, and his son Evan in 1976.
Courtesy estate of Bill Evans, copyright © Nenette Evans 1996

Oakland—this time their full symphony orchestra—for another performance of Claus Ogerman's *Symbiosis*.

A month later, Evans appeared on Johnny Carson's *Tonight Show* with Tony Bennett, as well as taking part in a one-night series called Concerts at the Grove in the Ambassador Hotel in Los Angeles. An increasing number of dates lately had been solo, and his thoughts turned again to the idea of a recording, particularly after hearing Marian McPartland play at Monterey. She was working solo in New York, and Evans wished he could do likewise. Helen Keane commented: "As much as Bill enjoyed playing alone at home, and although by this time he regularly included a solo section in his concert program, he found recording in this context very difficult. It was probably the only area he felt insecure about musically, and the fact that he'd gotten a Grammy for *Alone* didn't seem to help."[8]

He liked the full-sized Yamaha newly acquired by Fantasy for its studio, and in December 1975, at Helen's urging, he decided to risk himself solo on it with *Alone (Again)*. The weight of the album lay in Jule Styne's showstopper "People," from *Funny Girl*, here receiving the full rhapsodic treatment.

Rendering a Wagner opera at home Evans would have sounded much like this. On this track he hardly improvised in the usual jazz sense at all; rather, he created interest with inner figurations and fluctuating grades of tone color. He made the song see-saw several times between the keys of Bb and E, two tonalities that enjoy a special relationship for musicians, being equidistant by a tritone. Many factors influence a pianist's choice of key. There is the feel of the keyboard—the configurations of ebony and ivory—that renders certain passages more gratifying to the fingers; physiologically too, there are subtle connections between touch and sound vibration, producing sensations in the player that are unique to each key area. A further aspect, difficult to pin down and markedly personal, has to do with "color" and emotional resonance.

When *Alone (Again)* was released almost two years later, it was nominated for a Grammy.

⊂⊱ ⊂⊱ ⊂⊱

For the growing Evans family, the Riverdale apartment had become constrictingly small. Bill and Nenette, with their son Evan and Nenette's daughter Maxine, moved into a large, three-level house in Closter, a little town in Bergen County, New Jersey. It was a residential area in a valley—no apartments, no industry—about ten miles north of the George Washington Bridge. A forest and nature reserve bordered on their backyard. As Eliot Zigmund said, Bill was finally enjoying the fruits of his labors. Eliot saw a happy, almost bourgeois family man.

The only problem with the new home was that Evans had to work all the time in order to pay for it. For the most part this meant touring, so he hardly ever lived in the house, or played the Chickering baby grand he had inherited. When he was there, he enjoyed the location as a family person, keeping his customary low profile socially but more than willing to visit his stepdaughter's music class at school. He played for the children one day, to try and show them the difference between written and improvised music. He was concerned at the educational cutbacks. Citing his beloved Plato's dictum that a balanced personality may be created when music and gymnastics are in equilibrium, he observed that both were being phased out in schools.

It was around this time that Bill renewed his acquaintance with Warren Bernhardt, who visited the house in Closter. This time, as duettists, they were immersed in Rachmaninoff's Third Concerto, spending hours reading the score. "I remember how much Bill loved the harmonic construction of the second movement of the piece," said Bernhardt. Bill and

Nenette would go to hear Warren play at Bradley's in New York. Bernhardt recalled that Evan was still an infant and slept under the table during the dining and playing.

Another visitor to the house was the pianist Richie Beirach, to whom Evans introduced Scriabin's last set of piano Preludes, Op. 74. Beirach pays tribute: "He was very happy, and he was actually openly happy, which was completely unlike him. And it threw everybody. Anyway, it was great. He showed me his Chickering. He had pushed the keys down. They were like beautiful, old yellow keys, and you could see where his voicings would come from. He was a real poet. Sometimes less is less. Sometimes less is just not enough. But he would create an aura of silence around him. He would draw you in whether you wanted it or not. He was hypnotic."9

During 1975 a third volume of original tunes was printed by TRO, with the addition of a special section of Earl Zindars numbers that Evans played.

⋐⋐ ⋐⋐ ⋐⋐

The trio began 1976 with a typical chunk of globe-trotting time: a tour of Japan was followed by visits to Los Angeles, Minneapolis, and Boston, then on to Europe; then they were in South America and on the West Coast for two months or so. In all that time Evans would be lucky to get home for three or four weeks. Altogether, he spent a huge amount of time on the road, perhaps as much as half of it outside the United States.

In Tokyo the trio recorded privately for the Yamaha company archives, Evans playing one of their brand new pianos. Meanwhile, Eddie Gomez took Eliot Zigmund into another Tokyo studio to make *Down Stretch*, a trio record with Takehiro Honda on piano. Issued under Gomez's name, it was full of enterprising bass ideas, including overdubbing, and was indicative of his growing need to express himself in his own music.

By March 1976 the trio had reached Boston; at the Jazz Workshop it was standing room only for seven nights. Hot-footing from there, they played two weeks at Ronnie Scott's. The resident piano at the time was a Bechstein, in fair condition, once owned by Mike Hennessey. But Oscar Peterson was due to follow on at the club; a few days before his opening, Bösendorfer's London branch installed its Rolls-Royce of pianos, the Imperial. So once again Evans got to play on one of his favorite models. Hennessey asked whether his ideal playing environment included nobody listening except himself.

"Yes," Bill replied. "Especially with that piano. There's nothing more that you could wish than to be alone with that piano.... I think Oscar would have done a hell of a lot better on the Bechstein than I would (and vice versa), because his technique can just overcome a piano anyhow, and I love a piano with this kind of a tone, that speaks—really speaks."

Hennessey went on to other matters:

"So what's been happening since you were last over here?"

"Well mainly—I hate to bring it up—but the family thing has been primarily in my mind. I mean the musical thing, of course goes on..."

"Are you making a buck?"

"Oh, absolutely. Things are, without a doubt, better than they've ever been for me, career-wise."[10]

After Europe it was three weeks in South America, followed by several weeks on the West Coast. It was mid-May, and Evans was thinking about his next Fantasy album. For some time he had been mulling over the idea of a quintet recording along the lines of *Interplay*, made fourteen years before. Helen Keane suggested Harold Land on tenor sax and Kenny Burrell on guitar, while Evans was interested in the novelty of a fresh rhythm section, and suggested Ray Brown and Philly Joe Jones. It took all of a day in the studio to get these five giants working together smoothly and with a satisfactory balance, but some joyous music was eventually recorded for an album called *Quintessence*. Neither Land, Burrell, nor Brown had worked with Evans before. It has been said that Ray Brown defined bass playing in the pre-Evans style. Here he adjusted nothing, and Evans, away from his own trio setting, welcomed a straight blow. Philly Joe Jones played with sympathy and a delicate assurance that matched Evans's filigree strength.

One of the tracks—"The Second Time Around"—is for trio only. Here, Evans came just about as close as he ever would to sounding like the Oscar Peterson Trio, something he had always had a yen to do; on this number, the three players integrated with magical timing. Ray Brown's tenure with Oscar Peterson, incidentally, had been even longer than that of Gomez with Evans. "Why can't I get my rhythm section to sound like that?" Bill would wonder. It is perhaps to be regretted that he did not indulge in a straight swing more often; on the other hand, only with his own tightly knit chamber group could he nurture the slow development that was the central thread of his art.

In June 1976 the regular trio shared the opening concerts at Carnegie Hall of the fifth Newport–New York Jazz Festival with Tony Bennett. Singer and pianist alone, in the manner of their hit recording, began the concerts with "My Foolish Heart" and closed them with "But Beautiful" and "On the Sunny Side of the Street." As he frequently did when performing with just piano, Bennett chose to sing these without a microphone.

A week later, Evans and Gomez were further involved in the Newport

Festival program, joining saxophonists Lee Konitz and Warne Marsh with Elvin Jones on the drums for a spot at Radio City Music Hall. All the musicians gave their services for this fund-raising evening, introduced over the airwaves by Willis Conover for the Voice of America *Jazz Hour*. The reedmen revived an old standby of theirs, a forties bop number by Konitz called "Subconscious Lee."

From yet another European visit, a West Wind CD issued in 1989 and called *In His Own Way* presented performances from Cologne on September 6 (incorrectly identified as being from Rome). This fly-on-the-wall document preserves a thoroughly professional performance with occasional peaks. To describe it as unremarkable is only to judge it in the light of the trio's consistently high level. Such a set as this constituted a typical working night for Evans. Looked at coldly, he had put together a package that would impress a new audience with its professionalism, commitment, and variety of mood. With the resources of his trio he was able to entertain for an hour or so without resorting to gimmicks, musical or otherwise.

Returning to the States, Evans teamed up again with Tony Bennett for a second album called *Together Again,* this time for the singer's own Improv label. Like seasoned veterans of the cabaret stage, the two artists produced a recording at least as relaxed and mutually in tune as their first. Bennett gave a hushed rendering of one of Michel Legrand's finest songs, "You Must Believe in Spring," from the 1967 film *Les Demoiselles de Rochefort*. On his solo here, Evans began to get involved with the fertility of its harmonic sequence, perhaps unconsciously aware of its potential for the future, when it would turn out to be a trio-album title track.

We hear the words that shaped Bill's classic melody "The Two Lonely People." The pianist's attitude to lyrics was ambivalent: while prepared to be entertained by words, his true feelings were those of the committed instrumentalist. When asked how he felt about the lyrics to some of the old songs, he replied, "I never listen to lyrics. I'm seldom conscious of them at all. The vocalist might as well be a horn as far as I'm concerned."[11] Having said that, he provided lyrics for at least two of his own later compositions—the lighthearted "It's Love—It's Christmas," in which Bennett expressed an interest, and the heartfelt "Letter to Evan." He was also interested in other people's lyrics to his own tunes, as we have seen in connection with "Sugar Plum." The whole question of the relation between words and music is a thorny one, and the distinguished lyricist Gene Lees has written passionately about the ideal marriage that is possible. Evans was more than ready to compose from words, and was delighted with such reciprocal creations as Lees's own lyric to "Waltz for Debby."

In October, Evans, Gomez, and Zigmund played three nights at the Bottom Line in New York before crossing the Atlantic as part of George Wein's Newport Festival package, Newport à Paris. During the early sixties, Evans was better known in France, through his early albums, than in America. Every appearance at Radio France headquarters was an immediate sellout, and additional concerts sometimes had to be scheduled to accommodate the fans. The Evans group never sounded better in that venue than at this 1976 concert. *The Paris Concert* on Fantasy (not to be confused with the later one on Elektra-Musician) represents this underrecognized trio at its most energetically interactive. All three musicians played around the edges of the beat, pushing out the frontiers of what might be called a "controlled freedom," the governing factors being the fixed chord sequence and the implied pulse. "34 Skidoo," especially, benefited from this three-way fluidity of conception, realizing more invention than usual; frequently Evans got himself into a rut with this number, unable to find ideas capable of escaping a chord sequence that by its very nature trapped the improviser. His new melodic approach manifested an exciting obliquity, a seed that would be seen to germinate. A number of the tunes were recorded for the last or near-last time, presaging major repertoire changes.

Evans stayed with the quintet format for his next studio venture, calling on his old colleague Lee Konitz, a thought that had been at the back of his mind for a year or so. After the recent quintet performance at Newport–New York, what more logical than to include his saxophonist "big brother" from the fifties, Warne Marsh? In February 1977 the two reedmen joined the Evans trio to make *Crosscurrents*. It is a vexing album, for the saxophonists' tuning cannot be ignored. Since his early days with Miles Davis, Lee Konitz had made it a hallmark of his style to play sharp, but the upward pull had become more extreme over the years. Warne Marsh, in turn, seemed to be drawn pitchwise, as if by magnet, toward his colleague. There comes a point for the listener, however, when "expressive" intonation shades into torment, and enjoyment of *Crosscurrents* will be affected by one's degree of tolerance of the two "pitch camps" that obtain.

This project finally gave Eliot Zigmund, who had been with the trio since early in 1975, his first opportunity to record in the studio with Evans. He reflected on the frustration artists can feel when circumstances are beyond their control: "Bill was at a point in his life where each recording had to have some kind of a hook that would interest a record company or interest a market. So he couldn't just go in and do trio albums. I spent two years in the band without doing any recording, because every album he did was some kind of special project that didn't include me. There was a duo album with Eddie; there was an album with Kenny Burrell, Philly Joe and Harold Land; there was the stuff with Tony Bennett. So every time an album came out, it was like I was out in the cold. I was thinking, God, am I ever going to get to record with this guy?"[12]

Whenever he was recording for Fantasy, Evans tried to fit other local gigs into his schedule. Two days before these quintet sessions began, for example, he had given a fine solo piano set at Berkeley's Performing Arts Center. Then at the end of the week the trio played the Great American Music Hall in San Francisco, Warne Marsh sitting in to play some tunes from *Crosscurrents*, as well as "It's You or No One" from his fifties repertoire. Helen Keane often wished that they could have recorded that set. Evans went on to make one of his regular appearances at Joe Segal's Jazz Showcase in Chicago, while other spring venues included the Rising Sun in Montreal (with bassist Michel Donato) and the Scottsdale Center in Phoenix.

Fantasy released *Quintessence* quickly in May, but now Warner Brothers, venturing into jazz for the first time, made Evans an offer he could not refuse. Helen Keane spoke of Fantasy with affection: "We had spent over five years with the company and had come to feel like part of a family. The people who work there are warm, cooperative, and caring. Bill always looked forward to the time we spent in the Bay Area."[13]

But in the wake of what Keane called "a dazzling offer" from Warner, Evans made his last album for Fantasy; it was appropriate that it should be with his current trio and that it should be called *I Will Say Goodbye*, from the song by Michel Legrand. The Frenchman's songs have beguiling melodic appeal, and this, combined with their satisfying construction (Legrand has a strong sense of key relationships within a short span), is what persistently attracted Evans. His tunes also carry much sentiment, and the pianist could turn that to lyrical advantage while avoiding the maudlin. On this disc, the two versions of this haunting melody can be seen in retrospect to anticipate a new chapter in Evans's development—a final drive toward immediate connection with the listener. He had refined his harmonic language and was able at times to find a voicing that provided just enough information to orient the listener while adding a flavor peculiar to the moment. That flavor may be due to the choice of notes, or the conjuring of tone color from his imagination, or both.

The only original in this collection is "The Opener," toyed with on *Eloquence*. Like many of Evans's other tunes, as well as Legrand's "I Will Say Goodbye," it was built up from a germ motif and was another of those

Eliot Zigmund, Eddie Gomez, Helen Keane, and Bill Evans during playback at
Fantasy's Studio C while making *I Will Say Goodbye* in 1977.
Phil Bray, courtesy of Fantasy, Inc.

theater-style tunes of his, like "Show-Type Tune" and "Funny Man," that
conjured up the spectacle of Broadway.

The release of this album was delayed until January 1980, and it won
one of two Grammy Awards for the pianist that year. Although it was the last
time Helen Keane worked with Evans for Fantasy, in 1989 she produced *The
Complete Fantasy Recordings* (a nine-disc boxed set), as well as further issues
from the archives in ensuing years.

By way of a signing-on gift, Warner Brothers presented its new pianist
with an electronic console, an ARP Omni Synthesiser. Unlike his Fender-
Rhodes, though, it afforded him little pleasure, languishing untouched in
his music room. Meanwhile, albums were coming thick and fast, and the
first session for Warner Brothers was very much in the spirit of the last one for
Fantasy: at this time Evans seemed content to find new material and simply
play it beautifully. Once again the music of Michel Legrand provided the
title track for the album, *You Must Believe in Spring*. Legrand's way with a
melody was sinking deep into the pianist's psyche, for Evans's own new composition recorded here, "We Will Meet Again," pursued a similar contour to
Legrand's in its opening phrase. Furthermore, the other Evans original on
this album, "B Minor Waltz," absorbed a modulatory construct of Legrand's

by lifting the material bodily over to the flat-key side toward the end. It was several years since Evans had experienced a fertile period of composing, but the trickle begun by "The Opener" and the two tunes on this album presaged a flood that would sustain his imagination to the end.

Included on the album was "The Peacocks," which Bill had first played with Stan Getz in 1974. Jimmy Rowles, who wrote it, recalled how thrilled he was when he got the call about the recording license. "That really made me happy," he said. "When a guy like that takes your song it makes you feel good."[14] Evans added a devastating last chord on the flat fifth minor.

Then, leafing through the fake book, Evans found "Gary's Theme" by Gary McFarland; this gentle waltz, which Bill always referred to as "Gary's Waltz," contrasted a deliberately bland main section with a richly chromatic follow-on. Talking to Brian Priestley about choice of repertoire, Evans said: "Anytime that I come across a tune or anything that I really love and get into, by coincidence or whatever circumstance, I'll use it regardless."[15] A good example of this principle was the theme tune from his favorite TV program, M*A*S*H. The series had been spawned from the cinematic black comedy set in the Korean War, during which he had enlisted in 1951. The initials stand for Mobile Army Surgical Hospital, a unit, in the event, whose services he never required. Evans could not resist including Johnny Mandel's tune in his own programs. He would watch reruns of the show between sets in the dressing room at Ronnie's. Coincidentally, both the film and TV soundtrack performances employed the technique of putting the notes before the beat (prephrasing), an element of swing that Evans frequently adopted. Coproducer Tommy Lipuma got a lead sheet on the piece, and the trio threw together a routine of tried and trusted modulatory tricks, this time taking it through a cycle of descending major thirds. Compared with the bombshell it later became in clubs, this studio rendering was sedate in the extreme. More and more content to be himself, Evans was cultivating communion through simplicity. "B Minor Waltz" was dedicated to Ellaine. "We Will Meet Again" was written for his brother Harry, who died before it was issued and never knew about it. The album came out posthumously in 1981.

⫷ ⫷ ⫷

Eliot Zigmund and Eddie Gomez not only worked well together, but had become firm friends. Looking back, the drummer described the decision facing the bass player at that time: "Musically, it was great. The only possible thing I could say was, Eddie was kind of reaching a point where he was at the end of his tenure with Bill. So, I got a feeling at times that he was looking to move ahead, but yet the security of the gig was something that was keeping him there."[16] Gomez was beginning to feel pigeonholed as the bass player to Bill Evans, and the pianist himself felt that he was providing a limited setting for Eddie's talents. Gomez had to get out on his own, and at the same time he needed to travel less in order to spend more time with his family—the musician's chronic problem.

You Must Believe in Spring was Eddie's last album with Bill, and, along with *I Will Say Goodbye,* his most singing. Listening to his recordings throughout the eleven-year collaboration, one never ceases to admire his consistent energy and resource. On the bandstand he was a tower of strength, and for a while, in the early seventies, he carried the trio as much as Evans. During his time with Bill he found his lyricism and his own sound.

When *You're Gonna Hear from Me,* the second album from the Jazzhus Montmartre, was issued posthumously, Gomez wrote of his friend: "His demands were simple enough—show up and give one hundred percent, don't hold back, and take some chances now and then. He urged me to be myself and not dwell on the legacy of the late Scott LaFaro.

"Bill Evans was articulate, forthright, gentle, majestic, witty, and very supportive. His goal was to make music that balanced passion and intellect, that spoke directly to the heart."[17]

Part IV
The Last Trio, 1977–80

CHAPTER **19** Reflections in D

You keep pulling them out of the woodwork, you know!
     —Percy Heath to Bill Evans, referring to bassist Marc Johnson

Eddie Gomez had made his last recording with Evans, but he continued to play in the trio for a few more months. In autumn 1977 a date at the Eastman School of Music at Rochester, New York, was scheduled. But Gomez had a recording session fixed in California and was unable to play. Evans asked his former bassist Chuck Israels to fill in and, confident that the problem was solved, discussed repertoire with him on the flight from New York City.

Although it had been more than ten years since they had played together in a trio, it was easy to plan a program of items largely familiar to Israels. "Summertime" was revived, with its catchy bass riff intact from *How My Heart Sings*, as was Bernstein's "Some Other Time." Evans began the evening by telling the campus audience at the Eastman Theatre that the program would be unannounced, but then got into the swing of introducing each tune, taking care to credit each one with its composer. In a routine that would have confounded those critics who complained that he never spoke, he chattily introduced "Some Other Time" as "one of the three best songs which they left out of the movie" of *On the Town*. From the beginning he had been eager to praise Israels for his "true improvisation" in stepping in. In a number of fine solos, the bass player's grainy sound was unmistakable, as were his song lines.

This was one of Eliot Zigmund's last appearances with the trio, and all of a sudden the pianist was without a group. He said: "There was a lot of trauma when Eddie Gomez and Eliot Zigmund left almost simultaneously.... For the first time in eleven years I was faced with the prospect of reforming the entire trio. In that time Eddie and I had gotten so many million things together that it was a very difficult thing to contemplate."[1]

So it was, for a week in January 1978, that Evans held sway at the Village Vanguard, auditioning a different bass player each night. One of the most prized positions in jazz was up for grabs, and the cream of New York bass players climbed the stand, George Mraz and Rufus Reid among them. "When Eddie left," Evans said, "I was bombarded with calls, letters and demo tapes from aspiring bass players. I suppose sometimes this can work, but the truth is you pay your dues and you earn the respect of your peers. When something like this turns up, they think of you. You cannot force opportunities."[2]

I was lucky enough to catch a few of these sessions. Philly Joe Jones was behind the drums, and Evans and Helen Keane had arranged a nightly try-out schedule. There was no discussion on the stand, each candidate being expected to cope on the spot. Evans's own playing was rather routine; he was intent on placing settings at each bass player's disposal. After each set, he betrayed little, giving just a nod and a grunt.

On Sunday, the last day of tryouts, Michael Moore came onto the bandstand. It was a big occasion for him. His tone was softer than the others, molded with care, even love. There was a reason for this: the music of Bill Evans had inspired him to take up the bass in the first place, and he knew the trio's repertoire well. It was Helen who suggested that he should be given a shot. Evans had heard him play before, but Moore had never pestered him to play. Bill liked that.

At these auditions the pianist made no concessions in repertoire, mixing his usual proportion of standards, originals, and tunes he had made especially his own. In addition, there was one new item, a lovely rubato rumination that he had come across, a little-known composition by Duke Ellington called "Reflections in D." Ellington himself had recorded it in 1953, effectively as a piano solo, but with Wendell Marshall sustaining a D pedal point on bowed bass. When Evans tried it out at these auditions it sounded well enough accompanied by bass and drums, but it was to endure in his forthcoming programs as a peaceful yet searching solo haven.

Another tune that challenged all comers was "Gary's Theme." Michael Moore followed the chords through tentatively, but at the end of the set Bill's reaction was different: he nodded, smiled warmly, and said, "Thanks, Mike!" His complementary way with a fresh line, his quality of sound, his ability to carry a lyrical but strong solo, and his general sympathy won Moore the job, and he went on a five-month tour with Evans and Philly Joe Jones.

First, though, Evans had a solo project to complete for Warner Brothers, replacing a projected album with Johnny Mandel. It was a direct descendant of the 1963 album, *Conversations with Myself*, in that it made use of triple-tracking, but now varied by double-tracking, one solo track, and the use of the electric piano.

This radiant collection, called *New Conversations*, began with "Song for Helen," written specially for Helen Keane, his manager of sixteen years' standing. It was his second composition for her, and was, justly, a deeper, more golden affair than the earlier "One for Helen." The shimmering opening bars evoked the sound-world of the original *Conversations* album, in particular the introduction to the "*Spartacus* Love Theme." Now though, there was a new color, for the third keyboard was electric; at the end it projected the tune in relief from the proliferation of sixteenth notes surrounding it. The melody itself amounted to very little. A crude recipe would be: take the first three notes of "My Romance," repeat seventeen times at slightly different levels (varying the tones and semitones a bit), and briefly introduce a new shape (twice) at the apex. Specifically, a similar three-note figure permeates Scriabin's Prelude, Op. 74, No. 1, a piece Evans knew well, as testified by Richie Beirach. Evans took Scriabin's piece as his model, the contour rising slowly at first and leveling out to finish, when the motif was uttered thrice at the same pitch. In the case of each composer, this repetitive line, a kind of nontune in itself, came alive through the power of harmony (ex. 3).

"Maxine" was written to embody the spirit of Bill's stepdaughter, eleven years old at the time. "She's happy, full of life," he said. "The song has that spirit. It meanders a little, goes through a few channels, and ends playfully."[3] This three-keyboard celebration reflected Evans's newfound joy in family life. He played the piece for CBS-TV's *Camera Three* in a children's program on the poetry of e. e. cummings. Evans's comments on "For Nenette," written for his wife, may apply more generally to his melodic craftsmanship: "There was a danger of the melody being too sweet, and so I worked on this with a great deal of control and thought. The result, I hope, is a delicate balance of romanticism and discipline."[4] The complexity of the decoration is mesmerizing, as is the pianist's sense (in triplicate) of phrasing and emotional timing. A fourth offering from the revitalized composer was called "Remembering the Rain."

All these fresh compositions went into his own new publishing company, Teneten Music, the title being another of his anagrams, this time of his wife's name. Nenette was co-owner of the company, and after Bill died she assigned its catalogue to Ludlow Music, one of his earlier publishers. In 1981 the four new originals appeared in a volume called *Bill Evans/the 70s*, in versions that Art Murphy made playable for solo piano.

Ex. 3. The power of harmony: Evans's composition "Song for Helen," from the second statement of the tune on *New Conversations*. Someone once said that a chord in music cannot be verbalized; this was especially true of a Bill Evans chord, which invariably carried an emotional charge. His chords can at least, though, be notated.

On *New Conversations* only Ellington's "Reflections In D," the piece that Evans had been trying out at the Vanguard, was done on one piano, but whereas in the composer's hands the cameo had emerged as a set-piece, an easy reverie, Evans instilled a visionary depth, a glimpse of mysteries untold.

The earlier multitracked albums had contained some ragged ensemble playing, but now the pianist's control over the components and their assembly is nearly perfect, the whole album carefully honed and lovingly played. Although he has returned to the three keyboards of his first attempt, the overall effect is cleaner, less cluttered; problems of density are resolved by using a lot of solo sections, blending three pianos infrequently and not for long. "Playing by myself," he said, "I'm able to project my personal feelings more strongly. With a group, you have to bend and mix, and that can lead to very satisfying experiences, but you don't get as deeply into the essence of who you are as in a solo performance. This really is the essence of me."[5]

⋐ ⋐ ⋐

Evans had begun to use drugs again—cocaine this time—and it was an indulgence that Nenette could not handle. She would not expose the children, Maxine and Evan, to this way of life, and she moved to a house on Long Island Sound near New Haven, Connecticut. Evans took an apartment in Fort Lee, New Jersey, just across the Hudson River from Manhattan. But they shared the two homes, and in due course, the pianist moved a six-foot-three Baldwin grand, on loan from the company, into Nenette's home. He installed his Chickering in the Fort Lee apartment.

The current trio, with Mike Moore and Philly Joe Jones, played nationwide during the first few months of 1978. Besides playing the Ibis Club in New York and the Jazz Workshop in Boston, they had gigs in suburban Chicago (the Amazingrace Club in Evanston), Minneapolis, Seattle, San Francisco, and San Diego; they also played a week at Howard Rumsey's Concerts by the Sea in Redondo Beach.

Evans was conspicuously fashion conscious at this time. He dyed and set his hair, wore a medallion round his neck, and sported gold or silver matching sets of glasses, watch, and ring. Whatever he may have felt like, he was at least looking good. Nor had he lost his sense of humor: one evening a lady accosted him: "Why, Mr. Evans, you *are* looking well. Tell me, what do you do to keep in such good shape?"

"Well, I've been doing a lot of jogging..." (aside to Mike Moore) "... from the bed to the bathroom."

There were some bizarre occasions: in Seattle the trio participated in an event (the first of several) called a "Double Bill." The head of a dance company there happened to share Bill's name, and his troupe, the Bill Evans Modern Dance Company, performed choreography to Evans's compositions. This was the only context in which the pianist ever attempted a re-creation of his own "Peace Piece." For other reasons, Moore remembers that evening with a special twinge. "Bill went shopping in Sears with Philly Joe," he told me. "They got horrible polyester suits—powder blue coats, white trousers, and reversible vests (pink on one side). They decided it all—I had nothing to do with it, except I had to wear the damn things." It was the old junkie-buddy syndrome again: before, Evans and Jones had both been on heroin; now it was cocaine and alcohol, respectively. They were like a couple of vampires in their exclusive club, swapping stories on another planet.

In San Francisco, the trio and Tony Bennett did a benefit concert for the radio station KJAZ. "It was a disaster," Moore recounted. "At the last minute, everything was cut down from the orchestral arrangements. Bill, who was very nervous, tried to brief me so that I in turn could brief Philly Joe, who was not interested. 'Don't worry, I know Bill—I'll catch him,' he said. He never did—he missed everything."

When traveling by rental car, Evans did all the driving in spite of swollen feet and ankles. He had always had a taste for stylish cars, and he loved being behind the wheel. Philly Joe was always late, holding the others up, but Bill never said anything. When the trio did arrive, there was always a nine-foot Baldwin grand waiting, for Evans was now a Baldwin artist. He endorsed the firm's instruments in their advertisement that read simply: "Baldwin—Bill Evans' Accompanist."

Mike Moore rapidly became disillusioned about the joys of playing in the Bill Evans Trio. The pianist's tendency to rush the up-tempo numbers was readily abetted by Philly Joe Jones. Moore was happiest on ballads and asked Bill to include as many as possible. Evans agreed, but the drummer's barnstorming approach led Moore to quit after only a few months. If the performance at the Catamaran Hotel in San Diego was anything to go by, one could hardly blame him. The evening degenerated from the start, the Jones bombshells coming thicker and faster by the minute. By the time the fourth number ("Theme from *M*A*S*H*") had come up, it was not so much the Bill Evans Trio as the Philly Joe Jones Circus Band on stage. Jones had his own followers who egged him on relentlessly. On the other hand, no drummer could propel "Turn Out the Stars" quite like he did, and his sense of theater could instigate a hushed "But Beautiful" at just the right moment. Somehow Evans maintained his concentration on these gigs, and Moore doggedly turned in distinctive bass solos. Sometimes, the pianist would depart from his instincts and start talking to the audience, almost putting together an act; but the more he talked, the worse he played.

ᶜᴱ ᶜᴱ ᶜᴱ

After the departure of Michael Moore, Evans again needed a permanent replacement for Eddie Gomez, and he offered new tryout opportunities. Marc Johnson, a twenty-four-year-old bass player from Dallas, then with Woody Herman, was interested, to put it mildly. He had absorbed a classical background at North Texas State University. While playing professionally in the Fort Worth Symphony Orchestra he had gravitated toward the music of Bill Evans, and his fascination soon turned to reverence.

Johnson's mentor in Dallas was Fred Crane, a fine pianist who, coincidentally, had gone to college with Evans and who, like Evans, cultivated a beautiful sound. Crane contacted Bill and recommended Johnson. The Herman band was in a different place every night, and for weeks on end Johnson would call Evans from the road. Whenever he was near New York or free, the pianist was away somewhere else. Finally, in April, Johnson flew up from West Virginia to sit in at the Vanguard. He made an impact on Evans, who said, "Before we even finished the first number, I got the feeling immediately that this was the guy. I don't know how to explain what those decisions are based on. It's a lot of experience, and realizing how a guy approaches things and how he sounds, and all that. I'll tell you the truth—there were guys that worked with the trio that were better professional bass players than Marc was when he first came with the trio, but none of them indicated to me that they had the potential that he had for this music."[6]

Evans always had a sure nose for promise. Eddie Gomez had readily admitted that he was out of his depth when he joined, and Marc Johnson said the same: "In so many ways, I wasn't ready for the gig.... But I think Bill sensed in me a love and a drive and a concern and a care for him and the music. He knew I'd be there, and I wouldn't take some other gig over his— he was right."[7]

Evans, Philly Joe Jones, and Marc Johnson embarked on a festival tour of Europe, beginning with the Grande Parade du Jazz in Nice, under the aegis of the impresario George Wein. The trio was in residence on the Garden Stage of the Arènes de Cimiez, the Roman amphitheater behind the town. The whole tour was a disorganized and tiring affair. Evans had to lie down during the day when not traveling, and his aggravated hepatitis was sometimes so bad that he had to cancel parts of the schedule.

Lee Konitz joined them for most of the trip, but, as Mike Moore had been, he was troubled by Philly Joe Jones's inclination to push up the tempo. He explained: "Bill also had the tendency to play up on the top of the beat and I have a tendency to try to play in the middle of the beat and sometimes behind. So when people do that I feel like I have to run to keep up because that's not my comfortable feeling. So I was listening to Marc Johnson all the time—he was trying to hold it together. It was embarrassing; I was so uncomfortable that in Nice I felt I was having a heart attack after one set. I actually had to go to a hospital in an ambulance."[8] He eventually settled into playing duets with Evans.

When fit enough to appear, Bill was in adventurous form, the playing of Marc Johnson leading him into fresh ideas and new phrase structures. These two players were feeling their way together, melodically and rhythmically, in two-part counterpoint. There was a new element of risk taking from Evans, reminiscent of his all too brief interplay with Gary Peacock in the 1960s. Within his own harmonic framework, this was caution-to-the-winds, try-anything jazz; at this stage of the tour he was producing some of his most positive and creative playing in ages. Eliot Zigmund, who came back to play with Bill several times after Marc Johnson joined, put his finger on what was happening: "I think Bill was responding to Marc as much as a person as he was a musician. His interest in Marc was stirred by the fact that he was a great player, but also he was very young and open, and very, very respectful of Bill. He brought an openness to the music at a point when Bill was looking for it. Somewhere deep inside himself Bill was looking to really make a change, which is what happened with that trio."[9]

During one set, church bells pealed forth from the town. The players had just finished "Emily," and Bill paused to listen, then commented: "A real live scene here—Charles Ives!" Picking out the ringing tones of the bells on the piano and asking Johnson, "Is that your G natural there?" he advocated "Green Dolphin Street" and swung in accordingly. On its last date in Nice the trio was joined by Stan Getz, Curtis Fuller, and Christian Escoudé for a spirited if imprecise jam session. Incidentally, the pianist Jimmy Rowles was on the tour, unaware for a while that Evans was including his tune "The Peacocks" in his sets.

Evans made his fourth appearance at the Montreux Jazz Festival, notable for a rapt "Reflections in D" and the launch of "Nardis" into its final incarnation. On this number the tally for free, preamble choruses reached four, and the piece acquired a new logo in the shape of a rocking, semitonal riff behind the bass spot. Guitarist Kenny Burrell joined in for a couple of numbers from *Quintessence:* "A Child Is Born," done as a reflective guitar and piano duo—Bill looked happy with that one—and "Bass Face," nicely featuring Marc Johnson's funky line and firm tone.

The trio and Lee Konitz took part in festivals at Nîmes, North Sea, and Perugia. At Terni, in Umbria, all the ingredients of al fresco music making held sway: technicians on stage, photographers crowding the stand, and sheet music escaping in the wind. A vintage but robust Bechstein stood up valiantly to the heat of television lighting.

The next day they were booked into the Fairfield Halls, Croydon, in south London. Arriving late and exhausted from the airport, Evans announced to his audience, "I know you don't want to know this, but..." He recounted a string of on-the-road mishaps before, as if on cue, the sound system sabotaged his carefully judged piano opening. Professionalism in adversity saw him through, and he shrugged it off: "Well, that's killed that one"; it had been beautiful, too. He proceeded with patient resignation to a different number.

The one-nighters continued in the north of England at the Cleveland International Jazz Festival, on a huge stage (used previously for the Rolling Stones) erected in the center of Middlesbrough's hallowed turf at Ayresome Park football ground. Such a venue can hardly have been Evans's dream setting for music making, but he was better than most at ignoring his surroundings and getting on with the job. In any case, he was on tour, working and making money. The sound system conveyed over the yawning arena what the MC, George Melly, referred to as the "intimate speculations" of Evans and Konitz. The crowd was appreciative, but for a variety of reasons the four musicians were finding empathy difficult to achieve on this tour, both musically and personally. Johnson was still feeling his way on one or two numbers, in particular "Up with the Lark," but in general he had revealed himself as a powerful "walker" and a stunning soloist, exhibiting a wide range of tone, incisive energy (he had a snappy end to a note), and high lyricism. Evans felt him to be closer in spirit to Scott LaFaro than to Eddie Gomez.

That autumn, after a week at the Playboy Club in New York, it was time to visit Tokyo again. Percy Heath and Thad Jones were doing their own tour, and they attended the trio's concert in the wings. As Evans's group came off, the older bass player paid tribute to the younger, Heath addressing Evans with: "You keep pulling them out of the woodwork, you know!"[10]

⋹ ⋹ ⋹

Throughout his career, Evans nursed a constant grouse with record companies. He had been unimpressed with the marketing budget at

Fantasy—the backup for *Intuition*, for example—and now he complained of Warner Brothers' poor promotion of *New Conversations*. It was all the more galling because, in contrast to his early days, he was beginning to feel good about some of his records.

An album was planned with Michel Legrand, original music featuring Bill; it fell through. As yet unsettled regarding his trio lineup, he opted for another quintet album for his next Warner Brothers offering, even though *Crosscurrents* was about to be released. This time, for *Affinity*, Toots Thielemans was to be the frontliner. "He is the only harmonica player in jazz," said Evans. "And I just love his whole feeling for music and melody. How he does it on harmonica, nobody will ever know. I have stopped trying to figure it out."[11]

Aiming, as on *New Conversations*, for textural variety, Evans mixed up duos with Thielemans, numbers for trio and quartet, and quintets with the saxophonist Larry Schneider. Eliot Zigmund, who had really left the trio a year previously, was making a guest appearance, wearing his sober studio hat. He said, "I seemed to have developed a relationship with Bill where he would call me up to come back and play, which was a great thing. I didn't realize—I was too young to realize—how great it was!"[12]

Thielemans had worked with the singer-songwriter Paul Simon and had already treated his ballad "I Do It for Your Love" with some sophistication. He felt that it would suit Evans, and indeed, Paul Simon's statement, which said it all on his own terms, was enhanced structurally by the pianist's harmonic modifications. He took the song firmly into his own repertoire.

On "The Days of Wine and Roses" Evans brought a new dimension, developed from *Quintessence*, to the art of comping, indulging in an active brand that entertained without detracting from the soloist. It was Thielemans's idea to alternate half choruses in F and A♭, and in this form it became another regular for the trio.

On the sublime "Body and Soul," the music slows into eternity. Evans had entered his last great period. One manifestation was the recapturing of a sense of the unexpected in his timing, but with a new precision and a confident edge, left-hand displacements being placed against the beat with an outright intent that shocks us into acceptance, part of an accelerating trend toward the communicative point.

A few days later, he was the subject of Marian McPartland's charmingly hosted series of weekly conversations for National Public Radio, on which she persuaded her guests to play solo as well as in duet with herself. The shows were recorded at the Baldwin Piano Showroom on West 58th Street, and from about fifteen pianos in the building Marian selected one especially for Evans. The occasion, issued on Jazz Alliance as *Marian McPartland's Piano Jazz, with Guest Bill Evans,* brought out the graciousness of the man as well as what Helen Keane called his "forthright, gentle majesty."[13]

Bill got in gently with more or less the printed version of "Waltz for Debby" before the conversation turned toward rhythmic displacement. As demonstrated on the just-recorded *Affinity,* this pursuit was a higher priority for him than ever before. He explained: "I think the rhythmic construction of the thing has evolved quite a bit. Now, I don't know how obvious that would be to the listener, but the displacement of phrases, and the way phrases follow one another, and their placement against the meter and so forth, is something that I've worked on rather hard, and it's something I believe in. It has little to do with trends. It has more to do with my feeling about my basic conception of jazz structure and jazz melodies, and the way the rhythmic things follow one another. And so I just keep trying to get deeper into that, and as the years go by I seem to make some progress in that direction."[14]

There followed an astonishing display of deliberate phrase displacement, using "All of You," which Marian McPartland eventually slotted into with the melody itself. She did the same on Bill's next demonstration, a restructuring of "The Touch of Your Lips," using pedal points and chordal enhancements. For comparison, he played what the fake book might give. A discussion of key choice in general (Evans nominated A and E as two of his favorites) led to a complete solo performance of "Reflections in D." Along the way there were delightful two-piano explorations of some standards.

"Well—that's jazz!" said Bill after an easygoing jaunt through "In Your Own Sweet Way." The whole occasion was a happy one, and it was in that spirit, before everyone departed for dinner at the Russian Tea Room, that Marian wound up with: "I'll challenge you to a ballad sometime—but you'll win!"

"Oh, I don't like that idea," laughed Bill.[15]

CHAPTER **20** Twenty-One Cities in Twenty-Four Days

Believe me, if it wasn't for Helen, Bill would have been gone a long time before.
— Joe LaBarbera

Evans had found his bass player in Marc Johnson, but he was still looking for his drummer. He asked Eliot Zigmund to stay with the band, but Zigmund wanted to test his wings, feeling that there was not enough variation in the trio's repertoire and that in the course of a four-year span he had done what he wanted. In any case, he had a group going with Richie Beirach and Frank Tusa called Eon. Evans takes up the story:

> Marc came into the trio about six months before Philly Joe left, and we had some magnificent times with that trio. When Philly Joe left, after a Japanese tour we did, I was again looking for a drummer. I rely a lot on peer opinion. With Marc I relied on my college friend because he made a special effort to communicate with me, and in the same way I'm friendly with Joe Puma (we both like to go to the harness races once in a while) and I value his opinion about musicians. Joe said, "I hope you don't take this guy away from me, but as far as I'm concerned, Joe LaBarbera is the drummer who always does the right thing at the right time." So I had Joe come down and sit in at the Vanguard, and he attracted me very much the same way.[1]

Joe LaBarbera was born in New York in 1948 and studied with Alan Dawson at Berklee College of Music, just after Dawson himself had played briefly in the Bill Evans Trio. LaBarbera had played in the Woody Herman band a few years before Marc Johnson's tenure. More recently he had free-lanced with Jim Hall and Phil Woods, but he was perhaps best known for his time with Chuck Mangione. "I was aware of Bill's music from an early age," he recalls. "I started hearing him play when I was about twelve or thirteen, so, in the back of my mind, his sound was embedded. Maybe over the course of all those years, I was able to kind of figure out what it would be like to play with the guy, or what he would want."[2]

So it was that in January 1979 the new—the last—Bill Evans Trio began working together. One of their first gigs was a few days opposite the Russian trumpeter Valeri Ponomarev at a club in Philadelphia. Evans was astonished that such ability could be developed on the cultural "island" (jazzwise) of Russia. In front of a positive and discerning crowd the trio sounded relaxed, the ideas flowing easily within a spacious time scale. Evans was evidently in good creative humor, and several songs came off in that special way that can happen when conditions are right. Again he admitted the influence of crowd and ambience: "You're never going to hear on record what you may hear live. Our best performances have gone into the atmosphere, and we never have really gotten on record that special peak that happens fairly often (and you just never know), and there's just something about that physical contact, any-how—there's nothing like it."[3]

As with previous trios, the members got the formal details together on the job. A new series of engagements began at Rick's Café Americain at the Holiday Inn on Chicago's North Lake Shore Drive. This three-year-old venue had a fine piano and competed for a while with the city's most important jazz club, Joe Segal's Jazz Showcase, to which Evans had returned consistently over the years. The trio played a week at Rick's before visiting the town of Ames, home of Iowa State University. Iowa public radio and television recorded two hourlong sets, issued on KJazz video as *Jazz at the Maintenance Shop, Volumes 1 and 2*.

Evans's mood gradually soured during the course of the evening. In the first set (issued as volume 2), the out-of-tune piano came in for some criticism from the moody pianist, who was probably comparing it to the previous week's instrument in Chicago. During a typically concentrated "But Beautiful"—reputedly his favorite song—he alighted on a particularly tuneless high E♭, giving it a good thrashing while including it in the line. He was generally out of sorts, sighing from time to time during theme statements, as if to say, *This is hard work but we must keep going*. He delivered a warning: "We'd like to continue with an original by the late Gary McFarland. It's a tender waltz called 'Gary's Waltz'—although it was tender until tonight. I think there may be a bit of hostile frustration in the performance, because I'm dealing with a piano that I'm not too happy with tonight, but we'll do the best we can." In the event, hostility was tempered, though tenderness compromised.

The pianist's solo introduction to "Nardis" had been expanding since

1969, and on this occasion it took seven choruses. The primal energy of Marc Johnson's solo was firmly rooted in the open E of his bass. (Before his father tried to get him interested in jazz, Johnson had been a rock bass player.)

In the other set, it was the sound technicians who came under attack. Evans was unhappy with the level on the monitors and said so with good-natured sarcasm: "I'm glad we had a sound check, you know—spent about a half-hour down here getting it right. But we'll just go ahead and weather it through—'cause that's our job." The acerbic remarks were a verbal extension of his platform manner of the sixties; to those not familiar with his deadpan delivery, this could be off-putting.

Eventually, after an organically probing "The Peacocks" and a burning "Theme from M*A*S*H," Evans began to settle down. Joe LaBarbera could generate a steam-powered drive when moving to sticks, and the unit really came together on "In Your Own Sweet Way," seeking out textures and exploring creative spin-offs. Evans's displaced left hand sparred with the rock-steady Johnson, making for tough and resilient interplay; there was an inner fiber, a healthy three-way dynamism. Just as with Eliot Zigmund, the new trio had rapidly become an integrated unit. LaBarbera recalled his first experience of playing with Evans: "The minute you sat down and played with him, the minute the first note came out, he was so strong and so positive about his direction, that if you were any kind of a musician at all, you intuitively knew where he wanted it to go. He would never say anything to you like, 'Do this, do that.' He gave you the room to find it on your own."[4]

The early, whole-chorus trading on "My Romance" manifested a keen rapport between Johnson and LaBarbera. It was Evans's turn to be stunned; he could not quite believe his luck in having these two musicians from another generation in his group. He was thrilled and encouraged by their interest in his music and their ability to become a vibrant part of it.

In just three months, "I Do It for Your Love" had developed under the maturing Evans touch. He was digging into a fresh approach on ballads, moving concurrently through two time dimensions: while the changes glided infinitely slowly, the solo garland entwined at a rate befitting a four-fold-quicker pulse. The result was a rich proliferation executed in composure. More and more, there were new ways around corners, fresh approaches and departures.

At this televised performance in Ames, Evans had been testy, but at the end he said appreciatively, "You've been a very nice audience."

⊂⋷ ⊂⋷ ⊂⋷

In April, before a far-ranging tour of the American Northwest and parts of Canada, the trio began an engagement at Blues Alley, a jazz club in Washington, D.C. Willis Conover fixed an afternoon for Evans to visit his Georgetown apartment, the idea being to record an informal conversation for his program *The House of Sounds*. In the course of that interview, Evans talked perceptively and at length on questions of style and his own influence on younger players, as well as worldly cultural matters.

Back at the club that evening, he suffered a profound shock. The news came that his brother Harry, who had been severely depressed, had shot himself. Bill canceled the rest of his engagement at Blues Alley and much of the ensuing tour. He loved and admired his brother unconditionally, and he took his suicide very hard. First with Scott LaFaro, then Ellaine, and now Harry, tragedy hounded him. This latest blow robbed him of his remaining strength, and his spirit was finally broken. Only deep inside his music could he find consolation.

⊑ ⊑ ⊑

In the summer, he returned with his trio to the Hartford Jazz Festival in Connecticut, where he had played before with Gomez and Zigmund. Sometimes several thousand people attended these concerts at the city's Bushnell Park. The performance was broadcast on Public Alternative Radio in West Hartford, and chatting on air, the interviewer reassured the pianist that more people generally showed up as the evening progressed. "Well, sufficient," Evans chuckled. "Two or three people listening is enough for me." As it turned out, his patience was to be sorely tried by a hooligan element in the crowd. After a typically set-stopping "My Romance," he credited his colleagues over the PA system, followed by: "I'd like to add something. There seems to be a small group of (you might say) quote 'assholes' out there who think they should be the center of attention tonight. Now, we're going to take a twenty-minute break—if you think you should be the center of attention, come up on stage and entertain the people for the next twenty minutes."

Back in New York in July, WKCR-FM was replaying, day and night for almost a week, the complete recordings of Miles Davis. Evans was one of several musicians who contributed telephone interviews to this radio celebration, called the Miles Davis Festival. The trumpeter had been inactive for almost four years, and rumors abounded that he was in ill health, but Evans had visited him recently, along with Gil Evans, and had found him to be looking well and in good spirits. In the interview, Bill said that he had "somewhat prevailed upon him that the world was waiting for him," and

Davis did in fact make a start the following year on what turned out to be *The Man with the Horn.*

Evans was impatient to get his new trio on record, but *I Will Say Goodbye* had not been out long from Fantasy, and Warner Brothers was still holding *You Must Believe in Spring.* So he went into the studio to record another quintet album for Warner, which he designated "In loving dedication to my late brother, Harry L. Evans 1927–1979." *We Will Meet Again* was, for the most part, a straight blowing session, with a minimum of formatting, arranging, and editing, but there was nothing casual about it. Tom Harrell was the distinguished newcomer to what would prove to be the last Evans quintet lineup. He had played with the pianist before, contributing a delicately turned flugelhorn solo on Chuck Israels's arrangement of "Very Early" for the National Jazz Ensemble in 1975. On *We Will Meet Again*, Larry Schneider completed the lineup.

During the spring tour Evans had met his new young girlfriend, Laurie Verchomin, in Edmonton, Alberta. "Laurie," written for her, is a fine example of the composer's way with mutually supportive melody and harmony; it was hardly surprising that his creations should effect this union, in view of his long-standing ability to reconstruct standards by judicious harmonic substitution. So often with Evans, the first recording of a number was formally definitive, its freshness the key to its essence. It had been so with "I Do It for Your Love" on *Affinity,* and it was so now with "Laurie." On his solo the pianist penetrated the upper echelons of the keyboard like a delicate glistening rainbow. This was a recent preoccupation; during the sixties he rarely played outside the middle area, but he expanded slowly outward during the seventies.

Another newcomer was "Bill's Hit Tune" which assimilated Michel Legrand's way with cycles of fifths in the bass. Bill remarked that it had the "quality of a French movie theme if played slow." The tune was delivered in parallel thirds and sixths on soprano saxophone and trumpet, a compositional procedure stemming directly from the music of Frédéric Chopin. For his solo, Evans launched into a blinding cascade of notes. Never can he have packed so many notes into one solo, the most sustained rapid-scale onslaught of his career. Yet this was no facile garnish, but rather a regenerative outpouring of spiraling ideas always pertinent to the chord.

The Sam Lewis–J. Fred Coots song "For All We Know (We May Never Meet Again)" was done as a brief but yearning solo piano companion to "We Will Meet Again." These two brief tracks end the LP sides, functioning emotionally as "Epilogue" had done on *Everybody Digs Bill Evans.*

In 1980 the album won the Grammy Award for best jazz instrumental performance as a group, and Evans won as a soloist with the long-delayed *I Will Say Goodbye*.

⋐⋐ ⋐⋐ ⋐⋐

On August 16, Bill had his fiftieth birthday party in New York, attended by many of his fellow pianists and hosted by one of them, Garry Dial. It was a happy occasion, and he delighted everyone present with a potpourri of his recent compositions, including the very latest, which was to be called "Letter to Evan." Other sneak previews were "Bill's Hit Tune" and "Laurie," just recorded but still unknown. He played "For All We Know," Mercer Ellington's "Blue Serge," and his own "Fun Ride" before joining just about every pianist in the room for a duet.

There was a further celebration at Nenette's house near New Haven, attended by Warren Bernhardt. "Bill and I left the party early," he said. "We just drove around in his car, listening to Richard Pryor tapes and laughing for hours. We used to like to drive around and talk in the car. Bill had a terrific sense of humor and was always giving me humorous books by Thurber, Leacock, or Woody Allen."

⋐⋐ ⋐⋐ ⋐⋐

In September the new trio went to South America. One of the props Bill took with him was a solo piano album by Warren Bernhardt called *Floating*, which had been released in March. Evans loved it, and was inspired by it, particularly in the flourishing introductions to "Nardis." The Argentinian leg of the tour began at the Opera House in Buenos Aires, where Evans was received rapturously, as before. Concerts followed in nearby Rosario and San Nicolas before they returned to the capital and a different theater, where an unofficial recording was made. It was issued in 1989 on Yellow Note LPs as *Live in Buenos Aires 1979*. The group was peaking just then, and it is an especially magnificent example of their art.

Evans opened the second half with a solo performance of his new creation "Letter to Evan," written for his son's fourth birthday, September 13. While writing it, he consulted Warren Bernhardt. "He would play it over and over in various keys and ask my opinion," Warren recalls. "Then he'd ask me to play it and then transpose it and see what I thought. He really loved hearing these tunes of his over and over again. He'd get tied up in the most beastly keys. He got all the way into them, too. I remember him saying to me once—he may unfortunately have been referring to cocaine at the time, although it translates to all of his musical activities—'Yeah, Warren. When I get into something, I really get into it!'"

The recording continued with "I Loves You, Porgy," one of his most remarkable solo virtuoso indulgences. This impressive but curiously motivated assault on Gershwin's love song cleared the air for an astonishing piece of duo playing with Marc Johnson. The thrilling ride took place on "Up with the Lark," consistently aslant, with seemingly everything avoiding the beat— twos, threes, and fours tossed in the air and nonchalantly caught, both players conjuring with a beat that was not physically there. It all seemed so easy.

At such a juncture, the players must have been on a "high." Joe LaBarbera, however, had sat out four numbers, something he hated having to do, eager as he was to play. Coming in on "Someday My Prince Will Come," though, he had a tricky task to fulfill. Evans's tendency to rush could cause problems for his drummer, whose challenge was simultaneously to integrate and propel the group. Bill was well aware of the situation, admitted to Joe that he was rushing, and urged him to go along nevertheless. LaBarbera, who solved the dilemma brilliantly, gave his reaction: "It's tough for me to deal with that in any circumstance, because you're trained as a drummer to keep the beat steady and still propel the group. So, it was a conflict. But it was easily settled because Bill was very strong, and you just kind of went with him or else you were lost along the wayside. Also I have found, when I listen to some of those recordings where I am trying to hold it back, it kind of kills the groove. So I realized that it's not always the best thing to do. It's a tough thing to deal with, especially for younger players. They want to be correct, but it's not always the right solution to a musical problem."[5]

At the end of this Buenos Aires concert Bill yelled to his colleagues, "Beautiful!" as well he might.

In October, from Lulu White's club in Boston, the trio broadcast two calm and refined sets, much of the music turning softly inward upon itself. An album was a possibility, but there was a self-conscious air to the playing, the deliberate holding in of the reins lending a formality to the proceedings; the material was not issued.

⌁ ⌁ ⌁

Evans generally admired other pianists. He was able to open his mind to assimilate many ways of playing, considering "style" secondary to the communication of the artist's message. One night he had come across the pianist Joanne Brackeen playing with Joe Henderson at the Village Vanguard, and he pressed Helen Keane to become her manager. "It was an unspoken thing with Bill that I would never really have an interest in another pianist," Helen told Linda Dahl.[6] However, thus encouraged, she immediately took on Brackeen, a relationship sustained after Evans's death.

⊂⊢ ⊂⊢ ⊂⊢

In November and December, the trio embarked on a daunting schedule in Europe, the back-breaking itinerary taking in twenty-one cities in twenty-four days, in venues ranging from intimate jazz clubs to large concert halls.

Returning to the ever-welcoming Parisians, they gave two sets (recorded by Radio France) at Espace Cardin. Most of the material was issued in 1983 on two Elektra-Musician records (a new Warner Brothers label) as *The Paris Concert, Editions One and Two,* performances that have long been acclaimed as among the finest from the Bill Evans Trio. The pianist said that whereas the trio of the earlier seventies, for all its resourcefulness, tended to remain static, the new one was all the time manifesting an inner growth, and a willingness to expand. There was indeed an excitement in the air, a feeling that anything could be made to happen at any time. Burt Korall, in his sleeve note to *Edition Two,* noted the paradox that while being more experimental than ever before Evans seemed at the same time more accessible. "He more freely manipulated rhythmic sequences," he wrote. "He experimented with sonorities, moving with far less inhibition than in the early years. He seemed far less fearful of making mistakes or failing. The playing seemed to say, 'Let's do it!'"[7] Proving the point was a definitive trio version of "Laurie," imbued with a deep intensity of expression and full of daring and impulsive fantasy.

For some time the group's concert format had been carefully constructed. Spanning about two hours, it was in two parts. In the first half, six or more numbers would be chosen to contrast with one another rather like the movements of a classical suite (this portion would typically end with "My Romance"). Then Evans would build the second set, progressing from a solo number (or two), adding bass for one or two more, and finishing out with trio numbers, culminating usually at this time with a blockbusting "Nardis."

So it was that in Paris, after the concert interval, the pianist came out alone onto the stage to play "I Loves You, Porgy," a high spot of concentrated emotion. During the interval and throughout the following piano items the double bass was sitting out on stage under the lights, going gradually out of tune. When Marc Johnson joined Evans on the platform for their duo spot, it was for "Up with the Lark," which Evans pointedly commenced, as usual, on a reiterated G in the bass. Whether this was originally for tuning purposes or

With the pianist Walter Davis Jr. in Paris, November 25, 1979, the day before *The Paris Concert* with the last trio. Léon Terjanian was shooting a film with Davis, and Bill dropped by.

Léon Terjanian collection

not it became a curious feature of every performance. The trapeze act performed on this number in Buenos Aires could have sounded a warning; at any rate, this more controlled joyride from the Evans-Johnson duo gained in motivic development from its relative sobriety.

At this time, an earlier group innovation was revived and became an exhilarating feature of "My Romance": namely, the tempo change, controlled now by Joe LaBarbera, using a subdivision of the current tempo to link (either up or down) into the next one, a procedure used by previous trios on "Embraceable You" and "Stella by Starlight." From then on, in "My Romance," several such changes occurred, the excitement of each "upgrade" compounded by the overall accelerating momentum. A thrilling moment occurred when all three musicians changed gear in immaculate rhythmic unison.

Both "My Romance" and "Nardis" featured the three protagonists individually, and either number could function now as an extended set or concert closer. Evans declared "Nardis" as therapy for each of them—they played it almost nightly, staying close to the form yet finding a freedom related to it. He described each of Marc Johnson's solos on it as a finished work of art, as if the greatest bass virtuoso in the world had prepared a "piece" for two years and was finally ready to present it before the public—and yet it was a new solo, every time. Evans almost wished they could line up twenty or so of these recent "Nardis" performances and put out a four-album set.

These two LPs were the last to be approved and released by Helen Keane during Bill's lifetime, and *The Paris Concert, Edition One* was voted best album of the year by the Association of French Jazz Critics. Since *Further Conversations with Myself* in 1967, Helen had produced some two dozen of Bill's records on the Verve, Columbia, CTI, Fantasy, and Warner labels, as well as unofficially taking charge of several before that. Seven had been Grammy winners. She did indeed have the final word on what went out, and her cachet meant that Evans would be happy. Joe LaBarbera told Win Hinkle, "Bill trusted her to the extent that he would record the music and give the tapes to Helen and say, 'Helen, you've got it. You edit them, you mix them, and then show me what you've got.' She knew his music as well as anybody. Believe me, if it wasn't for Helen, Bill would have been gone a long time before."[8] Gene Lees goes so far as to say that if Helen had not taken over Bill's management in 1962, he would barely have lasted another six months.

A week into this tour of one-nighters, the trio broadcast a performance from Stuttgart's modern Liederhalle at least on a par with that in Paris. In fact, Evans's fantasia in front of "Nardis" became his most adventurous yet, truly inspired while satisfyingly organic. He was in outstanding form, radiating fresh perspectives and making the most of a superb instrument, and all with a touch at once quicksilver and gentle. Johnson's spontaneous rhythmic interplay with Evans had been a constant source of delight for some time. Under LaBarbera's heady propulsion they produced an "All of You" worthy to stand with the yardstick Vanguard tracks of 1961. To end the concert, "But Beautiful" came off miraculously—a deeply glowing and golden vignette; every night at this time it was a guaranteed gem of a ballad, just as "Alfie" had been a decade earlier.

Each day a new city awaited them: from Stuttgart they journeyed down to Lyon, where Léon Terjanian filmed their concert for a portrait movie to be called *Turn Out the Stars*. The next day they were back in Germany, at Hans Rossbach's jazzclub in Koblenz. The tour was taking its toll, the Lyon filming had tired him, and in Koblenz he had a cold and played rather mechanically. In 1990, West Wind included eight tracks from that evening (incorrectly designated as being from Rome) on a CD called *The Brilliant Bill Evans*.

For the following night's engagement in Holland, broadcast by TROS-Radio from Nick Vollebregt's Jazz Café in Laren, Evans was back in form. At his sharpest, the rhythmic displacement of a sequential phrase could be done

The last trio at Lyon,
December 4, 1979: Bill Evans,
Marc Johnson (bass), and Joe
LaBarbera (drums).

Léon Terjanian collection

with such uncompromising force as to emulate a bad edit. On "I Do It for
Your Love," a wild chunk of chording became compressed into a couple of
beats like a flurry of punches in the ring. After a considered "Laurie" and a
typical workout on "Nardis" from the trio, Toots Thielemans made up a quartet for some easily thrown together revivals from *Affinity*, as well as his own
classic "Bluesette." As always, it was good to hear Evans having a blow on different material, and it was a rare treat for him, too. As at Nîmes with Lee
Konitz, the pianist's well-formatted arrangement of "What Is This Thing
Called Love?" proved a fruitful number to have up his sleeve for a guest artist.

A few days (and cities) later the trio was onto the Spanish leg of the tour.
A private recording of their evening in Madrid was later issued as a limited

edition of three LPs on the Ivory label, called *Live at Balboa Jazz Club, Vols. 1, 2, and 3*. If the playing was solid and relatively straightforward rather than magical, it was nevertheless much appreciated by the hundred or so patrons huddled into the confines of this tiny club in the heart of the city. The "up" pace was dictated in part by the piano, not an instrument to encourage lingering or the savoring of color. One of the first numbers Evans ever recorded, "Like Someone in Love," was coming in for a late revival. He gave it the same treatment that Toots Thielemans had brought to "The Days of Wine and Roses," alternating the key every half-chorus.

In the light of the Evans group credo, Johnson and LaBarbera's adoption of a "play-along" stance on ballads might be seen as a curious trend, the more so as the pianist regarded this group as closest in spirit to his First Trio. Yet it was appropriate, Evans's own playing now having the strength and richness to stand in its own right. After coasting through some of the early seventies, the pianist had become the star of his own trio once again.

Andy LaVerne, who was playing the piano in Stan Getz's group on this tour (sometimes a day after Evans, sometimes as a double bill), recalls that Evans would tape the gig each night to listen to on the road, always intent on learning from his shortcomings. "He was working on some linear things at that point," said LaVerne. "What he was doing was playing ahead of the changes. His right-hand line would be ahead of where the changes were happening in the harmonic rhythm. That way he could create tension and release; when the changes caught up to his line, obviously that would be a release."[9] This displacement of phrases came absolutely naturally to Evans, developed through feeling, not intellect. He was not trying to throw his listeners but to say more within the form of jazz.

The unaccompanied items—"I Loves You, Porgy," "Noelle's Theme"— were delivered with the tonal and emotional range of a concert pianist exploring late Romantic repertoire. If Evans had ever made that trip to Russia, his audiences would surely have been moved by his portrayal of "Noelle's Theme." There was something in the touch and the spread-out use of the piano registers that recalled the poet in Horowitz. Even in rumination there was a clarity to the sound, an immediacy in the fingers.

The schedule was such that the players might drop their suitcases and go on stage. With strikes affecting Air France and the Italian trains, changes of clothes or dinner went by the board, and sleep was what they could grab here and there. Under these circumstances, Evans appreciated a JVC recorder given to him by the promoter on their last Japanese tour. On the move all the time, on trains and in the van, he listened with earphones.

Unable even to watch TV or register more than a hint of his surroundings, he found it a lifesaver. He was carrying Rachmaninoff playing his own Rhapsody on a Theme of Paganini and the Fourth Piano Concerto—"We really got to know those, man!"[10]

For much of the time they felt that they were not playing particularly well, and only after it was all over did they realize what fun it had been and what progress they had made. Evans declared it a favorite of his recent tours, and listening to the tapes back in the States he found the performances to have been surprisingly good. Although the most self-critical of artists, he even declared that he would have made a record out of some of them. By this token, it may be assumed that he would have approved *The Paris Concert, Editions One and Two,* but not *The Brilliant Bill Evans.*

CHAPTER **21**   Letter to Evan

*Some people just want to be hit over the head, and then if they're hit hard
enough maybe they feel something. But some people want to get inside of something and discover maybe more richness.*

—*Bill Evans*

In one respect, Evans had been fortunate throughout his life: he had always
had work. This is no mean achievement for any freelance musician, but it is
all the more remarkable considering the uncompromising dedication he
brought to his art. As a trio leader over two decades he had thrilled a dedicated band of enthusiasts, and their consistent following gave the lie to the
value of fashion, a commodity that never touched him. Through the sheer
quality of the music he had to offer he was able to maintain a full diary.

"The market doesn't influence my thinking in the slightest," he told
Brian Case, in one of his last interviews,

> except I'd suspect anything that makes it. I know where I came from, where I am and
> what I have to work with, and I try to make what I consider to be the most total kind
> of musical and human statement within the means and tradition from which I came.
>
> I love Bartók, Berg, Stravinsky. The fact that music is polytonal, atonal,
> polyrhythmic or whatever doesn't bother me—but it *must* say something. I work
> with very simple means because I'm a simple person, and I came from a simple tra-
> dition out of dance music and jobbing, and though I've sorta studied a lot of other
> music, I feel that I know my limitations and I try to work within them. Really, there's
> no limit to the expression I could make within the idiom if I had the inner need to
> say something.
>
> This is where I find the problem. More an emotional, a creative-emotional
> problem.[1]

Back in the States there was no letup, and the trio began 1980 in
remarkably fresh form. "Polka Dots and Moonbeams" assumed its final

mien, the changes strung out, hanging twice as slow as before. This was something that just happened somewhere one night, emulating the treatment already given to "If You Could See Me Now." Unbelievably, "Nardis" went from strength to strength, the piano preamble reaching epic proportions, the content further out than ever. At the end of January, this repertoire was taken into the Village Vanguard.

One-off events broke up the spring schedule: West German television, making a profile of Toots Thielemans, visited Evans's Fort Lee apartment. Expecting an interview, Bill was surprised to find the man himself on the doorstep with the crew. They duetted on "Laurie," Bill playing his beloved Chickering grand, which had recently been rebuilt. For another film documentary—about the pianist Jaki Byard—Evans contributed some off-the-cuff reflections on why some talents receive less recognition than others.

He visited Harvard University, playing a full set with his trio, some intriguing material with the campus orchestra, and piano duos with faculty member John Lewis. These two had duetted before, but this was their happiest hour, the dry Lewis touch acting as the perfect foil for a flighty Evans. "But Not for Me" was pure joy, Lewis tripping out delicato before stomping and strumming beneath his out-on-a-spree colleague; the irresistible combination brought the house down.

One other campus visit that April was especially emotive for Evans, a return to his alma mater, Southeastern Louisiana University at Hammond. He gave interviews, mingled with the staff and students, and played two sets with the trio. Inevitably, he included "Very Early," reminding his listeners that he had composed it when a student at the school.

⋲⋲ ⋲⋲ ⋲⋲

At Rick's Café Americain, fast becoming a regular Chicago gig, the trio was getting into gear for one of its finest club runs, two more weeks at the Village Vanguard beginning on May 27. The Wednesday and Thursday of the second week were scheduled for recording by Warner Brothers for a live double LP. Evans recalled to Ted O'Reilly:

> Well, the first night was practically meaningless; we were getting sound together and it just didn't seem to be getting there at all. However, things were better than I thought, when I go back and listen to the tape. But the next night was appreciably better, I think; by the last set it was beginning to get there. As it turns out, I think I used a couple of things from that set—the last set on Thursday night—in the album....
>
> So, I said to Helen, "Why don't we schedule this the rest of the week?" Well, she was a little bit hesitant because it's quite expensive, so I said, "Let's do tomorrow night anyhow, and then Sunday." So Friday night was quite a good night throughout

and, you know, it was all decent, but sure enough, Saturday night was the night. That was the one we didn't record. That was the peak night. But we got some good stuff on there.[2]

Some ninety-five titles were recorded over the four days that tapes were running. Evans was confident that there was enough, and more, for a double album, and in choosing the tracks he was even reluctant to have to exclude some material. With the sound engineer, Malcolm Addey, he mixed and edited the program, but, although imminent release was continually rumored over the years, the tapes remained in limbo. Finally in 1996, after protracted negotiations among various parties, Warner Brothers issued a boxed set of six CDs containing fifty-eight tracks, entitled *Turn Out the Stars: The Final Village Vanguard Recordings, June 1980*. Simultaneously, Evans's original track selection was compiled on a companion disc entitled *The Artist's Choice: Highlights from Turn Out the Stars*.

Four new compositions were on the Vanguard menu. "Tiffany" had recently been dedicated to Joe LaBarbera's baby daughter, born on February 29. The appeal of the piece lay in the playful journey taken by its all-pervading three-note motif. Bill had played a rough version over the phone to Joe and Carol the day after the birth, fixing it in manuscript just a few days later.

Then there was "Yet Ne'er Broken," another of those anagram titles, this time using the name of the connection who supplied his cocaine. For the final, explosive staccato chord of this number Evans extracted a leaf from Ahmad Jamal's book. Jamal had made a trademark of this kind of abrupt ending throughout his trio career, which ran parallel to that of Evans. Incidentally, although Evans admired and enjoyed Jamal's playing, he had never regarded him as a particular influence. It was the same with two of his other favorites, Thelonious Monk and Erroll Garner, of whom he wrote: "Each seems to me as great as any man can be great if he works true to his talents, neither over nor underestimating them and, most important, functions within his limitations."[3]

At first "Your Story" was just known as the "diddly-odd tune." The persistent mordent or twiddle from which it was constructed (already noted as an Evans trademark on many a tune's opening note) traveled with consummate ease through a forest of complementary keys before sinking home to roost with a contented sigh. The piece was always played rubato over just two choruses and without improvisation, sometimes amplified to a simulated slow-motion wave crash by Joe LaBarbera the second time round. In making a statement in its own right, it joined a handful of other tunes like "Minha," "Noelle's Theme," and "Theme from *M*A*S*H*."

"Knit for Mary F." was also first known by its identifying tag—in this case as "the repeated-note tune"—but was then titled for Mary Franksen of Omaha, Nebraska, in return for her motherly affection and "thousands" of clothing items she had knitted for Bill's family. It was another of those long melodies at which the composer was adept, affording gentle, harmonically instigated surprises and unified by the distinguishing shape of its opening motif: a bar of repeated notes, a single high leap, and a gentle fall by stages. As an improviser he discovered in it a fertile springboard for gnarled turns of invention.

By the final Sunday it was plain that Evans was very tired—he was producing some of his untidiest playing ever—but the overall impression from the run was of an artist pushing his imagination to the limit in communion with ideal partners. Their rapport was finely honed, secure, and yet open: the sense prevailed that anything could happen. Here, in creative terms, was a happy man at home again, one possessed of a compelling lyricism, elegant of tone even when strong. The invention was concentrated, avoiding conventional patterns and pursuing a freedom related to the form.

Nineteen years earlier, his playing with the First Trio in this very room had exemplified these qualities, but the texture now—the density of the fabric—had changed from the rare finesse of those days. The detail was running wilder, and the overtness had intensified. His comping afforded a keen extra pleasure, being compellingly structured in its own right; and he was pressing home his obsession with rhythmic displacement so that the listener had to hang on to the understood beat, at times tenaciously. Warren Bernhardt, who went in to hear him whenever he could, recalled: "He was playing magnificently then, and he spoke to me again (a recurring theme in my talks with him) about how, when things were just right, he could get every molecule in a given place to begin scintillating in a new and higher fashion, a quantum jump up from ordinary waking reality. This was something he could *see* when it was occurring." If this sounds like the cocaine talking, nevertheless we may connect such perception with the audacious and noble music being produced—a fitting resolution to two decades of trio artistry at the Vanguard.

⊂⊱ ⊂⊱ ⊂⊱

There ensued a month in Europe centered around a two-week residency at Ronnie Scott's. The artists had no knowledge of being recorded, but in 1993 Polygram issued two CDs on Dreyfus Jazz Line entitled *Letter to Evan* and *Turn Out the Stars*. At the club, the insistence of that reiterated note in "Knit for Mary F." was symptomatic of his burning urge to communicate, a recent, and now overwhelming, feature of the playing. Manifested as a

Close friend and pianist Warren Bernhardt was in on the beginnings
of many of Evans's compositions.
Courtesy of Warren Bernhardt

Slavic, impulsive approach to tone, it had been observed before, but now it
permeated the palette. The specifically Russian trait of emphasizing the
extremes was expressed by juxtaposing notes whispered pianissimo with those
aggressively etched. The oscillation between these two frontiers of tone, each
an emotional anchor point, was nervy and precipitate—voices could dart into
existence at any octave or intensity. Yet the pianist was acting according to an
inner scheme of phrasing, shaped in his imagination and made tangible in
the execution.

The presentation of "My Man's Gone Now" was a case in point, the
melody all but jabbed at us in splintered fragments of tone, as if to sing were
no longer enough, only a cry would do. For the coda he went back to the
score of the opera, falling infinitely from on high by the half-tone. Sometimes, as in "Your Story," the phrases themselves blew hot and cold, two bars
etched in steel, two shaded in dapper light; the full rainbow of color was
there, but now as if polarized to two alternating currents.

These long spells of touring kept him away from his son, and he played "Letter to Evan" every night. He took a renewed fancy to Steve Swallow's "Peau Douce," playing it as if waltzing on ice, the impeccable ensemble gliding through the sequence with the free-falling grace brought to "Up with the Lark."

Joe LaBarbera, in his eighteen-month association, had proved a perfect mirror of his pianist's moods and impetus. At times he seemed to be swamping the music with his driving cymbal work, but in a sense this was what Evans wanted—to be goaded every inch of the way. As at the Vanguard, many numbers were taken very fast indeed, engulfed in a flood of continuous energy. But now the notes were pouring out in a desperation born of inner fervor. Opening rhapsodies were massed in tiers, shifting tides around formal skeletons; piano solo codas were multilayered, like a one-man execution of *Conversations with Myself*.

To those of us privileged to attend this, his last run at the club, the sense was strong that he was bursting to play, play, play—albeit on a piano woefully sour in the mid-to-high register. Beyond such niceties, he grabbed us by the scruff of the neck as if to say, *Hey, listen to what I have to say to you!* Each time he took the stage, he entered that world he had created for himself and for which he lived, plugging into a continuous stream of consciousness on another plane, gathering up the reins of an ongoing creation.

We readily suspected that a joyful defiance in the face of death had set in. Brian Hennessey, for instance, remembers parting with Bill at the end of his London run: "When I said goodbye to him just before he left, we both knew that he didn't have much longer to live."[4] Pete King, who managed the business end of the club, told of a conversation with Bill at the end of the run:

> He didn't exactly tell me he was dying. But somehow or other you kind of accepted: this is what he was telling me. I remember crying, personally. It was terrible. Especially after how he'd played at the club. And to show what a guy he was, he told me at that backstage talk that he knew we were having a hard time, and he wanted to return in October, to do two weeks—absolutely free. You don't need to remind *me* about how well he played. You know, with my job I often don't get to hear even the big names very much. But even with my dashing about, every evening when his last set began, I was just *compelled* to sit down and just listen. And how he *played!* It was so compelling—he played in a much more intense, Bud Powell kind of bag. Absolutely tremendous.[5]

We could tell from the playing that the end was near. The sense of urgency to reach out to us through every phrase patently left no doubt. This was a man with a searing message to convey in the only way he knew and before it was too late.

They traveled to Belgium, where Léon Terjanian produced a short film, his second from the trio's performances, entitled *Bill Evans at Gouvy Jazz Festival*.

A few days later, they were among the fjords on the west coast of Norway, a country that, like its Scandinavian neighbors, held the pianist in high esteem. At the Molde International Jazz Festival the packed house was treated to the rare sight of Evans wearing a broad grin on stage; he was quite taken aback by the Norwegian style of rhythmic applause, which had reached thunderous levels after "Theme from *M*A*S*H*." As so often, "My Romance" concluded the set, Evans backing his colleagues' exchanges with ruthlessly displaced riff-style comping on the splendid Schimmel provided. This spontaneous play-along, combined with Joe LaBarbera's tempo switches, induced a heady blend of dizziness and exhilaration.

On stage after the concert, looking deceptively well, the pianist gave a short interview, revealing that in the past couple of years he had been listening to his own records more than before, going all the way back with a view to learning something. He still enjoyed *New Jazz Conceptions*, finding that he was now able to listen to himself more objectively. He reflected philosophically on audiences in general and his own in particular, asserting that most people do not want a challenge, do not want to participate, but simply want something done to them. There would always be some 15 percent, though, who desired something more and were prepared to search it out; herein lay the response to art.

He was into his last concerts now. After Reggio di Calabria at the foot of Italy, where he was consistently inspired, there was Barcelona, a rather formally staged television appearance before a token audience. Here he insisted on something that he had for a long time preferred—no applause during or between numbers. In spite of makeup and wardrobe, he looked ghastly—spaced out, gaunt, and turned in on his own anguish. Keyboard closeups exposed wrists and hands monstrously bloated, normal fingers protruding from the swelling like antennae from some grotesque and newly discovered creature of the deep. Against these odds, the playing was marvelous, "I Do It for Your Love" at once tortured and controlled, "Blue in Green" suspended into infinity. "Nardis" seemed, as it always did, the ultimate workout: no trio burned more fuel. The three were in mutual awe, each living the others' epic, Evans rocking slowly on his stool while Johnson unfolded his saga of the day. Over the rolling credits, the pianist doodled a protracted "Waltz for Debby," seemingly obeying the director's brief; but he was elsewhere, the glazed expression betraying a soul displaced beyond our understanding.

In Germany, on the Rhine, stands the spa town of Bad Hönningen, where lived Fritz Feltens, architect and jazz fan. Feltens had tried to engage the pianist for a private concert at his home the previous year. Evans should have taken a day off for his health, but he would not pass up a chance to play. His European tour organizer, Wim Wigt, found that he could just squeeze in an appearance for Evans at the end of the tour. Marc Johnson and Joe LaBarbera arrived in the afternoon to set up instruments and arrange the concert space, explaining that in order for Evans to best concentrate with a minimum of distraction he needed the piano to be turned around so that he could play with his back to the listeners. The pianist arrived looking ill indeed, the body wasted, the hands distended. It was the weakest his colleagues had seen him. Yet gathering his strength, he somehow found the energy to give his all.

The performance, on August 15, 1980, was issued on LP by West Wind in 1989 as *His Last Concert in Germany*. From this erratic evening, "Your Story" was never better, the piece digging deeper than ever before. Evans knew that it would be his last date on European soil. It was the eve of his fifty-first birthday, and at midnight the host presented him with a silver watch, engraved with a personal message. He was plainly delighted, expressing his gratitude repeatedly. In the early hours the musicians departed (they were flying to the States that day), and the audience dispersed. Evans had been totally focused while making music, but it was an increasing struggle for him to keep a grip on other things: in the light of dawn the birthday gift was found residing in the remains of the cold buffet.

⋴⋵ ⋴⋵ ⋴⋵

After an appearance in Portland, Oregon, the trio went on to Los Angeles to share a Hollywood Bowl concert with the George Shearing Duo and the Dave Brubeck Quartet. The contrasting styles of the three pianists attracted a large crowd, and they were congenially introduced by Shelly Manne. That was on August 27, just before a week's run for the trio at the Keystone Korner Jazz Club in San Francisco. There Herb Wong, a longtime friend of the pianist, found him in the worst shape he had ever seen him. Evans had demanded drugs as soon as he arrived in town, no longer caring what happened to him physically. Haggard, he was eating little more than candy. More than one doctor advised that he should withdraw from playing and enter hospital, but Evans was dismissive, being interested in only one thing: to play with his trio. Wong sat with him in the basement of the club, looked at his watch and said, "You know, you're going to have to get a little more rest before you get on stage."

"Let me tell you," Evans rejoined. "I can't wait to get on stage because of Joe LaBarbera and Marc Johnson. I have no words for it. Just to tell you that I admire these two young guys and I'm just a very lucky person. I can't wait to play with them."

The pianist's mood deepened. He spoke softly to his friend, drawing him in: "I don't want you to leave yet. I want to tell you something." Herb Wong waited.

"I want to thank you for all the conversations we've had all these years."

"You're thanking me?" said Herb. "You've got to be kidding. I'm the one that's so grateful to have the chances to chat with you about anything and everything."

Bill nodded. "Thanks a lot. I appreciate it, but I've got to go."[6]

Bill's friend was close to tears, and could only tell him to rest in order to play what he needed to play. Wong went upstairs and sat alone at the side waiting for the group to come on, aware that this might well be the last Bill Evans gig he would witness.

The trio played Keystone Korner for eight nights, starting on Sunday, August 31. All eight performances were recorded by the club owner, Todd Barkan, and issued in 1989, without authorization from the surviving artists, on an eight-CD set by Alfa Records of Tokyo called *Consecration: The Last Complete Collection*. Helen Keane told me specifically: "Bill was not happy with his playing while he was there, didn't know he was being recorded, and would never have approved the release of the material."

On the first night, a rendering of "My Foolish Heart" was conjured to compare with the classic 1961 performance from the Vanguard. Now, with continuity of feeling (and key, A major) over the intervening years, a more adventurous statement was being made, farther flung on the keyboard and freer rhythmically. The original conception had developed in complexity but not deepened in spirit: simply, its essence had remained intact, affirming the initial worth.

After "Knit for Mary F.," Bill ran down the set so far: "I know how curious people are about what's being played all the time…" His observation that the theme from M*A*S*H was also known as "Suicide Is Painless" extracted a wry chuckle from a few understanding souls. "Debatable," he proffered, with reason. At the end of the set he confided in his audience as though embracing them for the week: "You've been a superb audience; I got a good piano; should have a good time." On the third night he was late, and Denny Zeitlin sat in for a while. At the end of his own set, Bill paid tribute to his colleague: "I'm sorry I was late, though when I got here I was glad, because we all had the opportunity to hear a truly exceptional, marvelous creative talent and pianist, Denny Zeitlin."

On this run, the desperation, almost anger, exhibited at Ronnie's had dissipated, the tone now soberly controlled and unforced, the defiance more knowingly resigned. Paul Simon's song "I Do It for Your Love" continued to inspire the pianist's most complex thoughts, and the performance given on September 2 has been transcribed by Art Tofanelli Jr. for Win Hinkle's publication *Letter from Evans* (ex. 4). Its appearance on the printed page is remarkable, an amalgam of elements from the music of Chopin, Liszt, and Bartók, but above all the Romanian Georges Enescu. Evans's interpretation of this song defied categorization. The percussive, repeated note was much in evidence, better suited to vibraphone than piano technique, though one might rather cite the cimbalom, for this music represented, with its tremolos and swirling decoration, an uncanny return to those Eastern European roots that were so close to his ancestral Ukraine; more than a little of the gypsy within had surfaced.

Of scores of residences in clubs worldwide, this was the last one he completed. The Alfa boxed set (which won Japan's Gold Disc Award) documents virtually the whole run, revealing in the process a gradual winding down of inspiration. By the final Sunday the spark seemed to be largely gone, but the playing never fell below the pianist's root professional level, and it was in any case honorably carried by his colleagues. These two musicians, a generation younger, worshiped Bill and lent their support and youthful spirit to his own artistic energy. They both knew that any night could be his last.

Evans had been looking at transcriptions made by Peter Dreyfuss for a forthcoming music publication, to be called *Bill Evans 4*. (*Bill Evans 3* had appeared in 1975.) Judy Bell at TRO also prepared a volume called *The Last Compositions*, transcribed by Bob Bauer. In addition, Evans was working on an extended piece, emanating from the heart of his harmonic thinking. "There was for him this sense of something being just out of reach," explained his wife, Nenette. "Bill spoke of a large work, a work he always wanted to do. He would get enthused about it.... To quote his journals: 'Lately, I've been discovering something wonderfully basic...right in the middle of modern harmony.'"[7]

He was always so tired, though, and his playing diary was so full that he could never secure a long enough oasis of time during which to gather his thoughts. He felt obliged to satisfy his fans by continually playing. A Russian trip was planned to follow on the next Japanese tour; and then there were ideas for future projects, albums with Phil Woods, Oscar Peterson . . .

Ex. 4. The beginning of Paul Simon's "I Do It for Your Love" from *Consecration: The Last Complete Collection.* This particular outpouring is from the performance given September 2, 1980, at Keystone Korner, San Francisco.

On September 9, back in New York, he recorded a TV appearance on the *Merv Griffin Show* as one of three featured jazz artists, the others being Cal Tjader and George Shearing. On the studio's white Yamaha, wearing a suit to match, he played "Stompin' at the Savoy" and "Your Story." He justified his choice of "Your Story" on air to the audience: "You know, directors always panic about what you're going to play—*don't play anything slow*. I don't get a chance to play on shows like this too often, where I reach this many people, and I've been writing songs—they've been coming out lately like laying eggs. Once in a while I just go, prrk! prrk! prrk!—a new tune. So I would like to do this, which I think is a little more serious maybe for your audience."

"Play anything you want!" yelled someone from the floor.

Mundell Lowe, one of his very first friends in the business, was musical director for the show and was sitting in the house band. "I went backstage to see him," he recalls. "And I realized he was awfully ill—*awfully* ill. And, of course, Bill left the show and I gave him a big hug. I had a feeling that I might not see him again."[8]

The trio was booked into Fat Tuesday's for a week, starting that night, Tuesday, September 9. Marc Johnson recalls that Bill felt a little guilty for deserting the Vanguard. The television recording made it a long day for the weak and stricken musician. The following night he went in again and fulfilled his professional obligation at the club, but it was to be his last performance. On the Thursday he admitted defeat and declared himself unable to perform, a decision that he had never taken lightly throughout his life; all his colleagues knew that if Bill Evans could not play, something was seriously wrong. He hauled himself into the club by taxi to apologize to his waiting friends, in particular Marc Johnson, Joe LaBarbera, and Helen Keane. The club was run by Steve Getz, son of Stan, who called on Andy LaVerne to stand in for that night and the rest of the week if necessary. And so it proved, Evans languishing in his Fort Lee apartment for the next three days, attended by those closest to him.

On the Sunday, Laurie Verchomin and Joe LaBarbera persuaded Bill to go to Mount Sinai Hospital. On the way, although he was coughing up blood and complaining of a feeling of drowning, he was alert enough to give directions to LaBarbera, who was driving. Then he lost consciousness before Joe carried his frail body into the building.

Bill Evans died at approximately 3:30 P.M. the following day, Monday, September 15, 1980, officially from a hemorrhaging ulcer and bronchial pneumonia. His final condition arose as the culmination of many factors. The most critical of these was the damage to his liver, affected from youth by

Paris, fall 1979.

Léon Terjanian collection

hepatitis, its injury fearfully compounded by protracted drug use. In the final months he suffered, as so often before, from malnutrition. But there is a conviction among those who knew him well that it was the death of his dear brother that had undermined his will to live and led to the final decline. Nenette said, "Bill actively plotted an escape from pain."[9]

His slow suicide carried its own pain, but the agony was defied to the end by his artistic ecstasy.

⋵ ⋵ ⋵

Bill Evans rests in Baton Rouge, Louisiana.

Notes

Preface

Epigraph. *New York Times*, Sept. 25, 1977.

Prologue

Epigraph. Letter to the editor in "Chords and Discords," *Down Beat*, Oct. 1980, pp. 8, 70.
1. Chick Corea, interviewed in Paul Goldin, *Bill Evans*, French TV documentary, ARTE, 1996.
2. Letter to the editor, *Down Beat*, Oct. 1980, pp. 8, 70.
3. Mary Soroka, family letter to Irene Dent (cousin), courtesy of Dr. Earle Epps.
4. Earle W. Epps, interview by Win Hinkle, *Letter from Evans*, vol. 4, no. 3. Subsequent references to this bimonthly (later, quarterly) newsletter, edited by Win Hinkle from 1989 to 1994, abbreviated thus: *LFE* 4/3.
5. Ibid.
6. Epps, Soroka family genealogy.

1. The Kid from Plainfield

Epigraph. Quoted in Don DeMicheal, untitled essay accompanying *Bill Evans Plays*, Richmond Organization, 1969, pp. 29–30.
1. Epps, interview by Hinkle.
2. Quoted in Gene Lees, *Meet Me at Jim and Andy's* (New York: Oxford University Press, 1988), 150–51.
3. Quoted in Kitty Grime, *Jazz at Ronnie Scott's* (London: Hale, 1979), 94.
4. Quoted in Wayne Enstice and Paul Rubin, *Jazz Spoken Here* (Baton Rouge: Louisiana State University Press, 1992), 136.
5. In Louis Cavrell, *The Universal Mind of Bill Evans*, Rhapsody Films, 1966.
6. Ibid.
7. Quoted in DeMicheal, *Bill Evans Plays*.
8. Ibid.
9. Quoted in Don Nelsen, "Bill Evans: Intellect, Emotion, and Communication," *Down Beat*, Dec. 8, 1960, pp. 16–19.
10. Ibid.
11. Bill Evans, interview by Jean-Louis Ginibre, *Jazz Times*, Jan.–Feb. 1997, pp. 142–45; originally published in French in *Jazz* 116 (1965).
12. *Bill Evans Memorial Library*, unidentified U.S. radio program (Brian Hennessey).
13. Quoted in Nelsen, "Bill Evans."
14. Collection of Ron Nethercutt.
15. Mundell Lowe, interview by Ron Nethercutt, at National Association of Jazz Educators Convention, Jan. 1984.

2. Swing Pianist

Epigraph. In Cavrell, *The Universal Mind*.
1. Lowe, interview.
2. Evans, interview.
3. Quoted in Brian Hennessey, "Bill Evans: A Person I Knew," *Jazz Journal International*, March 1985, pp. 8–11.
4. Ibid.
5. Earl Zindars, interview by Win Hinkle, *LFE* 5/1.
6. Quoted in Nelsen, "Bill Evans."
7. Quoted in Brian Hennessey, "Bill Evans."
8. Pat Evans, interview by Ron Nethercutt, *LFE* 3/3.
9. Peri Cousins Harper, interview by Win Hinkle, *LFE* 4/3.
10. Bill Evans, interview with Brian Hennessey, *Along Came Bill*, program 2, BBC Radio, 1990.

3. New Jazz Conceptions

Epigraph. In Cavrell, *The Universal Mind*.
1. George Russell, interview by Ian Carr, *The Trail-Blazer*, program 2, BBC Radio, 1994.
2. Quoted in Burt Korall, liner note to *Jazz in the Space Age*, Decca DL 9219, 1960.
3. George Russell, liner note to *The Jazz Workshop*, RCA RD-7511, 1957.
4. Bill Evans, liner note to *Monk*, Columbia CL-2291, 1965.
5. Quoted in Nelsen, "Bill Evans."
6. In Cavrell, *The Universal Mind*.

4. Sideman

Epigraph. Milt Hinton, interview by Alyn Shipton, BBC Radio, 1992.
1. Jim Aikin, "Bill Evans," *Contemporary Keyboard*, June 1980, pp. 44–55.
2. Nat Hentoff, liner note to *Charles Mingus Sextet*, Polydor 623215, 1957.
3. Hinton, interview.
4. Jacket of *The Nearness of You*, EmArcy MG 36134, 1958.

5. A Call from Miles

Epigraph. Quoted in Nat Hentoff, "An Afternoon with Miles Davis," *Jazz Review*, Dec. 1958; reprinted in Martin Williams, ed., *Jazz Panorama* (New York: Da Capo, 1979), 164.
1. *Evans Memorial Library*.
2. Mike Hennessey, "Evans the Jazz," *Melody Maker*, Feb. 27, 1965, p. 12.
3. Quoted in Len Lyons, *The Great Jazz Pianists* (New York: Da Capo, 1983), 224–25.
4. Ibid.
5. Quoted in Sy Johnson, liner note to *Black Giants*, Columbia PG 33402, 1975.
6. Quoted in Brian Hennessey, "Bill Evans."
7. Miles Davis with Quincy Troupe, *Miles: The Autobiography* (New York: Simon and Schuster, 1989), 216.
8. Quoted in Goldin, *Bill Evans*.
9. Harper, interview.
10. Leonard Feather, "Jazz in American Society," *The Encyclopedia of Jazz* (New York: Da Capo, 1960), 79–88.
11. Davis with Troupe, *Miles*, 221.
12. Paul Wilner, "Jazz Pianist: Life on the Upbeat," *New York Times*, Sept. 25, 1977.

6. Everybody Digs Bill Evans

Epigraph. Quoted in Orrin Keepnews, liner note to *Peace Piece and Other Pieces*, Milestone M-47024, 1975.

1. Ibid.
2. Quoted in Leonard Feather, "Blindfold Test: Billy Taylor," *Down Beat*, Sept. 3, 1959, p. 31.
3. Quoted in Jim Aikin, "Bill Evans," *Contemporary Keyboard*, June 1980, pp. 44–55.
4. Quoted in Martin Williams, "Homage to Bill Evans," booklet accompanying *The Complete Riverside Recordings*, Riverside R-018, 1984.
5. Miles Davis, George Shearing, Ahmad Jamal, and Julian "Cannonball" Adderley, jacket of *Everybody Digs Bill Evans*, Riverside RLP 12-291, 1959.
6. Quoted in Orrin Keepnews, *Peace Piece*.
7. Ibid.

7. Miles Calls Back

Epigraph. Quoted in Brian Hennessey, "Bill Evans."
1. Zindars, interview.
2. Quoted in Orrin Keepnews, *Peace Piece*.
3. Ibid.
4. Quoted in Hanns Petrik, "Lee Konitz about Bill Evans," *LFE* 1/3.
5. Russell, interview, program 3.
6. Davis with Troupe, *Miles*, 223.
7. Jan Lohmann, *The Sound of Miles Davis: The Discography, 1945–1991* (Copenhagen: JazzMedia, 1992), 72–73.
8. Bill Evans, liner note to *Kind of Blue*, Columbia CL 1355, 1959.
9. Quoted in Brian Hennessey, "Bill Evans."
10. Quoted in Conrad Silvert, liner note to *Spring Leaves*, Milestone M-47034, 1976.
11. Zindars, interview.
12. Herb Wong, interview by Win Hinkle, *LFE* 4/3.
13. Evans, *Kind of Blue*.
14. Amy Herot, liner note to *Kind of Blue*, MasterSound Edition, Columbia CK 64403, 1992.
15. Quoted in Brian Hennessey, "Bill Evans."

8. Portrait in Jazz

Epigraph. Quoted in Williams, "Homage."
1. Evans, interview by Ginibre.
2. Dave Mackay, interview by Win Hinkle, *LFE* 5/1.
3. In Cavrell, *The Universal Mind*.
4. Ibid.
5. Quoted in Brian Case, "Johnny Appleseed of Bop," *Melody Maker*, March 14, 1981, pp. 26, 36.
6. Quoted in Lee Jeske, "Bill Evans: An Introspective Biography," *Goldmine*, Oct. 12, 1984, pp. 28–41.
7. Quoted in Williams, "Homage."
8. Quoted in Silvert, *Spring Leaves*.
9. Harper, interview.
10. Quoted in Silvert, *Spring Leaves*.
11. Quoted in Williams, "Homage."

9. Explorations

Epigraph. Quoted in Burt Korall, liner note to *Sung Heroes*, Sunnyside SSC 1015, 1986.
1. Ibid.
2. Quoted in Korall, *Space Age*.
3. Zindars, interview.
4. Quoted in Brian Hennessey, "Bill Evans."

10. Sunday at the Village Vanguard

Epigraph. Quoted in Nelsen, "Bill Evans."
1. Max Gordon, *Live at the Village Vanguard* (New York: Da Capo, 1980), caption 84–85.
2. Orrin Keepnews, booklet accompanying *The Complete Riverside Recordings*, Riverside Ro18, 1984.
3. Quoted in Brian Hennessey, "Bill Evans."
4. Quoted in Jack Maher, liner note to *Trio '65*, Verve V6–8613, 1965.
5. Quoted in Silvert, *Spring Leaves*.
6. Bill Goodwin, interview by Win Hinkle, *LFE* 1/5.
7. Quoted in Brian Hennessey, "Bill Evans."
8. Quoted in Silvert, *Spring Leaves*.
9. Quoted in Nelsen, "Bill Evans."
10. Bill Evans, interview by François Postif, *Jazz Hot*, April 1972.
11. Quoted in Silvert, *Spring Leaves*.
12. Whitney Balliett, *Such Sweet Thunder* (London: Macdonald, 1968), 80.

11. Moonbeams

Epigraph. Joe Goldberg, liner note to *Moonbeams*, Riverside RLP 428, 1962.
1. Quoted in Williams, "Homage."
2. Chuck Israels, interview by Ron Nethercutt, *LFE* 1/1.
3. Quoted ibid.
4. Ibid.
5. Peter Keepnews, liner note to *Conception*, Milestone M-47063, 1981.
6. Quoted in Jude Hibler, "Impressions of Bill Evans," *Jazz Link*, Oct. 1989, p. 3.
7. Linda Dahl, *Stormy Weather* (London: Quartet, 1984), 246.
8. Orrin Keepnews, *Complete Riverside*.
9. John S. Wilson, Record Reviews, *Down Beat*, Jan. 31, 1963, p. 25.
10. Quoted in Les Tomkins, "A Group Dialogue Featuring the Bill Evans 3," *Crescendo*, March 1965, pp. 28–30.
11. Quoted in Fred Binkley, liner note to *The Bill Evans Album*, Columbia C30855, 1971.
12. Quoted in Len Lyons, liner note to *The Second Trio*, Milestone HB 6121, 1977.

12. Conversations with Myself

Epigraph. Quoted in Lees, *Jim and Andy's*, 154.
1. Orrin Keepnews, *The Complete Riverside*.
2. Lees, *Jim and Andy's*, 152.
3. Quoted in Gene Lees, "Inside the New Bill Evans Trio," *Down Beat*, Nov. 22, 1962, pp. 24–26.
4. Bill Evans, "The House of Sounds," radio interview by Willis Conover, Washington, D.C., 1979.

5. Orrin Keepnews, liner note to *The Solo Sessions, Vol. 1*, Milestone M-9170, 1989.
6. Quoted in Binkley, *Album*.
7. Gene Lees, "Caught in the Act," *Down Beat*, Oct. 25, 1962, pp. 40–41.
8. Quoted in Dahl, *Stormy Weather*, 246.
9. Orrin Keepnews, *Solo Sessions*.
10. Bill Evans, liner note to *Conversations with Myself*, Verve V6-8526, 1963.

13. An American in Europe

Epigraph. Letter to the author.
1. Quoted in Doug Ramsey, booklet accompanying *The Secret Sessions*, Milestone 8MCD-4421-2, 1996.
2. Quoted in Leonard Feather, "Blindfold Test: Bill Evans," *Down Beat*, Nov. 5, 1964, p. 29.
3. Chuck Israels, liner note to *Bill Evans Trio at Shelly's Manne Hole*, Riverside RM 487, 1964.
4. Chuck Israels, liner note to *Time Remembered*, Milestone M-47068, 1983.
5. Goodwin, interview.
6. Bill Evans, interview by Ted O'Reilly, *Coda*, Feb. 1985.
7. Quoted in Orrin Keepnews, *Peace Piece*.
8. Lowe, interview.
9. Gene Lees, liner note to *The Paris Concert* (1976), VDJ-25035, 1976.
10. Balliett, *Such Sweet Thunder*, 83.
11. Quoted in Brian Hennessey, "Bill Evans."
12. Quoted in Gene Lees, "Bill Evans, the Pianist and the Man: Some Call It Genius," *International Musician*, 1965; reprinted in music folio: *Bill Evans, Piano Solos*, the Richmond Organization, 1965.
13. Dan Morgenstern, "The Art of Playing," *Down Beat*, Oct. 22, 1965, pp. 15–16.
14. Nat Hentoff, "Caught in the Act," *Down Beat*, Nov. 5, 1965, pp. 17, 31.
15. John S. Wilson, Record Reviews, *Down Beat*, July 15, 1965, p. 32.
16. Quoted in Brian Case, liner note to *In Your Own Sweet Way*, Affinity AFF 58, 1981.
17. Quoted in Valerie Wilmer, "Conversations with Bill Evans," *Jazzbeat*, March 1965, pp. 4–5.
18. Ronnie Scott, interview by Les Tomkins, *Crescendo International*, April 1979, p. 22.
19. Ronnie Scott, "Table Reserved—for Pianists Only," *Melody Maker*, March 20, 1965, p. 6.
20. Quoted in Mike Hennessey, "Evans the Jazz."
21. Bill Evans, interview by Peter Clayton, BBC Radio, 1972.

14. A Simple Matter of Conviction

Epigraph. In Cavrell, *The Universal Mind*.
1. Quoted in Brian Hennessey, "Bill Evans."
2. Quoted in Ramsey, *The Secret Sessions*.
3. Quoted in Jesse Hamlin, "The Secret Sound of Bill Evans," *San Francisco Sunday Examiner and Chronicle*, Nov. 10, 1996, Datebook, pp. 35–37.
4. Quoted in Marian McPartland, *All in Good Time* (New York: Oxford University Press, 1987), 121–23.
5. Quoted in Mark Gilbert, "Eddie Gomez," *Jazz Journal International*, March 1993, pp. 14–15.
6. Quoted in McPartland, *All in Good Time*, 123.
7. Quoted in Brian Hennessey, "Bill Evans."

8. Quoted in "News," *Down Beat*, Dec. 14, 1967, p. 9.
9. In Cavrell, *The Universal Mind*.
10. Ibid.
11. Ibid.
12. Quoted in Goldin, *Bill Evans*.

15. Quiet Now

Epigraph. Marty Morell, liner note to *Jazzhouse*, Milestone M-9151, 1987.
1. Quoted in Dahl, *Stormy Weather*, 247.
2. Ibid.
3. Sammy Mitchell, "Caught in the Act," *Down Beat*, May 16, 1968, pp. 34–35.
4. *Evans Memorial Library*.
5. Quoted in Thomas O'Neil, *The Grammys, for the Record* (New York: Penguin, 1993), 144.
6. Brian Priestley, "Caught in the Act," *Down Beat*, Oct. 17, 1968, p. 32.
7. Quoted in McPartland, *All in Good Time*, 107.
8. Bill Evans, liner note to *Alone*, Verve V6-8792, 1970.
9. *Evans Memorial Library*.
10. Gene Lees, "Montreux: The Swiss Festival That Runs Like Clockwork," *Down Beat*, Aug. 8, 1968, p. 19.
11. In Cavrell, *The Universal Mind*.
12. Morell, *Jazzhouse*.
13. Eddie Gomez, liner note to *You're Gonna Hear from Me*, Milestone M-9164, 1988.
14. Quoted in Brian Hennessey, "Bill Evans."

16. Living Time

Epigraph. Quoted in Brian Hennessey, "Bill Evans."
1. Brian Hennessey, *Along Came Bill*, program 4.
2. Harold Rhodes, liner note to *From Left to Right*, MGM SE-4723, 1970.
3. Helene Zindars, "The Genius of Bill Evans: In Retrospect," *LFE* 5/1.
4. Quoted in Leonard Feather, "Blindfold Test: Bill Evans, Pt. 1," *Down Beat*, May 28, 1970, p. 26.
5. Quoted in Brian Hennessey, "Bill Evans: A Person I Knew," part 2, *Jazz Journal International*, Oct. 1985, pp. 11–13.
6. "Goings on about Town (Night Life)," *New Yorker*, July 11, 1970, pp. 4–5.
7. Evans, *Alone*.
8. Quoted in Gilbert, "Eddie Gomez."
9. Quoted in Brian Hennessey, "Bill Evans," part 2.
10. Quoted in Jim Aikin, "Bill Evans."
11. Bill Evans, interview by Brian Priestley, BBC Radio, 1972.
12. Evans, interview by Postif.
13. Evans, interview by Priestley.
14. Evans, interview by Postif.
15. Ibid.
16. Quoted in Korall, *Space Age*.
17. Quoted in Orrin Keepnews, liner note to *Living Time*, Columbia KC 31490, 1972.
18. Russell, interview, program 8.
19. Quoted in Lyons, *Jazz Pianists*, 226.

17. You've Been a Fine Audience

Epigraph. Helen Keane, booklet accompanying *The Complete Fantasy Recordings*, Fantasy 9FCD-1012-2, 1989.
1. Evans, interview by Clayton.
2. Bill Evans, interview by Mike Hennessey, recorded at Ronnie Scott's club, London, 1975.
3. Evans, interview by O'Reilly.
4. Whitney Balliett, "Musical Events (Jazz)," *New Yorker*, July 22, 1972, pp. 40–46.
5. Keane, *Complete Fantasy*.
6. Max Gordon, liner note to *Since We Met*, Fantasy F-9501, 1976.
7. Evans, interview by Mike Hennessey.
8. Helen Keane, liner note to *The Bill Evans Trio Featuring Stan Getz: But Beautiful*, Milestone MCD 9249-2, 1996.
9. Evans, interview by Mike Hennessey.
10. Jimmy Rowles, interview by Win Hinkle, *LFE* 4/1.
11. Evans, interview by Mike Hennessey.

18. You Must Believe in Spring

Epigraph. Goodwin, interview.
1. Joe LaBarbera, interview by Win Hinkle, *LFE* 4/4.
2. Goodwin, interview.
3. Quoted in Lyons, *Jazz Pianists*, 223.
4. Quoted in Brian Hennessey, "Bill Evans," part 2.
5. Quoted in James Isaacs, liner note to *Tony Bennett/Jazz*, CBS 450465-1, 1987.
6. Quoted in Lyons, *Jazz Pianists*, 223.
7. Ibid., 220.
8. Keane, *Complete Fantasy*.
9. Richie Beirach, interview by Win Hinkle, *LFE* 5/3.
10. Evans, interview by Mike Hennessey.
11. Quoted in Lyons, *Jazz Pianists*, 224.
12. Eliot Zigmund, interview by Win Hinkle, *LFE* 5/2.
13. Keane, *Complete Fantasy*.
14. Rowles, interview.
15. Evans, interview by Priestley.
16. Zigmund, interview.
17. Gomez, *You're Gonna Hear*.

19. Reflections in D

Epigraph. In Marian McPartland, *Marian McPartland's Piano Jazz Interview*, Jazz Alliance TJA-12004, 1993.
1. Quoted in Aikin, "Bill Evans."
2. Quoted in Brian Hennessey, "Bill Evans," part 2.
3. Quoted in Nat Hentoff, insert notes to *New Conversations*, Warner Bros BSK 3177-Y, 1978.
4. Ibid.
5. Ibid.
6. Quoted in Aikin, "Bill Evans."
7. Marc Johnson, interview by Win Hinkle, *LFE* 2/1.
8. Lee Konitz, interview by Hanns Petrik, *LFE* 1/3.
9. Zigmund, interview.

10. In McPartland, *Piano Jazz.*
11. Quoted in Brian Hennessey, "Bill Evans," part 2.
12. Zigmund, interview.
13. Keane, *Complete Fantasy.*
14. In McPartland, *Piano Jazz.*
15. Ibid.

20. Twenty-One Cities in Twenty-Four Days

Epigraph. LaBarbera, interview.
1. Quoted in Aikin, "Bill Evans."
2. LaBarbera, interview.
3. Evans, interview by O'Reilly.
4. LaBarbera, interview.
5. Ibid.
6. Quoted in Dahl, *Stormy Weather,* 246.
7. Burt Korall, liner note to *The Paris Concert, Edition Two,* Elektra-Musician 1-60311-D, 1984.
8. LaBarbera, interview.
9. Andy LaVerne, interview by Win Hinkle, *LFE* 5/2.
10. Evans, interview by O'Reilly.

21. Letter to Evan

Epigraph. TV interview at Molde, Norway, private video, 1980.
1. Brian Case, "The Quiet Innovator," *Melody Maker,* Sept. 27, 1980, p. 28.
2. Evans, interview by O'Reilly.
3. Evans, *Monk.*
4. Brian Hennessey, *Along Came Bill,* program 1.
5. Quoted in Stan Britt, liner note to *Quiet Now,* Affinity AFF 73, 1981.
6. Wong, interview.
7. Quoted in Bonnie Biggs, "The Genius of Bill Evans," *Jazz Link,* Sept. 1989, pp. 3–5.
8. Lowe, interview.
9. Quoted in Biggs, "The Genius."

Discography

In compiling this listing, I am deeply indebted to Peter H. Larsen and his pioneering discography of Bill Evans, *Turn on the Stars*, published privately in Denmark in 1984.

The following is a list only of issued material that has at any time been available for public purchase, and it excludes reissues that do not add new material. Original LP issues are taken as the starting point and are the versions listed unless otherwise indicated. The CD version is listed when it contains extra tracks or when there is no LP version. In the murky field of bootlegs, the list does not claim to be comprehensive. Issued videos are included chronologically.

"Excerpt" after the record title indicates that there is other material on the disc, either by Bill Evans or by other artists. Dates of recording mostly follow the Larsen discography rather than the record sleeves. In the case of albums involving more than one recording date, the earliest date dictates the position of the entry. The names of the original producers and recording engineers are appended when known.

General Abbreviations

nc	not complete
#	take

Instrumental Abbreviations

tr	trumpet
frh	french horn
tb	trombone
b-tb	bass trombone
v-tb	valve trombone
tu	tuba
cl	clarinet
bcl	bass clarinet
bsn	bassoon
ss	soprano saxophone
as	alto saxophone
ts	tenor saxophone
brs	baritone saxophone
fl	flute

afl	alto flute
picc.	piccolo
hca	harmonica
mell.	mellophone
str.	strings
vln	violin
vla	viola
vib.	vibraphone
g	guitar
p	piano
el-p	electric piano
b	bass
el-b	electric bass
dr	drums
perc.	percussion
timp.	timpani
voc.	vocal
arr.	arranger
(asst.) cond.	(assistant) conductor
comp.	composer

Discography

1. *Listen to the Music of Jerry Wald*
Jerry Wald (cl & cond.); Bill Evans (p); probably Eddie Costa (vib.); Paul Motian (dr); with g, b, & str.

Who Cares?; If I Had You; Mad About the Boy; Dancing on the Ceiling; Lucky to Be Me; Three Little Words; Love for Sale; I've Got a Crush on You; You Brought a New Kind of Love to Me; Gloomy Sunday; Little Girl Blue; Maybe

1955, New York City

Kapp KL 1043

2. *The Singing Reed* (CD, excerpt)

Lucy Reed (voc.); Bill Evans (p); Howard Collins (g); Bob Carter (b); Sol Gubin (dr)

Inchworm; My Love Is a Wanderer; Because We're Kids; There's a Boat Dat's Leavin' Soon for New York; Little Girl Blue; Fools Fall in Love; Out of This World; You May Not Love Me; My Time of Day; No Moon at All; Tabby the Cat; Baltimore Oriole; That's How I Love the Blues

August 13–15, 1955, New York City

Fantasy OJCCD-1777-2 (Fantasy 3-212)

3. *A Message from Garcia* (excerpt)

Dick Garcia (g); Bill Evans (p); Jerry Bruno (b); Camille Morin (dr)

Kimona My House; Ev'ry Night About This Time; Like Someone in Love

1955, New York City

Recording Engineer: David Hancock

Producer: Chuck Darwin

Dawn DLP 1106

4. *The Jazz Workshop* (CD)

Art Farmer (tr); Hal McKusick (as); Bill Evans (p); Barry Galbraith (g); Milt Hinton (b); Joe Harris (dr); George Russell (comp. & cond.)

Ezz-thetic; Jack's Blues; Ye Hypocrite, Ye Beelzebub; Livingstone I Presume

March 31, 1956, New York City (Webster Hall)

Recording Engineer: Ray Hall

Producer: Jack Lewis

As above except Paul Motian (dr) replaces Harris

Round Johnny Rondo; Night Sound; Concerto for Billy the Kid; Witch Hunt

October 17, 1956, same location

Recording Engineer: Bernard Keville

Producer: Fred Reynolds

As above except McKusick also plays flute; Teddy Kotick (b) replaces Hinton; Osie Johnson (dr) replaces Motian; on "Fellow Delegates" George Russell plays boobams (chromatically tuned drums)

Fellow Delegates; Ballad of Hix Blewitt (2#s); Knights of the Steamtable; The Sad Sergeant; Concerto for Billy the Kid (alt.#)

December 21, 1956, same location ·

Recording Engineer: Ray Hall

Producer: Fred Reynolds

Blue Bird ND86467 (RCA-Victor LPM 1372)

5. *The Touch of Tony Scott*

Jimmy Maxwell, Jimmy Nottingham, Idrees Sulieman (tr); Jimmy Cleveland, Urbie Green, Rex

Peer (tb); Bart Warsalona (b-tb); Tony Scott (cl & cond.); Gigi Gryce, Sam Marowitz (as); Seldon Powell, Zoot Sims (ts); Danny Bank (brs); Bill Evans (p); Mundell Lowe (g); Milt Hinton (b); Osie Johnson (dr)

*You, You're Driving Me Crazy; *Poinciana; Rock Me but Don't Roll Me; *The Moon Walks; *Yesterdays

*These charts include important parts for harp which are convincingly done by an uncredited player.

July 2–3, 1956, New York City (Webster Hall)

Johnny Carisi, Joe Wilder (tr); Jimmy Cleveland, Urbie Green (tb); Tony Scott (cl & cond.); Danny Bank (brs); Bill Evans (p); Barry Galbraith (g); Milt Hinton (b); Osie Johnson (dr)

†The Jitterbug Waltz; My Old Flame; Walkin' on Air

†On this track there is an important vibraphone part, the player again unacknowledged.

July 5, 1956, same location

Tony Scott (cl); Bill Evans (p); Les Grinage (b); Lennie McBrowne (dr)

'Round Midnight; Vanilla Frosting on a Beef Pie; Deep Purple; Aeolian Drinking Song

July 6, 1956, same location

Recording Engineer: Fred Elasser

RCA-Victor LPM 1353

6. *New Jazz Conceptions* (CD)
Bill Evans (p); Teddy Kotick (b); Paul Motian (dr)

I Love You; Five; Conception; Easy Living; Displacement; Speak Low; Our Delight; No Cover, No Minimum (2#s); I Got It Bad (and That Ain't Good) (p solo); Waltz for Debby (p solo); My Romance (p solo)

September 11 and 27, 1956, New York City (Reeves Sound Studios)

Recording Engineer: Jack Higgins

Producer: Orrin Keepnews

In his book, *The View from Within* (pp. 167–68), Orrin Keepnews has cleared up some confusion over the recording dates of this album. The alt.# of "No Cover, No Minimum" first appeared on the Milestone double album *Conception* in 1981.

Riverside OJCCD 025-2 (RLP 12-223)

7. *The Complete Tony Scott*
Jimmy Nottingham, Clark Terry, Thad Jones, Johnny Carisi (tr); Henry Coker, Quentin Jackson, Sonny Truitt, Benny Powell (tb); Tony Scott (cl & cond.); Gigi Gryce (as); Zoot Sims, Frank Wess (ts); Danny Bank, Sahib Shihab (brs); Bill Evans (p); Freddie Green (g); Milt Hinton (b); Osie Johnson (dr)

Moonlight Cocktail; I Surrender Dear; Under a Blanket of Blue

December 11, 1956, New York City (Webster Hall)

As above except Bernie Glow (tr) replaces Nottingham; Les Grinage (b) replaces Hinton; Paul Motian (dr) replaces Johnson

I Found a Million Dollar Baby; Skylark; Finger Poppin' Blues

December 13, 1956, same location

As December 11, except Frank Foster (ts) replaces Sims

A Blues Serenade; Just One of Those Things; Walkin'

December 14, 1956, same location

As December 11, except Jimmy Maxwell (tr) replaces Nottingham; Joe Newman (tr) replaces Terry; Wendell Culley (tr) replaces Carisi; Bill Hughes (tb) replaces Truitt; Frank Foster (ts) replaces Sims; Frank Wess also plays flute; Charles Fowlkes (brs) replaces Bank; Les Grinage (b) replaces Hinton

The Lady Is a Tramp; Time to Go; I'll Remember April

February 6, 1957, same location

Producer: Tony Scott

RCA-Victor LPM 1452

8. *Brandeis Jazz Festival*
Louis Mucci, Art Farmer (tr); Jimmy Knepper (tb); John LaPorta, Hal McKusick, Teo Macero (reeds); Robert DiDomenica (fl); Manuel Zegler (bsn); Jimmy Buffington (frh); Bill Evans (p); Teddy Charles (vib.); Barry Galbraith (g); Joe Benjamin or Fred Zimmerman (b); Teddy Sommer (dr); Margaret Ross (harp); Charles Mingus (voc.); Gunther Schuller, George Russell (cond.)

All about Rosie; Suspensions; Revelations; All Set; Transformation; On Green Mountain

June 10, 18, and 20, 1957, New York City

Columbia WL 127

9. *Joe Puma/Jazz* (excerpt)
Joe Puma (g); Bill Evans (p); Oscar Pettiford (b); Paul Motian (dr)

I Got It Bad (and That Ain't Good); Mother of Earl; Indian Summer

Early summer 1957, New York City

Jubilee JLP-1070

10. *Eddie Costa, Mat Mathews, & Don Elliott at Newport* (excerpt)
Don Elliott (mell., vib. & *bongos); Bill Evans (p); Ernie Furtado (b); Al Beldini (dr)

Dancing in the Dark; I Love You (omit Elliott); *'S Wonderful

July 6, 1957, Newport, Rhode Island (Freebody Park)

Recorded by Voice of America

Verve MGV 8237

11. *East Coasting*
Clarence Shaw (tr); Jimmy Knepper (tb); Curtis Porter (Shafi Hadi) (as, ts); Bill Evans (p); Charles Mingus (b); Dannie Richmond (dr)

51st Street Blues; East Coasting; Memories of You; West Coast Ghost; Conversation; Celia

August 6, 1957, New York City

Bethlehem BTM 6814

12. *A Swinging Introduction* (excerpt)
Jimmy Knepper (tb); Gene Quill (as); Bill Evans (p); Teddy Kotick (b); Dannie Richmond (dr)

Love Letters; Ogling Ogre; You Stepped Out of a Dream; How High the Moon; Idol of the Flies; Avid Admirer

September 1957, New York City

Producer: Lee Kraft

Bethlehem BCP 77

13. *All-Star Sextets* (LP reissue, excerpt)
Phil Woods (as); Benny Golson (ts); Sahib Shihab (brs); Bill Evans (p); Oscar Pettiford (b); Art Taylor (dr)

Le Sneak; Ballad to the East; Blu-A-Round; Ba-Dut-Du-Dat

November 7, 1957, Hackensack, New Jersey

Recording Engineer: Rudy Van Gelder

Producer: Ozzie Cadena

Savoy/Arista SJL 2245 (first 3 tracks originally on *Jazz Sahib*, Savoy MGM 12124)

14a. *A Day in New York* (double CD)
Clark Terry (tr); Jimmy Knepper (tb); Tony Scott (cl & brs); Sahib Shihab (brs); Bill Evans (p); Milt Hinton or Henry Grimes (b); Paul Motian (dr)

(Scott, Evans, Motian on all tracks, others variable)

Franzy Pants (not previously issued)

and then comprising:

I. *The Modern Art of Jazz* (LP), Seeco CELP 425, producer: Chuck Darwin
She's Different; I Remember You; Lullaby of the Leaves; The Lady Is a Tramp; Tenderly; Five; Blues for Three Horns

II. *Free Blown Jazz* (LP), Carlton STLP 12/113
Portrait of Ravi; The Chant; I Can't Get Started; Body and Soul; Gone with the Wind; There Will Never Be Another You; The Explorer; If I'm Lucky

III. *My Kind of Jazz* (LP), Perfect PL 12010
Villa Jazz; Zonk; For Pete's Sake; Third Moon; Blues for Five; Just One of Those Things

IV. *Modern Jazz Festival* (LP, excerpt), Harmony HL 7196
At Home with the Blues; A Shoulder to Cry On

November 16, 1957, New York City

Fresh Sounds FSR CD-160/1/2

b. *Jazz Greats* (LP, excerpt)
Tony Scott and Sahib Shihab (brs); Bill Evans (p); prob. Milt Hinton (b); Paul Motian (dr)

Over and Over (omitted from CD)

Same date and location

Allegro ALL 737

15. *Roots* (excerpt)
Idrees Sulieman (tr); Frank Rehak (tb); Pepper Adams (brs); Bill Evans (p); Doug Watkins (b); Louis Hayes (dr)

Roots

December 6, 1957, Hackensack, New Jersey

Recording Engineer: Rudy Van Gelder

Prestige 8202

16. *Guys and Dolls Like Vibes*
Eddie Costa (vib.); Bill Evans (p); Wendell Marshall (b); Paul Motian (dr)

Guys and Dolls; I'll Know; I've Never Been in Love Before; Luck Be a Lady; Adelaide; If I Were a Bell

January 15–17, 1958, New York City

Coral CRL 57230

17. *The Mello Sound*

Don Elliott (tr, mell., vib. & voc.); Hal McKusick (fl, cl, bcl, as & ts); Bill Evans (p); Barry Galbraith (g); Ernie Furtado (b); Paul Motian (dr); Janet Putnam (harp); with 6-voice choir

Summer Scene; When the Sun Comes Out; Blue Waltz; A Million Dreams Ago; The Story of a Starry Night; Dinah; A Waltz; Poinciana; Tired of Me; Play Fiddle Play; I Don't Want to Walk Without You; It's Only a Paper Moon

February 10–11, 1958, New York City

Decca DL 9208

18. *The Nearness of You* (excerpt)

Helen Merrill (voc.); Bobby Jaspar (fl); Bill Evans (p); Barry Galbraith (g); Oscar Pettiford (b); Jo Jones (dr)

Let Me Love You; When the Sun Comes Out; All of You; The Nearness of You; Just Imagine

February 21, 1958, New York City

Producer: Hal Mooney

EmArcy MG 36134

19. *Cross Section–Saxes*

Art Farmer (tr); Hal McKusick (as & bcl); Bill Evans (p); Paul Chambers (b); Connie Kay (dr)

Sing Song; It Never Entered My Mind; Yesterdays

March 25, 1958, New York City

Hal McKusick (as); Frank Socolow (as); Dick Hafer (ts); Jay Cameron (brs); Bill Evans (p); Paul Chambers (b); Connie Kay (dr)

La Rue; Now's the Time; Whisper Not; The Last Day of Fall

March 28, 1958, New York City

Art Farmer (tr); Hal McKusick (as & cl); Bill Evans (p); Barry Galbraith (g); Milt Hinton (b); Charlie Persip (dr)

Stratusphunk; The End of a Love Affair; You're My Thrill

April 7, 1958, New York City

Producer: Marv Holzman

Decca DL 9209

20. *Four-Play* (CD, excerpt)

Miles Davis (tr); John Coltrane (ts); Bill Evans (p); Paul Chambers (b); Philly Joe Jones (dr)

Four (Four Plus One More); Bye Bye Blackbird; Walkin' (Rollin' and Blowin'); Two Bass Hit (nc)

May 17, 1958, New York City (Café Bohemia)

Recorded by Bandstand USA

Jazz Music Yesterday ME 6402 (first 3 tracks originally on *Makin' Wax*, Chakra CH 100 MD)

21. *'58 Miles* (CD, excerpt)

Miles Davis (tr); Cannonball Adderley (as); John Coltrane (ts); Bill Evans (p); Paul Chambers (b); Jimmy Cobb (dr)

including

I. *Jazz Track* (LP, excerpt)

On Green Dolphin Street; Fran-Dance; Stella by Starlight (omit Adderley)

Columbia CL 1268

II. *Black Giants* (double LP, excerpt)

Love for Sale

Columbia PG 33402

May 26, 1958, New York City

Producer: George Avakian and/or Teo Macero

Columbia 467918-2

22. *Legrand Jazz* (excerpt)

Miles Davis (tr); Jerome Richardson (bcl & brs); Phil Woods (as); John Coltrane (ts); Herbie Mann (fl); Eddie Costa (vib.); Barry Galbraith (g); Betty Glamann (harp); Bill Evans (p); Paul Chambers (b); Kenny Dennis (dr); Michel Legrand (arr. & cond.)

Wild Man Blues; 'Round Midnight; The Jitterbug Waltz; Django (omit Coltrane, Richardson, Woods, and Mann)

June 25, 1958, New York City

Producer: George Avakian and/or Teo Macero

Columbia CL 1250

23. *Portrait of Cannonball* (CD)

Cannonball Adderley (as); Blue Mitchell (tr); Bill Evans (p); Sam Jones (b); Philly Joe Jones (dr)

Minority (3#s, see below); Straight Life; Blue Funk; A Little Taste; People Will Say We're in Love; Nardis (2#s)

July 1, 1958, New York City (Reeves Sound Studios)

Recording Engineer: Jack Matthews

Producer: Orrin Keepnews

The originally issued version of "Minority" was a composite of #2 (theme and alto solo), followed by the balance of #3. The CD has this, and adds both of these takes individually complete.

Fantasy OJCCD 361-2 (RLP 12-269)

24. *Miles Davis & Thelonious Monk: Live at Newport 1958 & 1963* (double CD, excerpt)

Miles Davis (tr); Cannonball Adderley (as); John Coltrane (ts); Bill Evans (p); Paul Chambers (b); Jimmy Cobb (dr)

Ah-Leu-Cha; Straight, No Chaser; Fran-Dance; Two Bass Hit; Bye Bye Blackbird (omit Adderley); The Theme

July 3, 1958, Newport, Rhode Island (Freebody Park)

Producer: George Avakian and/or Teo Macero

Recorded by Voice of America

Columbia/Legacy C2K 53585 (CL 2178)

25. *Four-Play* (CD, excerpt)

Miles Davis (tr); Cannonball Adderley (as); John Coltrane (ts); Bill Evans (p); Paul Chambers (b); Jimmy Cobb (dr)

Walkin'; All of You; 'Round Midnight

Possibly August 9, 1958, Washington D.C. (Spotlite Lounge)

The sleeve gives June 30, which, being a Monday, seems unlikely. Jan Lohmann in his discography *The Sound of Miles Davis* gives August 9 as a probable date.

Jazz Music Yesterday ME 6402

26. *Jump for Joy*

Cannonball Adderley (as); Emmett Berry (tr); Gene Orloff, Leo Kruczek (vln); Dave Schwartz (vla); George Ricci (cello); Barry Galbraith (g); Bill Evans (p); Milt Hinton (b); Jimmy Cobb (dr); Bill Russo (arr. & cond.)

Nothin'; If Life Were All Peaches and Cream; Jump for Joy; Brownskin Gal in a Calico Gown; I Got It Bad (and That Ain't Good); Two Left Feet; Bli-Blip; The Tune of the Hickory Stick; Just Squeeze Me; Chocolate Shake

August 20–21, 1958, New York City (Fine Recording Studio)

Recording Engineer: George Piros

Producer: Jack Tracy

Mercury MG 20530

27. *Jazz at the Plaza, Vol. I*

Miles Davis (tr); Cannonball Adderley (as); John Coltrane (ts); Bill Evans (p); Paul Chambers (b); Jimmy Cobb (dr)

Straight, No Chaser; My Funny Valentine (omit Adderley and Coltrane); If I Were a Bell (omit Adderley); Oleo; The Theme

September 9, 1958, New York City (Plaza Hotel)

Producers: George Avakian, Teo Macero, and Irving Townsend

On the original issue, "Straight, No Chaser" was mistakenly called "Jazz at the Plaza" and credited to Davis instead of Thelonious Monk. *Jazz at the Plaza, Vol. 2* is by Duke Ellington and his Orchestra.

Columbia C 32470

28. *Modern Art*

Art Farmer (tr); Benny Golson (ts); Bill Evans (p); Addison Farmer (b); Dave Bailey (dr)

Mox Nix; Fair Weather; Darn That Dream; The Touch of Your Lips; Jubilation; Like Someone in Love; I Love You; Cold Breeze

September 10, 11, and 14, 1958, New York City (Nola Penthouse Sound Studio)

Recording Engineer: Tommy Nola

Producer: Jack Lewis

United Artists UAL 4007

29. *New York, N.Y.*

Art Farmer, Doc Severinsen, Ernie Royal (tr); Bob Brookmeyer, Frank Rehak, Tom Mitchell (tb); Hal McKusick (as); John Coltrane (ts); Sol Schlinger (brs); Bill Evans (p); Barry Galbraith (g); Milt Hinton (b); Charlie Persip (dr); Jon Hendricks (voc.); George Russell (arr. & cond.)

Manhattan

September 12, 1958, New York City

Art Farmer, Ernie Royal, Joe Wilder (tr); Bob Brookmeyer, Jimmy Cleveland, Tom Mitchell (tb); Hal McKusick, Phil Woods (as); Al Cohn (ts); Gene Allen (brs); Bill Evans (p); Barry Galbraith (g); George Duvivier (b); Max Roach (dr); Jon Hendricks (voc.); George Russell (comp. & cond.)

A Helluva Town

As above except Don Lamond (dr) replaces Roach; add Al Epstein (bongos); George Russell also plays chromatic drums

Manhatta-Rico

November 24, 1958, New York City

Art Farmer, Joe Wilder, Joe Ferrante (tr); Bob Brookmeyer, Frank Rehak, Tom Mitchell (tb); Hal McKusick, Phil Woods (as, fl & cl); Benny Golson (ts); Sol Schlinger (brs); Bill Evans (p); Barry Galbraith (g); Milt Hinton (b); Charlie Persip (dr); Jon Hendricks (voc.); George Russell (comp., arr., & cond.)

Big City Blues; (East Side Medley) Autumn in New York/How About You?

March 24, 1959, New York City

Decca DL 7-9216

30. *Everybody Digs Bill Evans* (CD)
Bill Evans (p); Sam Jones (b); Philly Joe Jones (dr)

Minority; Young and Foolish; Night and Day; Oleo; Tenderly; What Is There to Say?; Peace Piece (p solo); Lucky to Be Me (p solo); Some Other Time (p solo); Epilogue (p solo)

December 15, 1958, New York City (Reeves Sound Studios)

Recording Engineer: Jack Higgins

Producer: Orrin Keepnews

"Some Other Time" was first released on the Milestone double album *Conception* in 1981.

Riverside OJCCD 068-2 (RLP 12-291)

31. *Chet* (CD)
Chet Baker (tr); Herbie Mann (fl); Pepper Adams (brs); Bill Evans (p); Paul Chambers (b); Connie Kay (dr)

Alone Together; How High the Moon; If You Could See Me Now; You'd Be So Nice to Come Home To; Early Morning Mood

December 30, 1958, New York City (Reeves Sound Studios)

"Early Morning Mood" was originally issued separately on a Riverside "various artists" album called *New Blue Horns* (Riverside RLP 12-294).

Philly Joe Jones (dr) replaces Kay

'Tis Autumn; You and the Night and the Music; Time on My Hands (omit Mann and Adams)

January 19, 1959, same location

Recording Engineer: Jack Higgins

Producer: Orrin Keepnews

Riverside OJCCD 087-2 (RLP 12-299)

32. *The Jazz Soul of Porgy and Bess*
Art Farmer, Harry Edison, Bernie Glow, Marky Markowitz, Charlie Shavers (tr); Bob Brookmeyer (v-tb); Frank Rehak, Jimmy Cleveland, Earl Swope (tb); Rod Levitt (b-tb); Gene Quill, Phil Woods (as); Zoot Sims, Al Cohn (ts); Sol Schlinger (brs); Herbie Powell (g); Bill Evans (p); George Duvivier (b); Charlie Persip (dr); Bill Potts (arr. & cond.)

I Loves You, Porgy; Oh, Bess, Oh Where's My Bess; Summertime; A Woman Is a Sometime Thing; I Got Plenty o' Nuttin'; Bess, You Is My Woman Now; Clara, Clara; There's a Boat Dat's Leavin' Soon for New York; (Medley) Prayer/Strawberry Woman/Honey Man/Crab Man; Oh Lawd, I'm on My Way; My Man's Gone Now; It Takes a Long Pull to Get There; It Ain't Necessarily So

January 13–15, 1959, New York City (Webster Hall)

Recording Engineer: Ray Hall

Producer: Jack Lewis

United Artists UAL 4043

33. *Peace Piece and Other Pieces* (double LP, excerpt), or *Green Dolphin Street* (CD)
Bill Evans (p); Paul Chambers (b); Philly Joe Jones (dr)

You and the Night and the Music; How Am I to Know?; Woody'n You (2#s); My Heart Stood Still; On Green Dolphin Street

January 19, 1959, New York City (Reeves Sound Studios)

Recording Engineer: Jack Higgins

Producer: Orrin Keepnews

This double LP includes the album *Everybody Digs Bill Evans.*

Milestone M-47024 and MCD 9235-2

34. *Lee Konitz: Live at the Half Note* (double CD)
Lee Konitz (as); Warne Marsh (ts); Bill Evans (p); Jimmy Garrison (b); Paul Motian (dr)

Palo Alto; How About You?; My Melancholy Baby; Scrapple from the Apple; You Stepped Out of a Dream; 317 E 32nd; April; It's You or No One; Just Friends; Baby, Baby All the Time; Lennie-Bird; Subconscious-Lee

February 24 and possibly March 3, 1959, New York City (Half Note Café)

Recording Engineer: Peter Ind

Producer: Lee Konitz

Fragments from these sessions, edited by the pianist Lennie Tristano from a mono copy of the tapes, appeared on two LPs, each entitled *Warne Marsh/The Art of Improvising* (Revelation 22 and 27).

Verve 521 659-2

35. *Kind of Blue* (CD, excerpt)
Miles Davis (tr); Cannonball Adderley (as); John Coltrane (ts); Bill Evans (p); Paul Chambers (b); Jimmy Cobb (dr)

So What: Blue in Green

March 2, 1959, New York City (Columbia 30th Street Studio)

Same personnel and location

Flamenco Sketches (2#s); All Blues

April 6, 1959

Recording Engineer: Fred Plaut

Producers: Teo Macero and Irving Townsend

The second session is nearly always given as April 22, but according to the Columbia/Legacy

MasterSound Edition of *Kind of Blue* (CK 64403), sessions on that date and on March 10 may have been booked and canceled.

Columbia/Legacy CK 64935 (CL 1355)

36. *The Ivory Hunters*

Bill Evans, Bob Brookmeyer (p); Percy Heath (b); Connie Kay (dr)

Honeysuckle Rose; As Time Goes By; The Way You Look Tonight; It Could Happen to You; The Man I Love; I Got Rhythm

March 12, 1959, New York City

Recording Engineer: Dick Olmsted

Producer: Jack Lewis

Evans is heard on the right-hand channel.

United Artists UAL 4004

37. *Lee Konitz Meets Jimmy Giuffre*

Lee Konitz, Hal McKusick (as); Warne Marsh, Ted Brown (ts); Jimmy Giuffre (brs & arr.); Bill Evans (p); Buddy Clark (b); Ronnie Free (dr)

Moonlight in Vermont; The Song Is You; Somp'n Outa' Nothin'; Uncharted; Someone to Watch over Me; Palo Alto; When Your Lover Has Gone; Cork 'n' Bib; Darn That Dream (omit rhythm section)

May 12–13, 1959, New York City

Producer: Norman Granz

Verve MGV 8335

38. *Something New, Something Blue* (excerpt)

Art Farmer (tr); Frank Rehak (tb); Phil Woods (as); Al Cohn (ts, brs); Eddie Costa (vib.); Bill Evans (p); Addison Farmer (b); Ed Shaughnessy (dr); Manny Albam (arr. & cond.)

Night Crawlers; Tin Roof Blues

Teo Macero (arr. & cond.) replaces Albam

Blues for Amy; St. Louis Blues

May 15, 1959, New York City

Columbia CL 1388

39. *Odds Against Tomorrow*

Melvyn Broiles, Bernie Glow, John Ware, Joe Wilder (tr); John Clark, Thomas McIntosh (tb); Raymond Alonge, Paul Ingram, Al Richman, Gunther Schuller (frh); Harvey Phillips (tu); Robert DiDomenica (fl); Harvey Shapiro, Joe Tekula (cello); Ruth Berman (harp); Milt Jackson (vib.); Jim Hall (g); Bill Evans (p & steam calliope); Percy Heath (b); Connie Kay (dr); Walter Rosenberger (perc.); Richard Horowitz (timp.); John Lewis (comp. & cond.)

Prelude to *Odds Against Tomorrow*; A Cold Wind Is Blowing; Five Figure People Crossing Paths; How to Frame Pigeons; Morning Trip to Melton; Looking at the Caper; Johnny Ingram's Possessions; The Carousel Incident; Skating in Central Park; No Happiness for Slater; Odds Against Tomorrow; Games; Social Call; The Impractical Man; Advance on Melton; Waiting around the River; Distractions; The Caper Failure; Postlude

July 16, 17, and 20, 1959, New York City

Producer: Jack Lewis

United Artists UAL 4061

40. *Chet Baker Plays the Best of Lerner & Loewe* (excerpt)

Chet Baker (tr); Herbie Mann (fl, picc. & arr.); Zoot Sims (as & ts); Pepper Adams (brs); Bill Evans (p); Earl May (b); Clifford Jarvis (dr)

Show Me; I Talk to the Trees; Thank Heaven for Little Girls (omit Mann and Adams); I Could Have Danced All Night

July 22, 1959, New York City (Reeves Sound Studios)

Recording Engineer: Roy Friedman

Producer: Orrin Keepnews

The documentation to *The Complete Riverside Recordings* (see Collections) lists this date as July 12, and the recording engineer as Jack Higgins.

Riverside RLP 12-307

41a. *Golden Moments*

Tony Scott (cl); Bill Evans (p); Jimmy Garrison (b); Pete LaRoca (dr)

Like Someone in Love (omit Scott); Walkin'; I Can't Get Started; Free and Easy Blues; My Melancholy Baby

August 1 and 9, 1959, New York City (the Showplace)

b. *I'll Remember*

Same personnel, dates, and location

Stella by Starlight; I'll Remember April; A Night in Tunisia; Garrison's Raiders

Producer and Engineer: Tony Scott

Muse MR 5230 and MR 5266

42. *Sung Heroes* (excerpt)

Tony Scott (cl); Bill Evans (p); Scott LaFaro (b); Paul Motian (dr)

Misery (to Lady Day); Israel; Blues for an African Friend; Requiem for "Hot Lips" Page; For Stefan Wolpe

October 28 and possibly *29, 1959, New York City (Fine Studio)

Producer: Tony Scott

*On this date Evans was recording *You and Lee* with Lee Konitz.

Sunnyside SSC 1015

43. *You and Lee* (excerpt)

Ernie Royal, Marky Markowitz, Phil Sunkel (tr); Bob Brookmeyer, Eddie Bert, Billy Byers (tb); Lee Konitz (as); Bill Evans (p); Sonny Dallas (b); Roy Haynes (dr); Jimmy Giuffre (arr. & cond.)

I'm Getting Sentimental over You; You Don't Know What Love Is; I Didn't Know About You; Ev'rything I've Got (Belongs to You)

October 29, 1959, New York City

Verve MGV 8362

44. *Portrait in Jazz* (CD)

Bill Evans (p); Scott LaFaro (b); Paul Motian (dr)

Peri's Scope; Witchcraft; Spring Is Here; What Is This Thing Called Love?; Come Rain or Come Shine; Blue in Green (2#s); Autumn Leaves (2#s); Someday My Prince Will Come; When I Fall in Love

December 28, 1959, New York City (Reeves Sound Studios)

Recording Engineer: Jack Higgins

Producer: Orrin Keepnews

A 24-Karat Gold Disc of *Portrait in Jazz* was issued in 1995 by DCC Compact Classics Inc. under license from Fantasy, Inc.

Riverside OJCCD 088-2 (RLP 12-315)

45. *The Soft Land of Make Believe* (excerpt)
Frank Minion (voc.); Bill Evans (p); Paul Chambers (b); Jimmy Cobb (dr)

Flamenco Sketches; 'Round Midnight; So What

January 1960, New York City

Producer: Teddy Charles

Bethlehem BCP 6052

46. *The Legendary Bill Evans Trio: The 1960 Birdland Sessions* (CD)
comprising:

I. A *Rare Original* (LP), Alto AL 719
II. *Hooray for Bill Evans Trio* (LP), Session 113
Bill Evans (p); Scott LaFaro (b); Paul Motian (dr)

[I]Autumn Leaves [March 12th on the Books]; [I]Our Delight [Fingerology]; [I]Beautiful Love/Five [Ides of March]

March 12, 1960, New York City (Birdland)

[I]Autumn Leaves; [I]Come Rain or Come Shine/Five [March 19th Improvisations]

March 19, 1960, same location

[II]Come Rain or Come Shine; [I,II]Nardis [Billy Bounces Light]; [I,II]Blue in Green; [II]Autumn Leaves

April 30, 1960, same location

[II]All of You; [II]Come Rain or Come Shine; [II]Speak Low

May 7, 1960, same location

Titles in brackets are from the LPs. An affiliated LP, *John Handy/Bill Evans* (Ozone Records 20), includes the May 7 tracks only.

Cool & Blue C&B-CD 106

47. *The Soul of Jazz Percussion* (excerpt)
Donald Byrd (tr); Pepper Adams (brs); Bill Evans (p); Paul Chambers (b); Philly Joe Jones (dr); Earl Zindars (perc.)

Ping Pong Beer; Prophecy; Quiet Temple

Spring 1960, New York City

Producer: Teddy Charles

These tracks also appeared on the album *The Third World* (tcb Records 1004).

Warwick W-5003-ST

48. *Jazz in the Space Age*
Ernie Royal, Al Kiger (tr); Frank Rehak, Dave Baker (tb); Jimmy Buffington (frh); Walt Levinsky (as); Dave Young (ts); Sol Schlinger (brs); Bill Evans, Paul Bley (p); Milt Hinton (b); Barry Galbraith, Howard Collins (g); Don Lamond (dr); George Russell (comp., cond. & beads on tuned drums)

Chromatic Universe (Parts 1–3); The Lydiot

May 1960, New York City

As above except add Marky Markowitz (tr); Bob Brookmeyer (v-tb); omit Buffington, Bley, Collins; Hal McKusick (as) replaces Levinsky; Charlie Persip (dr) replaces Lamond

Dimensions; Waltz from Outer Space

August 1, 1960, New York City

Producer: Milton Gabler

In 1973 *New York, N.Y.* and *Jazz in the Space Age* were issued as a "twofer" in the Leonard Feather Series (MCA 2-4017).

Decca DL 7-9219

49. *The Great Kai and J.J.*
Kai Winding, J. J. Johnson (tb); Bill Evans (p); Paul Chambers (b); Roy Haynes (dr)

This Could Be the Start of Something; I Concentrate on You; Blue Monk; Side by Side

October 3 and November 2, 1960, New York City

As above except Tommy Williams (b) and Art Taylor (dr) replace Chambers and Haynes

Alone Together; Theme from *Picnic*; Going, Going, Going; Just for a Thrill; Judy; Georgia on My Mind; Trixie

November 4 and 8, 1960, New York City

Producer: Creed Taylor

Impulse A (S) 1

50. *The Incredible Kai Winding Trombones* (excerpt)
Kai Winding, Jimmy Knepper (tb); Dick Lieb, Paul Faulise (b-tb); Bill Evans (p); Ron Carter (b); Sticks Evans (dr)

Michie (slow version); Black Coffee; Bye Bye Blackbird

December 13, 1960, New York City

Producer: Creed Taylor

Impulse A (S) 3

51. *Jazz Abstractions* (excerpt)
Eric Dolphy, Robert DiDomenica (fl); Eddie Costa (vib.); Jim Hall (g); Bill Evans (p); George Duvivier, Scott LaFaro (b); Sticks Evans (dr); The Contemporary String Quartet (Charles Libove, Roland Vamos, Harry Zaratzian, and Joe Tekula)

Variants on a Theme of John Lewis (Django)

December 20, 1960, New York City

Add Ornette Coleman (as); Dolphy also plays as & bcl

Variants on a Theme of Thelonious Monk (Criss Cross)

Same date and location

Recording Engineer: Phil Ramone

Producers: John Lewis and Nesuhi Ertegun

Atlantic SD 1365

52. *Know What I Mean?* (CD)
Cannonball Adderley (as); Bill Evans (p); Percy Heath (b); Connie Kay (dr)

Who Cares (2#s); Goodbye; Nancy (with the Laughing Face); Toy; Elsa; Waltz for Debby; Venice; Know What I Mean? (2#s)

January 27, February 21, and March 13, 1961, New York City (Bell Sound Studios)

Recording Engineer: Bill Stoddard

Producer: Orrin Keepnews

Riverside OJCCD 105-2 (RLP 433)

53. *Explorations* (CD)
Bill Evans (p); Scott LaFaro (b); Paul Motian (dr)

Elsa; Sweet and Lovely; Beautiful Love (2#s); I Wish I Knew; The Boy Next Door; Haunted Heart; Nardis; How Deep Is the Ocean?; Israel

February 2, 1961, New York City (Bell Sound Studios)

Recording Engineer: Bill Stoddard

Producer: Orrin Keepnews

"The Boy Next Door" first appeared in 1976 on the "twofer" *Spring Leaves* (Milestone M-47034), which, besides *Explorations*, also contains the album *Portrait in Jazz*.

Riverside OJCCD 037-2 (RLP 351)

54. *The Blues and the Abstract Truth*
Freddie Hubbard (tr); Eric Dolphy (as & fl); Oliver Nelson (as, ts, comp. & arr.); George Barrow (brs); Bill Evans (p); Paul Chambers (b); Roy Haynes (dr)

Stolen Moments; Hoe-Down; Cascades; Yearnin'; Butch and Butch; Teenie's Blues (omit Hubbard and Barrow)

February 23, 1961, New York City

Sound Engineer: Rudy Van Gelder

Producer: Creed Taylor

Impulse A (S) 5

55a. *Sunday at the Village Vanguard*
Bill Evans (p); Scott LaFaro (b); Paul Motian (dr)

Gloria's Step (#2); My Man's Gone Now (#2); Solar; Alice in Wonderland (#2); All of You (#2); Jade Visions (#2)

June 25, 1961, New York City (the Village Vanguard)

b. *Waltz for Debby*
Same personnel, date, and location

My Foolish Heart; Waltz for Debby (#2); Detour Ahead (#2); My Romance (#1); Some Other Time; Milestones

c. *More from the Vanguard*
Same personnel, date, and location

Alice in Wonderland (#1); Detour Ahead (#1); All of You (#3); Gloria's Step (#3); My Romance (#2); Jade Visions (#1); Waltz for Debby (#1)

d. *The Village Vanguard Sessions* (double LP, excerpt)
Same personnel, date, and location

Porgy

e. *The Complete Riverside Recordings* (18-LP boxed set, excerpt)
Same personnel, date, and location

All of You (#1); . . . a few final bars

Recording Engineer: Dave Jones

Producer: Orrin Keepnews

All tracks are on *The Complete Riverside Recordings* (see Collections); "All of You" (#1) and " . . . a few final bars" are available nowhere else. The "twofer" *The Village Vanguard Sessions*, issued in 1973, contains, besides "Porgy," the albums *Sunday at the Village Vanguard* and *Waltz for Debby*. "Gloria's Step" (#1) is unissued (power out). "My Man's Gone Now" (#1) is also unissued (tape lost).

Riverside RLP 376, RLP 399, Milestone M-9125, M-47002, and Riverside R 018

56. *Rah* (excerpt)

Mark Murphy (voc.); Clark Terry, Bernie Glow, Ernie Royal (tr); Jimmy Cleveland, Melba Liston (tb); Bill Evans (p); Sam Herman (g); Wendell Marshall (b); Jimmy Cobb (dr); Ray Barretto (congas); Ernie Wilkins (arr. & cond.)

Out of This World; My Favorite Things

October 16, 1961, New York City (Plaza Sound Studio)

Recording Engineer: Ray Fowler

Producer: Orrin Keepnews

The Japanese CD of *Rah* (V VICJ-23695) has a longer version of "My Favorite Things."

Riverside RLP 395

57. *Nirvana*

Herbie Mann (fl & afl); Bill Evans (p); Chuck Israels (b); Paul Motian (dr)

Nirvana; I Love You; Lover Man; Willow Weep for Me; Cashmere; Gymnopédie No. 2

December 8, 1961, and May 4, 1962, New York City (Atlantic Studios)

Recording Engineers: Tom Dowd and Phil Iehle

Producer: Nesuhi Ertegun

Atlantic SD 1426

58. *Pike's Peak*

Dave Pike (vib.); Bill Evans (p); Herbie Lewis (b); Walter Perkins (dr)

Why Not; In a Sentimental Mood; Vierd Blues; Besame Mucho; Wild Is the Wind

February 6, 1962, New York City

Recording Engineers: Fred Plaut and Stan Weiss

Producer: Mike Berniker

Epic LA 16025

59. *Bill Evans Trio: Rare Broadcast Material* (excerpt)

Bill Evans (p); Chuck Israels (b); Paul Motian (dr)

Gloria's Step; Haunted Heart; Nardis

February 10, 1962, New York City (Birdland)

Chazzer 2007

60. *The Magic Touch* (CD)

Joe Wilder or Charlie Shavers, Clark Terry, Ernie Royal (tr); Jimmy Cleveland, Britt Woodman (tb); Julius Watkins (frh); Leo Wright, Jerry Dodgion (as & fl); Jerome Richardson (ts & fl); Johnny Griffin (ts); Tate Houston (brs); Bill Evans (p); Ron Carter or George Duvivier (b); Philly Joe Jones (dr); Barbara Winfield (voc.); Tadd Dameron (comp., arr. & cond.)

Our Delight (2#s); Dial B for Beauty; Bevan's Birthday; On a Misty Night (2#s); Swift as the Wind; Fontainebleau; Just Plain Talkin' (2#s); If You Could See Me Now; You're a Joy; Look, Stop and Listen

February 27, March 9, and April 16, 1962, New York City (Plaza Sound Studio)

Recording Engineer: Ray Fowler

Producer: Orrin Keepnews

Riverside OJCCD 143-2 (RLP 419)

61. *Conception* (double LP, excerpt)

Bill Evans (p)

Danny Boy; Like Someone in Love; In Your Own Sweet Way; Easy to Love

April 4, 1962, New York City (Plaza Sound Studios)

Recording Engineer: Ray Fowler

Producer: Orrin Keepnews

Orrin Keepnews documents the session as April 4; the sleeve has April 10. This double LP includes the whole of *New Jazz Conceptions*.

Milestone M-47063

62. *Just Jazz*

Freddie Hubbard or *Bill Hardman (tr); Curtis Fuller or *Grachan Moncur III (tb); Wayne Shorter (ts) or *Eric Dolphy (as); Bill Evans (p); Ron Carter or †Paul Chambers (b); Charlie Persip or †Jimmy Cobb (dr); Benny Golson (arr. & cond.)

Moten Swing; Out of Nowhere; *Groovin' High; Autumn Leaves; *Donna Lee; Quicksilver; Stella by Starlight; *Ornithology; *If I Should Lose You; †Walkin'

April, 1962, New York City

Recording Engineers: Richard B. Olmsted and William Hamilton

Producers: Barry D. Oslander and Tom Wilson

Another version of this recording was issued, called *Pop + Jazz = Swing* (AFLP 1978). It contains pop arrangements for strings and wind on a separate channel.

Audio Fidelity AFLP 2150

63. *Undercurrent* (CD)

Bill Evans (p); Jim Hall (g)

I Hear a Rhapsody; Stairway to the Stars; I'm Getting Sentimental over You; My Funny Valentine (2#s); Dream Gypsy; Romain (2#s); Skating in Central Park; Darn That Dream

April 24 and May 14, 1962, New York City (Sound Makers)

Recording Engineer: Bill Schwartau

Producer: Alan Douglas

Blue Note CDP7-90583-2 (United Artists UAJ 14003)

64a. *Moonbeams*

Bill Evans (p); Chuck Israels (b); Paul Motian (dr)

If You Could See Me Now; Very Early; Re: Person I Knew; Polka Dots and Moonbeams; I Fall In Love Too Easily; In Love in Vain; Stairway to the Stars; It Might as Well Be Spring

May 17, 29, and June 5, 1962, New York City (Sound Makers)

b. *How My Heart Sings* (CD)

Same personnel, dates, and location

How My Heart Sings; Summertime; Walkin' Up; Show-Type Tune; 34 Skidoo; I Should Care; Ev'rything I Love; In Your Own Sweet Way (2#s)

Recording Engineer: Bill Schwartau

Producer: Orrin Keepnews

Both these albums were reissued on a Milestone "twofer" called *The Second Trio* (M-47046).

Riverside RLP 428 and OJCCD 369-2 (RLP 473)

65. *Interplay* (CD)

Freddie Hubbard (tr); Jim Hall (g); Bill Evans (p); Percy Heath (b); Philly Joe Jones (dr)

Wrap Your Troubles in Dreams; When You Wish upon a Star; You Go to My Head; You and the Night and the Music; Interplay; I'll Never Smile Again (2#s)

July 16–17, 1962, New York City (Nola Penthouse Sound Studio)

Recording Engineer: Tommy Nola

Producer: Orrin Keepnews

Riverside OJCCD 308-2 (RLP 445)

66. *Empathy*

Bill Evans (p); Monty Budwig (b); Shelly Manne (dr)

The Washington Twist; Danny Boy; Let's Go Back to the Waltz; With a Song in My Heart; Goodbye; I Believe in You

August 20, 1962, New York City

Recording Engineer: Rudy Van Gelder

Producer: Creed Taylor

The sleeve gives the recording date as August 14.

Verve V6-8497

67. *Loose Bloose* (CD)

Zoot Sims (ts); Bill Evans (p); Jim Hall (g); Ron Carter (b); Philly Joe Jones (dr)

Loose Bloose (2#s); Fudgesickle Built for Four; Time Remembered; Funkallero; My Bells; There Came You; Fun Ride

August 21–22, 1962, New York City (Nola Penthouse Sound Studio)

Recording Engineer: Tommy Nola

Producer: Orrin Keepnews

Most of this material was first issued in 1982 on the double LP *The "Interplay" Sessions* (Milestone M-47066), also containing the album *Interplay*.

MCD 9200-2

68a. *The Solo Session, Vol. 1*

Bill Evans (p)

What Kind of Fool Am I? (2#s); (Medley) My Favorite Things/Easy to Love/Baubles, Bangles and Beads; When I Fall in Love; (Medley) *Spartacus* Love Theme/Nardis; Everything Happens to Me; April in Paris

January 10, 1963, New York City (Sound Makers Studio)

b. *The Solo Session, Vol. 2*

Same personnel, date, and location

All the Things You Are; Santa Claus Is Coming to Town; I Loves You, Porgy; Love Is Here to Stay; Ornithology; (Medley) Autumn in New York/How About You?

Recording Engineer: Bill Schwartau

Producer: Orrin Keepnews

Milestone MCD 9170 and 9195

69. *The Gary McFarland Orchestra*

Phil Woods (cl); Spencer Sinatra (afl); Jim Hall (g); Bill Evans (p); Richard Davis (b); Ed Shaughnessy (dr); Julian Barber, Alan Goldberg, Aaron Juvelier, Joe Tekula (str.); Gary McFarland (comp., arr., cond. & vib.)

A Moment Alone (omit Hall); Reflections in the Park; Peachtree; Night Images (omit Hall); Misplaced Cowpoke; Tree Patterns

January 24, 1963, New York City (Webster Hall)

Peter Larsen, in his discography, is adamant that all six tracks were recorded on the one January date according to the Verve record sheet. Some listings, as well as the record sleeve, assign three tunes to December 18, 1962.

Producer: Creed Taylor

Verve V6-8518

70. *Conversations with Myself* (CD)

Bill Evans (p) with two overdubbed tracks

N.Y.C.'s No Lark; How About You?; Just You, Just Me; Stella by Starlight; Hey There; 'Round Midnight; Bemsha Swing; *Spartacus* Love Theme; Blue Monk (one overdub only); A Sleepin' Bee

February 6, 9, and 20, 1963, New York City (Webster Hall)

Recording Engineer: Ray Hall

Producer: Creed Taylor

Verve 821 984-2 (V6-8526)

71a. *The V.I.P.s Theme*

Bill Evans (p); Claus Ogerman (arr. & cond.); unidentified orchestra, choir, and rhythm, but including Harry Lookofsky (concertmaster); Carl Lynch (g); Milt Hinton or Whitey Mitchell (b)

Theme from *The V.I.P.s*; On Broadway; Sweet September; Theme from *Mr. Novak*; *The Caretakers* Theme; More; Walk on the Wild Side; Hollywood; On Green Dolphin Street; The Days of Wine and Roses; The Man with the Golden Arm; Laura

b. (Verve single)

Same personnel, date, and location

55 Days in Peking

May 6 and summer 1963, New York City (A & R Studios and RCA Studios/Webster Hall)

Recording Engineers: Phil Ramone at A & R and Bob Simpson at RCA

Producer: Creed Taylor

"55 Days in Peking" is available only on the Verve single.

MGM E/SE 4184 and Verve V 10296

72a. *Bill Evans Trio at Shelly's Manne Hole* (CD)

Bill Evans (p); Chuck Israels (b); Larry Bunker (dr)

All the Things You Are; Love Is Here to Stay; 'Round Midnight; Stella by Starlight; The Boy Next Door; Isn't It Romantic?; Blues in F/Five; Wonder Why; Swedish Pastry

May 30 and 31, 1963, Los Angeles, California (Shelly's Manne Hole)

b. *Time Remembered* (double LP, excerpt)

Same personnel, dates, and location

Lover Man; Who Cares?; What Is This Thing Called Love?; How About You?; Everything Happens to Me; In a Sentimental Mood; My Heart Stood Still; Time Remembered

Recording Engineer: Wally Heider

Producers: Orrin Keepnews and Richard Bock

The double LP *Time Remembered* includes the LP *Bill Evans Trio at Shelly's Manne Hole.*

Riverside OJCCD 263-2 (RM 487) and Milestone M-47068

73. *Trio 64* (CD)

Bill Evans (p); Gary Peacock (b); Paul Motian (dr)

For Heaven's Sake; A Sleepin' Bee; Always (2#s); Everything Happens to Me; Dancing in the Dark; Santa Claus Is Coming to Town; I'll See You Again (2#s); Little Lulu (3#s); My Heart Stood Still

December 18, 1963, New York City

Recording Engineer: Bob Simpson

Producer: Creed Taylor

There are also incomplete selections of "Always," "I'll See You Again," and "My Heart Stood Still."

Verve 539 058-2 (V6-8578)

74. *Stan Getz and Bill Evans* (CD)

Stan Getz (ts); Bill Evans (p); Richard Davis or Ron Carter (b); Elvin Jones (dr)

My Heart Stood Still (2#s); Grandfather's Waltz (2#s); Melinda; Funkallero; But Beautiful; Night and Day (2#s); *Carpetbaggers* Theme; WNEW (Theme Song)

May 5–6, 1964, New Jersey (Van Gelder Studios, Englewood Cliffs)

Recording Engineer: Rudy Van Gelder

Producer: Creed Taylor

The Complete Bill Evans on Verve (see Collections) contains additional versions of "My Heart Stood Still," "Grandfather's Waltz," "Funkallero," "*Carpetbaggers* Theme," and "Night and Day."

Verve 833 802-2

75. *The Bill Evans Trio "Live"*

Bill Evans (p); Chuck Israels (b); Larry Bunker (dr)

Nardis; Someday My Prince Will Come; Stella by Starlight; How My Heart Sings; 'Round Midnight; What Kind of Fool Am I?; The Boy Next Door; How Deep Is the Ocean?

July 7 and 9, 1964, Sausalito, California (the Trident)

Recording Engineer: Wally Heider

Producer: Creed Taylor

The Complete Bill Evans on Verve (see Collections) contains 33 additional #s, including unique trio recordings of "Baubles, Bangles, and Beads," "My Love Is an April Song" (Earl Zindars), "What Kind of Fool Am I?" "'Deed I Do," and "Alone Together."

Verve V6-8803

76a. *Bill Evans in Europe* (Video, excerpt)
b. *Emily* (CD, excerpt)

Bill Evans (p); Chuck Israels (b); Larry Bunker (dr)

My Foolish Heart

August 1964, Stockholm, Sweden

Green Line VIDJAZZ 38 and Moon Records MCD 060-2

77. *Waltz for Debby*

Monica Zetterlund (voc.); Bill Evans (p); Chuck Israels (b); Larry Bunker (dr)

Come Rain or Come Shine; Jag Vet en Dejlig Rosa; Once upon a Summertime; So Long Big Time; Monicas Vals; Lucky to Be Me; Vindarne Sucka (omit Bunker); It Could Happen to You; Some Other Time; Om Natten (omit Israels and Bunker)

August 29, 1964, Stockholm (AB Europa Film Studio)

The Complete Bill Evans on Verve (see Collections) contains additional #s of "Come Rain or Come Shine," "Lucky to Be Me," and "It Could Happen to You," as well as a vocal rendering by Bill Evans of "Santa Claus Is Coming to Town." The recording date is given by Verve as August 23, 1964.

Philips 6378 508

78. *Trio '65*

Bill Evans (p); Chuck Israels (b); Larry Bunker (dr)

Israel; Elsa; 'Round Midnight; Love Is Here to Stay; How My Heart Sings; Who Can I Turn To?; Come Rain or Come Shine; If You Could See Me Now

February 3, 1965, New York City

Producer: Creed Taylor

Verve V6-8613

79. *Paris 1965* (CD)

Bill Evans (p); Chuck Israels (b); Larry Bunker (dr)

Elsa; I Should Care; Time Remembered; Come Rain or Come Shine; Some Other Time; Nardis; How Deep Is the Ocean?; Israel (nc)

February 13, 1965, Paris (Maison de l'ORTF)

Radio Production: Radio France

The wrong personnel is listed and "Time Remembered" is misnamed "Peace Piece." "Come Rain or Come Shine" is mutilated to cut out a radio announcement.

Royal Jazz RJ 503

80. *Two Super Bill Evans Trios: Live in Europe!* (excerpt)
Bill Evans (p); Chuck Israels (b); Larry Bunker (dr)

Nardis; Stella by Starlight; Someday My Prince Will Come; 'Round Midnight

Possibly February 1965, France

Unique Jazz UJ 24

81a. *Bill Evans Trio, Episode 1* (video)
Bill Evans (p); Chuck Israels (b); Larry Bunker (dr)

Five; How My Heart Sings; Nardis; Who Can I Turn To?; Someday My Prince Will Come; How Deep Is the Ocean?; Waltz for Debby; Five (theme) (nc)

March 19, 1965, London (Cine-Tele Sound Studios)

b. *Bill Evans Trio, Episode 2* (video)
Same personnel, date, and location

Elsa; Summertime; Come Rain or Come Shine; My Foolish Heart; Re: Person I Knew; Israel; Five (theme)

Sound Engineering: BBC Television

Producer: Terry Henebery

An edited version of *Episode 1* is included on *Bill Evans in Europe* (Green Line VIDJAZZ 38).

Pearson New Entertainment, PNV 1038 and 1039

82. *Bill Evans Trio with Symphony Orchestra*
Bill Evans (p); Chuck Israels (b); Grady Tate (dr); symphony orchestra arranged and conducted by Claus Ogerman

Prelude; Granados; Elegia; Pavane; Valse; Blue Interlude; Time Remembered; My Bells

September 29, October 18, and December 16, 1965, New Jersey (Van Gelder Studios, Englewood Cliffs)

Recording Engineer: Rudy Van Gelder

Producer: Creed Taylor

Verve V6-8640

83a. *Together Again* (excerpt)
b. *Piano Summit* (excerpt)
c. *Lee Konitz Trio and Quartet* (CD, excerpt)
Lee Konitz (as); Bill Evans (p); Niels-Henning Ørsted Pedersen (b); Alan Dawson (dr)

(Medley) How Deep Is the Ocean?/Detour Ahead/My Melancholy Baby

October 29, 1965, Berlin, Germany (Philharmonie)

Radio Production: Sender Freies Berlin

These medley numbers from Berlin appeared long before the above issues, scattered on the Unique Jazz label's *Lennie Tristano Solo in Europe and Lee Konitz Quartet in Europe* (UJ 21) and the related Jazz Connoisseur label's *Lee Konitz, Chet Baker, Keith Jarrett Quintet* (JC 113).

Earl Hines, Teddy Wilson, John Lewis, Lennie Tristano, Bill Evans, Jaki Byard (p); Niels-Henning Ørsted Pedersen (b); Alan Dawson (dr)

bBlues in D (actually in C)

October 30, 1965, same location

Bill Evans (p); Niels-Henning Ørsted Pedersen (b); Alan Dawson (dr)

[b]Beautiful Love; [b]Come Rain or Come Shine

Same date and location

Personnel as for October 29

[c]How Deep Is the Ocean?; Come Rain or Come Shine (omit Konitz); Beautiful Love (omit Konitz)

October 31 or November 1, 1965, Copenhagen, Denmark (Tivoli Gardens)

Radio Production: Danmarks Radio

[c]My Melancholy Baby

November 2, 1965, Stockholm, Sweden (Johanneshov Isstadion)

Radio Production: Sveriges Radio

Moon Records MLP 024-1, Philology W 102, and Magnetic Records MRCD 107

84. *Stockholm 1965* (CD)

Bill Evans (p); Palle Danielsson (b); Rune Carlsson (dr)

You and the Night and the Music; 'Round Midnight (2#s); Funkallero; What Is This Thing Called Love?; Very Early; Love Is Here to Stay; All of You (2#s); Elsa; Nardis; I Should Care; Time Remembered

November 15 and 19, 1965, Stockholm, Sweden (the Golden Circle)

Royal Jazz RJD 519

85. *Bill Evans at Town Hall* (CD)

Bill Evans (p); Chuck Israels (b); Arnie Wise (dr)

I Should Care; Spring Is Here; Who Can I Turn To?; Make Someone Happy; Solo—In Memory of His Father, Harry L. Evans, 1891–1966 (Medley): Prologue/Story Line/Turn Out the Stars/Epilogue (p solo); Beautiful Love; My Foolish Heart; One for Helen

February 21, 1966, New York City (Town Hall)

Recording Engineer: Val Valentin

Producers: Creed Taylor and Helen Keane

Verve 831 271-2 (V6-8683)

86. *The Secret Sessions* (8-CD boxed set, excerpt)

Bill Evans (p); Teddy Kotick (b); Arnie Wise (dr)

Very Early; 'Round Midnight; One for Helen; Blue in Green; Turn Out the Stars; Waltz for Debby; Time Remembered; Autumn Leaves

March, 1966, New York City (the Village Vanguard)

Recording Engineer: Mike Harris

Producer: Orrin Keepnews

8MCD-4421-2

87. *Intermodulation*

Bill Evans (p); Jim Hall (g)

Turn Out the Stars; All Across the City; I've Got You Under My Skin; My Man's Gone Now; Angel Face; Jazz Samba

April 7 and May 10, 1966, New Jersey (Van Gelder Studios, Englewood Cliffs)

Recording Engineer: Rudy Van Gelder

Producer: Creed Taylor

This album and *Trio 64* were issued as a "twofer" called *Trio (Peacock, Motian), Duo (Hall)* on Verve VE 2-2509.

Verve V6-8655

88. *The Secret Sessions,* continued (see 86)
Bill Evans (p); Eddie Gomez (b); Arnie Wise (dr)

I Should Care; Elsa; Who Can I Turn To?; My Foolish Heart; In Your Own Sweet Way; Five (theme)

July 3, 1966, New York City (the Village Vanguard)

89. *The Universal Mind of Bill Evans* (video)
Bill Evans (p) talking to Harry Evans

How About You?; Star Eyes; Very Early; Time Remembered; My Bells

Early autumn, 1966, New York City

Director: Louis Cavrell

Production: Charter Oak Telepictures Inc. in association with Helen Keane

Rhapsody Films 9015 (KJazz 101)

90. *A Simple Matter of Conviction*
Bill Evans (p); Eddie Gomez (b); Shelly Manne (dr)

A Simple Matter of Conviction; My Melancholy Baby; Only Child; Laura; Stella by Starlight; I'm Getting Sentimental over You; Star Eyes; Unless It's You (Orbit); These Things Called Changes

October 11, 1966, New Jersey (Van Gelder Studios, Englewood Cliffs)

The sleeve and various discographies are incorrect in giving October 4. Peter H. Larsen has personally looked through Creed Taylor's recording sheets and confirms October 11 as the correct date.

Recording Engineer: Rudy Van Gelder

Producer: Creed Taylor

Verve V6-8675

91. *The Secret Sessions,* continued (see 86)
Bill Evans (p); Eddie Gomez (b); Arnie Wise (dr)

Gloria's Step; Nardis; Someday My Prince Will Come

October 21, 1966, New York City (the Village Vanguard)

92. *Bill Evans Trio* (CD, excerpt)
Bill Evans (p); Eddie Gomez (b); Alex Riel (dr)

Elsa; Stella by Starlight; Detour Ahead; In a Sentimental Mood; Time Remembered; Nardis

October 24, 1966, Copenhagen, Denmark (Royal Theatre)

Radio Production: Danmarks Radio

Tempo di Jazz CDTJ 708

93. *Bill Evans Trio in Oslo* (video)
Bill Evans (p); Eddie Gomez (b); Alex Riel (dr)

Very Early; Stella by Starlight; If You Could See Me Now; Autumn Leaves; Time Remembered; Nardis; Five (theme)

October 28, 1966, Oslo, Norway (Munch-Museet)

TV Production by Norsk Rigskringkastning (NRK)

Directed by J. Bergh

KJazz 125

94. *The Secret Sessions,* continued (see 86)

Bill Evans (p); Eddie Gomez (b); Arnie Wise (dr)

Who Can I Turn To?; Come Rain or Come Shine; If You Could See Me Now; Spring Is Here; Re: Person I Knew; A Sleepin' Bee; Emily; Alfie; Walkin' Up; You're Gonna Hear from Me; Some Other Time; I'll Remember April; Alice in Wonderland; I Love You

November 10 and 12, 1966, New York City (the Village Vanguard)

Joe Hunt (dr) replaces Wise

Very Early; Time Remembered; 'Round Midnight (2#s); Stella by Starlight; Turn Out the Stars; My Man's Gone Now; In a Sentimental Mood; When I Fall in Love; Nardis; Come Rain or Come Shine; Gloria's Step

January 8, February 26, and March 5, 1967, same location

Philly Joe Jones (dr) replaces Hunt

Blue in Green; Waltz for Debby; Detour Ahead; On Green Dolphin Street; My Foolish Heart; If You Could See Me Now; Elsa; How Deep Is the Ocean?; Polka Dots and Moonbeams; I'm Getting Sentimental over You; I Should Care; Star Eyes; Peri's Scope; Haunted Heart; Airegin; Little Lulu; Five (theme); Turn Out the Stars; Nardis; California Here I Come; Very Early; Easy Living; Wonder Why

May 19, 21, 26, 28, and June 1, 1967, same location

95. *Further Conversations with Myself*

Bill Evans (p) with one overdubbed track

Emily; Yesterdays; Santa Claus Is Coming to Town; Funny Man; The Shadow of Your Smile; Little Lulu; Quiet Now

August 9, 1967, New York City (Webster Hall)

Recording Engineer: Ray Hall

Producer: Helen Keane

Verve V6-8727

96. *California Here I Come*

Bill Evans (p); Eddie Gomez (b); Philly Joe Jones (dr)

California Here I Come; Polka Dots and Moonbeams; Turn Out the Stars; Stella by Starlight; You're Gonna Hear from Me; In a Sentimental Mood; G Waltz; On Green Dolphin Street; Gone with the Wind; If You Could See Me Now; Alfie; Very Early; 'Round Midnight; Emily; Wrap Your Troubles in Dreams

August 17–18, 1967, New York City (the Village Vanguard)

Recording Engineer: Phil Ramone

Producer: Helen Keane

The Complete Bill Evans on Verve (see Collections) contains 31 extra #s, including a unique rendering of Harold Arlen's "Happiness Is a Thing Called Joe."

Verve VE 2-2545

97. *The Secret Sessions,* continued (see 86)
Bill Evans (p); Eddie Gomez (b); Philly Joe Jones (dr)

Time Remembered; You and the Night and the Music

September 3, 1967, New York City (the Village Vanguard)

Arnie Wise (dr) replaces Jones

Beautiful Love; Waltz for Debby; I Fall in Love Too Easily

February 4, 1968, same location

98. *At the Montreux Jazz Festival* (CD)
Bill Evans (p); Eddie Gomez (b); Jack DeJohnette (dr)

One for Helen; A Sleepin' Bee; Mother of Earl; Nardis; I Loves You, Porgy (piano solo); The Touch of Your Lips; Embraceable You; Someday My Prince Will Come; Walkin' Up; Quiet Now (piano solo)

June 15, 1968, Montreux, Switzerland (Casino de Montreux)

Recording Engineers: Pierre Grandjean and Jean-Claude Martin

Producer: Helen Keane

Verve 827 844-2 (V6-8762)

99. *Bill Evans Trio: Rare Broadcast Material* (excerpt)
Bill Evans, John Lewis (p); Eddie Gomez (b); Jack DeJohnette (dr); the CBS Orchestra, cond. Alfredo Antonini

Stella by Starlight (Bill Evans Trio only); Granados (omit Lewis); Almost Blues (omit Gomez and DeJohnette)

Possibly June, 1968, New York City (CBS Studios)

Taped and broadcast by CBS in the *Dial M for Music* TV series. Larsen gives July 13, but perhaps this was the transmission date, as the trio was playing at Ronnie Scott's club in London that night.

Chazzer 2007

100. *The Secret Sessions,* continued (see 86)
Bill Evans (p); Eddie Gomez (b); Jack DeJohnette (dr)

My Man's Gone Now; Who Can I Turn To?; Polka Dots and Moonbeams; Emily

August 23, 1968, New York City (the Village Vanguard)

John Dentz (dr) replaces DeJohnette

Ev'rything I Love; Someday My Prince Will Come; The Shadow of Your Smile

September 15, 1968, same location

101. *Alone* (CD)
Bill Evans (p)

Never Let Me Go; Here's That Rainy Day; On a Clear Day; A Time for Love (2#s); Midnight Mood; (Medley) All the Things You Are/Midnight Mood

September and October, 1968, New York City (Webster Hall)

Recording Engineer: Ray Hall

Producer: Helen Keane

Verve 833 801-2 (V6-8792)

102. *The Secret Sessions,* continued (see 86)

Bill Evans (p); Eddie Gomez (b); Marty Morell (dr)

A Sleepin' Bee; Blue in Green; For Heaven's Sake; Love Is Here to Stay

December 13 and 22, 1968, New York City (the Village Vanguard)

103. *What's New*

Jeremy Steig (fl); Bill Evans (p); Eddie Gomez (b); Marty Morell (dr)

So What; Lover Man; Time Out for Chris; Straight No Chaser; *Spartacus* Love Theme; What's New; Autumn Leaves

January 30, February 3–5, and March 3 or 11, 1969, New York City (Webster Hall)

Recording Engineer: Ray Hall

Producer: Helen Keane

Larsen gives the last date as March 3.

Verve V6-8777

104. *The Secret Sessions,* continued (see 86)

Bill Evans (p); Eddie Gomez (b); Marty Morell (dr)

In a Sentimental Mood; How My Heart Sings; On Green Dolphin Street

February 2, 1969, New York City (the Village Vanguard)

105a. *Piano Perspective*
b. *Autumn Leaves*
c. *It Happened in ... Pescara* (1969–1989) (double LP, excerpt)
d. *Two Super Bill Evans Trios: Live in Europe!* (excerpt)

Bill Evans (p); Eddie Gomez (b); Marty Morell (dr)

[c]So What; [a]Come Rain or Come Shine; [a]Nardis; [a]Quiet Now; [ab]'Round Midnight; [ab]Autumn Leaves; [b]Emily; [b]A Sleepin' Bee; [b]Alfie; [b]Who Can I Turn To?; [b]Very Early; [d]Waltz for Debby

July 18, 1969, Pescara, Italy

The Italian Lotus issue of *Autumn Leaves* assigns incorrect titles to four of the songs; those hoping, as a result, to hear "There'll Never Be Another You," "Stairway to the Stars," "Someday My Prince Will Come," and "Blue in Green" will be disappointed.

Joker UPS 2074, Joker UPS 2053, Philology W 100/101, and Unique Jazz UJ 24

106a. *Jazzhouse*

Bill Evans (p); Eddie Gomez (b); Marty Morell (dr)

How Deep Is the Ocean?; How My Heart Sings; Goodbye; Autumn Leaves; California Here I Come; A Sleepin' Bee; Polka Dots and Moonbeams; Stella by Starlight; Five/Oleo (theme)

November 24, 1969, Copenhagen, Denmark (Jazzhus Montmartre)

b. *You're Gonna Hear from Me*

Same personnel, date, and location

You're Gonna Hear from Me; 'Round Midnight; Waltz for Debby; Nardis; Time Remembered; Who Can I Turn To?; Emily; Love Is Here to Stay; Someday My Prince Will Come

Recording Engineer: Freddy Hansson

Producer: Helen Keane

Milestone M-9151 and M-9164

107a. *Bill Evans in Europe* (Video, excerpt)
b. *Emily* (CD, excerpt)
Bill Evans (p); Eddie Gomez (b); Marty Morell (dr)

Emily

Late November, 1969, Copenhagen, Denmark (TV-byen)

Green Line VIDJAZZ 38 and Moon Records MCD 060-2

108. *Quiet Now*
Bill Evans (p); Eddie Gomez (b); Marty Morell (dr)

Very Early; A Sleepin' Bee; Quiet Now; Turn Out the Stars; Autumn Leaves; Nardis

November 28, 1969, Amsterdam, Holland (RAI building)

The English label Affinity attributed these performances to Chuck Israels and Larry Bunker on its original LP. The 1986 Affinity CD release gets the artists right but still maintains that Evans is the composer of Denny Zeitlin's "Quiet Now."

Affinity AFF 73

109. *The Secret Sessions,* continued (see 86)
Bill Evans (p); Eddie Gomez (b); Marty Morell (dr)

My Foolish Heart; Stella by Starlight; Midnight Mood; What Are You Doing the Rest of Your Life?; I Should Care; Autumn Leaves

February 15 and April 18, 1970, New York City (the Village Vanguard)

110. *From Left to Right*
Bill Evans (p & el-p); Sam Brown (g); Eddie Gomez (b); *John Beal (el-b, overdubbed); Marty Morell (dr); orchestra arranged and conducted by Michael Leonard

*The Dolphin (before); *The Dolphin (after); What Are You Doing the Rest of Your Life?; I'm All Smiles; Why Did I Choose You?; Soirée; Lullaby for Helene; Like Someone in Love; Children's Play Song

October 1969–May 1970, New York City and San Francisco

Producer: Helen Keane

The Complete Bill Evans on Verve (see Collections) contains extra #s of "Why Did I Choose You?" "Soirée," "Lullaby for Helene," "What Are You Doing the Rest of Your Life?," and "The Dolphin." Locations included A & R Studios, Media Sound Studios, Century Sound, and RCA Studios in New York, as well as a studio in San Francisco.

MGM SE-4723

111. *Montreux II*
Bill Evans (p); Eddie Gomez (b); Marty Morell (dr)

Very Early; Alfie; 34 Skidoo; How My Heart Sings; Israel; I Hear a Rhapsody; Peri's Scope

June 19, 1970, Montreux, Switzerland (Casino de Montreux)

Recording Engineer: Pierre Grandjean

Producer: Helen Keane

CTI 6004

112. (MPS promotional record, excerpt)
Bill Evans (p); Eddie Gomez (b); Marty Morell (dr)

Turn Out the Stars

June 1970, Villingen, Germany (MPS Studios)

This was a private recording sent out to business associates.

MPS 0666041

113. *Homewood*

Bill Evans (p); Eddie Gomez (b); Marty Morell (dr)

Very Early; So What; Waltz for Debby; Like Someone in Love; Someday My Prince Will Come; Five (theme)

November 4, 1970, Chicago, Illinois

Red Bird Records RB-101

114. *The Bill Evans Album* (CD)

Bill Evans (p & el-p); Eddie Gomez (b); Marty Morell (dr)

Comrade Conrad; The Two Lonely People; Funkallero (2#s); Sugar Plum; Waltz for Debby (2#s); Re: Person I Knew (2#s); T.T.T. (Twelve Tone Tune)

May 11–12, 17, 19–20, and June 9, 1971, New York City (CBS 30th Street Studio)

Recording Engineer: Pete Weiss

Producer: Helen Keane

CD reissue produced by Orrin Keepnews in 1996.

Columbia CK 64963 (C 30855)

115. *The Secret Sessions,* continued (see 86)

Bill Evans (p); Eddie Gomez (b); Marty Morell (dr)

Re: Person I Knew; Alfie; Very Early

December 1971, New York City (the Village Vanguard)

116a. *Live in Paris 1972, Vol. 1*

Bill Evans (p); Eddie Gomez (b); Marty Morell (dr)

Re: Person I Knew; Turn Out the Stars; Gloria's Step; The Two Lonely People; Waltz for Debby; What Are You Doing the Rest of Your Life?

February 6, 1972, Paris (Maison de l'ORTF)

b. *Live in Paris 1972, Vol. 2*

Same personnel, date, and location

Twelve Tone Tune; Sugar Plum; Quiet Now; Very Early; Autumn Leaves; Time Remembered; My Romance; Someday My Prince Will Come

Production and Sound Engineering by Radio France

The announcer, André Francis, at the start of *Vol. 1*, recalls the first Parisian concert of Bill Evans at Maison de l'ORTF in 1965, but (curiously) assigns it to September 13, rather than February 13 as documented elsewhere.

France's Concert FC 107 and FC 114

117. *Emily* (CD, excerpt)

Herb Geller (afl); Bill Evans (p); Eddie Gomez (b); Marty Morell (dr)

Northern Trail

February c. 12, 1972, Hamburg, Germany (Funkhaus)

Recorded by Norddeutsche Rundfunk

This was recorded at a rehearsal session. The year is given as 1971, and the tune as "Quarter Tone Experiments," a tune which was played at the concert on February 14.

Moon Records MCD 060-2

118. *Two Super Bill Evans Trios: Live in Europe!* (excerpt)
Bill Evans (p); Eddie Gomez (b); Marty Morell (dr)

How My Heart Sings; Time Remembered; Twelve Tone Tune

February, 1972, Italy

Unique Jazz UJ 24

119. *Living Time*
Bill Evans (p & el-p); Eddie Gomez (b); Marty Morell (dr); The George Russell Orchestra, George Russell (comp. & cond.); Carl Atkins (asst. cond.)

Events I–VIII

May 1972, New York City (Columbia 30th Street Studio)

Recording Engineer: Pete Weiss

Producer: Helen Keane

Living Time and *The Bill Evans Album* were issued as a Columbia "twofer" on CG 33672.

Columbia KC 31490

120. *Live at the Festival* (excerpt)
Bill Evans (p); Eddie Gomez (b); Tony Oxley (dr)

Nardis

June 10, 1972, Ljubljana, Yugoslavia

Recorded by Radio Ljubljana

Enja 2030

121. *Bill Evans Trio: Rare Broadcast Material* (excerpt)
Bill Evans (p); Eddie Gomez (b); Marty Morell (dr)

How My Heart Sings; Gloria's Step; Time Remembered; My Romance

September 17, 1972, New York City (Top of the Gate)

As with similar bootlegs on the Alto, Session, and Unique labels, the sleeve information is inaccurate. "Gloria's Step" is not listed, and "Time Remembered" is called "Modal Original."

Chazzer 2007

122. *Live in Paris 1972, Vol. 3* (CD)
Bill Evans (p); Eddie Gomez (b); Marty Morell (dr)

Elsa; Detour Ahead; 34 Skidoo; Alfie; Peri's Scope; Blue in Green; Emily; Who Can I Turn To?; Some Other Time; Nardis; Waltz for Debby

December 17, 1972, Paris (Maison de l'ORTF)

Production and Sound Engineering by Radio France

France's Concert FCD 125

123. *The Tokyo Concert*
Bill Evans (p); Eddie Gomez (b); Marty Morell (dr)

Mornin' Glory; Up with the Lark; Yesterday I Heard the Rain; My Romance; When Autumn Comes;

T.T.T.T. (Twelve Tone Tune Two); Hullo Bolinas (p solo); Gloria's Step; On Green Dolphin Street

January 20, 1973, Tokyo, Japan (Yubin Chokin Hall)

Recording Engineers from CBS/Sony: Henichi Handa, Tomoo Suzuki, and Yuiichi Maejima

Producers: Kiyoshi Ito (CBS/Sony) and Helen Keane

Fantasy F-9457

124. *Buenos Aires Concert* 1973 (2-LP boxed set)
Bill Evans (p); Eddie Gomez (b); Marty Morell (dr)

Re: Person I Knew; Emily; Who Can I Turn To?; The Two Lonely People; What Are You Doing the Rest of Your Life?; My Romance; Mornin' Glory; Up with the Lark; Twelve Tone Tune; Yesterday I Heard the Rain; Beautiful Love; Waltz for Debby; My Foolish Heart

June 24, 1973, Buenos Aires, Argentina (Cine Teatro Gran Rex)

"Yesterday I Heard The Rain" is listed under its Spanish title, "Esta Tarde Vi Llover." "Mornin' Glory" and "Twelve Tone Tune" are incorrectly listed as "Time Remembered" and "34 Skidoo," respectively.

Yellow Note Y-201-1

125. *The Secret Sessions,* continued (see 86)
Bill Evans (p); Eddie Gomez (b); Marty Morell (dr)

Polka Dots and Moonbeams; Mornin' Glory; Yesterday I Heard the Rain; Emily; Time Remembered

August 12, 1973, New York City (the Village Vanguard)

126a. *From the Seventies* (excerpt)
Bill Evans (p); Eddie Gomez (b); Marty Morell (dr)

Up with the Lark; Quiet Now; Gloria's Step

November 19, 1973, Los Angeles, California (Shelly's Manne Hole)

b. *Eloquence* (excerpt)
Bill Evans (p)

(Medley) When in Rome/It Amazes Me

Recording Engineer: Jim Stern

Producer: Orrin Keepnews

Fantasy F-9630 and F-9618

127a. *Since We Met*
Bill Evans (p); Eddie Gomez (b); Marty Morell (dr)

Since We Met; Midnight Mood; Seesaw; Sareen Jurer; Time Remembered; Turn Out the Stars; But Beautiful

January 11–12, 1974, New York City (the Village Vanguard)

b. *Re: Person I Knew*
Same personnel, dates, and location

Re: Person I Knew; Sugar Plum; Alfie; Twelve Tone Tune; (Medley) Dolphin Dance (p solo)/Very Early; 34 Skidoo; Emily; Are You All the Things

c. *From the Seventies* (excerpt)
Same personnel, dates, and location

Elsa

d. *The Secret Sessions*, continued (see 86)

Same personnel, dates, and location

Who Can I Turn To?; Dolphin Dance

Recording Engineers: Michael De Lugg (except *The Secret Sessions*) and Mike Harris

Producers: Helen Keane and Orrin Keepnews

Fantasy F-9501, F-9608, F-9630, and 8MCD-4421-2

128. *Symbiosis*

Bill Evans (p & el-p); Eddie Gomez (b); Marty Morell (dr); orchestra conducted by Claus Ogerman

Symbiosis

February 11, 12, and 14, 1974, New York City (Columbia Recording Studios)

Recording Engineer: Frank Laico

Producer: Helen Keane

Pausa PR 7050 (US) or MPS-BASF 21 22094-3 (Europe)

129a. *Live in Europe, Vol. I*

Bill Evans (p); Eddie Gomez (b); Marty Morell (dr)

Emily; The Two Lonely People; Some Other Time; Time Remembered; Gloria's Step; My Romance; 34 Skidoo; Lover Man; Blue in Green; Re: Person I Knew; My Foolish Heart; Turn Out the Stars; Very Early

Summer (probably August), 1974, Europe

b. *Live in Europe, Vol. II*

Same personnel, date, and location

Up with the Lark; 34 Skidoo; Quiet Now; Twelve Tone Tune; Midnight Mood; Sugar Plum; Funkallero; The Two Lonely People; Waltz for Debby; Goodbye

On *Vol. I* there is no "Waltz for Debby" as listed, and the penultimate track (not listed) is "Turn Out the Stars." On *Vol. II* "Funkallero" is wrongly listed as "If You Could See Me Now."

EPM FDC 5712 and FDC 5713

130a. *Bill Evans with Stan Getz: Two Lonely People* (CD)
b. *The Bill Evans Trio Featuring Stan Getz: But Beautiful* (CD, excerpt)

Bill Evans (p); Eddie Gomez (b); Marty Morell (dr)

[b]See-saw; [ab]The Two Lonely People; [a]Turn Out the Stars; [a]34 Skidoo; [a]Twelve Tone Tune

Add Stan Getz (ts)

[ab]Grandfather's Waltz; [ab]Stan's Blues; [a]But Beautiful; [a]Funkallero; [a]The Peacocks (omit Gomez and Morell); [a]You and the Night and the Music

August 9, 1974, Laren, Holland (Singer Concertzaal)

Recording Engineers for Nederlandse Omroep Stichting (NOS): Tinus Bruyn and Cees van der Gragt

Producer for NOS: Joop de Roo

Bill Evans with Stan Getz: Two Lonely People was issued by Jazz Birdie's of Paradise in 1994, with "Twelve Tone Tune" and "Stan's Blues" wrongly listed as "Twelve Tone Tune Two" and "Peri's Scope," respectively. *The Bill Evans Trio Featuring Stan Getz: But Beautiful* (produced by Helen Keane) was issued by Milestone in 1995.

Jazz Birdie's of Paradise J-Bop 048 and Milestone MCD 9249-2

131. *The Bill Evans Trio Featuring Stan Getz: But Beautiful* (CD, excerpt)
Stan Getz (ts); Bill Evans (p); Eddie Gomez (b); Marty Morell (dr)

Emily; Lover Man; Funkallero; The Peacocks (omit Gomez and Morell); You and the Night and the Music; But Beautiful

August 16, 1974, Middelheim (Antwerp), Belgium

Recorded by Radiodiffusion Belgie

Producer: Helen Keane

Milestone MCD 9249-2

132. *Blue in Green*
Bill Evans (p); Eddie Gomez (b); Marty Morell (dr)

One for Helen; The Two Lonely People; What Are You Doing the Rest of Your Life?; So What; Very Early; If You Could See Me Now; 34 Skidoo; Blue in Green; Twelve Tone Tune

Various dates up to August 1974, Ottawa (Carleton University) and Hull, Canada (Camp Fortune, Gatineau Hills)

Recording Engineer for Canadian Broadcasting Corporation: Paul LaCroix

Producer: Helen Keane

Milestone M-9185

133. *The Canadian Concert*
Bill Evans (p); Eddie Gomez (b); Marty Morell (dr)

Midnight Mood; Elsa; Sugar Plum; Mornin' Glory; A Sleepin' Bee; How My Heart Sings; Time Remembered; Beautiful Love (nc)

July or August 1974, Hull, Canada (Camp Fortune, Gatineau Hills)

Recorded by Radio Canada

Can-Am CA 1200

134a. *Intuition*
Bill Evans (p & el-p); Eddie Gomez (b)

Invitation; Blue Serge; Show-Type Tune; The Nature of Things; Are You All the Things; A Face without a Name; Falling Grace; Hi Lili, Hi Lo

November 7–10, 1974, Berkeley, California (Fantasy Studios)

b. *Eloquence* (excerpt)
Same personnel, dates, and location

Gone with the Wind; Saudade Do Brasil

Recording Engineer: Don Cody

Producer: Helen Keane

Fantasy F-9475 and F-9618

135. *The Secret Sessions*, concluded (see 86)
Bill Evans (p); Eddie Gomez (b); Eliot Zigmund (dr)

Sugar Plum; Turn Out the Stars; Quiet Now; Waltz for Debby

January 26, 1975, New York City (the Village Vanguard)

136. *Switzerland 1975* (CD)

Bill Evans (p); Eddie Gomez (b); Eliot Zigmund (dr)

Sugar Plum; Midnight Mood; Turn Out the Stars; Gloria's Step; Up with the Lark; Twelve Tone Tune Two; Mornin' Glory; Sareen Jurer; Time Remembered; My Romance; Waltz for Debby; Yesterday I Heard the Rain

February 6, 1975, Epalinges, Switzerland (Maison des Spectacles)

Producer for Radio Suisse Romande: Pierre Grandjean

Jazz Helvet JH 01

137. *My Romance* (CD)

Bill Evans (p); Eddie Gomez (b); Eliot Zigmund (dr)

Gloria's Step; What Are You Doing the Rest of Your Life?; Who Can I Turn To?; My Romance; Twelve Tone Tune Two; My Foolish Heart; Up with the Lark; Sareen Jurer; Midnight Mood

February 16, 1975, Marseille, France (Théâtre des Variétés)

Originally recorded by Radio France

"Twelve Tone Tune Two" is incorrectly titled as "Mysterioso," "Up with The Lark" as "How My Heart Sings," "Sareen Jurer" as "Quiet Now," and "Midnight Mood" as "Quiet Again." No information is supplied regarding artists, place, and date; I have identified these from tapes in Brian Hennessey's collection, "The Bill Evans Memorial Library."

Zeta ZET 702

138. *Bill Evans, Monica Zetterlund* (CD)

Bill Evans (p); Eddie Gomez (b); Eliot Zigmund (dr)

Sugar Plum; Sareen Jurer; Very Early; Gloria's Step

Add Monica Zetterlund (voc.)

Come Rain or Come Shine; What's New; It Could Happen to You; Once upon a Summertime; The Second Time Around; Samba

February 22, 1975, Lund, Sweden (Konsthallen)

Recorded by Sveriges Radio

West Wind WW 2073

139. *The National Jazz Ensemble, Vol. 1* (excerpt)

Bill Evans (p); Chuck Israels (b, arr. & cond.); Bill Goodwin (dr); The National Jazz Ensemble

Very Early

April, 1975, New York City

Recording Engineer: Noel Edward Smith

Producers: Hank O'Neal and Chuck Israels

Chiaroscuro CR 140

140. *The Tony Bennett/Bill Evans Album*

Tony Bennett (voc.); Bill Evans (p)

Young and Foolish; The Touch of Your Lips; Some Other Time; When in Rome; We'll Be Together Again; My Foolish Heart; Waltz for Debby; But Beautiful; The Days of Wine and Roses

June 10–13, 1975, Berkeley, California (Fantasy Studios)

Recording Engineer: Don Cody

Producer: Helen Keane

Fantasy F-9489

141a. *Montreux III*
Bill Evans (p & el-p); Eddie Gomez (b)

Elsa; Milano; Venutian Rhythm Dance; Django; Minha (All Mine); Driftin'; I Love You; The Summer Knows

July 20, 1975, Montreux, Switzerland (Casino de Montreux)

b. *Eloquence* (excerpt)
Same date and location

In a Sentimental Mood; But Beautiful

Recording Engineer: John Timberly

Producer: Helen Keane

Fantasy F-9510 and F-9618

142. *Monterey Jazz Festival 75* (Video, excerpt)
Bill Evans (p); Eddie Gomez (b)

Up with the Lark

September 20, 1975, Monterey, California (County Fairgrounds)

Bill Evans, Patrice Rushen, John Lewis, and Marian McPartland (p)

Billie's Bounce

Same date and location

Recording Engineers: Wally Heider and Dave Mull

Director: Mark Massari

Storyville SV 6021

143a. *Alone (Again)*
Bill Evans (p)

The Touch of Your Lips; In Your Own Sweet Way; Make Someone Happy; What Kind of Fool Am I?; People

December 16–18, 1975, Berkeley, California (Fantasy Studios)

b. *Eloquence* (excerpt)
Same personnel, dates, and location

All of You; Since We Met; (Medley) But Not for Me/Isn't It Romantic?/The Opener

Recording Engineer: Don Cody

Producer: Helen Keane

Fantasy F-9542 and F-9618

144a. *Quintessence*
Harold Land (ts); Kenny Burrell (g); Bill Evans (p); Ray Brown (b); Philly Joe Jones (dr)

Sweet Dulcinea; Martina; The Second Time Around (omit Burrell and Land); A Child Is Born; Bass Face

May, 1976, Berkeley, California (Fantasy Studios)

b. *From the Seventies* (excerpt)
Same personnel, date, and location

Nobody Else but Me

Recording Engineer: Phil Kaffel

Producer: Helen Keane

On the CD version of *Quintessence* "Sweet Dulcinea" is called "Sweet Dulcinea Blue."

Fantasy F-9529 and F-9630

145. *In His Own Way* (CD)
Bill Evans (p); Eddie Gomez (b); Eliot Zigmund (dr)

Time Remembered; In Your Own Sweet Way; Sareen Jurer; Mornin' Glory; 34 Skidoo; Sugar Plum; Turn Out the Stars

September 6, 1976, Cologne, Germany

Although the sleeve says this set was recorded in Rome, I have identified its date and location from tapes in Brian Hennessey's collection, "The Bill Evans Memorial Library."

West Wind WW 2028

146. *Together Again*
Tony Bennett (voc.); Bill Evans (p)

The Bad and the Beautiful (p solo); Lucky to Be Me; Make Someone Happy; You're Nearer; A Child Is Born; The Two Lonely People; You Don't Know What Love Is; Maybe September; Lonely Girl; You Must Believe in Spring

September 27–30, 1976, San Francisco, California (Columbia Studios)

Recording Engineer: Don Cody

Producers: Helen Keane and Don Cody

Improv 7117

147. *The Paris Concert* [1976] (CD)
Bill Evans (p); Eddie Gomez (b); Eliot Zigmund (dr)

Sugar Plum; Time Remembered; 34 Skidoo; Twelve Tone Tune Two; Turn Out the Stars; Someday My Prince Will Come; Minha; All of You; Waltz for Debby

November 5, 1976, Paris (Maison de l'ORTF)

Producer for Radio France: André Francis

This session first appeared in *The Complete Fantasy Recordings* (see Collections).

Fantasy (Japan) VDJ-25035

148. *Crosscurrents* (CD)
Lee Konitz (as); Warne Marsh (ts); Bill Evans (p); Eddie Gomez (b); Eliot Zigmund (dr)

Eiderdown (2#s); Ev'ry Time We Say Goodbye (2#s, omit Konitz); Pensativa; Speak Low; When I Fall in Love (omit Marsh, Gomez, and Zigmund); Night and Day (2#s)

February 28, March 1 and 2, 1977, Berkeley, California (Fantasy Studios)

Recording Engineer: Phil Kaffel

Producer: Helen Keane

Fantasy OJCCD 718-2 (F-9568)

149a. *I Will Say Goodbye*
Bill Evans (p); Eddie Gomez (b); Eliot Zigmund (dr)

I Will Say Goodbye (2#s); Dolphin Dance; Seascape; Peau Douce; The Opener; Quiet Light; A House Is Not a Home

May 11–13, 1977, Berkeley, California (Fantasy Studios)

b. *From the Seventies* (excerpt)
Same personnel, dates, and location

Nobody Else but Me; Orson's Theme

Recording Engineer: Bruce Walford

Producer: Helen Keane

Fantasy F-9593 and F-9630

150. *You Must Believe in Spring*
Bill Evans (p); Eddie Gomez (b); Eliot Zigmund (dr)

B Minor Waltz; You Must Believe in Spring; Gary's Theme; We Will Meet Again; The Peacocks; Sometime Ago; Theme from *M*A*S*H* (aka Suicide Is Painless)

August 23–25, 1977, Hollywood, California (Capitol Studios)

Recording Engineer: Al Schmitt

Producers: Helen Keane and Tommy Lipuma

Warner Bros HS 3504-Y

151. *New Conversations*
Bill Evans (p & el-p) with one or two overdubbed tracks

Song for Helen; Nobody Else but Me; Maxine; For Nenette; I Love My Wife; Remembering the Rain; After You; Reflections in D (p solo)

January 26–28, 30, and February 13–16, 1978, New York City (Columbia 30th Street Studio)

Recording Engineer: Frank Laico

Producer: Helen Keane

Warner Bros BSK 3177-Y

152. *Affinity*
Toots Thielemans (hca); Larry Schneider (ts, ss & afl); Bill Evans (p & el-p); Marc Johnson (b); Eliot Zigmund (dr)

I Do It for Your Love (omit Schneider and Zigmund); Sno' Peas; This Is All I Ask (omit Schneider); The Days of Wine and Roses; Jesus' Last Ballad (el-p & hca only); Tomato Kiss; Noelle's Theme (The Other Side of Midnight) (el-p & hca only); Blue in Green (omit Schneider); Body and Soul (omit Schneider)

October 30, 31, and November 1 and 2, 1978, New York City (Columbia 30th Street Studio)

Recording Engineer: Frank Laico

Producer: Helen Keane

Warner Bros BSK 3293-Y

153. *Marian McPartland's Piano Jazz, with Guest Bill Evans* (CD)
Bill Evans (p)

Waltz for Debby; All of You (demo, add McPartland on p later); The Touch of Your Lips (demo, add McPartland on p later); Reflections in D

November 6, 1978, New York City (the Baldwin Piano Showroom)

Add Marian McPartland (p)

In Your Own Sweet Way; The Days of Wine and Roses; This Is All I Ask; I Love You

Same date and location

Recording Engineer: John J. Gelinas

Producer: Dick Phipps

This interview was first broadcast on National Public Radio on May 27, 1979, and was first issued on *The Complete Fantasy Recordings* (see Collections).

Jazz Alliance TJA 12004

154a. *Jazz at the Maintenance Shop, Volume 1* (video)
Bill Evans (p); Marc Johnson (b); Joe LaBarbera (dr)

Re: Person I Knew; Midnight Mood; The Peacocks; Theme from M*A*S*H; Quiet Now; Up with the Lark; In Your Own Sweet Way; I Do It for Your Love; My Romance

January 30, 1979, Ames, Iowa (the Maintenance Shop, Iowa State University)

b. *Jazz at the Maintenance Shop, Volume 2* (video)
Same personnel, date, and location

Mornin' Glory; 34 Skidoo; But Beautiful; Who Can I Turn To?; Gary's Theme; Turn Out the Stars; Someday My Prince Will Come; Minha (p, b only); Nardis

Producer/director: John Beyer (for Iowa Public Broadcasting Network)

This material was also issued on laser disc.

KJazz 120 and 135

155. *We Will Meet Again*
Tom Harrell (tr); Larry Schneider (ts, ss & afl); Bill Evans (p & el-p); Marc Johnson (b); Joe LaBarbera (dr)

Comrade Conrad; Laurie; Bill's Hit Tune; For All We Know (We May Never Meet Again) (p solo); Five; Only Child; Peri's Scope; We Will Meet Again (p solo)

August 6–9, 1979, New York City (Columbia 30th Street Studio)

Recording Engineer: Frank Laico

Producer: Helen Keane

Warner Bros HS 3411-Y

156. *Live in Buenos Aires 1979* (2-LP boxed set)
Bill Evans (p); Marc Johnson (b); Joe LaBarbera (dr)

Stella by Starlight; Laurie; Theme from M*A*S*H; Turn Out the Stars; I Do It for Your Love; My Romance; Letter to Evan (p solo); I Loves You, Porgy (p solo); Up with the Lark (p, b only); Minha (p, b only); Someday My Prince Will Come; If You Could See Me Now; Nardis

September 27, 1979, Buenos Aires, Argentina (Teatro Municipal General San Martin)

"Laurie" is wrongly listed as "Gary's Theme," "Turn Out the Stars" as "We Will Meet Again," "I Do It for Your Love" as "Letter to Evan," and "Letter to Evan" as "Noelle's Theme." These details are corrected on the West Wind 2-CD reissue (WW 2061) although Paul Simon's "I Do It for Your Love" is wrongly attributed to Evans.

Yellow Note Y-200-1

157a. *The Paris Concert, Edition One*

Bill Evans (p); Marc Johnson (b); Joe LaBarbera (dr)

I Do It for Your Love; Quiet Now; Noelle's Theme (p solo); My Romance; I Loves You, Porgy (p solo); Up with the Lark (p, b only); Minha (p, b only); Beautiful Love

November 26, 1979, Paris (Espace Pierre Cardin)

b. *The Paris Concert, Edition Two*

Same personnel, date, and location

Re: Person I Knew; Gary's Theme; Letter to Evan (p solo); 34 Skidoo; Laurie; Nardis

Sound Engineering by Radio France

Producers: Yves Abiteboul (Radio Concert) and Helen Keane (for Elektra Musician)

The Paris Concert, Edition One includes brief excerpts of a conversation between Bill and Harry Evans taken from the video *The Universal Mind of Bill Evans*.

Elektra Musician 1-60164-D, 1-60311-D

158. *The Brilliant Bill Evans* (CD, excerpt)

Bill Evans (p); Marc Johnson (b); Joe LaBarbera (dr)

My Romance; Re: Person I Knew; Laurie; Very Early; The Peacocks; On Green Dolphin Street; Mornin' Glory; Solar

December 5, 1979, Koblenz, Germany

Although the sleeve says this set was recorded in Rome, I have identified its date and location from tapes in the collection of Colin Kellam.

West Wind 2058

159. *Live at Balboa Jazz Club, Vols. 1, 2, and 3*

Bill Evans (p); Marc Johnson (b); Joe LaBarbera (dr)

If You Could See Me Now; Up with the Lark; I Do It for Your Love; Five; The Two Lonely People; Bill's Hit Tune; Gary's Theme; Laurie; Like Someone in Love; Nardis; Re: Person I Knew; When I Fall in Love; My Man's Gone Now; Theme from *M*A*S*H*; Blue in Green

December 12, 1979, Madrid (Balboa Jazz Club)

Ivory ILP 3000, 3001, and 3002

160. *Turn Out the Stars: The Final Village Vanguard Recordings, June 1980* (6-CD boxed set)

Bill Evans (p); Marc Johnson (b); Joe LaBarbera (dr)

Bill's Hit Tune (3#s); Nardis (4#s); If You Could See Me Now (2#s); The Two Lonely People (2#s); Laurie (2#s); My Romance (3#s); Tiffany (3#s); Like Someone in Love (3#s); Letter to Evan (2#s; #1 p, b only); The Days of Wine and Roses (3#s); Emily (2#s); My Foolish Heart; Yet Ne'er Broken (2#s); Quiet Now (2#s); But Not for Me (2#s); Spring Is Here; Autumn Leaves; Your Story (2#s); Re: Person I Knew; Polka Dots and Moonbeams (2#s); Theme from *M*A*S*H*; Turn Out the Stars (2#s); Knit for Mary F. (3#s); Midnight Mood; Time Remembered; Up with the Lark; In Your Own Sweet Way; I Do It for Your Love (2#s); Five (2#s); Minha; A Sleepin' Bee

June 4–6 and 8, 1980, New York City (the Village Vanguard)

Recording Engineer: Malcolm Addey

Producer: Helen Keane

Warner Bros 9 45925-2

161. *Letter to Evan* (CD)

Bill Evans (p); Marc Johnson (b); Joe LaBarbera (dr)

Emily; The Days of Wine and Roses; Knit for Mary F.; Like Someone in Love; Your Story; Stella by Starlight; My Man's Gone Now (p, b only); Letter to Evan

July 21, 1980, London (Ronnie Scott's club)

Producers: Francis Paudras and Léon Terjanian

Dreyfus 191 064-2

162. *Turn Out the Stars* (CD)

Bill Evans (p); Marc Johnson (b); Joe LaBarbera (dr)

I Do It for Your Love; Turn Out the Stars; My Romance; Laurie; The Two Lonely People; Peau Douce; But Beautiful

August 2, 1980, London (Ronnie Scott's club)

Producers: Francis Paudras and Léon Terjanian

Dreyfus 191 063-2

163a. *His Last Concert in Germany*

Bill Evans (p); Marc Johnson (b); Joe LaBarbera (dr)

(Medley) Noelle's Theme (p solo)/Letter to Evan; Yet Ne'er Broken; Laurie; Bill's Hit Tune; Knit for Mary F.; The Days of Wine and Roses; Your Story; But Beautiful; If You Could See Me Now; Waltz for Debby

August 15, 1980, Bad Hönningen, Germany

b. *The Brilliant Bill Evans* (CD, excerpt)

Same personnel, date, and location

Who Can I Turn To?; Theme from *M*A*S*H*; Five

Recording Engineer: Justus Liebig

On *The Brilliant Bill Evans* "Who Can I Turn To?" besides being mistitled "Who Can I Turn You," is mistakenly attributed to Evans.

West Wind 0022 and 2058

164. *Consecration: The Last Complete Collection* (8-CD boxed set)

Bill Evans (p); Marc Johnson (b); Joe LaBarbera (dr)

Re: Person I Knew (5#s); Tiffany (5#s); My Foolish Heart (3#s); Theme from *M*A*S*H* (3#s); Knit for Mary F. (5#s—#s 6 & 8 p, b only); The Days of Wine and Roses (4#s); Your Story (5#s—sometimes p, b only); The Two Lonely People (3#s—#4 p, b only); My Romance (6#s); Polka Dots and Moonbeams (4#s); Like Someone in Love (5#s); Letter to Evan; Gary's Theme; I Do It for Your Love (4#s); Someday My Prince Will Come; Up with the Lark; Mornin' Glory; Turn Out the Stars; Emily (3#s); Who Can I Turn To? (2#s); Laurie (2#s); You and the Night and the Music; Bill's Hit Tune; But Beautiful

August 31–September 7, 1980, San Francisco, California (Keystone Korner)

Producer: Todd Barkan

Each CD contains the music from each date chronologically.

Alfa Jazz OOR2-61-68

Collections

1. Bill Evans: The Complete Riverside Recordings (18-LP boxed set, issued in 1984)
Producer: Orrin Keepnews

Riverside R-O18

2. The Complete Bill Evans On Verve (18-CD boxed set, issued in 1997)
Producer: Michael Lang

This set includes a previously unissued session recorded (probably) on March 25, 1970, in San Francisco, consisting of 3 #s each of "Comrade Conrad" and "It Must Be Love." The artists were Bill Evans (p); Sam Brown (g); Eddie Gomez (b); Marty Morell (dr).

Verve 527 953-2

3. Bill Evans: The Secret Sessions (8-CD boxed set, issued in 1996)
Producer: Orrin Keepnews

Milestone 8MCD-4421-2

4. Bill Evans: The Complete Fantasy Recordings (9-CD boxed set, issued in 1989)
Producer: Helen Keane

Fantasy 9FCD-1012-2

Index